Quality Assurance Policies & Procedures for AMBULATORY HEALTH CARE

Judith M. Bulau, MSN, PHN
Health Care Program Investigator
Health Systems Development Division
Alternative Delivery Systems Section
Minnesota Department of Health
Minneapolis, Minnesota

AN ASPEN PUBLICATION®
Aspen Publishers, Inc.
Rockville, Maryland
1990

Library of Congress Cataloging - in - Publication Data

Bulau, Judith M.
Quality assurance policies and procedures for ambulatory health care / Judith M. Bulau.
p. cm.
"An Aspen publication."
Includes bibliographical references.
ISBN: 0-8342-0138-0
ISBN 13: 978-0-8342-0138-5

1. Ambulatory medical care — Quality control.
2. Ambulatory medical care. I. Title.
RA399.A1B84 1990
362.1' 2' 0685—dc20
89-18444
CIP

Editorial Services: Ruth Bloom
Library of Congress Catalog Card Number: 89-18444

Printed in the United States of America

1 2 3 4 5

With love
to
my dear friend,
Julie A. Lund

Table of Contents

Preface

Ambulatory health care agencies face significant challenges as they experience competitive demands to demonstrate their delivery of quality and safe services in a cost-effective manner. The continually changing health care environment confronts ambulatory health care providers with economic, political, and legal pressures to balance escalating health care costs without sacrificing quality and safety.

In addition, consumer needs and desires are dictating the delivery of ambulatory health care services. Knowledgeable, active consumers are replacing passive consumers who were once content to follow physician orders without questioning the merit of hospitalization and corresponding treatment plans. With such a knowledgeable and sophisticated approach toward active participation in their health care, consumers are expecting quality care. Quality assurance is welcomed by consumers of health care as a way of ensuring the delivery of quality health care services that allows them to participate actively in their treatment plans and to have control over their health care.

The response of ambulatory health care providers to these challenges has been delayed by the rapid growth of the managed health care industry and a corresponding critical need for expert management of quality ambulatory health care.

The ability of ambulatory health care providers to address quality health care issues has been significantly affected by the minimal availability of complete and practical information useful for the management of quality assurance programs and activities for ambulatory health care.

The intent of this author was to provide information concerning the management of quality assurance programs and activities for both established and developing ambulatory health care providers. The information is offered in the form of written policies and procedures that can be implemented by such providers. These policies and procedures constitute an ambulatory health care quality assurance policy and procedure manual that can be adapted to the needs of each ambulatory health care provider.

Several distinctive features are inherent in this manual. One distinctive feature is the practical application of quality assurance theory to realistic health care situations. Although the manual originates from the author's use of various sources of quality assurance literature that provides theoretical quality assurance concepts, it also reflects the necessity for those concepts to be applied in a useful manner to ambulatory health care practices.

In keeping with its practical application of quality assurance theory, this manual does not include a theoretical discussion of quality assurance concepts but instead refers the reader to a bibliography for the same. This manual is devoted to a strict application of quality assurance theory in order to provide complete information for developing and implementing the same.

A second distinctive feature is the author's attempt to address the conflict between rising health care costs and the need for quality and safe ambulatory health care services. This manual reflects the necessity for well-developed and well-implemented quality assurance programs that will ensure the provision of quality and safe ambulatory health care services while being responsive to the need for decreasing spiraling health care expenses. The author assumes that the inherent quality assurance monitoring approaches in this manual, which continually assess the delivery of ambulatory health care services, will promote reasonable health care expenditures. The author hopes that quality assurance controls will provide ambulatory health care managers with direction for making decisions about provider programs and services without compromising quality and safety.

Another distinctive feature of this manual is the adaptation of quality assurance policies and procedures to meet the needs of different types of ambulatory health care providers. Accordingly, the author acknowledged and promoted the development of various quality assurance programs while providing basic management information pertinent to all ambulatory health care provider quality assurance programs.

This manual's content is derived from the author's personal knowledge and health care administrative experience and expertise in quality assurance and ambulatory health care. This manual is primarily intended as a resource aid for ambulatory health care administrators, managers, physicians, staff members, and other health care professionals involved in the delivery of ambulatory health care services.

Acknowledgments

My sincere thanks go to those who granted permission to use their material in this manual. The material provided important supplementary information that ambulatory health care providers need in order to implement effective quality assurance programs.

My appreciation and thanks to Nancy Weisgerber, Sandy Cannon, Ruth Bloom, and the staff of Aspen Publishers, Inc., who have patiently provided their expertise and support for this manual to become a reality.

Special thanks and love go to Julie Lund, R.N., and Karen Hinze, R.N., whose professional practices always reflect the ideal quality standards for nursing and ambulatory health care. I am truly honored to be their colleague and friend.

My love goes to my mother, Anna Julia Bulau, for her love and encouragement, which richly nurtures my life.

I give my love to Julianne Bulau, my dear sister and friend, for her support and understanding of the sacrifices that are made to pursue dreams.

Finally, my love goes to Lisa Marie and Marlena Joi, my precious daughters, who again waited patiently for my work to be completed while continually giving me love and encouragement. Their sensitivity, independence, and strength become the wind beneath my wings.

Introduction

Emerging quality of health care concerns amid increasing expenditures of health care dollars have created a challenging opportunity for the ambulatory health care industry. This opportunity consists of the sharing of their individual and collective expertise, experience, and leadership for the refinement of ambulatory health care quality assurance programs and activities. This manual reflects a belief in such an opportunity and accordingly presents information regarding the management of quality assurance programs and activities by ambulatory health care providers.

Part I presents general information regarding the development of quality assurance policies and procedures and discusses their implementation, evaluation, and anticipated outcomes. First, some of the problems confronted in the development process are examined: inadequate ambulatory health care resource material for those planning to begin an ambulatory health care quality assurance program; inadequate administrative or writing experience of those who are given the responsibility for preparing the policies and procedures; and the need to incorporate federal, state, and local ambulatory health care provider rules and regulations in the projected policies and procedures. The advantages of having written policies and procedures available—both for those who are planning the development of an ambulatory health care quality assurance program and for those who are preparing revisions or additions to existing ambulatory health care quality assurance policies and procedures—are emphasized.

Next, the objectives and relevant strategies in the process of developing ambulatory health care quality assurance policies and procedures are examined. Following that, some of the essential elements of the process are detailed:

- need to reflect each ambulatory health care provider's unique quality assurance program
- administrative support
- structure and style
- writer's qualifications
- writer's responsibilities
- writer's accountability
- staff involvement
- flexibility in approach
- need to reflect current practices
- accessibility by staff

The general concepts underlying the writing of appropriate ambulatory health care quality assurance policies and procedures are also discussed.

Finally, the implementation, evaluation, and anticipated outcomes of appropriately developed quality assurance policies and procedures are considered. Again, the need to adapt the policies and procedures to reflect each provider's unique quality assurance program and activities is emphasized. Among the anticipated outcomes of such adaptation are a proactive management approach in the provider's operations, organizational stability, financial viability, and the establishment of common ambulatory health care quality assurance terminology and practices.

Following the general introductory material in Part I, the specific quality assurance policies and procedures for various functional and organizational areas in the ambulatory health care setting are provided in manual format in Part II. It is hoped that this material will be useful for all professionals and providers who are striving to deliver quality and safe ambulatory health care services in an increasingly competitive health care environment.

EFFECTS OF PLANNING POLICIES AND PROCEDURES

Ambulatory health care providers have a critical need for clearly written and well-developed quality assurance policies and procedures. These policies and procedures also need to be adequately implemented and evaluated in order for them to have a positive impact on the ambulatory health care provider.

Implementation

Policies and procedures need to be implemented in an organized manner after they have been written. A planned and organized approach will assist the ambulatory health care staff members to assimilate new and/or changed information. Utilizing change theory will create a sensitive and understanding environment for implementing the changes in policies and procedures. Such an environment is important in helping staff members assume responsibility for knowing and implementing the new and/or changed information. It is hoped that staff members will then be willing to participate in the evaluation of policies and procedures.

Evaluation

Evaluation of the ambulatory health care quality assurance policies and procedures is an ongoing process that involves specific criteria for assessing the effects of the defined policy and procedure development strategy.

Appropriate Times for Evaluation

Ambulatory health care quality assurance policies and procedures need to be evaluated at the following times:

- *When the policies and procedures have been developed and/or reviewed and revised but not yet implemented:* Careful analysis should be done to determine whether the revised and reviewed policies and procedures will meet the defined policy and procedure development strategy. Determining the effects of the development strategy will assist the staff members in anticipating problems and the need for changes before the developed policies and procedures are implemented. Evaluation at this time provides a final check to ensure that the policies and procedures will provide the efficient quality assurance management controls that are necessary for the ambulatory health care provider's operations.
- *When the policies and procedures have been developed and/or reviewed and revised and have been implemented:* Evaluation at this point is to determine if the implemented policies and procedures are truly functional for the ambulatory health care provider quality assurance program and activities. Corrective action can be implemented for the defined problems that surface through the evaluation process.
- *After the policies and procedures have been implemented and demonstrate apparent problems:* An evaluation needs to be done whenever implemented policies and procedures seem to be dysfunctional for the ambulatory health care provider's quality assurance program and activities so that specific problems may be identified and corrective action implemented as quickly as possible before problems disrupt operations and escalate to crisis proportions.
- *After corrective actions have been implemented to address demonstrated problems:* Evaluation is critical in order to determine if the corrective actions resolved the problems.

Results

Evaluation results need to be considered carefully if they indicate problems and a need for change. The need for evaluation does not cease after necessary changes have been implemented. Evaluation is a continuous process that determines the need for policy and procedure changes in response to changing health care delivery systems.

Anticipated Outcomes

Several outcomes can be anticipated when adequate time, energy, and administrative and financial support have been given to the development, implementation, and evaluation of clearly written policies and procedures. Some immediate effects are:

- a proactive management approach for the ambulatory health care provider's operation
- organizational stability within the provider's operations
- assurance of quality of ambulatory health care services as a result of the monitoring systems
- financial viability for the ambulatory health care provider
- common ambulatory health care quality assurance terminology and practice for the ambulatory health care provider

Proactive Management

Ambulatory health care quality assurance policies and procedures that have been thoughtfully developed to include planned action for the ambulatory health care provider's operations and potential quality assurance problems will provide an opportunity for the ambulatory health care management staff to respond to daily and emergency situations using a proactive management approach. Well-developed ambulatory health care quality assurance policies and procedures will have been designed with inherent action plans to be used as the ambulatory health care provider operations dictate.

In contrast, policies and procedures that have been hastily and thoughtlessly developed without consideration given to planning for operation and potential problems illustrate a reactive management approach. For example, unclear direction will prevent smooth operations and will precipitate crisis situations for which immediate decisions will need to be made. Decisions constantly made in response to crisis situations may not be the best decisions for the circumstances. Because of the critical lack of planning, a reactive management approach will lead to staff members spending the majority of their time maintaining operations and responding to operational difficulties and crisis situations, with minimal time and energy remaining for the development and growth of services and programs.

Proactive management is clearly the choice for efficient management of the ambulatory health care setting and is realized through well-developed quality assurance policies and procedures. Such a successful proactive management approach will promote organizational stability.

Organizational Stability

Organizational stability is enhanced by well-developed ambulatory health care quality assurance policies and procedures and the resulting proactive management approach. Such organizational stability is reflected in a clear delineation of staff roles and responsibilities in the delivery of quality ambulatory health care services, which in turn promote the efficient management of operations.

Monitoring Systems

Ambulatory health care provider quality assurance policies and procedures provide well-planned monitoring systems that control quality and the safe delivery of ambulatory health care services. For example, a policy and procedure regarding patient accidents monitors the safety of patients within the ambulatory health care environment, thereby ensuring adequate patient safety.

Another example is a policy and procedure regarding patient case conferences that monitors the patient plan of care given by ambulatory health care providers for the appropriate delivery of services. Quality and safety controls that are delineated will ensure adequate monitoring systems in the delivery of ambulatory health care services.

Financial Viability

Financial viability of the ambulatory health care provider is ensured with a proactive management philosophy, organizational stability, and monitoring systems that ensure quality of ambulatory health care services, all of which result from well-developed ambulatory health care quality assurance policies and procedures. Careful planning and development of policies and procedures build financial controls into the delivery of ambulatory health care services. For example, federal, state, local, and third party payor rules and regulations for the reimbursement of quality ambulatory health care services must be written into the policies and procedures so that compliance with the rules and regulations will occur. Compliance with the rules and regulations ensures reimbursement for the delivery of ambulatory health care services. If policies and procedures are developed without consideration of reimbursement rules and regulations, reimbursement for ambulatory health care services will not be forthcoming, and the provider's financial viability will be jeopardized. Financial viability is accomplished with well-developed policies and procedures and is a significant factor in determining if an ambulatory health care provider will survive in a competitive health care environment.

Common Terminology and Practice

Well-developed ambulatory health care quality assurance policies and procedures provide common ambulatory health care quality assurance terminology and practice. One problem that continues to face ambulatory health care providers is the inadequate development of ambulatory health care quality assurance terminology and practice. For example, ambulatory health care providers do not consistently interpret the meaning of *problem assessment*. For some ambulatory health care providers, *problem assessment* means the evaluation step of the quality assurance process that is implemented to determine if the problem has been resolved. For other providers, *problem assessment* means the initial step of the quality assurance process in which data are used to determine the existence, nature, and characteristics of a problem.

An example that relates to inconsistent practice is the different evaluation methods used by ambulatory health care providers to ascertain the effectiveness of their quality assurance program and activities. Some ambulatory health care providers conduct comprehensive evaluations of their quality assurance program and activities. Other providers conduct only partial evaluations of their quality assurance program and activities.

These examples illustrate the advantages of well-developed ambulatory health care quality assurance policies and procedures that will yield common ambulatory health care quality assurance terminology and practice for ambulatory health care providers. Common ambulatory health care terminology and practice will ultimately strengthen the quality and safe delivery of ambulatory health care services.

Survival

Ambulatory health care providers that incorporate well-developed policies and procedures into their operations will meet the survival challenge that exists in a competitive health care environment.

Part I

Ambulatory Health Care Quality Assurance Policy and Procedure Development

THE DEVELOPMENTAL PROCESS

The delivery of quality and safe ambulatory health care services to patients requires the efficient management of ambulatory health care provider operations. Efficient management begins with the development of clearly stated and organized quality assurance policies and procedures. Unfortunately, in many instances the development of ambulatory health care quality assurance policies and procedures is not given a high priority, with the result that the required effort becomes extremely difficult and is often abandoned.

Inhibiting Factors

There are numerous ways by which a low priority may inhibit the development of appropriate ambulatory health care quality assurance policies and procedures:

- The important task of writing the policies and procedures may be assigned to an individual who does not have the requisite qualifications.
- The individual who is given the responsibility of writing the policies and procedures may not be able to give adequate attention to the task because of other infringing work responsibilities. For example, the nursing manager may be inundated with ambulatory health care operational issues and thus be unable to devote enough time to the task of writing policies and procedures.
- Administrative endorsement and support for an appropriate time frame for writing the policies and procedures may be severely restricted or nonexistent. The administration may instead be focused on the need to provide immediate ambulatory health care services so that revenue can be generated regardless of whether adequate quality assurance policies and procedures exist to guide the delivery of such services.
- Administrative endorsement and financial support for the writing of the policies and procedures may be limited or nonexistent.
- The relevant resource material may be scarce or incomplete. In today's competitive ambulatory health care market, ambulatory health care providers may be reluctant to share information regarding policies and procedures. Providers may develop policies and procedures independently, thus wasting time and energy that might otherwise be spent on program development and marketing efforts.
- The independent development of policies and procedures by each ambulatory health care provider may not only suffer from the loss of the expertise of other providers but may also prevent the standardization of ambulatory health care quality assurance terminology and practice. For example, an ambulatory health care provider may experience difficulty in interpreting federal rules and regulations and their application by state authorities. The development of uniform ambulatory health care quality assurance policies and procedures would benefit both the ambulatory health care provider and licensing bodies by

providing the basis for common regulatory terminology and standards regarding the delivery of ambulatory health care services.

- The information needed to develop policies and procedures may seem overwhelming. This may tempt one to take shortcuts and decrease the policy and procedure development workload so that the provider's operations can begin or be maintained.
- The need to take into account a variety of content, including federal, state, and local rules and regulations, requires extensive time, planning, and organization.
- Ideally, the policies and procedures should be developed with the input of more than one individual, for example, members of the ambulatory health care staff or a committee representing the staff. Yet, if the provider is still in the process of development, the relevant staff or a committee may not yet be functioning and the task may thus be given to a single—perhaps the only—staff member functioning in the provider setting.
- The completed policies and procedures may be rushed carelessly through the review, revision, and approval system. The coordination and organization of the policies and procedures may thus be compromised, leading to fragmentation and confusion.
- The policies and procedures may not be written or cataloged in an appropriate format or cataloging system. This could make understanding and implementing them difficult.
- The writer of the policies and procedures may not be able to test them at an operational level, especially if they are applicable to a developing ambulatory health care provider.
- The writer of the policies and procedures may develop an "ownership" problem and resist input from other individuals. These various inadequacies and shortcomings in the process of developing quality assurance policies and procedures tend to produce the negative outcome of inefficient and reactive management of the ambulatory health care provider setting. In such an agency, management and staff time and energy that are directed at resolving current issues and concerns and responding to crisis situations would have been better spent in planning and writing clear ambulatory health care quality assurance policies and procedures aimed at ensuring the survival of the provider in a competitive ambulatory health care market.

Resulting Benefits

Important benefits can be gained from having well-developed ambulatory health care quality assurance policies and procedures. Such policies and procedures:

- provide flexibility in developing ambulatory health care provider needs, services, programs, and activities
- facilitate the acquisition of appropriate resource material for planning the development of an ambulatory health care quality assurance program or for revising or supplementing policy and procedure manuals for an existing provider
- provide common ambulatory health care quality assurance terminology and practices
- permit standardization of ambulatory health care quality assurance information, approaches, and interpretations for ambulatory health care and licensing agencies
- eliminate or at least minimize duplication of effort in the development of policies and procedures
- decrease the time, expense, and energy spent in the development of policies and procedures
- enable the ambulatory health care provider to begin quality assurance activities in a timely manner
- facilitate the review, revision, and approval process
- provide appropriate format, content, and cataloging systems

Development Strategies

These benefits suggest the type of development strategies that are available to a provider's management staff. There are, in effect, two major strategies that the ambulatory health care manager may select. The first gives top priority to the actual delivery of quality ambulatory health care services with only secondary attention to the development of quality assurance policies and procedures. The second strategy gives priority to the development of clearly stated and well-organized policies and procedures. In practice, the astute ambulatory health care manager will probably aim for a compromise between the development of adequate policies and procedures and the delivery of quality and safe services to patients. In any event, the priority given to the development of ambulatory health care quality assurance policies and procedures will have a significant impact on the ambulatory health care provider's ability to survive as a competitive health care provider.

DECISIONS AND OBJECTIVES

A careful review of the purposes of the projected ambulatory health care quality assurance policies and procedures is needed to enable the manager to make appropriate choices and decisions regarding the developmental process. Such a review will usually be guided by the particular provider's health care mission statement, philosophy, objectives, management approach, and organizational structure in the delivery of ambulatory health care services.

Definitions

For the purposes of this discussion, a *policy* is a definite course or method of action selected from among alternatives in light of given conditions to guide and determine present and future decisions. It is, in effect, a high-level, overall plan that embraces the general goals and procedures of an organization.

A *procedure* is a particular way of acting or accomplishing something to fulfill a policy. It is one of a series of steps arranged in a definite order to achieve a policy objective.

Objectives

Reflecting the particular ambulatory health care provider's mission statement, philosophy, objectives, management approach, and organizational structure and functions, the objectives of its quality assurance policies and procedures might include any of the following:

- to provide information to staff members during orientation, inservice training, and continuing education programs regarding the provider's quality assurance policies and operations
- to provide information regarding the provider's services to patients and patient families
- to provide information regarding the provider's quality assurance policies and operations to other health care providers
- to provide information regarding the provider's quality assurance practices to individuals, agencies, and institutions involved with education and research
- to provide information to licensing bodies regarding the provider's compliance with federal, state, and local rules and regulations
- to implement and reflect the provider's mission in the delivery of health care services
- to document the provider's history and continuing efforts to deliver ambulatory health care services
- to support the provider's management philosophy in the delivery of ambulatory health care services
- to document expectations and methods for implementing the provider's quality assurance program by (1) providing current task procedures; (2) facilitating the implementation of appropriate sequences of tasks; (3) providing a ready reference source for the provider's quality assurance activities and operations, thereby facilitating timely decision making; (4) establishing expectations for the provider's staff work performance; (5) fostering a provider team approach; (6) providing guidelines for the provider's operations in relation with other provider operations; (7) documenting infrequently used quality assurance activities and methods; (8) serving as a reference guide for policy and procedure review and revision; (9) serving as a reference guide for developing additional policies and procedures; (10) defining individual and group behavior and norms in quality assurance activities; and (11) facilitating communication among the provider's staff members and other health care providers
- to ensure the quality of the provider's services by (1) providing written and approved quality assurance standards and criteria; (2) providing a means of assessing the provider's clinical practices in the light of such standards and criteria; (3) reflecting continuity of the provider's quality assurance activities; (4) reflecting consistency in the provider's quality assurance activities; (5) minimizing duplication of quality assurance activities; (6) increasing the quality and productivity of the staff members' work performance; (7) providing protection in the event of legal issues and claims; (8) providing an established approach to deal with ethical issues and concerns; (9) ensuring compliance with federal, state, and local rules and regulations; and (10) providing standardized practices in the delivery of ambulatory health care services
- to clarify the provider's quality assurance organizational structure and lines of authority, responsibility, and accountability
- to provide similar ambulatory health care quality assurance terminology for patients, patient families, ambulatory health care providers, individuals involved with education and research, and licensing agencies

Strategies

A review of the purposes of the provider's policies and procedures enables the ambulatory health care manager to plan and implement individualized strategies for the particular provider. Given the widely differing missions and objectives among ambulatory health care providers, considerable variation in the planning of strategies is inevitable. Each ambulatory health care provider must be guided by its particular mission statement, philosophy, objectives, management approach, and organizational structure and functions. The ultimate decisions regarding the development of the provider's quality assurance policies and procedures will be based on and will reflect that provider's unique system for delivering ambulatory health care services.

ESSENTIAL ELEMENTS

The strategic decisions and objectives underlying the development of ambulatory health care quality assurance policies and procedures must take into account specific elements that are crucial to the realization of optimal benefits from the quality assurance policy and procedure process. In the light of these elements, further refinements can be made in the strategies selected by the providers.

Need To Reflect the Provider's Unique Services

As noted earlier, the policies and procedures must reflect the provider's particular mission statement, philosophy, objectives, management approach, and organizational structure and functions. The reader should keep this in mind in reviewing the specific policies and procedures presented in Part II, each of which is likely to require adaptation or refinement to meet the needs of a particular ambulatory health care provider.

Administrative Support

Strong administrative support is essential to procure the time, resources, and funds needed to develop appropriate ambulatory health care quality assurance policies and procedures. The visible organizational demonstration of such support is critical to successful policy and procedure development.

Structure and Style

To ensure structural clarity and stylistic consistency, the writing of the policies and procedures should be the responsibility of a single individual. This will also facilitate the necessary coordination of the policy and procedure content to permit efficient and unduplicated implementation of quality assurance activities.

The writer of the policies and procedures must have a demonstrated ability in program and policy development, in verbal and written communication, in quality assurance, in administrative practice, and in dealing with organizational structure and functions.

Writer's Responsibilities and Accountability

The responsibilities assumed by the writer of quality assurance policies and procedures include:

- developing a strategy for policy and procedure development
- procuring administrative support for the requisite time, resources, and funds
- implementing the approved strategy for policy and procedure development
- collecting information and other input from provider staff members and other individuals and providers as appropriate
- involving other staff members in the policy and procedure development process, as required
- preparing the policies and procedures
- procuring provider approval of the policies and procedures
- distributing the approved policies and procedures

The writer of the quality assurance policies and procedures is accountable to the staff members who will be implementing them. For example, if the staff members identify problems with regard to data collection activities, the writer must respond to their concern in the writing of the particular policy and procedure that deals with data collection.

Thus, to ensure appropriate use of the policies and procedures by the ambulatory health care staff members, their input and involvement are essential. If the provider is still in the development stage, staff participation may be difficult to obtain—especially if the full staff has not yet been hired. Whenever possible, however, staff participation should be actively enlisted in the creation, review, and revision of the policies and procedures.

Flexibility in Approach

The quality assurance policies and procedures must not only be clearly stated to provide guidance in specific situations, they must also be flexible in their adaptability to a variety of situations. Rigid guidelines are likely to promote inadequate management, leading to the implementation of policies and procedures that are inappropriate for specific circumstances. Though ambulatory health care quality assurance policies and procedures usually address major concerns and organizational operations and cannot deal with every situation that may arise, they should be designed to provide at least general guidelines for the quality delivery of all services within the scope of the provider's objectives and mission. Given this flexibility, sensible managers will be able to adapt successfully to changing concerns and circumstances.

Need To Reflect Current Practices

The policies and procedures must embody current descriptions of existing ambulatory health care quality assurance practices to ensure the continuation of quality and safe delivery of services. After the quality assurance policies and procedures have been approved, subsequent review and revision are needed to address further changes in the health care delivery system.

Accessibility to Staff

The established policies and procedures should be readily accessible to ambulatory health care staff members. To this end, they should:

- have clearly stated titles to permit cataloging
- be orderly arranged and numbered in a manual format to permit easy identification and reference
- be in a convenient location to permit easy retrieval and reference

THE WRITING PROCESS

Based on the strategic decisions and objectives and the developmental considerations discussed previously, the writing of ambulatory health care quality assurance policies and procedures should be guided by certain principles. At first, the writing process may seem fragmented and appear to be an overwhelming task. If it is properly approached and guided, however, the writer will discover that it is an organized process with a structure that can aid greatly in coordinating the writer's efforts to produce appropriate policies and procedures.

Content

The content of the policies and procedures should be:

- stated concisely and clearly in words that have precise meaning, thereby minimizing the chances of misinterpretation
- described in language that is familiar to and appropriate for the ambulatory health care staff members
- described in action terms
- written with consistent terminology
- written with minimal use of adjectives
- written with pronouns and antecedents kept close together
- written with correct word placement
- written with bias-free statements
- written with stereotype-free statements
- written with value-free statements
- coordinated with all other relevant policies and procedures

Format

The format of the policies and procedures should represent a logical sequence of action and thought. An outline format promotes this kind of logical sequence by ordering the content in short sentences, with each sentence containing one thought, and in short paragraphs, with each paragraph developing one idea. Examples of such a format are presented in Part II.

In the writing of policies and procedures, a consistent composition style should be maintained. The ambulatory health care quality assurance policies and procedures in Part II have been written in a narrative style to permit the presentation of action and thought in a logical sequence.

Organization

The policies and procedures should be organized in a way so as to be accessible and useful to all provider staff members. This requires a categorical arrangement and numbering system to facilitate placement in a manual format.

IMPLEMENTATION, EVALUATION, AND ANTICIPATED OUTCOMES

In the final stage of the process, the clearly written, well-developed, and appropriately coordinated and approved quality assurance policies and procedures are implemented and then evaluated to ensure the anticipated positive outcomes for the ambulatory health care provider.

Implementation

To assimilate new or revised information in a provider's ambulatory health care quality assurance policies and procedures, an organized approach is necessary. In this phase, it is necessary to create a sensitive and understanding environment that will accommodate the projected changes. Such an environment will help staff members assume responsibility for understanding and implementing the changes. This, in turn, will facilitate their participation in the subsequent evaluation of the policies and procedures.

Evaluation

Evaluation of the ambulatory health care quality assurance policies and procedures is an ongoing process in which specific criteria are used to measure the outcomes of defined policy and procedure development strategies.

Time Intervals

Evaluation may be performed at various time intervals. The initial evaluation may be done at the point at which the policies and procedures have been developed, reviewed, and revised but not yet implemented at an operational level. Careful analysis at this stage will determine if the policies and procedures are in accord with the established development strategy and will enable staff members to determine potential problems and consider the need for changes before the policies and procedures are implemented. This initial evaluation also provides a final check to ensure that the policies and procedures will provide the type of quality assurance controls necessary for efficient quality and safe provider operations.

After the quality assurance policies and procedures have been implemented at the operational level, an evaluation can determine whether the implemented policies and procedures are truly functional in terms of quality assurance activities; if not, corrective action can be taken. In such cases, the specific problems should be identified and the corrective action taken as quickly as possible to minimize disruption in provider operations and to prevent escalation of the problems to crisis proportions. Subsequently, a final evaluation is required to determine if the corrective action has in fact been effective in resolving the problems.

Results

If the evaluations indicate a need for changes in specific policies or procedures, such changes must be carefully considered in the context of an ongoing development and evaluation process. In short, evaluation is a continuous process that determines the need for changes in policies and procedures in response to dynamically changing health care delivery systems.

Anticipated Outcomes

If the appropriate time, energy, and administrative and financial support have been given to the development, implementation, and evaluation of clearly written policies and procedures, certain positive outcomes can be anticipated:

- a proactive management approach, resulting in organizational stability in ambulatory health care provider operations
- monitoring systems that ensure quality of services
- financial viability of the provider's operations
- standardized ambulatory health care quality assurance terminology and practices

Proactive Management and Organizational Stability

Ambulatory health care quality assurance policies and procedures that include planned action to monitor operations and deal with potential problems provide an excellent means for the management staff to respond to both routine and emergency situations using a proactive management approach. With such an approach, the available action plans can be used as the provider's operations dictate.

In contrast, policies and procedures that are hastily or thoughtlessly developed without planning with regard to quality assurance activities and potential problems are likely to result in a reactive management approach. In such cases, the provider's operations will be erratically managed, precipitating crisis situations in which hasty, and perhaps inappropriate, decisions will be made. The failure to include planning in the policies and procedures developmental process and the resulting reactive management approach will create a management environment in which staff members spend the majority of their time trying to maintain operations and responding to operational difficulties and crisis situations, leaving little time and energy for the continued development and growth of the provider's ambulatory health care services and programs.

Clearly, a proactive management approach is preferable. Such an approach, based on well-developed quality assurance policies and procedures, will maximize the opportunities and resources for an efficient management structure and the conditions for organizational stability. In this kind of management environment, the ambulatory health care provider staff members' roles and responsibilities in the delivery of services will be clearly delineated, further enhancing the efficient management of the provider's quality and safe operations.

Monitoring Systems

The quality assurance policies and procedures should include provisions for monitoring systems to control the quality and safety of the provider's services. For example, a procedure regarding patient accidents should include detailed provisions for monitoring patient accidents within the ambulatory health care environment. A procedure regarding patient case conferences should cite the means by which such conferences can monitor the delivery of ambulatory health care services under patient plans of care. In this way, the quality and safety controls embodied in the policies and procedures will ensure that appropriate monitoring systems are available and workable within the provider's health care delivery system.

Financial Viability

Well-developed policies and procedures that are implemented by proactive management and include appropriate monitoring mechanisms provide a sound basis for ensuring the financial viability of the ambulatory health care provider. For example, the financial controls incorporated in the policies and procedures can stipulate the means by which the provider complies with federal, state, local, and third party payor rules and regulations to ensure appropriate reimbursement. Through the continuous application of such procedural controls, the ambulatory health care provider can maximize its chances for survival in today's competitive health care environment.

Common Terminology and Practice

Inadequate development of standardized terminology and practices has posed continuing problems for ambulatory health care providers. For example, ambulatory health care providers do not have a consistent, standardized definition of *problem assessment*. For some providers, *problem assessment* means the evaluation step of the quality assurance process that is implemented to determine if a problem has been resolved. For other providers, it means the first step of the quality assurance process in which data are used to determine the existence, nature, and characteristics of a problem.

Another example of inconsistent quality assurance practice is the different evaluation methods implemented by ambulatory health care providers to determine the effectiveness of their quality assurance program and activities. Some providers have a practice of conducting comprehensive evaluations of their quality assurance program and activities, whereas other providers implement only partial evaluations. With carefully planned and coordinated quality assurance policies and procedures, ambulatory health care providers can do much to eliminate these kinds of inconsistencies. The resulting emergence of common ambulatory health care quality assurance terminology and practices will, in turn, provide a more reliable and comprehensive basis for the delivery of ambulatory health care services.

USE OF THE POLICY AND PROCEDURE MANUAL

The development process outlined for the writing, implementation, and evaluation of ambulatory health care quality assurance policies and procedures is adaptable to both existing and developing ambulatory health care providers, depending on the particular provider's mission statement, philosophy, objectives, management approach, and organizational structure and functions. Thus, based on these developmental principles, the specific policies and procedures presented in Part II of this manual are easily adaptable to a wide spectrum of ambulatory health care quality assurance functions in the areas of general administration, patient care, clinical records, education, personnel, and provider services. In each case, certain elements may need to be modified to fit a particular provider. For example, the quality assurance organizational chart or mission statement may have to be changed. Thus, with appropriate modifications, the Part II policies and procedures constitute an extensive resource tool to enable new and developing providers to develop appropriate policies and procedures and to assist established ambulatory health care providers in reviewing, supplementing, or revising existing policies and procedures. For both types of providers, the Part II material should also aid in the adaptation of new or revised policies and procedures to meet federal, state, local, and third party payor quality assurance requirements.

Thus, both existing and developing ambulatory health care providers can benefit by adapting and utilizing the policies and procedures provided in Part II. For both types of providers, the time, expense, and energy saved by using this resource manual can then be devoted to the achievement of their established objectives in the delivery of quality ambulatory health care services.

BIBLIOGRAPHY

American Medical Association. *Principles of Medical Ethics*. Chicago: American Medical Association, 1958.

American Nurses' Association. *Standards: Nursing Practice*. Kansas City, Mo.: American Nurses' Association, 1973.

Batalden, Paul B., and O'Connor, J. Paul. *Quality Assurance in Ambulatory Care*. Rockville, Md.: Aspen Publishers, Inc., 1980.

Bulau, Judith M. *Administrative Policies and Procedures for Home Health Care*. Rockville, Md.: Aspen Publishers, Inc., 1986.

Bulau, Judith M. *Quality Assurance Policies and Procedures for Home Health Care*. Rockville, Md.: Aspen Publishers, Inc., 1989.

Fox, Daniel J. *Fundamentals of Research in Nursing*. New York: Appleton-Century-Crofts, 1976.

Gould, E. Joyce, and Wargo, Joan. *Home Health Nursing Care Plans*. Rockville, Md.: Aspen Publishers, Inc., 1987.

Joint Commission on Accreditation of Healthcare Organizations. *Ambulatory Health Care Standards Manual*. Chicago: Joint Commission on Accreditation of Healthcare Organizations, 1987.

Lampe, Susan. *Focus Charting*. Minneapolis, Minn.: Eitel Hospital, 1982.

Lesikar, Raymond V. *Basic Business Communication*. Homewood, Ill.: Richard D. Irwin, 1982.

Meisenheimer, Claire Gavin. *Quality Assurance: A Complete Guide to Effective Programs*. Rockville, Md.: Aspen Publishers, Inc., 1985.

Meisenheimer, Claire Gavin. *Quality Assurance for Home Health Care*. Rockville, Md.: Aspen Publishers, Inc., 1989.

Personnel Management Communications. *Writing for the Workplace*. Sec. 10,001. Englewood Cliffs, N.J.: Prentice-Hall, 1983.

Polit, Denise F., and Hungler, Bernadette P. *Nursing Research: Principles and Methods*. Philadelphia: J.B. Lippincott, 1978.

Schroeder, Patricia S., and Maibusch, Regina M. *Nursing Quality Assurance: A Unit-Based Approach*. Rockville, Md.: Aspen Publishers, Inc., 1984.

Schroeder, Patricia S. "Standards of Practice," *Journal of Nursing Quality Assurance*. Vol. 1, Issue 2. Rockville, Md.: Aspen Publishers, Inc., 1987.

Solberg, Leif I., et al., *The Minnesota Project: A Focused Approach to Ambulatory Care Quality Assurance*. Minneapolis, Minn.: Group Health Plan, Inc., HMO Minnesota, and Share Health Plan, 1987.

Van Oosting, James. *The Business Report: Writer, Reader and Text*. Englewood Cliffs, N.J.: Prentice-Hall, 1983.

Wagner, Donna M. *Managing Quality in Home Health Care*. Rockville, Md.: Aspen Publishers, Inc., 1988.

Part II

Ambulatory Health Care Quality Assurance Policy and Procedure Manual

In Part II, specific ambulatory health care quality assurance policies and procedures that can be adapted for use by ambulatory health care providers are presented in manual format. Each section covers a particular area of policy and procedure development and implementation: section 1, general administration; section 2, patient care; section 3, clinical records; section 4, education; section 5, personnel; section 6, provider services. In each section, relevant administrative forms are included as exhibits following the policy and procedure pages on which they are cited.

Section 1000

General Administration

The following policies and procedures are adaptable to quality assurance functions in the area of general administration.

AMBULATORY HEALTH CARE PROVIDER
QUALITY ASSURANCE
POLICY AND PROCEDURE
1001

Subject: Administrative Control

Drafted by: ____________	Date drafted: ____________
Revised by: ____________	Date revised: ____________
Approved by: ____________	Date approved: ____________
Supersedes date: ____________	Page #: ____________
Date effective: ____________	Page: ______ of ____________

POLICY

The ambulatory health care administrative staff maintains administrative control and establishes lines of authority for the delegation of responsibility concerning quality assurance activities.

PURPOSE

To define ambulatory health care staff areas of responsibility concerning quality assurance activities.

PROCEDURE

1. The ambulatory health care provider's governing body assumes overall legal authority and responsibility for quality assurance activities.
2. The Administrator of Ambulatory Health Care assumes overall responsibility and authority for review and evaluation of the provider's ambulatory health care services.
3. The ambulatory health care provider's Medical Director assumes overall responsibility for review and evaluation of the provider's delivery of ambulatory health medical care services.
4. The Administrator of Ambulatory Health Care maintains a standing Ambulatory Health Care Quality Assurance (AHCQA) Committee to coordinate quality assurance activities.
5. The Nursing Manager maintains a standing Nursing Quality Assurance Committee to coordinate quality assurance activities.
6. The interdisciplinary team members/ancillary support services staff maintain standing quality assurance committees to coordinate each discipline's/service's quality assurance activities.
7. The Quality Assurance Manager and AHCQA Committee assume responsibility for the coordination of quality assurance activities.
8. The President of the ambulatory health care provider provides information about quality assurance activities to the provider's Board of Directors.
9. The Administrator of Ambulatory Health Care provides information about quality assurance activities to the Ambulatory Health Care Advisory Committee, AHCQA Committee, Ambulatory Health Care Risk Management (AHCRM) Committee, Ambulatory Health Care Utilization Review (AHCUR) Committee, Quality Assurance Manager, ambulatory health care provider nursing and ancillary support services management staff, and President of the ambulatory health care provider.
10. The Nursing Manager provides information about quality assurance activities to the Administrator of Ambulatory Health Care: Quality Assurance Manager; Ambulatory Health Care Advisory Committee, AHCQA Committee, AHCRM Committee, AHCUR Committee, ambulatory health care nursing staff, and interdisciplinary team members/ancillary support services staff.
11. The interdisciplinary team members/ancillary support services staff provide information about quality assurance activities to the Administrator of Ambulatory Health Care, Quality Assurance Manager, Ambulatory Health Care Advisory Committee, AHCQA Committee, AHCRM Committee, AHCUR Committee, and interdisciplinary team members/ancillary support services staff.
12. Responsibility and authority for quality assurance tasks are documented on a Responsibility and Authority for Quality Assurance Tasks Chart (see Exhibit 1001-1) and a Quality Assurance Organizational Chart (see Figure 1001-1).

Exhibit 1001-1 Responsibility and Authority for Quality Assurance Tasks Chart

AMBULATORY HEALTH CARE PROVIDER

RESPONSIBILITY AND AUTHORITY FOR QUALITY ASSURANCE TASKS

QUALITY ASSURANCE TASKS	AHCQA COMMITTEE		AMBULATORY HEALTH CARE PROVIDER ADMINISTRATION	
	RESPONSIBILITY	AUTHORITY	RESPONSIBILITY	AUTHORITY
Review data sources			X	X
Identify areas needing improvement	X	X		
Prioritize areas needing improvement			X	X
Investigate potential problems			X	X
Recommend corrective action			X	X
Implement corrective action			X	X
Recommend monitoring activities			X	X
Implement monitoring activities			X	X
Document impact on patient care and/or clinical performance			X	X
Assess results of monitoring activities	X	X		
Recommend further corrective action if initial action was not effective	X	X		
Implement further corrective action if initial action was not effective			X	
Report impact on patient care and/or clinical performance	X	X	X	X

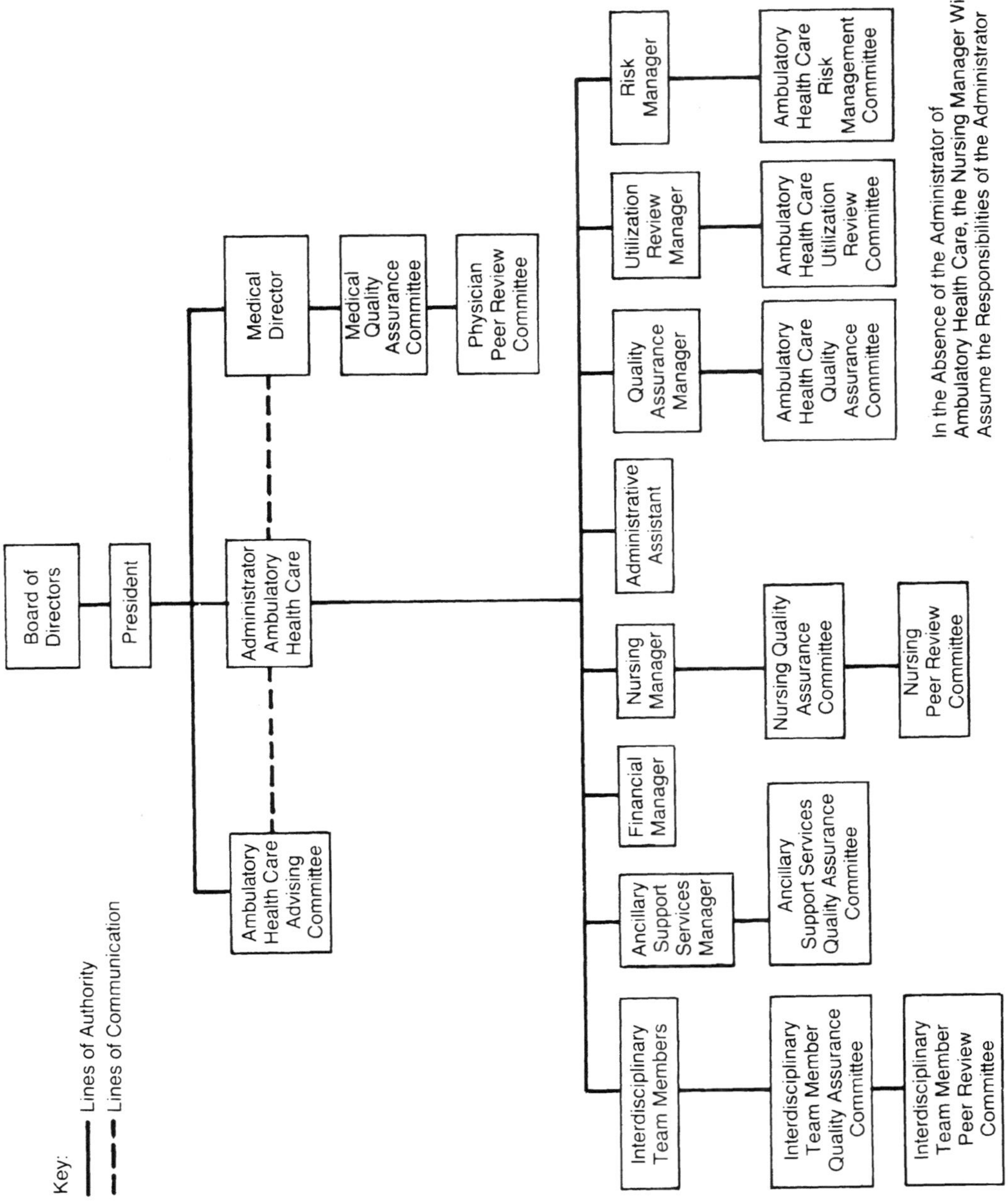

Figure 1001-1 Quality Assurance Organizational Chart

AMBULATORY HEALTH CARE PROVIDER
QUALITY ASSURANCE
POLICY AND PROCEDURE
1002

Subject: Ambulatory Health Care Advisory Committee

Drafted by: ______	Date drafted: ______
Revised by: ______	Date revised: ______
Approved by: ______	Date approved: ______
Supersedes date: ______	Page #: ______
Date effective: ______	Page: ______ of ______

POLICY

The ambulatory health care provider maintains an Ambulatory Health Care Advisory Committee.

PURPOSE

1. To advise ambulatory health care provider on professional issues.
2. To participate in evaluation of ambulatory health care provider programs.
3. To assist ambulatory health care provider in maintaining liaison with other health care providers.

PROCEDURE

1. The ambulatory health care Ambulatory Health Care Advisory Committee includes the following representatives:
   a. Administrator of Ambulatory Health Care
   b. Nursing Manager
   c. Medical Director
   d. physical therapist
   e. occupational therapist
   f. speech therapist
   g. dietician
   h. pharmacist
   i. laboratory technician
   j. radiology
   k. local community member(s) who is neither an owner nor employee of the ambulatory health care provider
2. The Ambulatory Health Care Advisory Committee coordinator is the Administrator of Ambulatory Health Care or Nursing Manager.
3. The Ambulatory Health Care Advisory Committee meets monthly.
4. The Ambulatory Health Care Advisory Committee establishes and annually reviews ambulatory health care provider policies and procedures governing:
   a. scope of services offered
   b. patient visits and transfers policies and procedures
   c. medical supervision
   d. plan of care
   e. emergency care
   f. clinical records
   g. personnel qualifications
   h. program evaluation
5. The Ambulatory Health Care Advisory Committee provides to the provider minutes of its monthly meetings (see Exhibit 1002-2).
6. Ambulatory Health Care Advisory Committee meeting agenda, minutes, and attendance records are filed in the ambulatory health care provider's Ambulatory Health Care Advisory Committee administrative file (see Exhibits 1002-1, 1002-2, and 1002-3).

Exhibit 1002-1 Ambulatory Health Care Advisory Committee Agenda Form

AMBULATORY HEALTH CARE PROVIDER
AMBULATORY HEALTH CARE ADVISORY COMMITTEE

Date:

Time:

AGENDA

Call to order

Approval of minutes

Committee reports:

Old Business: 1.

2.

3.

4.

5.

New Business: 1.

2.

3.

4.

5.

Adjournment

Exhibit 1002-2 Ambulatory Health Care Advisory Committee Meeting Minutes Form

AMBULATORY HEALTH CARE PROVIDER
AMBULATORY HEALTH CARE ADVISORY COMMITTEE MINUTES

Meeting Date:__________ Meeting Time:__________ Meeting Place:__________

Individuals present:____________________

____

____

____

ISSUE	DISCUSSION	ACTION

Exhibit 1002-3 Ambulatory Health Care Advisory Committee Member Attendance Form

AMBULATORY HEALTH CARE PROVIDER
AMBULATORY HEALTH CARE ADVISORY COMMITTEE
MEMBERSHIP ATTENDANCE

Date:

Members attending:

____
____
____
____
____
____
____
____

Members absent:

____
____
____
____
____
____

AMBULATORY HEALTH CARE PROVIDER
QUALITY ASSURANCE
POLICY AND PROCEDURE
1003

Subject: Ambulatory Health Care Advisory Committee Evaluation Function

Drafted by: ______	Date drafted: ______
Revised by: ______	Date revised: ______
Approved by: ______	Date approved: ______
Supersedes date: ______	Page #: ______
Date effective: ______	Page: ____ of ______

POLICY

The ambulatory health care provider's Ambulatory Health Care Advisory Committee provides a professional evaluation service to the provider.

PURPOSE

To assess the extent to which the ambulatory health care provider services are appropriate, adequate, effective, and efficient.

PROCEDURE

1. The Ambulatory Health Care Advisory Committee evaluates annually the ambulatory health care provider's total program based on a policy, administrative, and clinical record review:
   a. The overall policy and administrative review assesses:
      (1) extent to which provider's policy and administrative practices promote patient care that is appropriate, adequate, effective, and efficient
      (2) number of patients receiving each service offered
      (3) number of patient visits
      (4) reasons for patient transfers
      (5) breakdown by patient diagnosis
      (6) sources of patient referral
      (7) total staff days for each service offered
   b. The clinical record review:
      (1) is completed on a quarterly basis
      (2) is completed by appropriate health care professionals representing the scope of the program
      (3) assesses a sample of clinical records for adherence to established policies and procedures that define the provision of ambulatory health care services
      (4) includes a review of clinical records to ascertain adequacy of the care plan and appropriateness of continuing patient care
2. The Ambulatory Health Care Advisory Committee submits the following written reports to the Administrator of Ambulatory Health Care:
   a. annual report of its total program evaluation and recommendations for appropriate actions based on evaluation results, specifically addressing items 1a and 1b
   b. quarterly clinical record reviews with recommendations for appropriate actions based on results of reviews, specifically addressing item 1b
3. The Administrator of Ambulatory Health Care responds with appropriate action to the Ambulatory Health Care Advisory Committee's recommendations based on evaluation results.
4. Ambulatory Health Care Advisory Committee evaluation results are documented on an Evaluation of Ambulatory Health Care Provider's Total Program Form (see Exhibit 1003-1). These evaluation results include statistics as depicted on an Ambulatory Health Care Services Statistical Summary Form (see Exhibit 1003-2).
5. Problems identified through the Ambulatory Health Care Advisory Committee's evaluation function are referred to the Quality Assurance Manager for consideration as a continuous or special quality assurance activity.
6. Ambulatory Health Care Advisory Committee evaluation results are communicated to individuals, as appropriate, according to Policy and Procedure 1010: Confidentiality of Quality Assurance Information, and Policy and Procedure 1001: Administrative Control.
7. The completed Evaluation of Ambulatory Health Care Provider's Total Program Form is filed in the ambulatory health care provider's Evaluation of Ambulatory Health Care Provider's Total Program administrative file.

Exhibit 1003-1 Evaluation of Ambulatory Health Care Provider's Total Program Form

EVALUATION OF AMBULATORY HEALTH CARE PROVIDER'S TOTAL PROGRAM

YEAR OF EVALUATION: ____________

OBJECTIVE: To assess the extent to which the Ambulatory Health Care Provider's program is appropriate, adequate, effective, and efficient.

Topic	Topic Criteria	Topic Criteria Met			Topic Criteria Demonstrates Improvements				Corrective Action Taken	Comments
		Yes	No	Comments	Yes	No	N/A	Comments		
I. Organization Purpose: To ensure maximum efficiency in informing individuals of the organizational structure and lines of authority and their responsibilities and accountability.	1. There is an organizational or written description of the provider's organization.									
	2. The provider operates in accordance with the formal organizational plan.									
	3. The provider meets current legal requirements for operation.									
	4. All professional personnel hold a current license.									
	5. There are objectives that identify expected outcomes of the program.									
II. Administration Purpose: To ensure the provision, management, and support of the provider's operations. A. Governing Body	1. There is a governing body.									
	2. There are identified duties and responsibilities for the governing body.									
	3. The governing body functions in accordance with written rules and regulations.									

continues

Exhibit 1003-1 *continued*

Topic	Topic Criteria	Topic Criteria Met			Topic Criteria Demonstrates Improvements				Corrective Action Taken	Comments
		Yes	No	Comments	Yes	No	N/A	Comments		
	4. Minutes of meetings show that the members have taken action on all business for which they are responsible.									
B. Advisory Group	1. The advisory group is representative of the community served.									
	2. There are identified functions for the advisory group.									
	3. The advisory group functions in accordance with written rules and regulations.									
	4. Minutes of meetings show that the members have considered problems, offered recommendations to the governing body, and carried out their functions.									
C. Administrative Personnel	1. There is an appointed administrator and an alternate administrator.									
	2. The administrator functions in accordance with the job description.									
	3. There is an appointed Nursing Manager and an alternate Supervisor available during operating hours.									
	4. The Nursing Manager functions in accordance with the job description.									
D. Personnel	1. There are written personnel policies.									
	2. Personnel practices are carried out according to the written policies.									

continues

Exhibit 1003-1 *continued*

Topic	Topic Criteria	Topic Criteria Met			Topic Criteria Demonstrates Improvements				Corrective Action Taken	Comments
		Yes	No	Comments	Yes	No	N/A	Comments		
	3. There is a written job description that identifies current qualifications, duties, and functions.									
	4. There is an up-to-date personnel file for every employee.									
E. Reports and Records	1. Records and reports are kept according to policy guidelines, providing for:									
	a. maintenance and protection									
	b. retention									
	c. availability and confidentiality									
	2. Contracts:									
	a. are current									
	b. identify expectations of contractee and contractor									
F. Fiscal	1. Budgets, audits, accounting, and billing are carried out according to provider policy.									
	2. Billings are accurate and current.									
	3. There are established fees and a reasonable plan for collection.									
	4. Funding sources are multiple and adequate to meet costs.									

continues

Exhibit 1003-1 *continued*

Topic	Topic Criteria	Topic Criteria Met			Topic Criteria Demonstrates Improvements				Corrective Action Taken	Comments
		Yes	No	Comments	Yes	No	N/A	Comments		
G. Statistical Information	1. There is a description of service area and population served.									
	2. An annual report of service by age and diagnosis is provided.									
	3. The provider can identify the source of client referral.									
	4. The provider can identify the average lengths of care by diagnosis and age, and/or determine average number of visits/diagnoses.									
	5. The provider collects statistics that identify the number of visits made by each discipline.									
	6. There are statistics that identify the number and reason for transfer.									
	7. There are guidelines that identify how the statistical data are to be used and by whom.									
	8. Based on a review of gathered statistics and data:									
	a. The needs of the community served have been reviewed.									
	b. Services offered are adequate.									
	c. Staffing is adequate.									
	d. Operating hours are adequate.									
	e. Geographic area is adequate.									
	f. Population groups are being served adequately.									

continues

Exhibit 1003-1 *continued*

Topic	Topic Criteria	Topic Criteria Met			Topic Criteria Demonstrates Improvements				Corrective Action Taken	Comments
		Yes	No	Comments	Yes	No	N/A	Comments		
	g. Continuity of care systems is adequate.									
	h. Financial services are adequate.									
	9. There are statistics that identify staff recruitment.									
III. Patient Care and Transfer	1. Patients are accepted for care according to defined criteria.									
Purpose: To ensure appropriate utilization of services.	2. Patients are transferred according to transfer criteria.									
IV. Medical Service	1. There are written policies for medical care and treatment.									
Purpose: To ensure physician input and supervision of medical care.	2. There are written guidelines for medical emergencies.									
	3. The responsibilities of the attending physician are identified.									
	4. Medical consultation is available and utilized.									
	5. Patients are provided care only under current plans of treatment approved by attending physician.									
V. Service	1. There are written philosophy and objectives.									
Purpose: To ensure quality nursing care and adequate supervision of nursing care.	2. The nursing process (assessment, goal setting, planning, implementing, evaluating) is incorporated in policy and practice.									

continues

Exhibit 1003-1 *continued*

Topic	Topic Criteria	Topic Criteria Met			Topic Criteria Demonstrates Improvements				Corrective Action Taken	Comments
		Yes	No	Comments	Yes	No	N/A	Comments		
	3. There are written guidelines that describe expected nursing functions.									
	4. These guidelines are in accordance with current nursing practice.									
	5. The nursing staff keep current in knowledge and clinical competence by attending inservice meetings and by participating in continuing education.									
VI. Therapy Services Purpose: To ensure adequate provision of therapy services.	1. There are written guidelines that describe the scope of physical therapy, speech therapy, and/or occupational therapy services.									
	2. Current practice is in accordance with written policies.									
	3. The therapists keep current in knowledge and clinical competence by attending appropriate inservice meetings and by participating in continuing education.									
VII. Ancillary Support Services	1. There are written guidelines that describe the scope of ancillary support services.									
Purpose: To ensure adequate ancillary support services.	2. There are written guidelines that identify expected role functions of ancillary support services staff.									
	3. There is evidence of communication between the ancillary support services staff and patient family.									

continues

Exhibit 1003-1 *continued*

Topic	Topic Criteria	Topic Criteria Met			Topic Criteria Demonstrates Improvements				Corrective Action Taken	Comments
		Yes	No	Comments	Yes	No	N/A	Comments		
VIII. Other Services										
IX. Coordination of Patient Services	1. There are guidelines for liaison between and among all staff involved in the care of patients.									
Purpose: To ensure coordination of patient services so that efforts effectively complement all staff and support the objectives outlined in the plan of treatment.	2. Staff meetings and/or patient case conferences are held regularly.									
	3. There is an established method by which information is exchanged with other health care providers to ensure continuity of care for the patient.									

Signature of Administrator of Ambulatory Health Care

Date of Signature

continues

Exhibit 1003-1 *continued*

FOLLOWING SECTION TO BE COMPLETED BY AMBULATORY HEALTH CARE ADVISORY COMMITTEE

Date of Ambulatory Health Care Advisory Committee Review: ____________

______________________________ ______________________________
Ambulatory Health Care Advisory Committee Representative Signature Date of Signature

Ambulatory Health Care Advisory Committee Recommendations for Corrective Action:

CORRECTIVE ACTION RECOMMENDATIONS	DATE CORRECTIVE ACTION OUTCOME WILL BE ASSESSED	INDIVIDUAL RESPONSIBLE	DATE CORRECTIVE ACTION OUTCOME ASSESSED	CORRECTIVE ACTION EFFECTIVE		
				YES	NO	IF NO, EXPLAIN

FOLLOWING SECTION TO BE COMPLETED BY GOVERNING BODY

Date of Governing Body Review: ____________

______________________________ ______________________________
Signature of President Date of Signature

Exhibit 1003-2 Ambulatory Health Care Services Statistical Summary Form

AMBULATORY HEALTH CARE PROVIDER
AMBULATORY HEALTH CARE SERVICES STATISTICAL SUMMARY

Date: ____________

	Total Numbers		
Statistical Item	**Daily**	**Month to Date**	**Year to Date**
1. Patient visits			
2. Telephone calls regarding ambulatory health care services			
3. Referrals received			
4. Referral source: A. Self			
B. Family			
C. Attending physician			
D. Acute care facility			
E. Long-term care facility			
F. Other			
5. Patient visits by diagnosis: A.			
B.			
C.			
D.			
E.			
F.			
G.			
H.			
I.			
J.			
K.			
L.			
M.			
N.			
O.			
P. Other			
6. Sex: A. Male			
B. Female			
7. Total male and female			
8. Age: A. 16-21 years			
B. 22-32 years			
C. 33-43 years			
D. 44-54 years			
E. 55-65 years			

continues

Exhibit 1003-2 *continued*

Statistical Item	Total Numbers		
	Daily	Month to Date	Year to Date
F. 66-76 years			
G. 77-87 years			
H. 88+ years			
9. Average age			
10. Geographic location of patients A. Hennepin			
B. Ramsey			
C. Dakota			
D. Washington			
E. Scott			
F. Rice			
G. Carver			
H. Other			
11. Patients receiving each service offered: A. Skilled nursing service			
B. Laboratory			
C. Radiology			
D. Physical therapy			
E. Occupational therapy			
F. Social service			
G. Speech therapy			
H. Nutrition			
I. Pharmacy			
J. Other			
12. Total number of services patients receiving			
13. Total staff days for each service offered			
14. Visits A. Skilled nursing service			
B. Laboratory			
C. Radiology			
D. Physical therapy			
E. Occupational therapy			
F. Social service			
G. Speech therapy			
H. Nutrition			
I. Pharmacy			
J. Other			
15. Total visits			
16. Payment source A. Medicare			
B. Medicaid			
C. Insurance company			

continues

Exhibit 1003-2 *continued*

Statistical Item	Total Numbers		
	Daily	**Month to Date**	**Year to Date**
D. HMO			
E. Private pay			
F. Other			
17. Transfers			
18. Transfer reasons A. Patient admitted to acute care facility			
B. Patient admitted to extended care facility			
C. Patient admitted to outpatient care facility			
D. Patient moved out of ambulatory health care provider's geographic service area			
E. Patient obtaining ambulatory health care services from another source			
F. Patient condition does not require ambulatory health care services			
G. Patient needs cannot be met by ambulatory health care provider			
H. Patient noncompliant with the delivery of ambulatory health care services			
I. Patient reimbursement source for ambulatory health care services inadequate			
J. Other			
19. Transferred to: A. Physician			
B. Acute care facility			
C. Extended care facility			
D. Outpatient care facility			
E. Home health care agency			
F. Other			
20. Other			

AMBULATORY HEALTH CARE PROVIDER
QUALITY ASSURANCE
POLICY AND PROCEDURE
1004

Subject: Ambulatory Health Care Quality Assurance Committee

Drafted by: ______	Date drafted: ______
Revised by: ______	Date revised: ______
Approved by: ______	Date approved: ______
Supersedes date: ______	Page #: ______
Date effective: ______	Page: ____ of ______

POLICY

The ambulatory health care provider implements ambulatory health care activities through the Ambulatory Health Care Quality Assurance (AHCQA) Committee.

PURPOSE

1. To facilitate, coordinate, and integrate the ambulatory health care provider's quality assurance activities.
2. To develop, implement, and evaluate effective quality assurance activities according to the ambulatory health care provider's mission statement, philosophy, and objectives.

PROCEDURE

1. The AHCQA Committee includes the following members:
   a. Administrator of Ambulatory Health Care
   b. Nursing Manager
   c. Medical Director
   d. Quality Assurance Manager
   e. two ambulatory health care registered nurses
   f. two ambulatory health care licensed practical nurses
   g. two ambulatory health care aides
   h. interdisciplinary team members/ancillary support services staff:
      (1) physical therapist
      (2) occupational therapist
      (3) speech therapist
      (4) dietician
      (5) pharmacist
      (6) laboratory technician
      (7) radiology technician
      (8) Financial Manager
2. The ambulatory health care registered and licensed practical nurse, ambulatory health care aide, and interdisciplinary team members/ancillary support services staff AHCQA Committee member positions are selected by notifying individuals of the opportunity to serve on the committee.
3. The selection process used to give all eligible individuals an equal opportunity to be selected as a member of the AHCQA Committee is as follows:
   a. A Request for AHCQA Committee Members Memorandum (see Exhibit 1004-1) that discusses the opportunity for individuals to serve on the AHCQA Committee is distributed to eligible individuals in which they are asked to submit their names and job titles to the Quality Assurance Manager if they are interested in becoming AHCQA Committee members.
   b. Names of eligible individuals who express interest in serving on the AHCQA Committee are compiled.
   c. Where the available number of committee member positions equals the number of names submitted, those individuals who submitted their names are given the committee member positions.
   d. Where the available number of committee member positions is less than the number of names submitted, the following lottery method is used to provide an equal selection opportunity for all individuals who submitted their names for consideration:
      (1) All submitted names are written on individual pieces of paper of similar size.
      (2) All of the written names are put into a container and shuffled.
      (3) An individual draws the number of names required to fill the committee member positions out of the container.
      (4) The individuals whose names are drawn out of the container are selected to become AHCQA Committee members.

   e. Where the available number of committee member positions is greater than the number of names submitted, the Administrator of Ambulatory Health Care appoints the AHCQA Committee members.
   f. The outcome of the AHCQA Committee member selection process is communicated to all individuals who expressed an interest in serving on the AHCQA Committee on either an Appointment to the AHCQA Committee Memorandum (see Exhibit 1004-2) or an AHCQA Committee Membership Memorandum (see Exhibit 1004-3).
4. AHCQA Committee members serve on the committee for at least two years.
5. The AHCQA Committee chairperson is the Quality Assurance Manager.
6. AHCQA Committee membership terms expire on a rotation system in order to maintain maximum continuity in the committee membership.
7. Each AHCQA Committee member has one equal vote.
8. The AHCQA Committee quorum is not less than one half of the committee membership.
9. Recommendations of the AHCQA Committee are made by a vote of a majority of a quorum.
10. The AHCQA Committee meets on the third Tuesday of every month.
11. AHCQA Committee functions and responsibilities include the following:
   a. review and analysis of information from data sources
   b. assistance in problem assessment
   c. assistance in problem identification
   d. assistance in problem selection
   e. assistance in problem study
   f. assistance in development of valid clinical criteria
   g. recommendation for corrective actions to the Administrator of Ambulatory Health Care and Nursing Manager
   h. assistance in monitoring effectiveness of corrective actions
   i. assistance in problem evaluation
   j. assistance in problem reassessment
   k. annual review of AHCQA Committee functions and responsibilities relative to the ambulatory health care provider's quality assurance activities
   l. submission of documented annual AHCQA reviews to the Administrator of Ambulatory Health Care and Nursing Manager
   m. documentation and communication concerning quality assurance activities to the Administrator of Ambulatory Health Care and Nursing Manager
12. Meetings of the AHCQA Committee are documented in meeting minutes (see Exhibit 1004-4).
13. The AHCQA Committee provides minutes of its monthly meetings to the Ambulatory Health Care Advisory Committee.
14. AHCQA Committee meeting agenda, minutes, and attendance records are filed in the AHCQA Committee Meeting Minutes administrative file.
15. AHCQA Committee members serve as resource persons to other ambulatory health care provider staff members for problem assessment, identification, selection, study, corrective action, monitoring, evaluation, and reassessment according to each committee member's respective area of practice.
16. AHCQA Committee activities are conducted according to Policy and Procedure 1010: Confidentiality of Quality Assurance Information, and Policy and Procedure 1001: Administrative Control.

Exhibit 1004-1 Request for Ambulatory Health Care Quality Assurance Committee Members Memorandum

TO: Ambulatory Health Care Registered Nurses
Ambulatory Health Care Aides
Interdisciplinary Team Members/Ancillary Support Services Staff
FROM: Quality Assurance Manager
SUBJECT: Request for Ambulatory Health Care Quality Assurance Committee Members
DATE:

This is to inform you of an opportunity that is available to individuals who are interested in serving on the Ambulatory Health Care Quality Assurance (AHCQA) Committee to volunteer for open AHCQA Committee member positions. The available AHCQA Committee member positions are as follows:

Representative Position	Representative Position Available?		# of Representative Positions Available
	YES	NO	
Ambulatory Health Care Registered Nurse			
Ambulatory Health Care Licensed Practical Nurse			
Ambulatory Health Care Aide			
Physical Therapist			
Occupational Therapist			
Speech Therapist			
Dietician			
Pharmacist			
Laboratory Technician			
Radiology Technician			
Financial Manager			
Other			

The selection process that will be used to give all eligible individuals an equal opportunity to be selected as a member of the AHCQA Committee will be as follows:

1. Eligible individuals will be asked to submit their names and job titles to the Quality Assurance Manager if they are interested in becoming AHCQA Committee members.
2. The names of eligible individuals who express interest in serving on the AHCQA Committee will be compiled.
3. Where the available number of committee member positions equals the number of names submitted, those individuals who submitted their names will be given the committee member positions.
4. Where the available number of committee member positions is less than the number of names submitted, the following lottery method will be used to provide an equal selection opportunity for all individuals who submitted their names for consideration:
   a. All submitted names will be written on individual pieces of paper of similar size.
   b. All of the written names will be put into a container and shuffled.
   c. An individual will draw the number of names required to fill the committee member positions out of the container.
   d. The individuals whose names are drawn out of the container will be selected to become AHCQA Committee members.
5. Where the available number of committee member positions is greater than the number of names submitted, the Administrator of Ambulatory Health Care will appoint the AHCQA Committee members.
6. The outcome of the AHCQA Committee member selection process will be communicated to all individuals who expressed an interest in serving on the AHCQA Committee.

AHCQA Committee members serve on the committee for at least two years, and the AHCQA Committee meets on the third Tuesday of every month.

If you are interested in becoming an AHCQA Committee member, please give me your name and job title by __________.
(date)

Thank you for your consideration.

Exhibit 1004-2 Appointment to the Ambulatory Health Care Quality Assurance Committee Memorandum

TO:
FROM: Quality Assurance Manager
SUBJECT: Appointment to Ambulatory Health Care Quality Assurance Committee
DATE:

I want to thank you for your interest in serving as an Ambulatory Health Care Quality Assurance (AHCQA) Committee member.

I am pleased to inform you that you have been selected to become an AHCQA Committee member.

We will inform you when the next AHCQA meeting is scheduled and will send you the agenda for the same.

Thank you for your interest. I look forward to meeting with you.

Exhibit 1004-3 Ambulatory Health Care Quality Assurance Committee Membership Memorandum

TO:
FROM: Quality Assurance Manager
SUBJECT: Ambulatory Health Care Quality Assurance Committee Membership
DATE:

I want to thank you for your interest in serving as an Ambulatory Health Care Quality Assurance (AHCQA) Committee member.

We received an enthusiastic response to our request for AHCQA Committee members. Unfortunately, the number of committee member positions required to be filled was less than the number of names that were submitted. Therefore, we used a lottery method to provide an equal opportunity for all individuals who had submitted their names for consideration. I am sorry to inform you that your name was not drawn.

However, more opportunities will be available for you to serve on the AHCQA Committee whenever committee member positions become open. Your name will be placed on a waiting list so that you can be informed of future opportunities to serve as an AHCQA Committee member.

Once again, thank you for submitting your name for consideration in serving as an AHCQA Committee member.

Exhibit 1004-4 Ambulatory Health Care Quality Assurance Committee Minutes Form

AMBULATORY HEALTH CARE PROVIDER
AMBULATORY HEALTH CARE QUALITY ASSURANCE COMMITTEE MINUTES

Meeting Date:____________ Meeting Time:____________ Meeting Place:____________

Individuals Present:____________________________________

ISSUE	DISCUSSION	ACTION

AMBULATORY HEALTH CARE PROVIDER
QUALITY ASSURANCE
POLICY AND PROCEDURE
1005

Subject: Ambulatory Health Care Risk Management Committee	
Drafted by:	Date drafted:
Revised by:	Date revised:
Approved by:	Date approved:
Supersedes date:	Page #:
Date effective:	Page: ____ of ____

POLICY

The ambulatory health care provider implements ambulatory health care risk management activities through the Ambulatory Health Care Risk Management (AHCRM) Committee.

PURPOSE

1. To identify unsafe acts, conditions, and incidents that indicate operational errors.
2. To identify the primary cause of unsafe acts, conditions, and incidents.
3. To identify and control sets of circumstances that produce unsafe acts, conditions, and incidents.
4. To determine whether effective risk management controls are being used.
5. To incorporate patient safety into the provision of ambulatory health care services.
6. To define responsibility and accountability of management and line staff.
7. To decrease all exposed risks that would jeopardize the provider's income and assets.
8. To decrease the likelihood of litigation for a compensable event occurring in patient care, staff, financial, and criminal activities.

PROCEDURE

1. The AHCRM Committee includes the following:
   a. Nursing Manager
   b. Medical Director
   c. Quality Assurance Manager
   d. two ambulatory health care registered nurses
   e. two ambulatory health care licensed practical nurses
   f. two ambulatory health care aides
   g. interdisciplinary team members/ancillary support services staff:
      (1) physical therapist
      (2) occupational therapist
      (3) speech therapist
      (4) dietician
      (5) pharmacist
      (6) laboratory technician
      (7) radiology technician
      (8) Financial Manager
2. The ambulatory health care registered and licensed practical nurse, ambulatory health care aide, and interdisciplinary team members/ancillary support services staff AHCRM Committee member positions are selected by notifying individuals of the opportunity to serve on the committee.
3. The selection process used to give all eligible individuals an equal opportunity to be selected as a member of the AHCRM Committee is as follows:
   a. A Request for AHCRM Committee Members Memorandum (see Exhibit 1005-1) that discusses the opportunity for individuals to serve on the AHCRM Committee is distributed to eligible individuals in which they are asked to submit their names and job titles to the Quality Assurance Manager if they are interested in becoming AHCRM Committee members.
   b. Names of eligible individuals who express interest in serving on the AHCRM Committee are compiled.
   c. Where the available number of committee member positions equals the number of names submitted, those individuals who submitted their names are given the committee member positions.
   d. Where the available number of committee member positions is less than the number of names submitted, the following lottery method is used to provide an equal selection opportunity for all individuals who submitted their names for consideration:

(1) All submitted names are written on individual pieces of paper of similar size.
(2) All of the written names are put into a container and shuffled.
(3) An individual draws the number of names required to fill the committee member positions out of the container.
(4) The individuals whose names are drawn out of the container are selected to become AHCRM Committee members.

e. Where the available number of committee member positions is greater than the number of names submitted, the Administrator of Ambulatory Health Care appoints the AHCRM Committee members.
f. The outcome of the AHCRM Committee member selection process is communicated to all individuals who expressed an interest in serving on the AHCRM Committee on either an Appointment to the AHCRM Committee Memorandum (see Exhibit 1005-2) or an AHCRM Committee Membership Memorandum (see Exhibit 1005-3).

4. AHCRM Committee members serve on the committee for at least two years.
5. AHCRM Committee membership terms expire on a rotation system in order to maintain maximum continuity in the committee membership.
6. The AHCRM Committee chairperson is the Risk Manager.
7. Each AHCRM Committee member has one equal vote.
8. The AHCRM Committee quorum is not less than one half of the committee membership.
9. Recommendations of the AHCRM Committee are made by a vote of a majority of a quorum.
10. The AHCRM Committee meets on the first Tuesday of every month.
11. AHCRM Committee functions and responsibilities include analysis and review of the following:
    a. patient quality of care outcomes
    b. high risk/volume/problem areas in providing patient care
    c. patient satisfaction surveys
    d. staff satisfaction surveys
    e. physician satisfaction surveys
    f. patient concerns
    g. staff concerns
    h. physician concerns
    i. clinical record reviews
    j. patient care plan reviews
    k. patient incidents/accidents and claims
    l. medication errors
    m. malpractice claims, litigation, settlements, and judgments
    n. equipment malfunction statistics
    o. documentation
    p. infection statistics
    q. unanticipated patient hospitalizations
    r. unanticipated patient deaths
    s. caregiver competency
    t. on-call system
    u. staff competency and job performance
    v. staff turnover
12. Meetings of the AHCRM Committee are documented in meeting minutes (see Exhibit 1005-4).
13. The AHCRM Committee provides minutes of its monthly meetings to the Ambulatory Health Care Quality Assurance Committee and Ambulatory Health Care Advisory Committee.
14. AHCRM Committee meeting agenda, minutes, and attendance records are filed in the AHCRM Committee Meeting Minutes administrative file.
15. AHCRM Committee members serve as resource persons to other ambulatory health care provider staff members for risk management activities according to each committee member's respective area of practice.
16. AHCRM Committee activities are conducted according to Policy and Procedure 1010: Confidentiality of Quality Assurance Information, and Policy and Procedure 1001: Administrative Control.

Exhibit 1005-1 Request for Ambulatory Health Care Risk Management Committee Members Memorandum

TO: Ambulatory Health Care Registered Nurses
Ambulatory Health Care Licensed Practical Nurses
Ambulatory Health Care Aides
Interdisciplinary Team Members/Ancillary Support Services Staff
FROM: Quality Assurance Manager
SUBJECT: Request for Ambulatory Health Care Risk Management Committee Members
DATE:

This is to inform you of an opportunity that is available to individuals who are interested in serving on the Ambulatory Health Care Risk Management (AHCRM) Committee to volunteer for open AHCRM Committee member positions. The available AHCRM Committee member positions are as follows:

Representative Position	Representative Position Available?		# of Representative Positions Available
	YES	NO	
Ambulatory Health Care Registered Nurse			
Ambulatory Health Care Licensed Practical Nurse			
Ambulatory Health Care Aide			
Physical Therapist			
Occupational Therapist			
Speech Therapist			
Dietician			
Pharmacist			
Laboratory Technician			
Radiology Technician			
Financial Manager			
Other			

The selection process that will be used to give all eligible individuals an equal opportunity to be selected as a member of the AHCRM Committee will be as follows:

1. Eligible individuals will be asked to submit their names and job titles to the Quality Assurance Manager if they are interested in becoming AHCRM Committee members.
2. The names of eligible individuals who express interest in serving on the AHCRM Committee will be compiled.
3. Where the available number of committee member positions equals the number of names submitted, those individuals who submitted their names will be given the committee member positions.
4. Where the available number of committee member positions is less than the number of names submitted, the following lottery method will be used to provide an equal selection opportunity for all individuals who submitted their names for consideration:
   a. All submitted names will be written on individual pieces of paper of similar size.
   b. All of the written names will be put into a container and shuffled.
   c. An individual will draw the number of names required to fill the committee member positions out of the container.
   d. The individuals whose names are drawn out of the container will be selected to become AHCRM Committee members.
5. Where the available number of committee member positions is greater than the number of names submitted, the Administrator of Ambulatory Health Care will appoint the AHCRM Committee members.
6. The outcome of the AHCRM Committee member selection process will be communicated to all individuals who expressed an interest in serving on the AHCRM Committee.

AHCRM Committee members serve on the committee for at least two years, and the AHCRM Committee meets on the first Tuesday of every month.

If you are interested in becoming an AHCRM Committee member, please give me your name and job title by ___________.
(date)

Thank you for your consideration.

Exhibit 1005-2 Appointment to the Ambulatory Health Care Risk Management Committee Memorandum

TO:
FROM: Quality Assurance Manager
SUBJECT: Appointment to Ambulatory Health Care Risk Management Committee
DATE:

I want to thank you for your interest in serving as an Ambulatory Health Care Risk Management (AHCRM) Committee member.

I am pleased to inform you that you have been selected to become an AHCRM Committee member.

We will inform you when the next AHCRM meeting is scheduled and will send you the agenda for the same.

Thank you for your interest. I look forward to meeting with you.

Exhibit 1005-3 Ambulatory Health Care Risk Management Committee Membership Memorandum

TO:
FROM: Quality Assurance Manager
SUBJECT: Ambulatory Health Care Risk Management Committee Membership
DATE:

I want to thank you for your interest in serving as an Ambulatory Health Care Risk Management (AHCRM) Committee member.

We received an enthusiastic response to our request for AHCRM Committee members. Unfortunately, the number of committee member positions required to be filled was less than the number of names that were submitted. Therefore, we used a lottery method to provide an equal opportunity for all individuals who had submitted their names for consideration. I am sorry to inform you that your name was not drawn.

However, more opportunities will be available for you to serve on the AHCRM Committee whenever committee member positions become open. Your name will be placed on a waiting list so that you can be informed of future opportunities to serve as an AHCRM Committee member.

Once again, thank you for submitting your name for consideration in serving as an AHCRM Committee member.

Exhibit 1005-4 Ambulatory Health Care Risk Management Committee Minutes Form

AMBULATORY HEALTH CARE PROVIDER
AMBULATORY HEALTH CARE RISK MANAGEMENT ASSURANCE COMMITTEE MINUTES

Meeting Date:________________ Meeting Time:________________ Meeting Place:________________

Individuals Present:____

ISSUE	DISCUSSION	ACTION

AMBULATORY HEALTH CARE PROVIDER
QUALITY ASSURANCE
POLICY AND PROCEDURE
1006

Subject: Ambulatory Health Care Utilization Review Committee	
Drafted by: ______	Date drafted: ______
Revised by: ______	Date revised: ______
Approved by: ______	Date approved: ______
Supersedes date: ______	Page #: ______
Date effective: ______	Page: ____ of ______

POLICY

The ambulatory health care provider implements ambulatory health care utilization review activities through the Ambulatory Health Care Utilization Review (AHCUR) Committee.

PURPOSE

1. To determine adequacy of patient care.
2. To determine effectiveness of patient care.
3. To identify problems with patient care.
4. To establish a system for problem resolution.
5. To ensure peer review of patient care.
6. To identify gaps in ambulatory health care services.
7. To ensure that established policies and procedures are followed in the provision of ambulatory health care services.
8. To provide information required for planning, developing, implementing, evaluating, and monitoring ambulatory health care staff development and services.

PROCEDURE

1. The AHCUR Committee includes the following members:
   a. Nursing Manager
   b. Medical Director
   c. Quality Assurance Manager
   d. two ambulatory health care registered nurses
   e. two ambulatory health care licensed practical nurses
   f. two ambulatory health care aides
   g. interdisciplinary team members:
      (1) physical therapist
      (2) occupational therapist
      (3) speech therapist
      (4) dietician
      (5) pharmacist
   h. laboratory technician
   i. radiology technician
   j. Financial Manager
   k. one ambulatory health care professional not employed by the ambulatory health care provider
2. The ambulatory health care registered and licensed practical nurse and interdisciplinary team members AHCUR Committee member positions are selected by notifying individuals of the opportunity to serve on the committee.
3. The selection process used to give all eligible individuals an equal opportunity to be selected as a member of the AHCUR Committee is as follows:
   a. A Request for AHCUR Committee Members Memorandum (see Exhibit 1006-1) that discusses the opportunity for individuals to serve on the AHCUR Committee is distributed to eligible individuals in which they are asked to submit their names and job titles to the Quality Assurance Manager if they are interested in becoming AHCUR Committee members.
   b. Names of eligible individuals who express interest in serving on the AHCUR Committee are compiled.
   c. Where the available number of committee member positions equals the number of names submitted, those individuals who submitted their names are given the committee member positions.
   d. Where the available number of committee member positions is less than the number of names submitted, the following lottery method is used to provide an equal selection opportunity for all individuals who submitted their names for consideration:
      (1) All submitted names are written on individual pieces of paper of similar size.
      (2) All of the written names are put into a container and shuffled.

   (3) An individual draws the number of names required to fill the committee member positions out of the container.
   (4) The individuals whose names are drawn out of the container are selected to become AHCUR Committee members.
   e. Where the available number of committee member positions is greater than the number of names submitted, the Administrator of Ambulatory Health Care appoints the AHCUR Committee members.
   f. The outcome of the AHCUR Committee member selection is communicated to all individuals who expressed an interest in serving on the AHCUR Committee on either an Appointment to the AHCUR Committee Memorandum (see Exhibit 1006-2) or an AHCUR Committee Membership Memorandum (see Exhibit 1006-3).
4. AHCUR Committee members serve on the committee for at least two years.
5. AHCUR Committee membership terms expire on a rotation system in order to maintain continuity in the committee membership.
6. The AHCUR Committee chairperson is the Utilization Review Manager.
7. Each AHCUR Committee member has one equal vote.
8. The AHCUR Committee quorum is not less than one half of the committee membership.
9. Recommendations of the AHCUR Committee are made by a vote of a majority of a quorum.
10. The AHCUR Committee meets on the second Wednesday of every month.
11. AHCUR Committee functions and responsibilities include analysis and review of the following:
   a. ambulatory health care provider patient visits, transfers, hospitalizations, and deaths, as reflected in statistics derived from but not limited to the following data sources:
      (1) Ambulatory Health Care Patient Register Log (see Exhibit 1006-4)
      (2) Daily Ambulatory Health Care Patient Census Form (see Exhibit 1006-5)
   b. appropriateness of delays in the provision of ambulatory health care services
   c. referral/intake process, such as number of provider visits, referral sources, and efficiency of patient visits and transfer processes, obtained by compiling statistics from the Ambulatory Health Care Patient Register Log
   d. operating costs, such as fluctuations in costs and high costs
   e. high risk/volume/problem prone areas in providing patient care
   f. outcome-oriented reviews of patient nursing care plans
   g. outcome-oriented reviews of patient medical care plans
   h. appropriateness of length and cost of ambulatory health care visits
   i. process-oriented reviews of individualized patient care
   j. process- and/or outcome-oriented reviews of specific patient diagnoses or categories
   k. interdisciplinary team care plan reviews
12. Meetings of the AHCUR Committee are documented in meeting minutes (see Exhibit 1006-6).
13. The AHCUR Committee provides minutes of its monthly meeting to the Ambulatory Health Care Quality Assurance Committee and Ambulatory Health Care Advisory Committee.
14. AHCUR Committee meeting agenda, minutes, and attendance records are filed in the AHCUR Committee Meeting Minutes administrative file.
15. AHCUR Committee members serve as resource persons to other ambulatory health care provider staff members for utilization review activities according to each committee member's respective area of practice.
16. AHCUR Committee activities are conducted according to Policy and Procedure 1010: Confidentiality of Quality Assurance Information, and Policy and Procedure 1001: Administrative Control.

Exhibit 1006-1 Request for Ambulatory Health Care Utilization Review Committee Members Memorandum

TO: Ambulatory Health Care Registered Nurses
Ambulatory Health Care Licensed Practical Nurses
Ambulatory Health Care Aides
Interdisciplinary Team Members/Ancillary Support Services Staff
FROM: Quality Assurance Manager
SUBJECT: Request for Ambulatory Health Care Utilization Review Committee Members
DATE:

This is to inform you of an opportunity that is available to individuals who are interested in serving on the Ambulatory Health Care Utilization Review (AHCUR) Committee to volunteer for open AHCUR Committee member positions. The available AHCUR Committee member positions are as follows:

Representative Position	Representative Position Available?		# of Representative Positions Available
	YES	NO	
Ambulatory Health Care Registered Nurse			
Ambulatory Health Care Licensed Practical Nurse			
Ambulatory Health Care Aide			
Physical Therapist			
Occupational Therapist			
Speech Therapist			
Dietician			
Pharmacist			
Laboratory Technician			
Radiology Technician			
Financial Manager			
Other			

The selection process that will be used to give all eligible individuals an equal opportunity to be selected as a member of the AHCUR Committee will be as follows:

1. Eligible individuals will be asked to submit their names and job titles to the Quality Assurance Manager if they are interested in becoming AHCUR Committee members.
2. The names of eligible individuals who express interest in serving on the AHCUR Committee will be compiled.
3. Where the available number of committee member positions equals the number of names submitted, those individuals who submitted their names will be given the committee member positions.
4. Where the available number of committee member positions is less than the number of names submitted, the following lottery method will be used to provide an equal selection opportunity for all individuals who submitted their names for consideration:
   a. All submitted names will be written on individual pieces of paper of similar size.
   b. All of the written names will be put into a container and shuffled.
   c. An individual will draw the number of names required to fill the committee member positions out of the container.
   d. The individuals whose names are drawn out of the container will be selected to become AHCUR Committee members.
5. Where the available number of committee member positions is greater than the number of names submitted, the Administrator of Ambulatory Health Care will appoint the AHCUR Committee members.
6. The outcome of the AHCUR Committee member selection process will be communicated to all individuals who expressed an interest in serving on the AHCUR Committee.

AHCUR Committee members serve on the committee for at least two years, and the AHCUR Committee meets on the third Tuesday of every month.

If you are interested in becoming an AHCUR Committee member, please give me your name and job title by ________.
(date)

Thank you for your consideration.

Exhibit 1006-2 Appointment to the Ambulatory Health Care Utilization Review Committee Membership Memorandum

TO:
FROM: Quality Assurance Manager
SUBJECT: Appointment to Ambulatory Health Care Utilization Review Committee
DATE:

I want to thank you for your interest in serving as an Ambulatory Health Care Utilization Review (AHCUR) Committee member.

I am pleased to inform you that you have been selected to become an AHCUR Committee member.

We will inform you when the next AHCUR meeting is scheduled and will send you the agenda for the same.

Thank you for your interest. I look forward to meeting with you.

Exhibit 1006-3 Ambulatory Health Care Utilization Review Committee Membership Memorandum

TO:
FROM: Quality Assurance Manager
SUBJECT: Ambulatory Health Care Utilization Review Committee Membership
DATE:

I want to thank you for your interest in serving as an Ambulatory Health Care Utilization Review (AHCUR) Committee member.

We received an enthusiastic response to our request for AHCUR Committee members. Unfortunately, the number of committee member positions required to be filled was less than the number of names that were submitted. Therefore, we used a lottery method to provide an equal opportunity for all individuals who had submitted their names for consideration. I am sorry to inform you that your name was not drawn.

However, more opportunities will be available for you to serve on the AHCUR Committee whenever committee member positions become open. Your name will be placed on a waiting list so that you can be informed of future opportunities to serve as an AHCUR Committee member.

Once again, thank you for submitting your name for consideration in serving as an AHCUR Committee member.

Exhibit 1006-4 Ambulatory Health Care Patient Register Log

AMBULATORY HEALTH CARE PATIENT REGISTER

NO.	DATE OF APPOINTMENT REQUEST	REFERRAL SOURCE	DATE OF ACTUAL PATIENT VISIT	PATIENT NAME	PATIENT CLINICAL RECORD NO.	PATIENT ADDRESS	PATIENT TELEPHONE NO.	PATIENT BIRTH DATE	PATIENT DIAGNOSIS	PATIENT SEX		PATIENT NATIONAL ORIGIN					
										F	M	WHITE	BLACK	ASIAN	HISPANIC	AMER. INDIAN	OTHER (PLEASE DESCRIBE)

AMBULATORY HEALTH CARE PATIENT REGISTER

PATIENT'S PHYSICIAN			PATIENT PAYMENT SOURCE							DATE SERVICES COMPLETED	TRANSFERRED TO	TRANSFER REASON
			PRIVATE PAY	INS. CO.	MEDICARE	MEDICAID	WORKER'S COMP.	AUTO INS.	OTHER (PLEASE DESCRIBE)			

Source: Reprinted with permission from Briggs Corporation, Des Moines, Iowa, © 1989.

Exhibit 1006-5 Daily Ambulatory Health Care Patient Census Form

DAILY AMBULATORY HEALTH CARE PATIENT CENSUS

DATE ______________________ , 19 ________

NEW PATIENTS (RECORD TOTAL ON LINE 1 OF SUMMARY)

NO.	TIME	PATIENT NAME

NEW PATIENTS (RECORD TOTAL ON LINE 1 OF SUMMARY)

NO.	TIME	PATIENT NAME

HOSPITALIZATIONS (RECORD TOTAL ON LINE 2 OF SUMMARY)

NO.	TIME	PATIENT NAME

TRANSFERS (RECORD TOTAL ON LINE 3 OF SUMMARY)

NO.	TIME	PATIENT NAME

DEATHS (RECORD TOTAL ON LINE 4 OF SUMMARY)

NO.	TIME	PATIENT NAME

DAILY PATIENT SUMMARY

LINE NO.	ITEM	NO. OF: ADULTS	CHILDREN	NEWBORNS
1	Total New Patients			
2	Hospitalizations			
3	Transfers			
4	Deaths			
5	Total Transfers and Deaths (Sum of Lines 3 & 4)			
6	Total Patient Visits (From Patient Register Log)			

Signature of Individual Completing This Form | Date of Signature

Form 3374/2 BRIGGS, Des Moines, IA 50306 (800) 247-2343
PRINTED IN U.S.A.

Source: Reprinted with permission from Briggs Corporation, Des Moines, Iowa, © 1989.

Exhibit 1006-6 Ambulatory Health Care Utilization Review Committee Minutes Form

AMBULATORY HEALTH CARE PROVIDER
AMBULATORY HEALTH CARE UTILIZATION REVIEW COMMITTEE MINUTES

Meeting Date:__________ Meeting Time:__________ Meeting Place:__________

Individuals Present:______________________________

____

____

____

ISSUE	DISCUSSION	ACTION

AMBULATORY HEALTH CARE PROVIDER
QUALITY ASSURANCE
POLICY AND PROCEDURE
1007

Subject: Available and Accessible Ambulatory Health Care Services	
Drafted by: ______	Date drafted: ______
Revised by: ______	Date revised: ______
Approved by: ______	Date approved: ______
Supersedes date: ______	Page #: ______
Date effective: ______	Page: ______ of ______

POLICY

Available and accessible ambulatory health care services are provided to patients.

PURPOSE

1. To ensure that health care services are readily available to meet the health care needs of patients.
2. To ensure that health care services are provided in a timely manner in consideration of convenience for patients.
3. To ensure that urgent/emergency health care services are provided in an expedient manner.
4. To provide patients with appropriate referrals to health care providers whenever necessary.

PROCEDURE

1. Adequate available and accessible comprehensive ambulatory health care services are facilitated by sufficent existing:
   a. ambulatory health care policies and procedures that address available and accessible ambulatory health care services
   b. number and type of health care providers
   c. primary and specialty physicians/other health care providers
   d. diagnostic, urgent, and emergency services, supplies, equipment, and medications
   e. preventive equipment maintenance policies and procedures
   f. ancillary support services
   g. provider environment conducive for patients to safely access, move about, and function in provider premises
   h. provider telephone resource services
   i. provider referral system
2. Information is given to patients regarding the provision of 24 hours a day, seven days a week ambulatory health care services, and including:
   a. provider's office hours of operation
   b. list of primary and specialty physicians/other health care providers
   c. instructions for scheduling appointments with their physician/health care provider
   d. instructions for obtaining telephone health care information from the provider
   e. instructions for obtaining after office hours urgent/emergency health care from the provider
   f. instructions for obtaining appropriate referrals to other providers
3. Patients are triaged in order to determine priorities for providing available and accessible health care services to meet their health care needs.
4. Patients are encouraged to schedule their appointments for health care services with their health care provider as desired and necessary.
5. Patients are assisted to schedule appointments for health care services within a reasonable timeframe of the patient's request for an appointment, as follows:
   a. urgent health care visit where patient is presenting with symptoms (e.g., urinary symptoms): schedule appointment within 24 hours of patient request for appointment
   b. nonurgent health care visit where patient is presenting with symptoms (e.g., painful joint symptoms with no obvious history of illness or injury): schedule appointment within one week of patient request for appointment
   c. nonurgent health care visit where patient is not presenting with symptoms (e.g., history and physical): schedule appointment within six weeks of patient request for appointment

6. Scheduled appointments for health care visits are conducted within a reasonable timeframe of patient's arrival for scheduled appointment, as follows:
   a. urgent health care visit where patient is presenting with symptoms (e.g., urinary symptoms): conduct visit within ten minutes of patient's arrival for scheduled appointment
   b. nonurgent health care visit where patient is presenting with symptoms (e.g., painful joint symptoms with no obvious history of illness or injury): conduct visit within twenty minutes of patient's arrival for scheduled appointment
   c. nonurgent health care visit where patient is not presenting with symptoms (e.g., history and physical): conduct visit within twenty minutes of patient's arrival for scheduled appointment
7. Emergency health care services are provided in an expedient manner for patients requiring them.

AMBULATORY HEALTH CARE PROVIDER
QUALITY ASSURANCE
POLICY AND PROCEDURE
1008

Subject: Conclusions	
Drafted by: ____________	Date drafted: ____________
Revised by: ____________	Date revised: ____________
Approved by: ____________	Date approved: ____________
Supersedes date: ____________	Page #: ____________
Date effective: ____________	Page: ______ of ______

POLICY

Conclusions are based on analyzed and interpreted study topic data.

PURPOSE

1. To present study topic results in the context of the specific study topic.
2. To formulate judgment or opinions based on the study topic.
3. To explain formulated study topic conclusions and the rationale for the same.
4. To answer the study topic question, problem, or hypothesis.

PROCEDURE

1. Conclusions are derived from analyzed and interpreted study topic data.
2. Conclusions focus on:
   a. presentation and interpretation of study topic results
   b. implications of study topic results within a broader context
   c. application of conclusions to study topic question, problem, or hypothesis
   d. generalization of study topic results to comparable situations
3. Conclusions are documented on a Special Quality Assurance Study Form (see Exhibit 1037-1).
4. Conclusions are communicated to individuals, as appropriate, according to Policy and Procedure 1010: Confidentiality of Quality Assurance Information, and Policy and Procedure 1001: Administrative Control.

AMBULATORY HEALTH CARE PROVIDER
QUALITY ASSURANCE
POLICY AND PROCEDURE
1009

Subject: Confidentiality for Patients	
Drafted by:	Date drafted:
Revised by:	Date revised:
Approved by:	Date approved:
Supersedes date:	Page #:
Date effective:	Page: ____ of ____

POLICY

Ambulatory health care staff and interdisciplinary team members/ancillary support services staff provide confidentiality for patients and patient clinical records.

PURPOSE

1. To protect the patient's right to privacy.
2. To protect patient clinical records from loss, alteration, unauthorized use, or damage.

PROCEDURE

1. All requests for patient information are reviewed to determine whether or not the individual requesting the information will be allowed access to the information.
2. Access to patient information is determined in the light of the requesting individual's or provider's involvement with the patient's clinical care and the nature of the patient's health insurance program:
   a. Involvement with patient clinical care:
      (1) Professional personnel directly involved with the patient's care—for example, the attending physician; social worker; physical and occupational therapists; and laboratory, radiology, and pharmacy staff members—are permitted access to the patient's clinical record.
      (2) Telephone requests for access to patient clinical information by professional personnel directly involved with the patient's clinical care are referred to the Nursing Manager.
      (3) Professional personnel not directly involved with the patient's clinical care are not permitted access to the patient's clinical record without a completed and signed Patient Consent Form allowing such access (see Exhibit 1009-1).
   b. The nature of the patient's health insurance program:
      (1) Governmental and private agencies and individuals are permitted access to patient information regarding health insurance claims in the light of current rules and regulations of the Social Security Administration regarding the disclosure of such information.
      (2) Disclosure of such patient information regarding a health insurance claim according to Social Security rules and regulations requires a completed and signed Patient Consent Form.
      (3) Requests for information about a Medicare beneficiary, a Medicare claim, or other related information that may not be disclosed are referred to the Administrator of Ambulatory Health Care.
      (4) Individuals not directly involved with the patient's clinical care are not permitted access to the patient's clinical record without a completed and signed Patient Consent Form permitting such access.
3. A completed and signed Patient Consent Form must:
   a. specify the patient's name
   b. be signed and dated by the patient or by someone authorized to act in the patient's behalf:
      (1) If the patient is a minor, the consent form is signed by the patient's parent or guardian.
      (2) If the patient has a legally appointed guardian, the consent form is signed by that guardian.
      (3) If the patient is unable to sign the consent form but uses some other means to indicate approval, such means must be witnessed or notarized.
      (4) If the validity of a signature is questioned, the ambulatory health care provider may require a notarized signature.

(5) If the patient is deceased, signed consent is given by the person representing the patient's estate.

c. specify that the ambulatory health care provider is authorized to disclose the patient information
d. specify the information that the patient is authorizing the ambulatory health care provider to disclose
e. specify the individual and/or agency to whom the information is being released
f. specify the purpose for which the information is being released
g. specify an expiration date for the consent that will not exceed two years from the date the consent form was signed
h. specify that the consent form may be revoked at any time

4. Additional release of patient information is dependent on further patient consent.
5. Completed and signed consent forms and released patient information are protected against their unauthorized use.
6. The original patient clinical record is filed and locked in the ambulatory health care provider office.
7. The entire original patient clinical record must not be removed from the ambulatory health care provider office except under subpoena for court cases when the court does not accept certified Xerox copies for the record.
8. Original patient clinical records are filed and locked in the ambulatory health care provider office for seven years.

Exhibit 1009-1 Patient Consent Form

AMBULATORY HEALTH CARE PROVIDER
PATIENT CONSENT FORM

Patient name: __________
Patient clinical record no: __________
Patient Social Security no: __________
Patient Medicare no: __________
Patient insurance no: __________

PERMISSION FOR DISCLOSURE AND USE OF INFORMATION

I consent to the release of my ambulatory health care provider records to be reviewed by authorized representatives of Medicare/Medicaid, Medicare intermediary, and/or my private insurance company(ies) for use in determining my ambulatory health care benefits. Specifically, I authorize and request the ambulatory health care provider to allow

____
(name of individual/agency requesting to review patient clinical records)

to examine my personal and medical records now held by the ambulatory health care provider and to make machine or photographic copies of said records.

I understand that I have the legal right to refuse the release of my personal and medical records now held by the ambulatory health care provider and that I am waiving this legal right by signing this consent. I authorize

____
(name of individual/agency requesting to review patient clinical records)

to examine said records for the following purpose(s) only:

1. __________
2. __________
3. __________

This consent shall be valid whatever period of time is reasonably necessary for

____
(name of individual/agency requesting to review patient clinical records)

to fulfill the above described purpose(s), such period not to exceed two (2) years from the date of signature, or until I revoke this consent in writing. Such a revocation of this consent shall have a prospective effect only.

I consent to the review of my ambulatory health care provider records for any necessary audits within the ambulatory health care provider.

PERMISSION TO PROVIDE THE AMBULATORY HEALTH CARE PROVIDER SERVICES TO PATIENT

I consent to have the ambulatory health care provider provide me with emergency and nonemergency ambulatory health care services according to ambulatory health care provider policies and procedures and approval of my physician.

I consent to abide by the ambulatory health care provider's specific policies and procedures relating to ambulatory health care which have been reviewed with me and which include provisions for termination of ambulatory health care services at my request, my physician's request, and/or the ambulatory health care provider's request.

PERMISSION TO PAY MEDICARE AMBULATORY HEALTH CARE BENEFITS
TO THE AMBULATORY HEALTH CARE PROVIDER

I certify that the information given to me in applying for payment under Title XVIII of the Social Security Act is correct.

I request that payment of authorized ambulatory health care benefits be made in my behalf.

I also understand that I am responsible for any health insurance deductible and coinsurance.

continues

Exhibit 1009-1 *continued*

PATIENT RESPONSIBILITY FOR PAYMENT OF AMBULATORY HEALTH CARE PROVIDER SERVICES

I understand that the ambulatory health care provider will promptly present claims for the payment of my ambulatory health care services to my private insurance company(ies) or through contracts that may be available to the ambulatory health care provider.

I also understand that I am responsible for the entire ambulatory health care provider bill or balance of the same bill as determined by the ambulatory health care provider, if the submitted claims or any part of them are denied for payment.

I understand that the ambulatory health care provider's failure to request immediate payment shall not release me or my estate from the obligation to pay the ambulatory health care provider.

I understand that this consent may be revoked by me at any time.

I agree to abide by all of the above conditions and I acknowledge that this agreement shall bind me and my heirs, executors, administrators, and assigns.

I hereby certify that I have read and understand the above agreement and I have executed said agreement of my own free will effective of the date below.

Signature of Patient/Guardian — Date of Signature

Signature of Witness — Date of Signature

AMBULATORY HEALTH CARE PROVIDER
QUALITY ASSURANCE
POLICY AND PROCEDURE
1010

Subject: Confidentiality of Quality Assurance Information

Drafted by: ______	Date drafted: ______
Revised by: ______	Date revised: ______
Approved by: ______	Date approved: ______
Supersedes date: ______	Page #: ______
Date effective: ______	Page: ____ of ______

POLICY

Ambulatory health care staff and interdisciplinary team members/ancillary support services staff provide confidentiality for quality assurance activities.

PURPOSE

1. To protect patients' right to privacy.
2. To protect quality assurance information from loss, alterations, unauthorized use, and damage.

PROCEDURE

1. Patient/ambulatory health care provider staff member identifiable information is not included in written or computerized information/reports.
2. A coding system for written/computerized information/reports is used to identify patients or ambulatory health care provider staff members, with the coding system key held confidential by the Administrator of Ambulatory Health Care, Nursing Manager, and Quality Assurance Manager.
3. Quality assurance activity worksheets are destroyed after quality assurance data are analyzed and final results are summarized.
4. Legal issues and concerns regarding internal and external review activities are addressed in accordance with legal standards established for review organizations (see Exhibit 1010-1).
5. All requests for quality assurance information are reviewed to determine whether or not the individual requesting the information will be allowed access to the information.
6. Access to quality assurance information is determined in light of the requesting individual's or agency's involvement with the quality assurance activities.
7. The following individuals are permitted access to quality assurance information:
   a. Ambulatory Health Care Quality Assurance Committee members
   b. Quality Assurance Manager
   c. Administrator of Ambulatory Health Care
   d. Nursing Manager
   e. Ambulatory Health Care Advisory Committee members
   f. external ambulatory health care review agencies, such as local or state health department or Medicare agencies, during on-site reviews of provider's activities
   g. President of the ambulatory health care provider
   h. Board of Directors of the ambulatory health care provider
   i. individuals assigned to work on the provider's quality assurance activities
8. All requests for quality assurance information by individuals not included in item 7 above are referred to the Administrator of Ambulatory Health Care for approval/disapproval of the same.
9. Released quality assurance information:
   a. is protected against unauthorized use
   b. is reviewed in the presence of an ambulatory health care provider administrative staff member
   c. is not removed from the ambulatory health care provider office except upon approval of the Administrator of Ambulatory Health Care
10. Documents concerning quality assurance activities are filed in the ambulatory health care provider's Quality Assurance Activities administrative file.

Exhibit 1010-1 Legal Health Care Information Standards for Review Organizations

HEALTH CARE INFORMATION; REVIEW ORGANIZATION

145.61 DEFINITIONS.

Subdivision 1. As used in sections 145.61 to 145.67 the terms defined in this section have the meanings given them.

Subd. 2. **Professional**. "Professional" means a person licensed or registered to practice a healing art under chapter 147 or 148, to practice dentistry under chapter 150A, to practice as a pharmacist under chapter 151, or to practice podiatry under chapter 153.

Subd. 3. "Professional service" means service rendered by a professional of the type such professional is licensed to perform.

Subd. 4. "Health care" means professional services rendered by a professional or an employee of a professional and services furnished by a hospital, sanatorium, nursing home or other institution for the hospitalization or care of human beings.

Subd. 4a. "Administrative staff" means the staff of a hospital or clinic.

Subd. 5. "Review organization" means a nonprofit organization acting according to clause (k) or a committee whose membership is limited to professionals and administrative staff, except where otherwise provided for by state or federal law, and which is established by a hospital, by a clinic, by one or more state or local associations of professionals, by an organization of professionals from a particular area or medical institution, by a health maintenance organization as defined in chapter 62D, by a nonprofit health service plan corporation as defined in chapter 62C, by a professional standards review organization established pursuant to United States Code, title 42, section 1320c-1 et seq., or by a medical review agent established to meet the requirements of section 256B.04, subdivision 15, or 256D.03, subdivision 7, paragraph (b), or by the department of human services, to gather and review information relating to the care and treatment of patients for the purposes of:

(a) evaluating and improving the quality of health care rendered in the area or medical institution;

(b) reducing morbidity or mortality;

(c) obtaining and disseminating statistics and information relative to the treatment and prevention of diseases, illness and injuries;

(d) developing and publishing guidelines showing the norms of health care in the area or medical institution;

(e) developing and publishing guidelines designed to keep within reasonable bounds the cost of health care;

(f) reviewing the quality or cost of health care services provided to enrollees of health maintenance organizations;

(g) acting as a professional standards review organization pursuant to United States Code, title 42, section 1320c-1 et seq.;

(h) determining whether a professional shall be granted staff privileges in a medical institution or whether a professional's staff privileges should be limited, suspended or revoked;

(i) reviewing, ruling on, or advising on controversies, disputes or questions between:

(1) health insurance carriers or health maintenance organizations and their insureds or enrollees;

(2) professional licensing boards acting under their powers including disciplinary, license revocation or suspension procedures and health providers licensed by them when the matter is referred to a review committee by the professional licensing board;

(3) professionals and their patients concerning diagnosis, treatment or care, or the charges or fees therefor;

(4) professionals and health insurance carriers or health maintenance organizations concerning a charge or fee for health care services provided to an insured or enrollee;

(5) professionals or their patients and the federal, state, or local government, or agencies thereof;

(j) providing underwriting assistance in connection with professional liability insurance coverage applied for or obtained by dentists, or providing assistance to underwriters in evaluating claims against dentists;

(k) acting as a medical review agent under section 256B.04, subdivision 15, or 256D.03, subdivision 7, paragraph (b); or

(l) providing recommendations on the medical necessity of a health service, or the relevant prevailing community standard for a health service.

History: *1971 c 283 s 1; 1974 c 295 s 1,2; 1975 c 73 s 1; 1976 c 173 s 49; 1982 c 424 s 133; 1982 c 546 s 1; 1985 c 184 s 1; 1989 c 282 art 3 s 30*

145.62 LIMITATION ON LIABILITY FOR PERSONS PROVIDING INFORMATION TO REVIEW ORGANIZATION.

No person, firm, or corporation providing information to a review organization shall be subject to any action for damages or other relief, by reason of having furnished such information, unless such information is false and the person providing such information knew, or had reason to believe, such information was false.

History: *1971 c 283 s 2*

145.63 LIMITATION ON LIABILITY FOR MEMBERS OF REVIEW ORGANIZATIONS.

No person who is a member or employee of, who acts in an advisory capacity to or who furnishes counsel or services to, a review organization shall be liable for damages or other relief in any action brought by a person or persons whose activities have been or are being scrutinized or reviewed by a review organization, by reason of the performance by the person of any duty, function or activity of such review organization, unless the performance of such duty, function or activity was motivated by malice toward the person affected thereby. No person shall be liable for damages or other relief in any action by reason of the performance of the person of any duty, function, or activity as a member of a review committee or by reason of any recommendation or action of the review committee when the person acts in the reasonable belief that the action or recommendation is warranted by facts known to the person or the review organization after reasonable efforts to ascertain the facts upon which the review organization's action or recommendation is made, except that any corporation designated as a review organization under the Code of Federal Regulations, title 42, section 466 (1983) shall be subject to actions for damages or other relief by reason of any failure of a person, whose care or treatment is required to be scrutinized or reviewed by the review organization, to receive medical care or treatment as a result of a determination by the review organization that medical care was unnecessary or inappropriate.

History: *1971 c 283 s 3; 1974 c 295 s 3; 1985 c 184 s 2; 1986 c 444*

145.64 CONFIDENTIALITY OF RECORDS OF REVIEW ORGANIZATION.

All data and information acquired by a review organization, in the exercise of its duties and functions, shall be held in confidence, shall not be disclosed to anyone except to the extent necessary to carry out one or more of the purposes of the review organization, and shall not be subject to subpoena or discovery. No person described in

continues

Exhibit 1010-1 *continued*

section 145.63 shall disclose what transpired at a meeting of a review organization except to the extent necessary to carry out one or more of the purposes of a review organization. The proceedings and records of a review organization shall not be subject to discovery or introduction into evidence in any civil action against a professional arising out of the matter or matters which are the subject of consideration by the review organization. Information, documents or records otherwise available from original sources shall not be immune from discovery or use in any civil action merely because they were presented during proceedings of a review organization, nor shall any person who testified before a review organization or who is a member of it be prevented from testifying as to matters within the person's knowledge, but a witness cannot be asked about the witness' testimony before a review organization or opinions formed by the witness as a result of its hearings. The provisions of this section shall not apply to a review organization of the type described in section 145.61, subdivision 5, clause (h).

History: *1971 c 283 s 4; 1974 c 295 s 4; 1975 c 73 s 2; 1986 c 444*

145.65 GUIDELINES NOT ADMISSIBLE IN EVIDENCE.

No guideline established by a review organization shall be admissible in evidence in any proceeding brought by or against a professional by a person to whom such professional has rendered professional services.

History: *1971 c 283 s 5*

145.66 PENALTY FOR VIOLATION.

Any disclosure other than that authorized by section 145.64, of data and information acquired by a review committee or of what transpired at a review meeting, is a misdemeanor.

History: *1971 c 283 s 6*

145.67 PROTECTION OF PATIENT.

Nothing contained in sections 145.61 to 145.67 shall be construed to relieve any person of any liability which the person has incurred or may incur to a patient as a result of furnishing health care to such patient.

History: *1971 c 283 s 7; 1986 c 444*

MALPRACTICE ACTIONS; EXPERT REVIEW

145.682 CERTIFICATION OF EXPERT REVIEW; AFFIDAVIT.

Subdivision 1. **Definition.** For purposes of this section, "health care provider" means a physician, surgeon, dentist, or other health care professional or hospital, including all persons or entities providing health care as defined in section 145.61, subdivisions 2 and 4, or a certified health care professional employed by or providing services as an independent contractor in a hospital.

Subd. 2. **Requirement.** In an action alleging malpractice, error, mistake, or failure to cure, whether based on contract or tort, against a health care provider which includes a cause of action as to which expert testimony is necessary to establish a prima facie case, the plaintiff must: (1) unless otherwise provided in subdivision 3, paragraph (b), serve upon defendant with the summons and complaint an affidavit as provided in subdivision 3; and (2) serve upon defendant within 180 days after commencement of the suit an affidavit as provided by subdivision 4.

Subd. 3. **Affidavit of expert review.** The affidavit required by subdivision 2, clause (1), must be by plaintiff's attorney and state that:

(a) the facts of the case have been reviewed by the plaintiff's attorney with an expert whose qualifications provide a reasonable expectation that the expert's opinions could be admissible at trial and that, in the opinion of this expert, one or more defendants deviated from the applicable standard of care and by that action caused injury to the plaintiff; or

(b) the expert review required by paragraph (a) could not reasonably be obtained before the action was commenced because of the applicable statute of limitations. If an affidavit is executed pursuant to this paragraph, the affidavit in paragraph (a) must be served on defendant or the defendant's counsel within 90 days after service of the summons and complaint.

Subd. 4. **Identification of experts to be called.** The affidavit required by subdivision 2, clause (2), must be by the plaintiff's attorney and state the identity of each person whom plaintiff expects to call as an expert witness at trial to testify with respect to the issues of malpractice or causation, the substance of the facts and opinions to which the expert is expected to testify, and a summary of the grounds for each opinion. Answers to interrogatories that state the information required by this subdivision satisfy the requirements of this subdivision if they are signed by the plaintiff's attorney and served upon the defendant within 180 days after commencement of the suit against the defendant.

The parties or the court for good cause shown, may by agreement, provide for extensions of the time limits specified in subdivision 2, 3, or this subdivision. Nothing in this subdivision may be construed to prevent either party from calling additional expert witnesses or substituting other expert witnesses.

Subd. 5. **Responsibilities of plaintiff as attorney.** If the plaintiff is acting pro se, the plaintiff shall sign the affidavit or answers to interrogatories referred to in this section and is bound by those provisions as if represented by an attorney.

Subd. 6. **Penalty for noncompliance.** Failure to comply with subdivision 2, clause (1), within 60 days after demand for the affidavit results, upon motion, in mandatory dismissal with prejudice of each cause of action as to which expert testimony is necessary to establish a prima facie case.

Failure to comply with subdivision 2, clause (2), and subdivision 4 results, upon motion, in mandatory dismissal with prejudice of each cause of action as to which expert testimony is necessary to establish a prima facie case.

Subd. 7. **Consequences of signing affidavit.** The signature of the plaintiff or the plaintiff's attorney constitutes a certification that the person has read the affidavit or answers to interrogatories, and that to the best of the person's knowledge, information, and belief formed after a reasonable inquiry, it is true, accurate, and made in good faith. A certification made in violation of this subdivision subjects the attorney or plaintiff responsible for such conduct to reasonable attorney's fees, costs, and disbursements.

History: *1986 c 455 s 60*

Source: Minnesota State Register and Public Documents Division.

AMBULATORY HEALTH CARE PROVIDER
QUALITY ASSURANCE
POLICY AND PROCEDURE
1011

Subject: Continuous Quality Assurance Activities

Drafted by: ____________ Date drafted: ____________

Revised by: ____________ Date revised: ____________

Approved by: ____________ Date approved: ____________

Supersedes date: ____________ Page #: ____________

Date effective: ____________ Page: ______ of ______

POLICY

The ambulatory health care provider conducts continuous quality assurance activities.

PURPOSE

1. To ensure quality of ambulatory health care to all patients.
2. To monitor continuously problems with delivery of quality health care.
3. To monitor health care trends that warrant study, particularly in relationship to quality of care.
4. To monitor continuously diagnoses and clinical procedures and treatments that demonstrate significant risk for complications, frequency of occurrence, and adverse health outcomes.
5. To monitor continuously problems that have potentially adverse patient outcomes.
6. To identify problems for special quality assurance studies.

PROCEDURE

1. An available, accessible, and appropriate data collection and retrieval system is maintained to support continuous quality assurance activities.
2. Specific quality assurance steps are used for continuous quality assurance activities, which incorporate the following:
   a. problem assessment
   b. problem identification
   c. problem selection
   d. problem study
   e. problem corrective action
   f. problem monitoring
   g. problem evaluation
   h. problem reassessment
3. Continuous quality assurance activities:
   a. are integrated with special quality assurance studies, as necessary
   b. address health care trends that warrant study, particularly in relationship to quality of care
   c. address diagnoses, treatments, and procedures that demonstrate significant risk for complications, frequency of occurrence, and adverse health outcomes
   d. address improved delivery of health care services that has a positive impact on patient care and/or clinical practice
4. Ambulatory health care provider nursing, interdisciplinary team, and ancillary support services staff members:
   a. document continuous quality assurance activities on a Problem Identification Form (see Exhibit 1029-1)
   b. submit the completed Problem Identification Form to the appropriate nursing/interdisciplinary team/ancillary support services management staff member
5. The nursing/interdisciplinary team/ancillary support services management staff member:
   a. reviews the completed Problem Identification Form
   b. initiates a Continuous Quality Assurance Activity Form (see Exhibit 1011-1)
   c. submits the reviewed Problem Identification Form and the Continuous Quality Assurance Activity Form to the Administrator of Ambulatory Health Care
6. The Administrator of Ambulatory Health Care:
   a. reviews the submitted Problem Identification Form and the Continuous Quality Assurance Activity Form
   b. submits the reviewed Continuous Quality Assurance Activity Form to the Quality Assurance Manager
   c. presents information regarding continuous quality assurance activities to the President and Board of Directors of the ambulatory health care provider

7. The Quality Assurance Manager:
   a. reviews the submitted Continuous Quality Assurance Activity Form
   b. presents the Continuous Quality Assurance Activity Form to the Ambulatory Health Care Quality Assurance (AHCQA) Committee
   c. monitors quality assurance activities using a Quality Assurance Activities Monitoring Log (see Exhibit 1011-2)
8. The AHCQA Committee:
   a. reviews information regarding the continuous quality assurance activity
   b. makes recommendations relative to the continuous quality assurance activity, as appropriate
   c. presents information regarding the continuous quality assurance activity to the ambulatory health care provider's Ambulatory Health Care Advisory Committee
9. The ambulatory health care provider's Ambulatory Health Care Advisory Committee:
   a. reviews information regarding the continuous quality assurance activity
   b. makes recommendations relative to the continuous quality assurance activity, as appropriate
   c. presents information regarding recommendations for the continuous quality assurance activity to the Administrator of Ambulatory Health Care
10. The President and Board of Directors of the ambulatory health care provider:
    a. review information regarding continuous quality assurance activities
    b. make recommendations relative to continuous quality assurance activities
11. Continuous quality assurance activities are communicated to individuals, as appropriate, according to Policy and Procedure 1010: Confidentiality of Quality Assurance Information, and Policy and Procedure 1001: Administrative Control.
12. The completed Problem Identification Form and the Continuous Quality Assurance Activity Form are filed in the ambulatory health care provider's Problem Identification and Continuous Quality Assurance Activity administrative files.

Exhibit 1011-1 Continuous Quality Assurance Activity Form

AMBULATORY HEALTH CARE PROVIDER
CONTINUOUS QUALITY ASSURANCE ACTIVITY

Following Section To Be Completed by Manager Initiating Quality Assurance Activity

Date of Problem Identification Review	Date Quality Assurance Activity Implemented
Quality Assurance Activity Approach (Please check [√] one) ☐ Structure ☐ Process ☐ Outcome	Quality Assurance Activity Time Frame ☐ Prospective ☐ Concurrent ☐ Retrospective

Reason(s) Quality Assurance Activity Selected and Warranted (Please check [√] one or more)
- ☐ Health care trends' relationship to quality of care
- ☐ Diagnoses, treatments, and procedures demonstrate actual/potential adverse health care outcomes
- ☐ Diagnoses, treatments, and procedures demonstrate significant risk for complications
- ☐ Adverse diagnoses, treatments, and procedures demonstrate significant frequency of occurrence
- ☐ Improvement in delivery of health care would have a positive impact on patient care and/or clinical practice
- ☐ Benefits for patient care and/or clinical practices worthy of cost expenditures for quality assurance study
- ☐ Probability exists that adequate resources exist to achieve completion of quality assurance activity

Identified Problem (please describe only *one* problem per form)

Criteria Used for Problem Identification, e.g., from Standard, Policy, and Procedure, Patient Bill of Rights, Code of Ethics

Cause of Identified Problem

Corrective Action Objective(s) (please include information regarding who, what, when, where, and how)

Description of Expected Outcome(s) after Corrective Action Implemented

Implementation Date of Corrective Action	Projected Evaluation Date of Implemented Corrective Action

Name of Individual Responsible for Implementation of Corrective Action

Description of Actual Outcome(s) after Corrective Action Implemented, Including Relevant Statistical Data (please attach supporting information, as appropriate)

continues

Exhibit 1011-1 *continued*

Description Regarding Impact of Quality Assurance Activity on Patient Ambulatory Health Care and/or Clinical Practice

Manager's Evaluation Regarding Resolution of Problem As Result of Quality Assurance Activity (please check [√] one)
☐ Identified Problem Resolved
☐ Identified Problem Not Resolved

Manager's Recommendation Regarding Disposition of Quality Assurance Activity (please check [√] one)
☐ Discontinue quality assurance activity
☐ Continue quality assurance activity for interval problem assessment
☐ Continue quality assurance activity for constant problem assessment

Signature of Manager	Date of Signature

Following Section To Be Completed by AHCQA Committee Chairperson

Date of AHCQA Committee Review of Quality Assurance Activity

Description Regarding Impact of Quality Assurance Activity on Patient Ambulatory Health Care and/or Clinical Practice

AHCQA Committee Evaluation Regarding Resolution of Problem As Result of Quality Assurance Activity (please check [√] one)
☐ Identified Problem Resolved
☐ Identified Problem Not Resolved

AHCQA Committee Recommendation Regarding Disposition of Quality Assurance Activity (please check [√] one)
☐ Discontinue quality assurance activity
☐ Continue quality assurance activity for interval problem assessment
☐ Continue quality assurance activity for constant problem assessment

Signature of AHCQA Committee Chairperson	Date of Signature

Following Section To Be Completed by Ambulatory Health Care Advisory Committee

Ambulatory Health Care Advisory Committee Evaluation Regarding Resolution of Problem As Result of Quality Assurance Activity (please check [√] one)
☐ Identified Problem Resolved
☐ Identified Problem Not Resolved

Ambulatory Health Care Advisory Committee Recommendation Regarding Disposition of Quality Assurance Activity (please check [√] one)
☐ Discontinue quality assurance activity
☐ Continue quality assurance activity for interval problem assessment
☐ Continue quality assurance activity for constant problem assessment

Signature of Ambulatory Health Care Advisory Committee Chairperson	Date of Signature

continues

Exhibit 1011-1 *continued*

Following Section To Be Completed by Administrator of Ambulatory Health Care

Ambulatory Health Care Advisory Committee Recommendation Regarding Disposition of Quality Assurance Activity (please check [√] one)

☐ Approved and Referred to Quality Assurance Manager for Disposition

☐ Not Approved (please explain) ________

Signature of Administrator of Ambulatory Health Care	Date of Signature

Following Section To Be Completed by Quality Assurance Manager

Disposition of Quality Assurance Activity per Administrator of Ambulatory Health Care Approval (please check [√] one)

☐ Discontinued; Manager Notified

☐ Continued for Interval Problem Assessment; Manager Notified

☐ Continued for Constant Problem Assessment; Manager Notified

Date Quality Assurance Activity:

__Discontinued

__Continued for Interval Problem Assessment; New Continuous Quality Assurance Activity Form Initiated for Completion by Appropriate Manager

__Continued for Constant Problem Assessment; New Continuous Quality Assurance Activity Form Initiated for Completion by Appropriate Manager

Signature of Quality Assurance Manager	Date of Signature

Exhibit 1011-2 Quality Assurance Activities Monitoring Log

AMBULATORY HEALTH CARE PROVIDER
QUALITY ASSURANCE ACTIVITIES MONITORING LOG

Title/Number of QA Activity	Date QA Activity Initiated	Individual(s) Responsible	Date of Problem:							
			Assessment	Identification	Selection	Study	Correct Action	Monitoring	Evaluation	Reassessment

continues

Exhibit 1011-2 *continued*

Individual(s) Responsible for Corrective Action	Date Submitted to:				Date of Final Problem Resolution	Impact on Patient Care/ Clinical Practice
	AHCQA Committee	Ambulatory Health Care Advisory Committee	Governing Body	Administrator of AHC		

AMBULATORY HEALTH CARE PROVIDER
QUALITY ASSURANCE
POLICY AND PROCEDURE
1012

Subject: Data Analysis and Interpretation	
Drafted by:	Date drafted:
Revised by:	Date revised:
Approved by:	Date approved:
Supersedes date:	Page #:
Date effective:	Page: ______ of

POLICY

Data are analyzed and interpreted using data collected from study topic.

PURPOSE

1. To select appropriate and adequate data analysis and interpretation methods.
2. To analyze and interpret data that will answer study topic question, problem, or hypothesis.

PROCEDURE

1. Data analysis and interpretation methods are developed while considering:
   a. data analysis and interpretation skills required
   b. data analysis and interpretation time required
   c. statistical techniques that the data analysis and interpretation methods permit
   d. nature of generalizations that can be made from the data
2. Data analysis and interpretation methods are implemented using data collected from study topic.
3. Statistical data are analyzed according to selected data analysis and interpretation methods.
4. Analyzed data are summarized in preparation for reaching conclusions.
5. Data analysis and interpretation information is documented on a Special Quality Assurance Study Form (see Exhibit 1037-1).
6. Data analysis and interpretation information is communicated to individuals, as appropriate, according to Policy and Procedure 1010: Confidentiality of Quality Assurance Information, and Policy and Procedure 1001: Administrative Control.

AMBULATORY HEALTH CARE PROVIDER
QUALITY ASSURANCE
POLICY AND PROCEDURE
1013

Subject: Data Collection	
Drafted by:	Date drafted:
Revised by:	Date revised:
Approved by:	Date approved:
Supersedes date:	Page #:
Date effective:	Page: ____ of ____

POLICY

Data are collected by gathering information from a sample that is representative of the total population under study.

PURPOSE

1. To select a reliable and valid data collection method for the type of data needed to answer study topic question, problem, or hypothesis.
2. To collect data needed to answer study topic question, problem, or hypothesis.

PROCEDURE

1. Data collection involves five steps, as follows:
   a. selection of data collection method:
      (1) questioning method, where there is verbal interaction between interviewer and participant (e.g., interviews, questionnaires)
      (2) observation method, where observer watches participant function in study situation
      (3) measuring method, where there is an intervening device that individual doing measuring applies to participant to obtain participant's measurements
   b. selection of data gathering instruments, while considering:
      (1) available instruments to provide necessary data
      (2) most appropriate instrument in terms of cost in time and money of different instruments
      (3) demands each instrument makes on subjects of study topic
      (4) skills and knowledge needed to analyze and interpret the data
   c. development of data collection method
   d. development of data gathering instruments
   e. implementation of data collection method through use of data gathering instruments
2. Data collection information is documented on a Special Quality Assurance Study Form (see Exhibit 1037-1).
3. Data collection information is communicated to individuals, as appropriate, according to Policy and Procedure 1010: Confidentiality of Quality Assurance Information, and Policy and Procedure 1001: Administrative Control.

AMBULATORY HEALTH CARE PROVIDER
QUALITY ASSURANCE
POLICY AND PROCEDURE
1014

Subject: Evaluation of Quality Assurance Program

Drafted by: ______	Date drafted: ______
Revised by: ______	Date revised: ______
Approved by: ______	Date approved: ______
Supersedes date: ______	Page #: ______
Date effective: ______	Page: ______ of ______

POLICY

The Ambulatory Health Care Quality Assurance (AHCQA) Committee evaluates ambulatory health care provider quality assurance activities.

PURPOSE

1. To assess extent to which ambulatory health care provider quality assurance activities are appropriate, adequate, effective, and efficient.
2. To assess extent to which ambulatory health care provider resources for quality assurance activities are appropriate, available, and adequate.
3. To identify unnecessary duplicate quality assurance activities.
4. To ensure coordination and integration of quality assurance activities.
5. To determine if quality assurance program objectives are being met.
6. To ensure that the quality assurance program is consistent with internal and external legal and third party payor requirements.

PROCEDURE

1. The AHCQA Committee evaluates annually the ambulatory health care provider's total quality assurance program.
2. The AHCQA Committee review evaluates at least the following:
   a. written quality assurance plan, which includes:
      (1) mission statement
      (2) philosophy
      (3) objectives
      (4) administrative control
      (5) scope of quality assurance activities
      (6) standards
      (7) continuous quality assurance activities: problem assessment, identification, selection, study, corrective action, monitoring, evaluation, and reassessment
      (8) special quality assurance studies: study topic selection; study topic; data collection, analysis, and interpretation; conclusions; and recommendations
      (9) communication of quality assurance results
      (10) education
      (11) quality assurance policies and procedures
   b. organization
   c. administration
   d. medical quality assurance activities
   e. nursing quality assurance activities
   f. therapy quality assurance activities
   g. ancillary support services quality assurance activities
   h. other activities
   i. coordination of quality assurance activities
3. The AHCQA Committee submits the following report to the Administrator of Ambulatory Health Care and to the ambulatory health care provider's Ambulatory Health Care Advisory Committee: written report of its total evaluation and its recommendations for appropriate corrective action based on the evaluation results that specifically addressed item 2 above.
4. The Administrator of Ambulatory Health Care and Ambulatory Health Care Advisory Committee respond with appropriate action to the AHCQA Committee.
5. The AHCQA Committee evaluation results are documented on an Evaluation of Ambulatory Health Care Provider's Quality Assurance Program Form (see Exhibit 1014-1).
6. The AHCQA Committee evaluation results are communicated to ambulatory health care staff members.

7. Continuing education classes are offered to ambulatory health care staff members, as necessary, to address educational needs identified by the AHCQA Committee evaluation results.
8. Evaluation of Quality Assurance Program information is communicated to individuals, as appropriate, according to Policy and Procedure 1010: Confidentiality of Quality Assurance Information, and Policy and Procedure 1001: Administrative Control.
9. The completed Evaluation of Ambulatory Health Care Provider's Quality Assurance Program Form is filed in the ambulatory health care provider's Evaluation of Ambulatory Health Care Quality Assurance Activities administrative file.

Exhibit 1014-1 Evaluation of Ambulatory Health Care Provider's Quality Assurance Program Form

EVALUATION OF AMBULATORY HEALTH CARE PROVIDER'S QUALITY ASSURANCE PROGRAM
YEAR OF EVALUATION: ________

OBJECTIVE: To assess the extent to which the ambulatory health care provider's quality assurance program is appropriate, adequate, effective, and efficient.

Topic	Topic Criteria	Topic Criteria Met			Topic Criteria Demonstrate Improvements				Corrective Action Taken	Comments
		Yes	No	Comments	Yes	No	N/A	Comments		
I. Quality Assurance Program Purpose: To ensure quality of ambulatory health care to all patients.	1. There is a written Quality Assurance Plan that includes: a. Mission statement									
	b. Philosophy									
	c. Objectives									
	d. Administrative control									
	e. Scope of quality assurance activities									
	f. Standards									
	g. Problem assessment, identification, selection, study, corrective action, monitoring, evaluation, and reassessment									
	h. Study topic selection; study topic; data collection analysis and interpretation; conclusions; and recommendations									
	i. Communication of quality assurance results									
	j. Education									
	k. Quality assurance policies and procedures									
	2. The written Quality Assurance Plan is implemented.									
II. Organization Purpose: To ensure maximum efficiency in informing individuals of the organizational structure and lines of authority and their responsibilities and accountability.	1. There is an organizational or written description of the provider's Quality Assurance Program structure.									
	2. The provider operates in accordance with the formal Quality Assurance Plan.									
	3. There are objectives that identify expected outcomes of the Quality Assurance Program.									
III. Administration Purpose: To ensure the provision, management, and support of the provider's Quality Assurance Program. A. Governing Body	1. There is a governing body.									
	2. There are identified duties and responsibilities for the governing body.									
	3. The governing body functions in accordance with written rules and regulations.									

continues

Exhibit 1014-1 *continued*

Topic	Topic Criteria	Topic Criteria Met			Topic Criteria Demonstrate Improvements				Corrective Action Taken	Comments
		Yes	No	Comments	Yes	No	N/A	Comments		
	4. Minutes of meetings show that the members have taken action on all business for which they are responsible.									
B. Advisory Group	1. The advisory group is representative of the community served.									
	2. There are identified quality assurance functions for the advisory group.									
	3. The advisory group functions in accordance with written rules and regulations.									
	4. Minutes of meetings show that the members have considered problems, offered recommendations to the governing body, and carried out their functions.									
C. Administrative Personnel	1. There is an appointed administrator and an alternate administrator.									
	2. There is an appointed Nursing Manager and an alternate supervisor available during operating hours.									
	3. There are identified quality assurance functions for administrative personnel.									
	4. Administrative personnel function in accordance with written rules and regulations.									
	5. Minutes of meetings show that the members have considered problems, offered recommendations to the governing body, and carried out their functions.									
D. Personnel	1. There are written job descriptions that identify current quality assurance qualifications, duties, and functions.									
E. Reports and Records	1. Quality assurance records and reports are kept according to policy guidelines, providing for a. maintenance and protection									
	b. retention									
	c. availability and confidentiality									
	2. Contracts relative to quality assurance a. are current									
	b. identify expectations of contractee and contractor									
F. Fiscal	1. Quality assurance budgets, audits, accounting, and billing are carried out according to provider policy.									
	2. Funding sources are multiple and adequate to meet costs.									

continues

Exhibit 1014-1 *continued*

Topic	Topic Criteria	Topic Criteria Met: Yes	No	Comments	Topic Criteria Demonstrate Improvements: Yes	No	N/A	Comments	Corrective Action Taken	Comments
G. Statistical Information	1. There is a description of Quality Assurance Program statistical record keeping.									
	2. An annual report of Quality Assurance statistics is provided.									
	3. There are guidelines that identify how the statistical data are to be used and by whom.									
	4. Review of gathered statistics and data assists in the evaluation of quality health care.									
IV. Medical Quality Assurance Activities Purpose: To ensure physician input and supervision of medical Quality Assurance Activities.	1. There are written Quality Assurance Philosophy, Objectives, and Policies.									
	2. There are written guidelines that describe expected medical staff quality assurance functions.									
	3. These guidelines are implemented in accordance with current medical practice.									
	4. Medical consultation is available and utilized.									
V. Nursing Quality Assurance Activities Purpose: To ensure nursing input and supervision of nursing Quality Assurance Activities.	1. There are written Quality Assurance philosophy, objectives, and policies.									
	2. The nursing process (assessment, goal setting, planning, implementing, evaluating) is incorporated in quality assurance activities.									
	3. There are written guidelines that describe expected nursing quality assurance functions.									
	4. These guidelines are implemented in accordance with current nursing practice.									
	5. The nursing staff keep current in quality assurance theory and application by attending inservice meetings and by participating in continuing education.									
VI. Therapy Quality Assurance Activities Purpose: To ensure therapist input and supervision of therapy Quality Assurance Activities.	1. There are written guidelines that describe the scope of physical therapy, speech therapy, and/or occupational therapy quality assurance functions.									
	2. These guidelines are implemented in accordance with current therapy practice.									
	3. Therapists keep current in quality assurance theory and application by attending appropriate inservice meetings and by participating in continuing education.									

continues

Exhibit 1014-1 *continued*

Topic	Topic Criteria	Topic Criteria Met			Topic Criteria Demonstrate Improvements				Corrective Action Taken	Comments
		Yes	No	Comments	Yes	No	N/A	Comments		
VII. Ancillary Support Quality Assurance Activities Purpose: To ensure ancillary support input and supervision of ancillary support quality assurance activities.	1. There are written guidelines that describe the scope of ancillary support quality assurance functions.									
	2. These guidelines are implemented in accordance with current ancillary support standards.									
	3. Ancillary support services staff keep current in quality assurance theory and application by attending appropriate inservice meetings and by participating in continuing education.									
VIII. Other Quality Assurance Activities										
IX. Coordination of Quality Assurance Activities Purpose: To ensure coordination of quality assurance activities so that efforts effectively complement all staff and support the objectives outlined in the Quality Assurance Program.	1. There are guidelines for liaison between and among all staff involved in quality assurance activities.									
	2. Staff meetings, including discussion of quality assurance activities, are held regularly.									
	3. There is an established method by which information is exchanged with other health care providers to ensure continuity of quality assurance activities.									

Signature of Administrator of Ambulatory Health Care ______ Date of Signature ______

Signature of Ambulatory Health Care Quality Assurance Committee Chairperson ______ Date of Signature ______

Following Section To Be Completed by Ambulatory Health Care Advisory Committee

Date of Ambulatory Health Care Advisory Committee Review: ______

Ambulatory Health Care Advisory Committee Chairperson Signature ______ Date of Signature ______

Ambulatory Health Care Advisory Committee Recommendations for Corrective Action:

CORRECTIVE ACTION RECOMMENDATIONS	DATE CORRECTIVE ACTION OUTCOME WILL BE ASSESSED	INDIVIDUAL RESPONSIBLE	DATE CORRECTIVE ACTION OUTCOME ASSESSED	CORRECTIVE ACTION EFFECTIVE		
				YES	NO	IF NO, EXPLAIN

Following Section To Be Completed by Governing Body

Date of Governing Body Review: ______

Signature of President ______ Date of Signature ______

AMBULATORY HEALTH CARE PROVIDER
QUALITY ASSURANCE
POLICY AND PROCEDURE
1015

Subject: External Review of Ambulatory Health Care Provider Services	
Drafted by:	Date drafted:
Revised by:	Date revised:
Approved by:	Date approved:
Supersedes date:	Page #:
Date effective:	Page: ____ of ____

POLICY

Ambulatory health care staff and interdisciplinary team members/ancillary support services staff facilitate external review of ambulatory health care provider services.

PURPOSE

1. To provide information to external review agencies regarding ambulatory health care provider's delivery of ambulatory health care services.
2. To facilitate external review of ambulatory health care provider's services in consideration of the provider's confidentiality policy and procedure.
3. To receive information regarding the external review and evaluation of the quality and appropriateness of ambulatory health care services provided.
4. To strengthen ambulatory health care services and quality assurance activities based on external review results.

PROCEDURE

1. External review agency requests to conduct an external review visit of the ambulatory health care provider are communicated to and approved by the Administrator of Ambulatory Health Care or the Nursing Manager.
2. Ambulatory health care staff members immediately inform the Administrator of Ambulatory Health Care or the Nursing Manager of external review visits occurring that had not been announced prior to the actual visit.
3. Legal issues and concerns regarding external review activities are addressed in accordance with legal standards established for review organizations (see Exhibit 1010-1).
4. Ambulatory health care staff members assist and cooperate with individuals conducting external review visits.
5. Problems identified through external review visits are referred to the Quality Assurance Manager for consideration as a continuous or special quality assurance activity/study.
6. External review activities information is communicated to individuals, as appropriate, according to Policy and Procedure 1010: Confidentiality of Quality Assurance Information, and Policy and Procedure 1001: Administrative Control.
7. External review activity information is filed in the ambulatory health care provider's External Review Activity administrative file.

AMBULATORY HEALTH CARE PROVIDER
QUALITY ASSURANCE
POLICY AND PROCEDURE
1016

Subject: Financial Planning	
Drafted by: ______	Date drafted: ______
Revised by: ______	Date revised: ______
Approved by: ______	Date approved: ______
Supersedes date: ______	Page #: ______
Date effective: ______	Page: ______ of ______

POLICY

The ambulatory health care provider implements a financial planning process for financial decision making and budget preparation for quality assurance activities.

PURPOSE

1. To ensure that the financial planning process is designed and implemented in a manner conducive to meeting the ambulatory health care provider's quality assurance program objectives and goals.
2. To ensure compliance with budgetary guidelines and limitations regarding quality assurance activities.
3. To identify costs of quality assurance activities.
4. To justify quality assurance costs.
5. To justify anticipatory expenditures for quality assurance activities.
6. To assess less costly alternatives for quality assurance activities.
7. To identify required resources for quality assurance activities.

PROCEDURE

1. The Board of Directors, President, Administrator of Ambulatory Health Care, Nursing Manager, Quality Assurance Manager, interdisciplinary team/ancillary support services staff department heads, and Financial Manager provide budget information for the financial planning process for quality assurance activities, including:
   a. direct costs for quality assurance activities:
      (1) labor
      (2) printing
      (3) typing
      (4) data tabulation and analysis
      (5) photocopying
      (6) audiovisual aids
   b. indirect costs:
      (1) donated staff time
      (2) absorbed staff time
2. The Administrator of Ambulatory Health Care submits the ambulatory health care provider's objectives for quality assurance activities to the President of the ambulatory health care provider on a yearly basis.
3. Quality assurance budget recommendations are reviewed by the Administrator of Ambulatory Health Care and the President of the ambulatory health care provider based on budget recommendations relative to:
   a. ambulatory health care provider's objectives
   b. federal/state/local regulations
   c. corporate financial solvency

AMBULATORY HEALTH CARE PROVIDER
QUALITY ASSURANCE
POLICY AND PROCEDURE
1017

Subject: Interdisciplinary Team Member Peer Review Committees	
Drafted by: ______	Date drafted: ______
Revised by: ______	Date revised: ______
Approved by: ______	Date approved: ______
Supersedes date: ______	Page #: ______
Date effective: ______	Page: ______ of ______

POLICY

The ambulatory health care provider's interdisciplinary team members implement peer review activities through interdisciplinary team member peer review (ITMPR) committees.

PURPOSE

1. To determine adequacy of patient care.
2. To determine effectiveness of patient care.
3. To identify problems with patient care.
4. To identify problems with continuity of patient care.
5. To establish a system for problem resolution.
6. To assess patient outcomes against established patient outcome standards.
7. To ensure peer review of patient care.
8. To ensure that established policies and procedures are followed in the provision of ambulatory health care services.
9. To provide information required for planning, developing, implementing, evaluating, and monitoring interdisciplinary team member staff development and services.

PROCEDURE

1. ITMPR committees consist of three members from the same discipline and one professional who represents the discipline and who is not employed by the ambulatory health care provider for each ITMPR Committee to ensure peer review of each discipline as follows:
   a. physical therapy
   b. occupational therapy
   c. speech therapy
   d. nutrition services
   e. pharmacy services
2. ITMPR Committee members are selected by notifying individuals of the opportunity to serve on the committee.
3. The selection process used to give all eligible individuals an equal opportunity to be selected as a member of the ITMPR Committee is as follows:
   a. A Request for ITMPR Committee Members Memorandum (see Exhibit 1017-1) that discusses the opportunity for individuals to serve on the ITMPR Committee is distributed to eligible individuals in which they are asked to submit their names and job titles to the Quality Assurance Manager if they are interested in becoming ITMPR Committee members.
   b. Names of eligible individuals who express interest in serving on the ITMPR Committee are compiled.
   c. Where the available number of committee member positions equals the number of names submitted, those individuals who submitted their names are given the committee member positions.
   d. Where the available number of committee member positions is less than the number of names submitted, the following lottery method is used to provide an equal selection opportunity for all individuals who submitted their names for consideration:
      (1) All submitted names are written on individual pieces of paper of similar size.
      (2) All of the written names are put into a container and shuffled.
      (3) An individual draws the number of names required to fill the committee member positions out of the container.
      (4) The individuals whose names are drawn out of the container are selected to become ITMPR Committee members.
   e. Where the available number of committee member positions is greater than the number of names submitted, the Administrator of Ambulatory Health Care appoints the ITMPR Committee members.

   f. The outcome of the ITMPR Committee member selection process is communicated to all individuals who expressed an interest in serving on the ITMPR Committee on either an Appointment to the ITMPR Committee Memorandum (see Exhibit 1017-2) or an ITMPR Committee Membership Memorandum (see Exhibit 1017-3).
4. ITMPR Committee members serve on the committee for at least two years.
5. ITMPR Committee membership terms expire on a rotation system in order to maintain continuity in the committee membership.
6. The ITMPR Committee chairperson is chosen by the ITMPR Committee members.
7. Each ITMPR Committee member has one equal vote.
8. The ITMPR Committee quorum is not less than one half of the committee membership.
9. Recommendations of the ITMPR Committee are made by a vote of a majority of a quorum.
10. The ITMPR Committee meets on the second Thursday of every month.
11. ITMPR Committee functions and responsibilities include analysis and review of the following:
    a. appropriateness of the provision of the interdisciplinary team services
    b. appropriateness of delays in the provision of interdisciplinary team services
    c. process-oriented reviews of individualized patient care
    d. process- and/or outcome-oriented reviews of specific patient diagnoses or categories
    e. interdisciplinary team care plan reviews
    f. patient clinical record reviews for compliance with accepted professional and legal standards
12. Meetings of the ITMPR Committee are documented in meeting minutes (see Exhibit 1017-4).
13. The ITMPR Committee provides minutes of its monthly meetings to the Ambulatory Health Care Utilization Review Committee.
14. ITMPR Committee meeting agenda, minutes, and attendance records are filed in the ITMPR Committee Meeting Minutes administrative file.
15. ITMPR Committee members serve as resource persons to other ambulatory health care provider staff members for peer review activities.
16. ITMPR Committee activities are conducted according to Policy and Procedure 1010: Confidentiality of Quality Assurance Information, and Policy and Procedure 1001: Administrative Control.

Exhibit 1017-1 Request for Interdisciplinary Team Member Peer Review Committee Members Memorandum

TO: Interdisciplinary Team Members

FROM: Quality Assurance Manager

SUBJECT: Request for Interdisciplinary Team Member Peer Review Committee Members

DATE:

This is to inform you of an opportunity that is available to individuals who are interested in serving on the Interdisciplinary Team Member Peer Review (ITMPR) Committee to volunteer for open ITMPR Committee member positions. The available ITMPR Committee member positions are as follows:

Representative Position	Representative Position Available?		# of Representative Positions Available
	YES	NO	
Physical Therapist			
Occupational Therapist			
Speech Therapist			
Dietician			
Pharmacist			
Other			

The selection process that will be used to give all eligible individuals an equal opportunity to be selected as a member of the ITMPR Committee will be as follows:

1. Eligible individuals will be asked to submit their names and job titles to the Quality Assurance Manager if they are interested in becoming ITMPR Committee members.
2. The names of eligible individuals who express interest in serving on the ITMPR Committee will be compiled.
3. Where the available number of committee member positions equals the number of names submitted, those individuals who submitted their names will be given the committee member positions.
4. Where the available number of committee member positions is less than the number of names submitted, the following lottery method will be used to provide an equal selection opportunity for all individuals who submitted their names for consideration:
   a. All submitted names will be written on individual pieces of paper of similar size.
   b. All of the written names will be put into a container and shuffled.
   c. An individual will draw the number of names required to fill the committee member positions out of the container.
   d. The individuals whose names are drawn out of the container will be selected to become ITMPR Committee members.
5. Where the available number of committee member positions is greater than the number of names submitted, the Administrator of Ambulatory Health Care will appoint the ITMPR Committee members.
6. The outcome of the ITMPR Committee member selection process will be communicated to all individuals who expressed an interest in serving on the ITMPR Committee.

ITMPR Committee members serve on the committee for at least two years, and the ITMPR Committee meets on the second Thursday of every month.

If you are interested in becoming an ITMPR Committee member, please give me your name and job title by ________________.
(date)

Thank you for your consideration.

Exhibit 1017-2 Appointment to the Interdisciplinary Team Member Peer Review Committee Memorandum

TO:
FROM: Quality Assurance Manager
SUBJECT: Appointment to Interdisciplinary Team Member Peer Review Committee
DATE:

I want to thank you for your interest in serving as an Interdisciplinary Team Member Peer Review (ITMPR) Committee member.

I am pleased to inform you that you have been selected to become an ITMPR Committee member.

We will inform you when the next ITMPR meeting is scheduled and will send you the agenda for the same.

Thank you for your interest. I look forward to meeting with you.

Exhibit 1017-3 Interdisciplinary Team Member Peer Review Committee Membership Memorandum

TO:
FROM: Quality Assurance Manager
SUBJECT: Interdisciplinary Team Member Peer Review Committee Membership
DATE:

I want to thank you for your interest in serving as an Interdisciplinary Team Member Peer Review (ITMPR) Committee member.

We received an enthusiastic response to our request for ITMPR Committee members. Unfortunately, the number of committee member positions required to be filled was less than the number of names that were submitted. Therefore, we used a lottery method to provide an equal opportunity for all individuals who had submitted their names for consideration. I am sorry to inform you that your name was not drawn.

However, more opportunities will be available for you to serve on the ITMPR Committee whenever committee member positions become open. Your name will be placed on a waiting list so that you can be informed of future opportunities to serve as an ITMPR Committee member.

Once again, thank you for submitting your name for consideration in serving as an ITMPR Committee member.

Exhibit 1017-4 Interdisciplinary Team Member Peer Review Committee Minutes Form

AMBULATORY HEALTH CARE PROVIDER
INTERDISCIPLINARY TEAM MEMBER PEER REVIEW COMMITTEE MINUTES

Meeting Date:________________ Meeting Time:________________ Meeting Place:________________

Individuals Present:____

____

____

____

ISSUE	DISCUSSION	ACTION

AMBULATORY HEALTH CARE PROVIDER
QUALITY ASSURANCE
POLICY AND PROCEDURE
1018

Subject: Internal Review of Ambulatory Health Care Provider Services	
Drafted by: ______	Date drafted: ______
Revised by: ______	Date revised: ______
Approved by: ______	Date approved: ______
Supersedes date: ______	Page #: ______
Date effective: ______	Page: ______ of ______

POLICY

Internal review of patient care is conducted through ongoing quality assurance activities.

PURPOSE

1. To ensure delivery of quality and safe patient care.
2. To assess problems in the delivery of quality and safe patient care.
3. To assess patient outcomes.
4. To monitor ambulatory health care provider operations.
5. To assess high volume/risk/problem factors that may be associated with the delivery of ambulatory health care services.
6. To strengthen ambulatory health care services and quality assurance activities based on internal review results.

PROCEDURE

1. Quality assurance activities are implemented for the ambulatory health care provider's internal review of patient care through established structure, process, and outcome monitoring systems including but not limited to:
   a. administrative and operational policies and procedures
   b. patient care policies and procedures
   c. clinical records policies and procedures
   d. education policies and procedures
   e. personnel policies and procedures
   f. provider services policies and procedures
2. Legal issues and concerns regarding internal review activities are addressed in accordance with legal standards established for review organizations (see Exhibit 1010-1).
3. Ambulatory health care staff members assist and cooperate with individuals conducting internal review activities.
4. Problems identified through internal review activities are referred to the Quality Assurance Manager for consideration as a continuous or special quality assurance activity/study.
5. Internal review activities information is communicated to individuals, as appropriate, according to Policy and Procedure 1010: Confidentiality of Quality Assurance Information, and Policy and Procedure 1001: Administrative Control.
6. Internal review activity information is filed in the ambulatory health care provider's Internal Review Activity administrative file.

AMBULATORY HEALTH CARE PROVIDER
QUALITY ASSURANCE
POLICY AND PROCEDURE
1019

Subject: Management Assessment of Ambulatory Health Care Services	
Drafted by: ______	Date drafted: ______
Revised by: ______	Date revised: ______
Approved by: ______	Date approved: ______
Supersedes date: ______	Page #: ______
Date effective: ______	Page: ____ of ______

POLICY

The ambulatory health care provider's management staff assess the delivery of ambulatory health care services.

PURPOSE

1. To collect/give information about the delivery of ambulatory health care services.
2. To identify interdepartmental/intradepartmental trends of concerns/problems with the delivery of ambulatory health care services.
3. To assess progress in meeting current objectives for the delivery of ambulatory health care services.
4. To develop new objectives based on identified needs for the delivery of ambulatory health care services.

PROCEDURE

1. Each ambulatory health care provider manager assesses the delivery of ambulatory health care services on a quarterly basis relative to and as applicable to:
   a. quality assurance activities, which include the following steps:
      (1) problem assessment
      (2) problem identification
      (3) problem selection
      (4) problem study
      (5) problem corrective action
      (6) problem monitoring
      (7) problem evaluation
      (8) problem reassessment
   b. development of new objectives and goals
   c. achievement of established objectives and goals
   d. patient care
   e. patient acuity levels
   f. patient/staff caseload/assignment ratios
   g. patient population
   h. patient, patient family, ambulatory health care staff, and community education
   i. ambulatory health care staff meeting activity
   j. committee activity
   k. community/professional association activity
   l. policy and procedure changes/development, implementation, and evaluation
   m. equipment/service changes
   n. financial/budget activity
   o. public relations/marketing activity
   p. special projects/assignments
   q. interdepartmental/intradepartmental activity
   r. research activity
2. The manager documents the assessment of the delivery of ambulatory health care on an Assessment of Ambulatory Health Care Services Form (see Exhibit 1019-1).
3. The Assessment of Ambulatory Health Care Services Form:
   a. is written in an informative, concise style
   b. may be typed or legibly handwritten
4. The completed Assessment of Ambulatory Health Care Services Form is due in the office of the Administrator of Ambulatory Health Care the third Wednesday of the following months:

April:	1st quarter
July:	2nd quarter
October:	3rd quarter
January:	4th quarter

5. The Administrator of Ambulatory Health Care:
   a. reviews the completed Assessment of Ambulatory Health Care Services Form
   b. provides a verbal and written response to each ambulatory health care provider manager who has submitted a completed Assessment of Ambulatory Health Care Services Form

c. documents the written response to the ambulatory health care provider manager on a Response to Assessment of Ambulatory Health Care Services Form (see Exhibit 1019-2).

d. recommends quality assurance activities based on information received from the ambulatory health care provider managers

6. Problems identified through management assessment of ambulatory health care services are referred to the Quality Assurance Manager for consideration as a continuous or special quality assurance activity.
7. Management assessment of ambulatory health care services information is communicated to individuals, as appropriate, according to Policy and Procedure 1010: Confidentiality of Quality Assurance Information, and Policy and Procedure 1001: Administrative Control.
8. The completed Assessment of Ambulatory Health Care Services Form and Response to Assessment of Ambulatory Health Care Services Form are filed in the ambulatory health care provider's Assessment of Ambulatory Health Care Services and Response to Assessment of Ambulatory Health Care Services administrative files.

Exhibit 1019-1 Assessment of Ambulatory Health Care Services Form

AMBULATORY HEALTH CARE PROVIDER
ASSESSMENT OF AMBULATORY HEALTH CARE SERVICES

Name	Title
Date of Report	Quarter of Report (please check [√] one) ☐ 1st ☐ 2nd ☐ 3rd ☐ 4th

Area(s) of Responsibility

Achievement of Established Objectives and Goals, Including Quality Assurance

Developed Objectives and Goals, Including Quality Assurance for Next Quarter

Status of Quality Assurance Activities

	STEP OF QA PROCESS COMPLETED (please check [✓] one or more)								
	Problem								
DESCRIPTION OF QA ACTIVITY	ASSESSMENT	IDENTIFICATION	SELECTION	STUDY	COR-RECT-TIVE ACTION	MONI-TORING	EVALUATION	REASSESSMENT	COMMENTS

Patient Care

Patient Acuity Levels

Patient/Staff Caseload/Assignment Ratios

Patient Population

Patient, Patient Family, AHC Staff, and Community Education

AHC Staff Meeting Activity

continues

Exhibit 1019-1 *continued*

Committee Activity

Community/Professional Association Activity

Policy and Procedure Changes/Development, Implementation, and Evaluation

Equipment/Service Changes

Financial/Budget Activity

Public Relations/Marketing Activity

Special Projects/Assignments

Interdepartmental/Intradepartmental Activity

Recommendations for Changes To Facilitate Quality Patient Care

Signature of Individual Completing This Form	Date of Signature
Signature of Administrator of Ambulatory Health Care	Date of Signature

Exhibit 1019-2 Response to Assessment of Ambulatory Health Care Services Form

AMBULATORY HEALTH CARE PROVIDER
RESPONSE TO ASSESSMENT OF AMBULATORY HEALTH CARE SERVICES

Name		Title
Date of Report	Date of Response to Report	Quarter of Report (please check [√] one) ☐ 1st ☐ 2nd ☐ 3rd ☐ 4th

Response to Report

ITEM	RESPONSE
Achievement of Established Objectives and Goals	
Developed Objectives and Goals for Next Quarter	
Status of Quality Assurance Activities	
Patient Care	
Patient Acuity Levels	
Patient/Staff Caseload/Assignment Ratios	
Patient Population	
Patient, Patient Family, AHC Staff, and Community Education	
AHC Staff Meeting Activity	
Committee Activity	
Community/Professional Association Activity	
Policy and Procedure Changes/Development, Implementation, and Evaluation	
Equipment/Service Changes	
Financial/Budget Activity	
Public Relations/Marketing Activity	
Special Projects/Assignments	
Interdepartmental/Intradepartmental Activity	
Recommendations for Changes To Facilitate Quality Patient Care	
Other	

Signature of Administrator of Ambulatory Health Care	Date of Signature

AMBULATORY HEALTH CARE PROVIDER
QUALITY ASSURANCE
POLICY AND PROCEDURE
1020

Subject: Mission Statement

Drafted by: ______	Date drafted: ______
Revised by: ______	Date revised: ______
Approved by: ______	Date approved: ______
Supersedes date: ______	Page #: ______
Date effective: ______	Page: ______ of ______

POLICY

Ambulatory health care quality assurance activities are guided by the ambulatory health care provider's mission statement.

PURPOSE

To ensure delivery of quality, safe, and cost-effective ambulatory health care services to patients.

PROCEDURE

The mission of the ambulatory health care provider is to provide quality, safe, and cost-effective delivery of ambulatory health care services to individuals in need of those services.

The ambulatory health care provider's Board of Directors and administrative staff are committed to the provision of ambulatory health care services that are guided by a quality assurance program in order to ensure that the delivered services constitute quality, safe, and cost-effective services for the provider's patients.

AMBULATORY HEALTH CARE PROVIDER
QUALITY ASSURANCE
POLICY AND PROCEDURE
1021

Subject: Nursing Peer Review Committee	
Drafted by: ______	Date drafted: ______
Revised by: ______	Date revised: ______
Approved by: ______	Date approved: ______
Supersedes date: ______	Page #: ______
Date effective: ______	Page: ____ of ______

POLICY

The ambulatory health care provider's nursing staff implements peer review activities through the Nursing Peer Review Committee.

PURPOSE

1. To determine adequacy of patient nursing care.
2. To determine effectiveness of patient nursing care.
3. To identify problems with patient nursing care.
4. To identify problems with continuity of patient nursing care.
5. To establish a system for problem resolution.
6. To assess patient outcomes against established patient outcome standards.
7. To ensure peer review of patient nursing care.
8. To ensure that established nursing policies and procedures are followed in the provision of ambulatory health care services.
9. To provide information required for planning, developing, implementing, evaluating, and monitoring ambulatory health care nursing staff development and services.

PROCEDURE

1. The Nursing Peer Review (NPR) Committee includes the following members:
   a. five ambulatory health care registered nurses actively participating in nursing practice
   b. one ambulatory health care nurse not employed by the ambulatory health care provider and actively participating in nursing practice
2. The Ambulatory Health Care Registered Nurse NPR Committee members are selected by notifying individuals of the opportunity to serve on the committee.
3. The selection process used to give all eligible individuals an equal opportunity to be selected as a member of the NPR Committee is as follows:
   a. A Request for Nursing Peer Review Committee Members Memorandum (see Exhibit 1021-1) that discusses the opportunity for individuals to serve on the NPR Committee is distributed to eligible individuals in which they are asked to submit their names and job titles to the Quality Assurance Manager if they are interested in becoming NPR Committee members.
   b. Names of eligible individuals who express an interest in serving on the NPR Committee are compiled.
   c. Where the available number of committee member positions equals the number of names submitted, those individuals who submitted their names are given the committee member positions.
   d. Where the available number of committee member positions is less than the number of names submitted, the following lottery method is used to provide an equal selection opportunity for all individuals who submitted their names for consideration:
      (1) All submitted names are written on individual pieces of paper of similar size.
      (2) All of the written names are put into a container and shuffled.
      (3) An individual draws the number of names required to fill the committee member positions out of the container.
      (4) The individuals whose names are drawn out of the container are selected to become NPR Committee members.
   e. Where the available number of committee member positions is greater than the number of names submit-

ted, the Nursing Manager appoints the NPR Committee members.

f. The outcome of the NPR Committee member selection process is communicated to all individuals who expressed an interest in serving on the NPR Committee on either an Appointment to the Nursing Peer Review Committee Memorandum (see Exhibit 1021-2) or a Nursing Peer Review Committee Membership Memorandum (see Exhibit 1021-3).

4. NPR Committee members serve on the committee for at least two years.
5. NPR Committee membership terms expire on a rotation system in order to maintain continuity in the committee membership.
6. The NPR Committee chairperson is chosen by the NPR Committee members.
7. Each NPR Committee member has one equal vote.
8. The NPR Committee quorum is not less than one half of the committee membership.
9. Recommendations of the NPR Committee are made by a vote of a majority of a quorum.
10. The NPR Committee meets on the first Thursday of every month.
11. NPR Committee functions and responsibilities include analysis and review of the following:
    a. appropriateness of delays in the provision of ambulatory health care services
    b. outcome-oriented reviews of patient nursing care plans
    c. process-oriented reviews of individualized patient care
    d. process- and/or outcome-oriented reviews of specific patient diagnoses or categories
    e. interdisciplinary team care plan reviews
    f. patient clinical record reviews for compliance with accepted professional and legal standards
12. Meetings of the NPR Committee are documented in meeting minutes (see Exhibit 1021-4).
13. The NPR Committee provides minutes of its monthly meetings to the Ambulatory Health Care Utilization Review Committee.
14. NPR Committee meeting agenda, minutes, and attendance records are filed in the NPR Committee Meeting Minutes administrative file.
15. NPR Committee members serve as resource persons to other ambulatory health care provider staff members for peer review activities.
16. NPR Committee activities are conducted according to Policy and Procedure 1010: Confidentiality of Quality Assurance Information, and Policy and Procedure 1001: Administrative Control.

Exhibit 1021-1 Request for Nursing Peer Review Committee Members Memorandum

TO: Ambulatory Health Care Registered Nurses
FROM: Quality Assurance Manager
SUBJECT: Request for Nursing Peer Review Committee Members
DATE:

This is to inform you of an opportunity that is available to individuals who are interested in serving on the Nursing Peer Review (NPR) Committee to volunteer for open NPR Committee member positions. The available NPR Committee member positions are as follows:

Representative Position	Representative Position Available?		# of Representative Positions Available
	YES	NO	
Ambulatory Health Care Registered Nurse			

The selection process that will be used to give all eligible individuals an equal opportunity to be selected as a member of the NPR Committee will be as follows:

1. Eligible individuals will be asked to submit their names and job titles to the Quality Assurance Manager if they are interested in becoming NPR Committee members.
2. The names of eligible individuals who express interest in serving on the NPR Committee will be compiled.
3. Where the available number of committee member positions equals the number of names submitted, those individuals who submitted their names will be given the committee member positions.
4. Where the available number of committee member positions is less than the number of names submitted, the following lottery method will be used to provide an equal selection opportunity for all individuals who submitted their names for consideration:
   a. All submitted names will be written on individual pieces of paper of similar size.
   b. All of the written names will be put into a container and shuffled.
   c. An individual will draw the number of names required to fill the committee member positions out of the container.
   d. The individuals whose names are drawn out of the container will be selected to become NPR Committee members.
5. Where the available number of committee member positions is greater than the number of names submitted, the Nursing Manager will appoint the NPR Committee members.
6. The outcome of the NPR Committee member selection process will be communicated to all individuals who expressed an interest in serving on the NPR Committee.

NPR Committee members serve on the committee for at least two years, and the NPR Committee meets on the first Thursday of every month.

If you are interested in becoming an NPR Committee member, please give me your name and your job title by __________.
(date)

Thank you for your consideration.

Exhibit 1021-2 Appointment to the Nursing Peer Review Committee Memorandum

TO:
FROM: Quality Assurance Manager
SUBJECT: Appointment to Nursing Peer Review Committee
DATE:

I want to thank you for your interest in serving as a Nursing Peer Review (NPR) Committee member.

I am pleased to inform you that you have been selected to become an NPR Committee member.

We will inform you when the next NPR meeting is scheduled and will send you the agenda for the same.

Thank you for your interest. I look forward to meeting with you.

Exhibit 1021-3 Nursing Peer Review Committee Membership Memorandum

TO:
FROM: Quality Assurance Manager
SUBJECT: Nursing Peer Review Committee Membership
DATE:

I want to thank you for your interest in serving as a Nursing Peer Review (NPR) Committee member.

We received an enthusiastic response to our request for NPR Committee members. Unfortunately, the number of committee member positions required to be filled was less than the number of names that were submitted. Therefore, we used a lottery method to provide an equal opportunity for all individuals who had submitted their names for consideration. I am sorry to inform you that your name was not drawn.

However, more opportunities will be available for you to serve on the NPR Committee whenever committee member positions become open. Your name will be placed on a waiting list so that you can be informed of future opportunities to serve as an NPR Committee member.

Once again, thank you for submitting your name for consideration in serving as an NPR Committee member.

Exhibit 1021-4 Nursing Peer Review Committee Meeting Minutes Form

AMBULATORY HEALTH CARE PROVIDER
NURSING PEER REVIEW COMMITTEE MINUTES

Meeting Date:____________ Meeting Time:____________ Meeting Place:____________

Individuals Present:____

ISSUE	DISCUSSION	ACTION

AMBULATORY HEALTH CARE PROVIDER
QUALITY ASSURANCE
POLICY AND PROCEDURE
1022

Subject: Objectives for Quality Assurance Program

Drafted by: ______	Date drafted: ______
Revised by: ______	Date revised: ______
Approved by: ______	Date approved: ______
Supersedes date: ______	Page #: ______
Date effective: ______	Page: ______ of ______

POLICY

The ambulatory health care provider's Quality Assurance Program is guided by the objectives of the provider.

PURPOSE

1. To ensure that the ambulatory health care provider's Quality Assurance Program is consistent with the provider's mission statement, philosophy, and objectives.
2. To ensure achievement of quality assurance activities.

PROCEDURE

1. Quality assurance activities are guided by the overall objectives of the ambulatory health care provider, which are as follows:
   a. to provide comprehensive quality patient-centered and patient family-centered ambulatory health care
   b. to address the patient's unique physiological, safety, psychological, self-esteem, and self-actualization needs in a patient plan of ambulatory health care
   c. to provide ambulatory health care services that promote the patient's value of life by:
      (1) minimizing negative patient illness and disability outcomes
      (2) maximizing potential patient level-of-independence outcomes
      (3) restoring, maintaining, and promoting patient health
   d. to assist the patient to search for meaning in personal life experiences surrounding the patient's illness or disability, as appropriate
   e. to assist the patient in making choices and decisions about ambulatory health care services relative to the patient's self-defined unique needs
   f. to encourage the patient to collaborate actively with ambulatory health care staff members and other health care providers regarding the provision of ambulatory health care services
   g. to involve the patient family in the patient plan of care whenever possible
   h. to advise the patient family regarding community support services, as needed
   i. to serve as a resource for the patient, the patient family, and the community
   j. to provide health care education for the patient, the patient family, and the community
2. The ambulatory health care provider implements quality assurance activities to achieve the following objectives:
   a. to develop, implement, and evaluate standards to measure nursing practice and delivery of ambulatory health care services
   b. to develop, implement, and evaluate effective quality assurance activities according to the ambulatory health care provider's mission statement, philosophy, and objectives
   c. to develop effective systems for problem assessment, identification, selection, study, corrective action, monitoring, evaluation, and reassessment of nursing/interdisciplinary team practice and ambulatory health care services
   d. to provide focus and direction for quality assurance activities
   e. to develop effective verbal/written information systems to communicate quality assurance activity outcomes to appropriate individuals and committees
   f. to provide educational opportunities for all ambulatory health care staff members to increase knowledge and participation in quality assurance activities
   g. to correlate the findings of quality assurance activities with the content of the ambulatory health care provider's continuing education programs

h. to encourage input and participation of all ambulatory health care staff relative to quality assurance activities
i. to coordinate and integrate the ambulatory health care provider's interdepartmental/intradepartmental quality assurance activities with overall provider quality assurance activities
j. to ensure administrative commitment and support for quality assurance activities

AMBULATORY HEALTH CARE PROVIDER
QUALITY ASSURANCE
POLICY AND PROCEDURE
1023

Subject: Philosophy	
Drafted by: ______	Date drafted: ______
Revised by: ______	Date revised: ______
Approved by: ______	Date approved: ______
Supersedes date: ______	Page #: ______
Date effective: ______	Page: ______ of ______

POLICY

Quality assurance activities are guided by the overall philosophy of the ambulatory health care provider.

PURPOSE

1. To adopt the appropriate philosophical approach to providing quality ambulatory health care services.
2. To ensure quality of ambulatory health care to all patients.

PROCEDURE

Quality assurance activities are guided by the overall philosophy of the ambulatory health care provider. The adoption of the appropriate philosophical approach to providing quality ambulatory health care services is based on the following basic assumptions:

1. The realization and maintenance of the full potential of human life are supreme values.
2. Humans possess a unique hierarchy of needs, as defined by Maslow:
   a. physiological needs
   b. safety needs
   c. belongingness and love needs
   d. self-esteem needs
   e. self-actualization needs
3. Humans search for meaning in personal life experiences.
4. Humans make choices and decisions based on their individual beliefs and values.
5. Humans exert personal control over their lives in making such choices and decisions.

The philosophy of the ambulatory health care provider, based on these assumptions, stipulates that each ambulatory health care patient:

1. desires ambulatory health care services that promote the patient's value of life by:
   a. minimizing negative patient illness and disability outcomes
   b. maximizing potential patient level-of-independence outcomes
   c. restoring, maintaining, and promoting patient health
2. possesses unique physiological, safety, psychological, self-esteem, and self-actualization needs that require consideration in the patient's plan of ambulatory health care
3. searches for meaning in the personal life experiences surrounding the patient's illness or disability
4. makes choices and decisions about the provision of ambulatory health care services relative to the patient's self-defined unique needs and according to the patient's personal beliefs and values
5. exerts personal control over the patient's personal life in collaborating with ambulatory health care staff members regarding the provision of services

In support of the ambulatory health care provider's philosophy, the provider is dedicated to the provision of comprehensive quality patient-centered and patient family-centered ambulatory health care that is focused on the patient's unique physiological, safety, psychological, self-esteem, and self-actualization needs. The provider is committed to the provision of ambulatory health care services that will assist the patient in searching for meaning in the personal life experiences surrounding the patient's illness or disability, to make choices and decisions about the provision of ambulatory health care services based on the patient's self-defined unique needs, and to collaborate actively with the ambulatory health care provider staff and other health care providers regarding the provision of appropriate services. The ambulatory health care provider is also dedicated to the provision of ambulatory health care education to the patient, patient family, and community.

AMBULATORY HEALTH CARE PROVIDER
QUALITY ASSURANCE
POLICY AND PROCEDURE
1024

Subject: Physician Peer Review Committee

Drafted by:	Date drafted:
Revised by:	Date revised:
Approved by:	Date approved:
Supersedes date:	Page #:
Date effective:	Page: ____ of

POLICY

The ambulatory health care provider's physician staff implements peer review activities through the Physician Peer Review Committee.

PURPOSE

1. To determine adequacy of patient medical care.
2. To determine effectiveness of patient medical care.
3. To identify problems with patient medical care.
4. To identify problems with continuity of patient medical care.
5. To establish a system for problem resolution.
6. To assess patient outcomes against established patient outcome standards.
7. To ensure peer review of patient medical care.
8. To ensure that established medical policies and procedures are followed in the provision of ambulatory health care services.
9. To provide information required for planning, developing, implementing, evaluating, and monitoring ambulatory health care medical staff development and services.

PROCEDURE

1. The Physician Peer Review (PPR) Committee includes the following members:
   a. five ambulatory health care physicians actively participating in medical practice
   b. one ambulatory health care physician not employed by the ambulatory health care provider and actively participating in medical practice
2. The PPR Committee members are selected by notifying individuals of the opportunity to serve on the committee.
3. The selection process used to give all eligible individuals an equal opportunity to be selected as a member of the PPR Committee is as follows:
   a. A Request for Physician Peer Review Committee Members Memorandum (see Exhibit 1024-1) that discusses the opportunity for individuals to serve on the PPR Committee is distributed to eligible individuals in which they are asked to submit their names and specialty to the Quality Assurance Manager if they are interested in becoming PPR Committee members.
   b. Names of eligible individuals who express an interest in serving on the PPR Committee are compiled.
   c. Where the available number of committee member positions equals the number of names submitted, those individuals who submitted their names are given the committee member positions.
   d. Where the available number of committee member positions is less than the number of names submitted, the following lottery method is used to provide an equal selection opportunity for all individuals who submitted their names for consideration:
      (1) All submitted names are written on individual pieces of paper of similar size.
      (2) All of the written names are put into a container and shuffled.
      (3) An individual draws the number of names required to fill the committee member positions out of the container.
      (4) The individuals whose names are drawn out of the container are selected to become PPR Committee members.
   e. Where the available number of committee member positions is greater than the number of names submitted, the Medical Director appoints the PPR Committee members.
   f. The outcome of the PPR Committee member selection process is communicated to all individuals who expressed an interest in serving on the PPR Commit-

tee on either an Appointment to the Physician Peer Review Committee Memorandum (see Exhibit 1024-2) or a Physician Peer Review Committee Membership Memorandum (see Exhibit 1024-3).

4. PPR Committee members serve on the committee for at least two years.
5. PPR Committee membership terms expire on a rotation system in order to maintain continuity in the committee membership.
6. The PPR Committee chairperson is chosen by the PPR Committee members.
7. Each PPR Committee member has one equal vote.
8. The PPR Committee quorum is not less than one half of the committee membership.
9. Recommendations of the PPR Committee are made by a vote of a majority of a quorum.
10. The PPR Committee meets on the first Wednesday of every month.
11. PPR Committee functions and responsibilities include analysis and review of the following:
    a. appropriateness of delays in the provision of ambulatory health care services
    b. outcome-oriented reviews of patient medical care
    c. process-oriented reviews of individualized patient care
    d. process- and/or outcome-oriented reviews of specific patient diagnoses or categories
    e. interdisciplinary team care plan reviews
    f. patient clinical record reviews for compliance with accepted professional and legal standards
12. Meetings of the PPR Committee are documented in meeting minutes (see Exhibit 1024-4).
13. The PPR Committee provides minutes of its monthly meetings to the Ambulatory Health Care Utilization Review Committee.
14. PPR Committee meeting agenda, minutes, and attendance records are filed in the PPR Committee Meeting Minutes administrative file.
15. PPR Committee members serve as resource persons to other ambulatory health care provider staff members for peer review activities.
16. PPR Committee activities are conducted according to Policy and Procedure 1010: Confidentiality of Quality Assurance Information, and Policy and Procedure 1001: Administrative Control.

Exhibit 1024-1 Request for Physician Peer Review Committee Members Memorandum

TO: Ambulatory Health Care Physicians
FROM: Quality Assurance Manager
SUBJECT: Request for Physician Peer Review Committee Members
DATE:

This is to inform you of an opportunity that is available to individuals who are interested in serving on the Physician Peer Review (PPR) Committee to volunteer for open PPR committee member positions. The available PPR committee member positions are as follows:

Representative Position	Representative Position Available? YES	NO	# of Representative Positions Available
Ambulatory Health Care Physician			

The selection process that will be used to give all eligible individuals an equal opportunity to be selected as a member of the PPR Committee will be as follows:

1. Eligible individuals will be asked to submit their names and job titles to the Quality Assurance Manager if they are interested in becoming PPR Committee members.
2. The names of eligible individuals who express interest in serving on the PPR Committee will be compiled.
3. Where the available number of committee member positions equals the number of names submitted, those individuals who submitted their names will be given the committee member positions.
4. Where the available number of committee member positions is less than the number of names submitted, the following lottery method will be used to provide an equal selection opportunity for all individuals who submitted their names for consideration:
   a. All submitted names will be written on individual pieces of paper of similar size.
   b. All of the written names will be put into a container and shuffled.
   c. An individual will draw the number of names required to fill the committee member positions out of the container.
   d. The individuals whose names are drawn out of the container will be selected to become PPR Committee members.
5. Where the available number of committee member positions is greater than the number of names submitted, the Medical Director will appoint the PPR Committee members.
6. The outcome of the PPR Committee member selection process will be communicated to all individuals who expressed an interest in serving on the PPR Committee.

PPR Committee members serve on the committee for at least two years, and the PPR Committee meets on the first Wednesday of every month.

If you are interested in becoming a PPR Committee member, please give me your name and your speciality by __________.
(date)

Thank you for your consideration.

Exhibit 1024-2 Appointment to the Physician Peer Review Committee Memorandum

TO:
FROM: Quality Assurance Manager
SUBJECT: Appointment to Physician Peer Review Committee
DATE:

I want to thank you for your interest in serving as a Physician Peer Review (PPR) Committee member.

I am pleased to inform you that you have been selected to become a PPR Committee member.

We will inform you when the next PPR meeting is scheduled and will send you the agenda for the same.

Thank you for your interest. I look forward to meeting with you.

Exhibit 1024-3 Physician Peer Review Committee Membership Memorandum

TO:
FROM: Quality Assurance Manager
SUBJECT: Physician Peer Review Committee Membership
DATE:

I want to thank you for your interest in serving as a Physician Peer Review (PPR) Committee member.

We received an enthusiastic response to our request for PPR Committee members. Unfortunately, the number of committee member positions required to be filled was less than the number of names that were submitted. Therefore, we used a lottery method to provide an equal opportunity for all individuals who had submitted their names for consideration. I am sorry to inform you that your name was not drawn.

However, more opportunities will be available for you to serve on the PPR Committee whenever committee member positions become open. Your name will be placed on a waiting list so that you can be informed of future opportunities to serve as a PPR Committee member.

Once again, thank you for submitting your name for consideration in serving as a PPR Committee member.

Exhibit 1024-4 Physician Peer Review Committee Meeting Minutes Form

AMBULATORY HEALTH CARE PROVIDER
PHYSICIAN PEER REVIEW COMMITTEE MINUTES

Meeting Date:__________________ Meeting Time:__________________ Meeting Place:__________________

Individuals Present:____

ISSUE	DISCUSSION	ACTION

AMBULATORY HEALTH CARE PROVIDER
QUALITY ASSURANCE
POLICY AND PROCEDURE
1025

Subject: Problem Assessment	
Drafted by: ________	Date drafted: ________
Revised by: ________	Date revised: ________
Approved by: ________	Date approved: ________
Supersedes date: ________	Page #: ________
Date effective: ________	Page: ____ of ________

POLICY

Problems are monitored and assessed for identification and selection as a quality assurance activity.

PURPOSE

1. To assess problem's impact on patient care and clinical practice.
2. To determine problem's existence, scope, type, characteristics, complexity, and prevalence.

PROCEDURE

1. Multiple internal/external data sources are organized to monitor and assess ambulatory health care services for quality of health care problems relative to:
   a. problem's relationship to quality of delivered care
   b. problem's prevalence that would warrant correction
   c. problem's propensity to be resolved
   d. benefit to patient care that would result from resolving problem versus the cost of assessing and resolving problem
2. Problems are assessed for identification and selection through utilization of:
   a. internal data sources, which include but are not limited to the following:
      (1) patient clinical records
      (2) patient accident/incident reports
      (3) medication error reports
      (4) infection control reports
      (5) Patient Concerns Form (see Policy and Procedure 2010: Patient Concerns, and Exhibit 2010-1)
      (6) patient letters and/or comments regarding ambulatory health care services
      (7) Patient Evaluation of Ambulatory Health Care Services Form (see Exhibit 2011-1)
      (8) ambulatory health care staff and interdisciplinary team/ancillary support services staff member credentials
      (9) Problem Identification Form (see Exhibit 1029-1)
      (10) Continuous Quality Assurance Activity Form (see Exhibit 1011-1)
      (11) ambulatory health care staff orientation, inservice, and continuing education records
      (12) interdepartmental and intradepartmental committee meeting minutes
      (13) formal group meetings
      (14) informal group meetings:
         (a) lunch
         (b) breaks
         (c) any gathering where two or more persons are communicating
      (15) patient case conferences
      (16) mortality reports
      (17) utilization review reports
      (18) drug utilization review reports
      (19) blood utilization review reports
      (20) surgical case review reports
      (21) medical record review reports
      (22) pharmacy and therapeutics evaluation reports
      (23) structure, process, and outcome study data
      (24) accreditation/licensure/certification survey reports
      (25) PSRO/PRO data
      (26) patient classification data
      (27) research studies
      (28) ambulatory health care standards

(29) personnel records
(30) financial reports
(31) quality assurance suggestion box
(32) personal knowledge/expertise
(33) personal experience
(34) other data relating directly or indirectly to patient ambulatory health care

b. external data sources, which include but are not limited to the following:
   (1) professional organizations
   (2) regulatory agencies
   (3) review agencies
   (4) cost review agencies
   (5) third party payors
   (6) literature
   (7) local, state, and national PSRO profiles
   (8) National Center for Health Statistics reports
   (9) Department of Public Health reports
   (10) data routinely collected from other ambulatory health care providers
   (11) diagnostic and surgical procedure indices
   (12) continuing education conferences
   (13) professional conferences
c. valid and relevant structure, process, and outcome of patient care/clinical practice criteria that:
   (1) are developed to define the focus for monitoring and assessing quality of health care problems
   (2) are appropriately implemented to monitor and assess quality of health care problems
   (3) include objective and measurable statements
d. prospective, concurrent, and retrospective monitoring activities that are appropriately implemented to assess quality of health care problems
e. appropriate study sample that:
   (1) is representative of the assessed problem
   (2) has adequate number of representative cases with which to study problem
   (3) has sufficient quality of representative cases with which to study problem
   (4) can be studied with adequate resources in a cost-effective manner

3. Problem assessment information is documented on a Continuous Quality Assurance Activity Form.
4. Problem assessment information is communicated to individuals, as appropriate, according to Policy and Procedure 1010: Confidentiality of Quality Assurance Information, and Policy and Procedure 1001: Administrative Control.

AMBULATORY HEALTH CARE PROVIDER
QUALITY ASSURANCE
POLICY AND PROCEDURE
1026

Subject: Problem Corrective Action	
Drafted by: ______	Date drafted: ______
Revised by: ______	Date revised: ______
Approved by: ______	Date approved: ______
Supersedes date: ______	Page #: ______
Date effective: ______	Page: ______ of ______

POLICY

Corrective action is developed and implemented based on study outcomes.

PURPOSE

1. To determine appropriate corrective action for identified problems.
2. To correct knowledge, performance, and/or system deficiencies that caused identified problems.
3. To resolve identified problems.

PROCEDURE

1. Corrective action is developed and implemented after the identified problem has been studied according to Policy and Procedure 1033: Problem Study.
2. Appropriate corrective action is developed to correct defined knowledge, performance, and systems problem causes.
3. Developed corrective action describes:
   a. all corrective actions required to resolve knowledge, performance, and systems problem causes
   b. measurable objectives for each corrective action, including degree of expected change in patient care and/or clinical practices
   c. person(s) responsible for implementing/monitoring/evaluating/reassessing corrective actions
   d. date corrective action is to be implemented
   e. date corrective action is to be evaluated for effectiveness in problem resolution
4. Developed corrective action is implemented to correct defined knowledge, performance, and systems problem causes.
5. Developed corrective action is implemented to correct defined knowledge, performance, and systems problem causes on the date the corrective action was scheduled to be implemented.
6. Corrective action information is documented on a Continuous Quality Assurance Activity Form (see Exhibit 1011-1).
7. Corrective action information is communicated to individuals, as appropriate, according to Policy and Procedure 1010: Confidentiality of Quality Assurance Information, and Policy and Procedure 1001: Administrative Control.

AMBULATORY HEALTH CARE PROVIDER
QUALITY ASSURANCE
POLICY AND PROCEDURE
1027

Subject: Problem Evaluation	
Drafted by:	Date drafted:
Revised by:	Date revised:
Approved by:	Date approved:
Supersedes date:	Page #:
Date effective:	Page: of

POLICY

Monitored corrective action is evaluated for effectiveness in problem resolution.

PURPOSE

1. To ensure effective problem resolution.
2. To ensure that desired outcome has been achieved and sustained.
3. To obtain cooperation for further corrective action as necessary.
4. To develop and implement alternative corrective action as necessary.
5. To validate effectiveness of overall quality assurance program that enhances quality patient care and clinical practice.

PROCEDURE

1. Corrective action is evaluated for effectiveness in problem resolution after the corrective action has been monitored according to Policy and Procedure 1030: Problem Monitoring.
2. Monitored corrective action is evaluated for effectiveness in problem resolution focusing on:
   a. problem assessment, identification, selection, study, corrective action, monitoring, evaluation, and reassessment information pertinent to each problem
   b. improvement in the delivery of health care that has had a positive impact on patient care and/or clinical practices
   c. positive problem resolution outcomes
3. Monitored corrective action is evaluated for effectiveness in problem resolution on the date the corrective action is scheduled to be evaluated.
4. Evaluation information is documented on a Continuous Quality Assurance Activity Form (see Exhibit 1011-1).
5. Evaluation information is communicated to individuals, as appropriate, according to Policy and Procedure 1010: Confidentiality of Quality Assurance Information, and Policy and Procedure 1001: Administrative Control.

AMBURLATORY HEALTH CARE PROVIDER
QUALITY ASSURANCE
POLICY AND PROCEDURE
1028

Subject: Problem Identification	
Drafted by: ______	Date drafted: ______
Revised by: ______	Date revised: ______
Approved by: ______	Date approved: ______
Supersedes date: ______	Page #: ______
Date effective: ______	Page: ______ of ______

POLICY

Problems are identified for possible selection as a quality assurance activity.

PURPOSE

To select problems for quality assurance activities according to their impact on patient care and clinical practice.

PROCEDURE

1. Problems are identified for possible selection as a quality assurance activity after they have been assessed according to Policy and Procedure 1025: Problem Assessment.
2. Implemented measurable health care standards are compared with implemented process, structure, and outcome criteria to identify quality of health care problems.
3. An appropriate representative sample of health care standards compared with structure, process, and outcome criteria is obtained to identify quality of health care problems.
4. Problem identification information is documented on a Continuous Quality Assurance Activity Form (see Exhibit 1010-1).
5. Problem identification information is communicated to individuals, as appropriate, according to Policy and Procedure 1010: Confidentiality of Quality Assurance Information, and Policy and Procedure 1001: Administrative Control.

AMBULATORY HEALTH CARE PROVIDER
QUALITY ASSURANCE
POLICY AND PROCEDURE
1029

Subject: Problem Identification by Ambulatory Health Care Staff Members	
Drafted by:	Date drafted:
Revised by:	Date revised:
Approved by:	Date approved:
Supersedes date:	Page #:
Date effective:	Page: ______ of

POLICY

Ambulatory health care staff members are encouraged to identify problems for quality assurance activities.

PURPOSE

1. To identify problems with delivery of ambulatory health care services for problem resolution.
2. To ensure ambulatory health care staff participation in quality assurance activities.

PROCEDURE

1. Problems are identified for possible selection as a quality assurance activity after they have been assessed according to Policy and Procedure 1025: Problem Assessment.
2. The ambulatory health care staff member:
   a. informs the Nursing Manager/interdisciplinary team/ancillary support services department head, as appropriate, of the identified problem
   b. documents the incident on a Problem Identification Form (see Exhibit 1029-1)
   c. submits the completed Problem Identification Form to the Nursing Manager/interdisciplinary team/ancillary support services department head, as appropriate
3. The Nursing Manager/interdisciplinary team/ancillary support services department head:
   a. reviews the completed Problem Identification Form while considering the identified problem's impact on patient care and clinical practice
   b. considers the identified problem's impact on patient care and clinical practice
   c. investigates the problem
   d. documents the problem investigation on the Problem Identification Form
   e. makes decisions/recommendations for selection of identified problem as a problem to study
   f. documents whether or not identified problem has been recommended as a problem to study on the Problem Identification Form
   g. submits the completed Problem Identification Form to the Administrator of Ambulatory Health Care
4. The Administrator of Ambulatory Health Care:
   a. reviews the completed Problem Identification Form
   b. conducts further investigation of problem as necessary
   c. considers identified problem's impact on patient care and clinical practice
   d. makes decisions/recommendations for selecting identified problem as a problem to study
   e. documents whether or not identified problem has been selected as a problem to study on the Problem Identification Form
   f. initiates a Continuous Quality Assurance Activity Form (see Exhibit 1011-1) if the identified problem has been selected as a problem to study
   g. sends the initiated Continuous Quality Assurance Activity Form to the Quality Assurance Manager
   h. files the completed Problem Identification Form in the ambulatory health care provider's Problem Identification administrative file
5. The Quality Assurance Manager reviews the completed Continuous Quality Assurance Activity Form according to Policy and Procedure 1032: Problem Selection.
6. Quality assurance information is communicated to individuals, as appropriate, according to Policy and Procedure 1010: Confidentiality of Quality Assurance Information, and Policy and Procedure 1001: Administrative Control.
7. Documents concerning quality assurance activities are filed in the ambulatory health care provider's Quality Assurance Activities administrative file.

Exhibit 1029-1 Problem Identification Form

AMBULATORY HEALTH CARE PROVIDER
PROBLEM IDENTIFICATION FORM

Following Section To Be Completed by Individual Reporting the Problem

Name of Individual(s) Involved in Incident		Place of Incident	
Date of Incident	Time of Incident A.M. P.M.	Date This Form Completed	Time This Form Completed A.M. P.M.

Objective Narrative Description of Incident

Narrative Description of Identified Problems Resulting from Incident

Criteria Used for Problem Identification, e.g., from Standard, Policy and Procedure, Patient Bill of Rights, Code of Ethics

Corrective Action Implemented? ☐ Yes ☐ No (please explain) ____	Date Corrective Action Implemented

Narrative Description of Implemented Corrective Action

Recommendations for Additional Corrective Action

Following Section To Be Completed by Manager Reviewing Identified Problem

Review Date of This Form	Review Time of This Form

Narrative Description of Incident Investigation

Additional Corrective Action Implemented? ☐ Yes ☐ No (please explain) ____	Date Corrective Action Implemented

Narrative Description of Additional Corrective Action

continues

Exhibit 1029-1 *continued*

Description of Outcome(s) Resulting from Additional Corrective Action
Description Regarding Potential Impact of Quality Assurance Activity on Patient Ambulatory Health Care and/or Clinical Practice
Identified Problem Referred for Quality Assurance Activity? ☐ Yes ☐ No (please explain) ____

Signature of Manager	Date of Signature

Following Section To Be Completed by Administrator of Ambulatory Health Care
Identified Problem Referred for Quality Assurance Activity? ☐ Yes ☐ No (please explain) ____
Signature of Administrator of Ambulatory Health Care

AMBULATORY HEALTH CARE PROVIDER
QUALITY ASSURANCE
POLICY AND PROCEDURE
1030

Subject: Problem Monitoring

Drafted by: ______	Date drafted: ______
Revised by: ______	Date revised: ______
Approved by: ______	Date approved: ______
Supersedes date: ______	Page #: ______
Date effective: ______	Page: ______ of ______

POLICY

Implemented corrective action is monitored on an ongoing basis.

PURPOSE

To assess actual/potential effectiveness of problem resolution.

PROCEDURE

1. Corrective action is monitored on an ongoing basis after it has been implemented according to Policy and Procedure 1026: Problem Corrective Action.
2. Implemented corrective action is monitored on an ongoing basis to assess actual/potential effectiveness of problem resolution.
3. Monitored corrective action that is determined to be actually/potentially ineffective in problem resolution is discontinued in a timely manner, as appropriate.
4. Discontinued/new corrective action is revised/developed in a timely manner as a substitute for monitored corrective action that has been determined to be ineffective in problem resolution.
5. Revised corrective action is implemented to correct knowledge, performance, and systems problem causes.
6. Revised corrective action is monitored on an ongoing basis to assess actual/potential effectiveness of problem resolution.
7. Implemented corrective action is monitored and appropriately discontinued/revised as often as necessary, in a timely manner, to assess actual/potential effectiveness of problem resolution.
8. Monitoring information is documented on a Continuous Quality Assurance Activity Form (see Exhibit 1011-1).
9. Monitoring information is communicated to individuals, as appropriate, according to Policy and Procedure 1010: Confidentiality of Quality Assurance Information, and Policy and Procedure 1001: Administrative Control.

AMBULATORY HEALTH CARE PROVIDER
QUALITY ASSURANCE
POLICY AND PROCEDURE
1031

Subject: Problem Reassessment

Drafted by:	Date drafted:
Revised by:	Date revised:
Approved by:	Date approved:
Supersedes date:	Page #:
Date effective:	Page: ____ of ____

POLICY

Actual/apparent resolved problems are reassessed as necessary.

PURPOSE

1. To ensure sustained problem resolution.
2. To restudy problem as necessary.
3. To develop and implement alternative corrective action as necessary.
4. To monitor problem as necessary.
5. To reevaluate problem as necessary.
6. To reassess problem for sustained problem resolution as necessary.

PROCEDURE

1. Actual/apparent resolved problems are reassessed as necessary after the problems have been evaluated according to Policy and Procedure 1027: Problem Evaluation.
2. Actual/apparent resolved problems are reassessed to determine sustained problem resolution through an examination of the system for ongoing quality assurance activities, including, as necessary, the following areas:
   a. problem assessment
   b. problem identification
   c. problem selection
   d. problem study
   e. problem corrective action
   f. problem monitoring
   g. problem evaluation
   h. problem reassessment
3. The system for ongoing quality assurance activities is repeatedly implemented, as necessary, until actual problem resolution occurs for those actual/apparent resolved problems that are determined to lack sustained problem resolution.
4. Reassessment information is documented on a Continuous Quality Assurance Activity Form (see Exhibit 1011-1).
5. Reassessment information is communicated to individuals, as appropriate, according to Policy and Procedure 1010: Confidentiality of Quality Assurance Information, and Policy and Procedure 1001: Administrative Control.

AMBULATORY HEALTH CARE PROVIDER
QUALITY ASSURANCE
POLICY AND PROCEDURE
1032

Subject: Problem Selection	
Drafted by: ______	Date drafted: ______
Revised by: ______	Date revised: ______
Approved by: ______	Date approved: ______
Supersedes date: ______	Page #: ______
Date effective: ______	Page: ______ of ______

POLICY

Identified problems are selected for study relative to their impact on patient care and clinical practice.

PURPOSE

1. To select appropriate identified problems for problem study.
2. To coordinate the selection of problem studies for quality assurance activities.

PROCEDURE

1. Problems are selected for study after they have been identified according to Policy and Procedure 1028: Problem Identification.
2. Identified problems are selected for study in consideration of but not limited to the following:
   a. frequency of problem occurrence that would warrant problem resolution
   b. trend of problem occurrence that would warrant problem resolution
   c. actual/potential adverse health outcomes resulting from identified problems that would warrant problem resolution
   d. probability that improved delivery of health care would have a positive impact on patient care and/or clinical practices
   e. benefits for patient care and/or clinical practices that would be worthy of cost expenditures for problem resolution
   f. probability that adequate resources exist to achieve problem resolution
3. The Quality Assurance Manager:
   a. reviews completed Continuous Quality Assurance Activity Form (see Exhibit 1011-1).
   b. considers impact of identified problem on patient care and clinical practice
   c. makes recommendations for selecting identified problem as a problem to study
   d. documents recommendations for selecting identified problem as a problem to study on the Continuous Quality Assurance Activity Form
   e. presents completed Continuous Quality Assurance Activity Form to the Ambulatory Health Care Quality Assurance (AHCQA) Committee for review and recommendations
4. The AHCQA Committee:
   a. reviews completed Continuous Quality Assurance Activity Form
   b. considers impact of identified problem on patient care and clinical practice
   c. makes recommendations for selecting identified problem as a problem to study
   d. documents AHCQA Committee review and recommendations for selecting identified problem as a problem to study on the Continuous Quality Assurance Activity Form
5. Problem selection information is documented on a Continuous Quality Assurance Activity Form.
6. Problem selection information is communicated to individuals, as appropriate, according to Policy and Procedure 1010: Confidentiality of Quality Assurance Information, and Policy and Procedure 1001: Administrative Control.

AMBULATORY HEALTH CARE PROVIDER
QUALITY ASSURANCE
POLICY AND PROCEDURE
1033

Subject: Problem Study	
Drafted by:	Date drafted:
Revised by:	Date revised:
Approved by:	Date approved:
Supersedes date:	Page #:
Date effective:	Page: ____ of ____

POLICY

Selected problems are studied relative to their impact on patient care and clinical practice.

PURPOSE

1. To study selected problem's impact on patient care and/or clinical practice.
2. To determine actual cause of identified problem.
3. To assist in determining appropriate corrective action for identified problem.
4. To ensure that the problem is studied adequately in order to measure effectively the quality of care delivered.

PROCEDURE

1. Problems are studied after they have been selected for study according to Policy and Procedure 1032: Problem Selection.
2. Selected problems are studied using appropriate and valid study methods to determine actual causes of problems.
3. Appropriate and valid study methods are individually chosen and implemented for each selected problem according to but not limited to the following factors:
   a. adequacy of data sources
   b. quantity of data sources
   c. availability of data sources
   d. reliability of data sources
   e. staff resources
   f. time
   g. cost
   h. ambulatory health care staff knowledge and ability to implement study methodology
4. Appropriate and valid study methods include but are not limited to the following:
   a. audits
   b. patient interviews
   c. patient concerns
   d. patient survey forms
   e. ambulatory health care staff survey forms
   f. community survey forms
   g. individual interviews:
      (1) telephone
      (2) in person
   h. patient transfer interviews
   i. group interviews
   j. ambulatory health care staff exit interviews
   k. ambulatory health care staff discipline meetings
   l. patient/family case conferences
   m. direct/indirect observation
   n. patient education surveys
   o. criteria maps
   p. computer-assisted random selection of criteria
   q. computer-assisted data sorting that examines relationship of study variables
5. The chosen study method is implemented to study the selected problem.
6. Implementation/monitoring of the chosen study method is according to a defined timeframe, as follows:
   a. *prospective:* the study of a selected problem from a certain point toward the future, e.g., the next 50 patients who are transferred from the ambulatory health care provider to an acute care facility
   b. *concurrent:* the study of a selected problem while care is being delivered, e.g., patients who are currently receiving chemotherapy
   c. *retrospective:* the study of a selected problem after care has been delivered, e.g., patients who have been seen by the ambulatory health care provider with a diabetes diagnosis
7. Implementation of the chosen study method focuses on three approaches to be used, as appropriate:

a. *structure:* focus is on the framework that provides support for the actual provision of ambulatory health care services, e.g., delivery care system, ambulatory health care staff qualifications, ambulatory health care policies and procedures
b. *process:* focus is on the standards and process used by the ambulatory health care staff to deliver ambulatory health care services, e.g., implementation of chemotherapy standards by registered nurses
c. *outcome:* focus is on anticipated changes in patient's condition after patient has been seen by the ambulatory health care provider, e.g., patient accurately states signs and symptoms for wound infection

8. Actual causes of problems are determined from the problem study, which identifies deficiencies in:
   a. knowledge, where deficits in theory or practice information exist, creating a negative impact on patient care and/or clinical practices
   b. performance, where deficits in behavior/practice exist, creating a negative impact on patient care and/or clinical practices
   c. systems, where deficits in organizational, administrative, or environmental factors exist, creating a negative impact on patient care and/or clinical practices
9. Problem study information is documented on a Continuous Quality Assurance Activity Form (see Exhibit 1011-1).
10. Problem study information is communicated to individuals, as appropriate, according to Policy and Procedure 1010: Confidentiality of Quality Assurance Information, and Policy and Procedure 1001: Administrative Control.

AMBULATORY HEALTH CARE PROVIDER
QUALITY ASSURANCE
POLICY AND PROCEDURE
1034

Subject: Quality Assurance Plan	
Drafted by:	Date drafted:
Revised by:	Date revised:
Approved by:	Date approved:
Supersedes date:	Page #:
Date effective:	Page: ____ of

POLICY

The ambulatory health care provider maintains an established Quality Assurance Program through a written Quality Assurance Plan.

PURPOSE

1. To describe the ambulatory health care provider's Quality Assurance Program.
2. To ensure a planned, systematic approach for quality assurance.
3. To coordinate quality assurance activities.
4. To define expectations for quality assurance activities.

PROCEDURE

1. The ambulatory health care provider's Quality Assurance Program is implemented and evaluated on an ongoing basis according to a written Quality Assurance Plan (see Exhibit 1034-1), which includes descriptions of its:
   a. administrative control
   b. mission statement
   c. philosophy
   d. objectives
   e. scope
   f. Quality Assurance Committee
   g. continuous quality assurance activities: problem assessment, identification, selection, study, corrective action, monitoring, evaluation, and reassessment
   h. special quality assurance studies: study topic selection; study topic; data collection, analysis, and interpretation; conclusions; and recommendations
   i. confidentiality policy for quality assurance information
   j. documentation methods for quality assurance activities
   k. system for communicating quality assurance information
   l. quality assurance program evaluation method
2. A quality assurance policy and procedure manual is written and maintained in order to implement the written Quality Assurance Plan.
3. The Quality Assurance Plan is reviewed, revised, and approved, annually, by the Ambulatory Health Care Quality Assurance Committee, Ambulatory Health Care Advisory Committee, Administrator of Ambulatory Health Care, President of the ambulatory health care provider, and Board of Directors.

Exhibit 1034-1 Quality Assurance Plan

AMBULATORY HEALTH CARE PROVIDER
Quality Assurance Plan

Administrative Control

The ambulatory health care provider's Board of Directors is ultimately responsible for the quality of ambulatory health care services delivered. The President of the ambulatory health care provider is responsible for the overall Quality Assurance Program. The Administrator of Ambulatory Health Care is responsible for establishing the Quality Assurance Program. The Quality Assurance Manager is responsible for the operations of the Quality Assurance Program. The ambulatory health care staff and interdisciplinary team members are responsible for conducting quality assurance activities according to the provider's Quality Assurance Program. Communication of quality assurance information occurs according to the organizational structure.

Mission Statement

The mission of the ambulatory health care provider is to provide for the quality, safe, and cost-effective delivery of ambulatory health care services to individuals in need of those services. The ambulatory health care provider's Board of Directors and administrative staff are committed to the provision of ambulatory health care services that are guided by a Quality Assurance Program in order to ensure that the delivered services constitute quality, safe, and cost-effective services for the provider's patients.

Philosophy

Quality assurance activities are guided by the overall philosophy of the ambulatory health care provider. The adoption of the appropriate philosophical approach in providing quality ambulatory health care services is based on the following basic assumptions:

1. The maintenance and realization of the full potential of human life are supreme values.
2. Humans possess a unique hierarchy of needs, as defined by Maslow:
   a. physiological needs
   b. safety needs
   c. belongingness and love needs
   d. self-esteem needs
   e. self-actualization needs
3. Humans search for meaning in personal life experiences.
4. Humans make choices and decisions based on their individual beliefs and values.
5. Humans exert personal control over their lives in making such choices and decisions.

The philosophy of the ambulatory health care provider, based on these assumptions, stipulates that each ambulatory health care patient:

1. desires ambulatory health care services that promote the patient's value of life by:
   a. minimizing negative patient illness and disability outcomes
   b. maximizing potential patient level-of-independence outcomes
   c. restoring, maintaining, and promoting patient health
2. possesses unique physiological, safety, psychological, self-esteem, and self-actualization needs that require consideration in the patient's plan of ambulatory health care
3. searches for meaning in the personal life experiences surrounding the patient's illness or disability
4. makes choices and decisions about the provision of ambulatory health care services relative to the patient's self-defined unique needs and according to the patient's personal beliefs and values
5. exerts personal control over the patient's personal life in collaborating with ambulatory health care staff members regarding the provision of services

In support of the ambulatory health care provider's philosophy, the provider is dedicated to the provision of comprehensive quality patient-centered and patient family-centered ambulatory health care that is focused on the patient's unique physiological, safety, psychological, self-esteem, and self-actualization needs. The provider is committed to the provision of ambulatory health care services that will assist the patient in searching for meaning in the personal life experiences surrounding the patient's illness or disability; to make choices and decisions about the provision of ambulatory health care services based on the patient's self-defined unique needs; and to collaborate actively with the ambulatory health care provider staff and other health care providers regarding the provision of appropriate services. The ambulatory health care provider is also dedicated to the provision of ambulatory health care education to the patient, the patient's family, and the community.

Objectives

The ambulatory health care provider implements quality assurance activities to achieve the following objectives:

1. To develop, implement, and evaluate standards to measure medical, nursing, and therapy practice and delivery of ambulatory health care services.
2. To develop, implement, and evaluate effective quality assurance activities according to the ambulatory health care provider's mission statement, philosophy, and objectives.
3. To develop effective systems for problem assessment, identification, selection, study, corrective action, monitoring, evaluation, and reassessment of nursing/interdisciplinary team practice and ambulatory health care services.
4. To provide focus and direction for quality assurance activities.
5. To develop effective verbal/written information systems to communicate quality assurance activity outcomes to appropriate individuals and committees.
6. To provide educational opportunities for all ambulatory health care staff members to increase their knowledge and participation in quality assurance activities.
7. To correlate the findings of quality assurance activities with the content of ambulatory health care provider continuing education programs.
8. To encourage input and participation of all ambulatory health care staff relative to quality assurance activities.
9. To coordinate and integrate ambulatory health care provider interdepartmental/intradepartmental quality assurance activities with overall provider quality assurance activities.
10. To ensure administrative commitment and support for quality assurance activities.

continues

Exhibit 1032-1 *continued*

Scope

The scope of the Quality Assurance Program includes all of the services provided by the ambulatory health care provider, such as medical; nursing; physical, occupational, and speech therapy; and nutrition, pharmacy, laboratory, and radiology services.

Quality Assurance Committee

The Ambulatory Health Care Quality Assurance Committee will consist of:

1. Administrator of Ambulatory Health Care
2. Nursing Manager
3. Medical Director
4. Quality Assurance Manager
5. two ambulatory health care registered nurses
6. two ambulatory health care licensed practical nurses
7. two ambulatory health care aides
8. interdisciplinary team members/ancillary support services staff:
   a. physical therapist
   b. occupational therapist
   c. speech therapist
   d. dietician
   e. pharmacist
   f. laboratory technician
   g. radiology technician
   h. Financial Manager

Quality Assurance Activities

Quality assurance activities are established by developing, implementing, and evaluating:

1. Quality Assurance Program
2. quality assurance policies and procedures
3. continuous quality assurance activities: problem assessment, identification, selection, study, corrective action, monitoring, evaluation, and reassessment
4. special quality assurance studies: study topic selection; study topic; data collection, analysis, and interpretation; conclusions; and recommendations
5. confidentiality of quality assurance information
6. administrative policies and procedures
7. clinical policies and procedures

Approval

The ambulatory health care provider Quality Assurance Program as outlined in this plan is approved and will become effective on (Date Quality Assurance Program Will Become Effective).

____________________ Signature of President	____________________ Date of Signature
____________________ Signature of Board of Directors Representative	____________________ Date of Signature

AMBULATORY HEALTH CARE PROVIDER
QUALITY ASSURANCE
POLICY AND PROCEDURE
1035

Subject: Recommendations	
Drafted by: ______	Date drafted: ______
Revised by: ______	Date revised: ______
Approved by: ______	Date approved: ______
Supersedes date: ______	Page #: ______
Date effective: ______	Page: ______ of ______

POLICY

Recommendations are based on study topic conclusions.

PURPOSE

1. To formulate recommendations for further study.
2. To provide direction for further studies to gain increased insight into the study topic.

PROCEDURE

1. Recommendations are derived from study topic conclusions.
2. Recommendations focus on the positive impact on patient care and/or clinical practice and include the following:
   a. description of specific action to correct or eliminate identified problem
   b. identification of the following:
      (1) individual(s) responsible for implementation of the recommendations
      (2) dates for implementation of recommendations
      (3) dates for implementation of special quality assurance study evaluation
   c. prioritization of recommendations
3. Recommendations are documented on a Special Quality Assurance Study Form (see Exhibit 1037-1).
4. Recommendations are communicated to individuals, as appropriate, according to Policy and Procedure 1010: Confidentiality of Quality Assurance Information, and Policy and Procedure 1001: Administrative Control.

AMBULATORY HEALTH CARE PROVIDER
QUALITY ASSURANCE
POLICY AND PROCEDURE
1036

Subject: Scope of Quality Assurance Program	
Drafted by: ______	Date drafted: ______
Revised by: ______	Date revised: ______
Approved by: ______	Date approved: ______
Supersedes date: ______	Page #: ______
Date effective: ______	Page: ______ of ______

POLICY

The scope of the ambulatory health care provider's Quality Assurance Program encompasses assessment of the total provider's operations, programs, and services.

PURPOSE

1. To define the scope of the ambulatory health care provider's Quality Assurance Program.
2. To coordinate and integrate the ambulatory health care provider's interdepartmental/intradepartmental quality assurance activities with overall provider quality assurance activities.

PROCEDURE

1. The ambulatory health care provider develops and implements a Quality Assurance Program.
2. Assessment of the ambulatory health care provider's operations, programs, and services occurs according to the ambulatory health care provider's Quality Assurance Program.
3. The ambulatory health care provider's nursing department develops and implements a written quality assurance plan.
4. The ambulatory health care provider's interdisciplinary team members develop and implement a written quality assurance plan.
5. The ambulatory health care provider's ancillary support services staff develop and implement a written quality assurance plan.
6. Interdepartmental quality assurance activities are developed, implemented, and evaluated according to each department's quality assurance plan in conjunction with the overall ambulatory health care provider's Quality Assurance Program.
7. Intradepartmental quality assurance activities are developed, implemented, and evaluated in conjunction with the ambulatory health care provider's overall Quality Assurance Program.
8. All ambulatory health care staff members participate in ambulatory health care quality assurance activities.

AMBULATORY HEALTH CARE PROVIDER
QUALITY ASSURANCE
POLICY AND PROCEDURE
1037

Subject: Special Quality Assurance Studies	
Drafted by: ______	Date drafted: ______
Revised by: ______	Date revised: ______
Approved by: ______	Date approved: ______
Supersedes date: ______	Page #: ______
Date effective: ______	Page: ______ of ______

POLICY

The ambulatory health care provider conducts special quality assurance studies.

PURPOSE

1. To develop research studies based on findings or problems identified through quality assurance activities.
2. To provide direction for future studies designed to gain greater insight into the topic under investigation.
3. To answer questions of ambulatory health care and clinical practice.
4. To advance the scientific base of ambulatory health care and clinical practice.
5. To generate new knowledge for the purpose of developing or refining relevant theories.
6. To improve validity and credibility of quality assurance activities.

PROCEDURE

1. An available, accessible, and appropriate data collection and retrieval system is maintained to support special quality assurance studies.
2. The scientific method is used for special quality assurance studies, which incorporates the following:
   a. study topic selection
   b. study topic
   c. data collection
   d. data analysis and interpretation
   e. conclusions
   f. recommendations
3. A minimum of five quality assurance studies:
   a. are implemented annually, of which three are based on patient care outcomes
   b. are controlled studies to acquire significant and useful information relevant to quality of ambulatory health care
   c. are integrated with continuous quality assurance activities, as necessary
   d. address diagnoses, treatments, and procedures that demonstrate significant risk for complications, frequency of occurrence, and adverse health outcomes
   e. address improved delivery of health care services that has a positive impact on patient care and/or clinical practice
4. Special quality assurance studies are documented on a Special Quality Assurance Study Form (see Exhibit 1037-1).
5. Special quality assurance studies are communicated to individuals, as appropriate, according to Policy and Procedure 1010: Confidentiality of Quality Assurance Information, and Policy and Procedure 1001: Administrative Control.
6. Completed special quality assurance studies are filed in the ambulatory health care provider's Special Quality Assurance Study administrative file.

Exhibit 1037-1 Special Quality Assurance Study Form

AMBULATORY HEALTH CARE PROVIDER
SPECIAL QUALITY ASSURANCE STUDY

Following Section To Be Completed by Quality Assurance Manager

Date Study Implemented	Date Study Completed

Study Topic

Reason(s) Study Topic Selected and Study Warranted (please check [√] one or more)
☐ Health care trends' relationship to quality of care
☐ Diagnoses, treatments, and procedures demonstrate actual/potential adverse health care outcomes
☐ Diagnoses, treatments, and procedures demonstrate significant risk for complications
☐ Adverse diagnoses, treatments, and procedures demonstrate significant frequency of occurrence
☐ Improvement in delivery of health care would have a positive impact on patient care and/or clinical practice
☐ Benefit for patient care and/or clinical practice worthy of cost expenditures for study
☐ Probability that adequate resources exist to achieve completion of study

Purpose of Study

Population(s) Studied

Study Topic Question, Problem, or Hypothesis

Study Topic Approach (please check [√] one)	Data Collection Method (please check [√] one)
☐ Historical ☐ Survey ☐ Experimental	☐ Questioning ☐ Observing ☐ Measuring

Narrative Description of Data Collection, Including Relevant Statistical Data (please attach supporting information)

Data Gathering Instruments Used

Description of Sample Participants

Pilot Study Implemented?
☐ Yes ☐ No (please explain) ________________

Data Analysis and Interpretation

Conclusions

Description of How Study Addressed Improved Delivery of Health Care Services Having a Positive Impact on Patient Care and/or Clinical Practice

continues

Exhibit 1037-1 *continued*

Recommendations for Improving Patient Care and/or Clinical Practice

Recommendations Regarding Disposition of Study
☐ Discontinue ☐ Continue

Signature of Quality Assurance Manager	Date of Signature

Following Section To Be Completed by AHCQA Committee Chairperson

Date of AHCQA Committee Review of Study	AHCQA Committee Recommendation Regarding Disposition of Study (please check [√] one) ☐ Discontinue ☐ Continue
Signature of AHCQA Committee Chairperson	Date of Signature

Following Section To Be Completed by Ambulatory Health Care Advisory Committee Chairperson

Date of Ambulatory Health Care Advisory Committee Review of Study	Ambulatory Health Care Advisory Committee Recommendation Regarding Disposition of Study (please check [√] one) ☐ Discontinue ☐ Continue
Signature of Ambulatory Health Care Advisory Committee Chairperson	Date of Signature

Following Section To Be Completed by Administrator of Ambulatory Health Care

Ambulatory Health Care Advisory Committee Recommendation Regarding Disposition of Study (please check [√] one)
☐ Approved and Referred to Quality Assurance Manager for Disposition ☐ Not Approved (please explain) ____________

Signature of Administrator of Ambulatory Health Care	Date of Signature

Following Section To Be Completed by Quality Assurance Manager

Disposition of Study per Administrator of Ambulatory Health Care Approval (please check [√] one)
☐ Discontinued; Appropriate Individuals Notified ☐ Continued; Appropriate Individuals Notified

Date Study
____________Discontinued ____________Continued

Signature of Quality Assurance Manager	Date of Signature

AMBULATORY HEALTH CARE PROVIDER
QUALITY ASSURANCE
POLICY AND PROCEDURE
1038

Subject: Staff Member Assessment of Ambulatory Health Care Services

Drafted by: ______	Date drafted: ______
Revised by: ______	Date revised: ______
Approved by: ______	Date approved: ______
Supersedes date: ______	Page #: ______
Date effective: ______	Page: ______ of ______

POLICY

Ambulatory health care staff members assess the delivery of ambulatory health care services.

PURPOSE

To collect/give information about the delivery of ambulatory health care services.

PROCEDURE

1. Each ambulatory health care staff member assesses the delivery of ambulatory health care services on a quarterly basis relative to:
   a. development of new objectives and goals
   b. achievement of established objectives and goals
   c. patient care
   d. patient acuity levels
   e. patient/staff caseload/assignment ratios
   f. patient population
   g. patient, patient family, ambulatory health care staff, and community education
   h. ambulatory health care staff meeting activity
   i. committee activity
   j. community/professional association activity
   k. policy and procedure changes/development, implementation, and evaluation
   l. equipment/service changes
   m. financial/budget activity
   n. public relations/marketing activity
   o. special projects/assignments
   p. interdepartmental/intradepartmental activity
   q. research activity
2. The ambulatory health care staff member documents the assessment of the delivery of ambulatory health care services on an Assessment of Ambulatory Health Care Services Form (see Exhibit 1019-1), excluding the "Status of Quality Assurance Activities" section of the form.
3. The Assessment of Ambulatory Health Care Services Form:
   a. is written in an informative and concise style
   b. may be typed or legibly handwritten
4. The completed Assessment of Ambulatory Health Care Services Form is due in the office of the ambulatory health care staff member's manager by the first Wednesday of the following months:

April:	1st quarter
July:	2nd quarter
October:	3rd quarter
January:	4th quarter

5. The ambulatory health care staff member's manager:
   a. reviews the completed Assessment of Ambulatory Health Care Services Form
   b. provides a verbal and written response to each ambulatory health care staff member who has submitted a completed Assessment of Ambulatory Health Care Services Form
   c. documents the written response to the ambulatory health care staff member on a Response to Assessment of Ambulatory Health Care Services Form (see Exhibit 1019-2)
   d. assesses/incorporates the ambulatory health care staff member's assessments into the manager's Assessment of Ambulatory Health Care Services Form, as appropriate
   e. submits the ambulatory health care staff member's completed Assessment of Ambulatory Health Care Services Form and Response to Assessment of Ambulatory Health Care Services Form to the

Administrator of Ambulatory Health Care along with the manager's completed Assessment of Ambulatory Health Care Services Form

6. The Administrator of Ambulatory Health Care reviews the submitted Assessment of Ambulatory Health Care Services Form and Response to Assessment of Ambulatory Health Care Services Form.
7. Problems identified through the staff member's assessment of ambulatory health care services are referred to the Quality Assurance Manager for consideration as a continuous or special quality assurance activity/study.
8. Staff member assessment of ambulatory health care services is communicated to individuals, as appropriate, according to Policy and Procedure 1010: Confidentiality of Quality Assurance Information, and Policy and Procedure 1001: Administrative Control.
9. The completed Assessment of Ambulatory Health Care Services Form and Response to Assessment of Ambulatory Health Care Services Form are filed in the ambulatory health care provider's Staff Member Assessment of Ambulatory Health Care Services and Response to Assessment of Ambulatory Health Care Services administrative files.

AMBULATORY HEALTH CARE PROVIDER
QUALITY ASSURANCE
POLICY AND PROCEDURE
1039

Subject: Staff Member Quality Assurance Concerns/Suggestions	
Drafted by: ______	Date drafted: ______
Revised by: ______	Date revised: ______
Approved by: ______	Date approved: ______
Supersedes date: ______	Page #: ______
Date effective: ______	Page: ______ of ______

POLICY

Ambulatory health care staff members are encouraged to contribute information regarding quality assurance concerns/suggestions.

PURPOSE

1. To ensure ambulatory health care staff member participation in the ambulatory health care provider's Quality Assurance Program.
2. To obtain information about quality assurance concerns and suggestions to strengthen quality assurance activities.

PROCEDURE

1. Ambulatory health care staff members are encouraged to complete a Staff Member Quality Assurance Concern/Suggestion Form (see Exhibit 1039-1).
2. Quality assurance concerns/suggestions are referred to the Quality Assurance Manager for consideration as a continuous or special quality assurance activity/study.
3. Staff member quality assurance concerns/suggestions are communicated to individuals, as appropriate, according to Policy and Procedure 1010: Confidentiality of Quality Assurance Information, and Policy and Procedure 1001: Administrative Control.
4. The completed Staff Member Quality Assurance Concern/Suggestion Form is filed in the ambulatory health care provider's Staff Member Quality Assurance Concern/Suggestion administrative file.

Exhibit 1039-1 Staff Member Quality Assurance Concern/Suggestion Form

AMBULATORY HEALTH CARE PROVIDER
STAFF MEMBER QUALITY ASSURANCE CONCERN/SUGGESTION FORM

The ambulatory health care provider staff strive to ensure quality ambulatory health care for patients that is consistent with the ambulatory health care provider philosophy. In order to assist the ambulatory health care staff in addressing quality assurance concerns/suggestions, it will be helpful if you provide information regarding any concerns or suggestions you may have regarding quality assurance. Please complete and return this form to the Quality Assurance Manager. Thank you for your assistance in our continuing efforts to provide quality ambulatory health care services to patients.

Date This Form Completed	Date Quality Assurance Concern/Suggestion Became Apparent

Description of Quality Assurance Concern/Suggestion

Your Name (optional)	Your Position (optional)

AMBULATORY HEALTH CARE PROVIDER
QUALITY ASSURANCE
POLICY AND PROCEDURE
1040

Subject: Standards	
Drafted by:	Date drafted:
Revised by:	Date revised:
Approved by:	Date approved:
Supersedes date:	Page #:
Date effective:	Page: ___ of

POLICY

The ambulatory health care provider's quality assurance activities are guided by ambulatory health care and nursing/interdisciplinary team/ancillary support services staff standards.

PURPOSE

1. To maintain accountability for nursing/interdisciplinary team/ancillary support services staff practice.
2. To provide ambulatory health care staff members with current health care standards.
3. To define and measure quality of ambulatory health care.
4. To define and measure quality of nursing/interdisciplinary team/ancillary support services staff practice.
5. To assist ambulatory health care staff members in clarifying individual, societal, professional, and provider values.
6. To assist ambulatory health care staff members in integrating individual, societal, professional, and provider values into practice.
7. To provide information to patients; patient families; external review agencies; federal, state, and local government; and the community regarding the quality of ambulatory health care services that is available from ambulatory health care staff.

PROCEDURE

1. The ambulatory health care provider's quality assurance activities are developed, implemented, and evaluated according to:
   a. American Medical Association's ethical standards established for medical practice (see Exhibit 1040-1)
   b. legal standards established for medical practice (see Exhibit 1040-2)
   c. American Nurses' Association standards established for nursing practice (see Exhibit 1040-3)
   d. American Nurses' Association ethical standards established for nursing practice (see Exhibit 1040-4)
   e. professional national standards established for the respective interdisciplinary team practice (i.e., physical, occupational, and speech therapy and social and nutrition services)
   f. professional national standards established for the respective ancillary support services staff practice (i.e., pharmacy, laboratory, and radiology services)
   g. professional state standards established for ambulatory health care nursing practice
   h. professional state standards established for the respective interdisciplinary team ambulatory health care practice (i.e., physical, occupational, and speech therapy and social and nutrition services)
   i. professional state standards established for the respective ancillary support services staff practice (i.e., pharmacy, laboratory, and radiology services)
   j. legal standards established for ambulatory health care provider licensure
   k. regulatory standards established for ambulatory health care provider participation
   l. legal standards established for the respective ancillary support services practice (i.e., pharmacy, laboratory, and radiology services)
   m. legal standards established for nursing practice (see Exhibit 1040-5)
   n. legal standards established for the respective interdisciplinary team practice (i.e., physical, occupational, and speech therapy and social and nutrition services)
   o. accreditation standards established for ambulatory health providers

p. mission statement of the ambulatory health care provider
q. philosophy of the ambulatory health care provider
r. objectives of the ambulatory health care provider

2. The standards that are developed, implemented, and evaluated:
   a. are well defined
   b. are relevant
   c. are achievable
   d. are measurable
   e. are reviewed and revised as necessary
3. The adopted ambulatory health care provider standards are reviewed and discussed with ambulatory health care staff members during orientation.
4. Revisions in the adopted ambulatory health care provider standards are given to, reviewed with, and discussed with ambulatory health care staff members, whenever necessary.
5. Ambulatory health care staff members are responsible and held accountable for assuring compliance with the adopted ambulatory health care provider standards.
6. Appropriate disciplinary action is taken when there is reasonable cause to believe that an ambulatory health care staff member has not complied with the provider's adopted ambulatory health care standards, according to Policy and Procedure 5003: Discipline of Home Health Care Staff Members.

Exhibit 1040-1 American Medical Association Principles of Medical Ethics

AMERICAN MEDICAL ASSOCIATION
PRINCIPLES OF MEDICAL ETHICS

PREAMBLE:

The medical profession has long subscribed to a body of ethical statements developed primarily for the benefit of the patient. As a member of this profession, a physician must recognize responsibility not only to patients, but also to society, to other health professionals, and to self. The following Principles adopted by the American Medical Association are not laws, but standards of conduct which define the essentials of honorable behavior for the physician.

I. A physician shall be dedicated to providing competent medical service with compassion and respect for human dignity.
II. A physician shall deal honestly with patients and colleagues, and strive to expose those physicians deficient in character or competence, or who engage in fraud or deception.
III. A physician shall respect the law and also recognize a responsibility to seek changes in those requirements which are contrary to the best interests of the patient.
IV. A physician shall respect the rights of patients, of colleagues, and of other health professionals, and shall safeguard patient confidences within the constraints of the law.
V. A physician shall continue to study, apply and advance scientific knowledge, make relevant information available to patients, colleagues, and the public, obtain consultation, and use the talents of other health professionals when indicated.
VI. A physician shall, in the provision of appropriate patient care, except in emergencies, be free to choose whom to serve, with whom to associate, and the environment in which to provide medical services.
VII. A physician shall recognize a responsibility to participate in activities contributing to an improved community.

Source: Reprinted from *Principles of Medical Ethics* with permission of the American Medical Association.

Exhibit 1040-2 Legal Standards for Physician Practice Laws as Indicated by the State of Minnesota Physician Practice Act

CHAPTER 147
PHYSICIANS AND SURGEONS, OSTEOPATHS

147.01 BOARD OF MEDICAL EXAMINERS.

Subdivision 1. **Creation; terms.** The board of medical examiners consists of 11 residents of the state of Minnesota appointed by the governor. Seven board members must hold a degree of doctor of medicine and be licensed to practice medicine under this chapter. One board member must hold a degree of doctor of osteopathy and either be licensed to practice osteopathy under Minnesota Statutes 1961, sections 148.11 to 148.16; prior to May 1, 1963, or be licensed to practice medicine under this chapter. Three board members must be public members as defined by section 214.02. One of the public members must represent a mental health and consumer advocacy organization. A member may serve more than one term but shall not serve more than two terms consecutively. Membership terms, compensation of members, removal of members, the filling of membership vacancies, and fiscal year and reporting requirements are as provided in sections 214.07 to 214.09. The provision of staff, administrative services and office space; the review and processing of complaints; the setting of board fees; and other provisions relating to board operations are as provided in chapter 214 and Laws 1976, chapter 222, sections 2 to 7.

Subd. 2. **Recommendations for appointment.** Prior to the end of the term of a doctor of medicine or public member on the board, or within 60 days after a doctor of medicine or public member position on the board becomes vacant, the state medical association, the mental health association of Minnesota, and other interested persons and organizations may recommend to the governor doctors of medicine and public members qualified to serve on the board. Prior to the end of the term of a doctor of osteopathy, or within 60 days after a doctor of osteopathy membership becomes vacant, the Minnesota osteopathic medical society may recommend to the governor three doctors of osteopathy qualified to serve on the board. The governor may appoint members to the board from the list of persons recommended or from among other qualified candidates.

Subd. 3. **Board administration.** The board shall elect from among its number a president, a vice-president, and a secretary-treasurer, who shall each serve for one year, or until a successor is elected and qualifies. The board shall have authority to adopt rules as may be found necessary to carry out the purposes of this chapter. The members of the board shall have authority to administer oaths and the board, in session, to take testimony as to matters pertaining to the duties of the board. Six members of the board shall constitute a quorum for the transaction of business. The board shall have a common seal, which shall be kept by the executive secretary, whose duty it shall be to keep a record of all proceedings of the board, including a register of all applicants for license under this chapter, giving their names, addresses, ages, educational qualifications, and the result of their examination. These books and registers shall be prima facie evidence of all the matters therein recorded.

Subd. 4. **Disclosure.** Subject to the exceptions listed in this subdivision, all communications or information received by or disclosed to the board relating to any person or matter subject to its regulatory jurisdiction, and all records of any action or proceedings thereon, except a final decision of the board, are confidential and privileged and any disciplinary hearing shall be closed to the public.

(a) Upon application of a party in a proceeding before the board under section 147.091, the board shall produce and permit the inspection and copying, by or on behalf of the moving party, of any designated documents or papers relevant to the proceedings, in accordance with the provisions of rule 34, Minnesota rules of civil procedure.

(b) If the board imposes disciplinary measures of any kind, the name and business address of the licensee, the nature of the misconduct, and the action taken by the board are public data.

(c) The board shall exchange information with other licensing boards, agencies, or departments within the state, as required under section 214.10, subdivision 8, paragraph (d), and may release information in the reports required under sections 147.02, subdivision 6, and 214.10, subdivision 8, paragraph (b).

(d) The board shall furnish to a person who made a complaint a summary of the results of an investigation of that complaint, a description of the activities and actions of the board relating to that complaint, and the reasons for actions taken by the board.

Subd. 5. The board of medical examiners shall provide blanks, books, certificates, and such stationery and assistance as is necessary for the transaction of the business pertaining to the duties of such board. The expenses of administering sections 147.01 to 147.29 shall be paid from the appropriations made to the board of medical examiners. The board shall employ an executive director.

History: *(5706) RL s 2295; 1921 c 68 s 1; 1927 c 188 s 1; 1963 c 45 s 1; 1967 c 416 s 1; 1969 c 927 s 1; 1973 c 638 s 6; 1975 c 136 s 5; 1976 c 2 s 65; 1976 c 222 s 32; 1976 c 239 s 53; 1984 c 588 s 1; 1985 c 247 s 1-3,24; 1986 c 444; 1Sp1986 c 3 art 1 s 22; 1987 c 86 s 1*

continues

Exhibit 1040-2 *continued*

147.02 EXAMINATION; LICENSING.

Subdivision 1. **United States or Canadian medical school graduates.** The board shall, with the consent of six of its members, issue a license to practice medicine to a person who meets the following requirements:

(a) An applicant for a license shall file a written application on forms provided by the board, showing to the board's satisfaction that the applicant is of good moral character and satisfies the requirements of this section.

(b) The applicant shall present evidence satisfactory to the board of being a graduate of a medical or osteopathic school located in the United States, its territories or Canada, and approved by the board based upon its faculty, curriculum, facilities, accreditation by a recognized national accrediting organization approved by the board, and other relevant data, or is currently enrolled in the final year of study at the school.

(c) The applicant must have passed an examination prepared and graded by the national board of medical examiners or the federation of state medical boards. The board shall by rule determine what constitutes a passing score in the examination.

(d) The applicant shall present evidence satisfactory to the board of the completion of one year of graduate, clinical medical training in a program accredited by a national accrediting organization approved by the board or other graduate training approved in advance by the board as meeting standards similar to those of a national accrediting organization.

(e) The applicant shall make arrangements with the executive director to appear in person before the board or its designated representative to show that the applicant satisfies the requirements of this section. The board may establish as internal operating procedures the procedures or requirements for the applicant's personal presentation.

(f) The applicant shall pay a fee established by the board by rule. The fee may not be refunded.

(g) The applicant must not have engaged in conduct warranting disciplinary action against a licensee. If the applicant does not satisfy the requirements of this paragraph, the board may refuse to issue a license unless it determines that the public will be protected through issuance of a license with conditions and limitations the board considers appropriate.

Subd. 2. [Repealed, 1985 c 247 s 26]

Subd. 3. [Repealed, 1971 c 485 s 6]

Subd. 4. [Repealed, 1984 c 432 art 2 s 55]

Subd. 5. **Procedures.** The board shall adopt a written statement of internal operating procedures describing procedures for receiving and investigating complaints, reviewing misconduct cases, and imposing disciplinary actions.

Subd. 6. **Disciplinary actions must be published.** At least annually, the board shall publish and release to the public a description of all disciplinary measures taken by the board. The publication must include, for each disciplinary measure taken, the name and business address of the licensee, the nature of the misconduct, and the disciplinary measure taken by the board.

Subd. 6a. **Exception to publication requirement.** The publication requirement does not apply to disciplinary measures by the board which are based exclusively upon grounds listed in section 147.091, subdivision 1, clause (l) or (r).

History: *(5707) RL s 2296; 1909 c 474 s 1; 1927 c 188 s 2; 1937 c 203 s 1; 1953 c 290 s 1; 1959 c 346 s 1; 1963 c 45 s 2; 1967 c 416 s 2; 1969 c 6 s 25; 1969 c 927 s 2; 1971 c 485 s 2; 1973 c 638 s 7; 1974 c 42 s 1; 1975 c 93 s 1,2; 1976 c 222 s 33; 1983 c 290 s 17; 1985 c 247 s 4-6; 1986 c 444; 1988 c 557 s 1*

NOTE: Subdivision 6a, as added by Laws 1988, chapter 557, section 1, is repealed effective August 1, 1990. See Laws 1988, chapter 557, section 6.

147.021 [Renumbered 147.091]

147.025 EVIDENCE OF PAST SEXUAL CONDUCT.

In a proceeding for the suspension or revocation of a license or other disciplinary action for unethical or unprofessional conduct involving sexual contact with a patient or former patient, the board or administrative law judge shall not consider evidence of the patient's previous sexual conduct nor shall any reference to this conduct be made during the proceedings or in the findings, except by motion of the complainant, unless the evidence would be admissible under the applicable provisions of section 609.347, subdivision 3.

History: *1984 c 556 s 1; 1984 c 640 s 32*

147.03 LICENSURE BY ENDORSEMENT; RECIPROCITY.

The board, with the consent of six of its members, may issue a license to practice medicine to any person who satisfies the following requirements:

(a) The applicant shall satisfy all the requirements established in section 147.02, subdivision 1, paragraphs (a), (b), (d), (e), and (f).

(b) The applicant shall present evidence satisfactory to the board that the applicant has a valid license to practice medicine issued by the proper agency in another state or by a province of Canada; or is a diplomate of the national board of medical examiners, the national board of examiners for osteopathic physicians and surgeons, or the licensure medical council of Canada.

(c) The applicant shall present evidence satisfactory to the board that the applicant passed an examination as determined by the endorsing examining board or licensing agency. The board, at its discretion, may establish by rule passing grade levels higher than those determined by an examining board or agency or may require the applicant to be examined in subjects not previously covered in an examination.

(d) The applicant shall pay a fee established by the board by rule. The fee may not be refunded.

(e) The applicant must not have engaged in conduct warranting disciplinary action against a licensee, or have been subject to disciplinary action in another state. If an applicant does not satisfy the requirements stated in this clause, the board may refuse to issue a license unless it determines that the public will be protected through issuance of a license with conditions or limitations the board considers appropriate.

The board may issue a temporary permit to practice medicine to a physician eligible for licensure under this section upon payment of a fee set by the board. The permit remains valid only until the next meeting of the board.

History: *(5709) 1905 c 236 s 1; 1913 c 139 s 1; 1919 c 251 s 1; 1927 c 188 s 3; 1953 c 290 s 2; 1963 c 45 s 3; 1975 c 92 s 1; 1977 c 7 s 1; 1985 c 247 s 8; 1986 c 444*

147.031 EXAMINATIONS AND LICENSES OF OSTEOPATHS.

Subdivision 1. Any doctor of osteopathy licensed by the state board of osteopathy under Minnesota Statutes 1961, Sections 148.11 to 148.16, desiring to obtain a license to practice medicine shall apply to the secretary of the board and pay a fee of $50 for the use of the board, which in no case shall be refunded. The applicant shall be examined in the subjects that the board then examines applicants under section 147.02 in which the applicant

continues

Exhibit 1040-2 *continued*

was not examined by the state board of osteopathy prior to the issuance of a license under Minnesota Statutes 1961, sections 148.11 to 148.16, prior to May 1, 1963. All applicants shall be known to the board members or examiners only by number, without names, or other methods of identification on examination papers by which board members or examiners may be able to identify such applicants, until the final grades of all the examination papers have been determined, and the licenses granted or refused. After such examination, the board, if eight members thereof consent, shall grant such doctor of osteopathy a license to practice medicine. The board may refuse to grant such a license to any person guilty of immoral, dishonorable, or unprofessional conduct, as defined in Minnesota Statutes 1961, chapter 147, but subject to the right of the applicant to appeal to the district court in the county in which the principal office of the board is located on the questions of law and fact.

Subd. 2. Any such doctor of osteopathy may, until so granted a license to practice medicine, continue to practice osteopathy as taught in reputable colleges of osteopathy, including the use and administration, in connection with the practice of obstetrics, minor surgery, and toxicology only, of anesthetics, narcotics, antidotes, and antiseptics subject to the same state and federal restrictions and limitations as are by law applicable to physicians licensed to practice medicine and shall have the same rights and powers and be subject to the same duties as physicians licensed to practice medicine with reference to matters pertaining to the public health, including the reporting of births and deaths. The board shall by rule determine what constitutes minor surgery, anesthetics, narcotics, antidotes, and antiseptics.

Subd. 3. No person who is not on May 1, 1963, licensed by the state board of osteopathy under Minnesota Statutes 1961, sections 148.11 to 148.16, shall engage in the practice of osteopathy or by use of titles or initials indicating degrees, or in any other way, hold out as being so engaged.

Subd. 4. Every person who shall violate any provisions of this section shall be guilty of a gross misdemeanor.

Subd. 5. The board shall investigate suspected violations of this section and institute proceedings thereunder.

History: *1963 c 45 s 4; 1973 c 638 s 8; 1985 c 248 s 70; 1986 c 444*

147.035 MALPRACTICE HISTORY.

Subdivision 1. **Submission.** A person desiring to practice medicine in this state who has previously practiced in another state shall submit the following additional information with the license application for the five-year period of active practice preceding the date of filing such application:

(a) The name and address of the person's professional liability insurer in the other state.

(b) The number, date, and disposition of any medical malpractice settlement or award made to the plaintiff relating to the quality of medical treatment.

Subd. 2. **Board action.** The board shall give due consideration to the information submitted pursuant to section 147.03 and this section. An applicant who willfully submits incorrect information shall be subject to disciplinary action pursuant to section 147.091.

History: *1976 c 222 s 35; 1985 c 247 s 24; 1986 s 444*

147.037 LICENSING OF FOREIGN MEDICAL SCHOOL GRADUATES.

Subdivision 1. **Requirements.** The board shall, with the consent of six of its members, issue a license to practice medicine to any person who satisfies the following requirements:

(a) The applicant shall satisfy all the requirements established in section 147.02, subdivision 1, paragraphs (a), (e), (f), and (g):

(b) The applicant shall present evidence satisfactory to the board that the applicant is a graduate of a medical or osteopathic school approved by the board as equivalent to accredited United States or Canadian schools based upon its faculty, curriculum, facilities, accreditation, or other relevant data.

(c) The applicant shall present evidence satisfactory to the board that the applicant has been awarded a certificate by the educational council for foreign medical graduates, and the applicant has a working ability in the English language sufficient to communicate with patients and physicians and to engage in the practice of medicine.

(d) The applicant shall present evidence satisfactory to the board of the completion of two years of graduate, clinical medical training in a program located in the United States, its territories, or Canada and accredited by a national accrediting organization approved by the board or other graduate training approved in advance by the board as meeting standards similar to those of a national accrediting organization. This requirement shall not apply to an applicant who is admitted as a permanent immigrant to the United States as a person of exceptional ability in the sciences pursuant to rules of the United States Department of Labor and who has completed one year of the graduate, clinical medical training required by this paragraph.

(e) The applicant must have passed an examination prepared and graded by the federation of state medical boards, the licensure medical council of Canada, or shall establish eligibility through reciprocity with another state using an examination equivalent to Minnesota's at the time the applicant was licensed in that state.

Subd. 2. **Medical school review.** The board may contract with any qualified person or organization for the performance of a review or investigation, including site visits if necessary, of any medical or osteopathic school prior to approving the school under section 147.02, subdivision 1, paragraph (b), or subdivision 1, paragraph (b), of this section. To the extent possible, the board shall require the school being reviewed to pay the costs of the review or investigation.

History: *1985 c 247 s 9; 1986 c 444*

147.04 RETALIATORY PROVISIONS.

If by the laws of any state or the rulings or decisions of the appropriate officers or boards thereof, any burden, obligation, requirement, disqualification, or disability is put upon physicians registered in this state or holding diplomas from medical colleges in this state which are in good standing therein, affecting the right of these physicians to be registered or admitted to practice in that state, then the same or like burdens, obligations, requirements, disqualification, or disability may be put upon the registration in this state of physicians registered in that state or holding diplomas from medical colleges situated therein.

History: *(5710) 1905 c 236; 1913 c 139 s 2; 1959 c 346 s 2*

147.05 [Renumbered 147.01, subd 5]
147.06 [Repealed, 1985 c 247 s 26]
147.07 [Repealed, 1985 c 247 s 26]
147.072 [Repealed, 1985 c 247 s 26]
147.073 [Renumbered 147.161]
147.074 [Renumbered 147.162]
147.075 [Repealed, 1981 c 323 s 4; 1983 c 312 art 1 s 27]
147.08 [Repealed, 1974 c 61 s 2]

147.081 PRACTICING WITHOUT LICENSE; PENALTY.

Subdivision 1. **Unlawful practice of medicine.** It is unlawful for any person not holding a valid license issued in accordance with this chapter to practice medicine as defined in subdivision 3 in this state.

continues

Exhibit 1040-2 *continued*

Subd. 2. **Penalty**. Any person violating the provisions of subdivision 1 is guilty of a gross misdemeanor.

Subd. 3. **Practice of medicine defined.** For purposes of this chapter, a person not exempted under section 147.09 is "practicing medicine" or engaged in the "practice of medicine" if the person does any of the following:

(1) advertises, holds out to the public, or represents in any manner that the person is authorized to practice medicine in this state;

(2) offers or undertakes to prescribe, give, or administer any drug or medicine for the use of another;

(3) offers or undertakes to prevent or to diagnose, correct, or treat in any manner or by any means, methods, devices, or instrumentalities, any disease, illness, pain, wound, fracture, infirmity, deformity or defect of any person;

(4) offers or undertakes to perform any surgical operation upon any person;

(5) offers to undertake to use hypnosis for the treatment or relief of any wound, fracture, or bodily injury, infirmity, or disease; or

(6) uses in the conduct of any occupation or profession pertaining to the diagnosis of human disease or conditions, the designation "doctor of medicine," "medical doctor," "doctor of osteopathy," "osteopath," "osteopathic physician," "physician," "surgeon," "M.D.," "D.O.," or any combination of these designations.

History: *(5717) RL s 2300; 1927 c 188 s 4; 1963 c 45 s 6; 1971 c 485 s 5; 1974 c 43 s 1; 1985 c 247 s 13,24; 1986 c 444*

147.09 EXEMPTIONS.

Section 147.081 does not apply to, control, prevent or restrict the practice, service, or activities of:

(1) A person who is a commissioned medical officer of, a member of, or employed by, the armed forces of the United States, the United States Public Health Service, the Veterans Administration, any federal institution or any federal agency while engaged in the performance of official duties within this state, if the person is licensed elsewhere.

(2) A licensed physician from a state or country who is in actual consultation here.

(3) A licensed or registered physician who treats the physician's home state patients or other participating patients while the physicians and those patients are participating together in outdoor recreation in this state as defined by section 86A.03, subdivision 3. A physician shall first register with the board on a form developed by the board for that purpose. The board shall not be required to promulgate the contents of that form by rule. No fee shall be charged for this registration.

(4) A student practicing under the direct supervision of a preceptor while the student is enrolled in and regularly attending a recognized medical school.

(5) A student who is in continuing training and performing the duties of an intern or resident or engaged in postgraduate work considered by the board to be the equivalent of an internship or residency in any hospital or institution approved for training by the board.

(6) A person employed in a scientific, sanitary or teaching capacity by the state university, the state department of education, or by any public or private school, college, or other bona fide educational institution, or the state department of health, whose duties are entirely of a public health or educational character, while engaged in such duties.

(7) Physician's assistants registered in this state.

(8) A doctor of osteopathy duly licensed by the state board of osteopathy under Minnesota Statutes 1961, sections 148.11 to 148.16, prior to May 1, 1963, who has not been granted a license to practice medicine in accordance with this chapter provided that the doctor confines activities within the scope of the license.

(9) Any person licensed by a health related licensing board, as defined in section 214.01, subdivision 2, or registered by the commissioner of health pursuant to section 214.13, including licensed psychologists with respect to the use of hypnosis; provided that the person confines activities within the scope of the license.

(10) A Christian Scientist or other person who endeavors to prevent or cure disease or suffering exclusively by mental or spiritual means or by prayer, or who practices ritual circumcision pursuant to the requirements or tenets of any established religion.

History: *(5716) RL s 2299; 1971 c 485 s 4; 1980 c 567 s 1; 1981 c 23 s 4; 1985 c 247 s 12; 1986 c 444; 1987 c 384 art 1 s 17*

147.091 GROUNDS FOR DISCIPLINARY ACTION.

Subdivision 1. **Grounds listed.** The board may refuse to grant a license or may impose disciplinary action as described in section 147.141 against any physician. The following conduct is prohibited and is grounds for disciplinary action:

(a) Failure to demonstrate the qualifications or satisfy the requirements for a license contained in this chapter or rules of the board. The burden of proof shall be upon the applicant to demonstrate such qualifications or satisfaction of such requirements.

(b) Obtaining a license by fraud or cheating, or attempting to subvert the licensing examination process. Conduct which subverts or attempts to subvert the licensing examination process includes, but is not limited to: (1) conduct which violates the security of the examination materials, such as removing examination materials from the examination room or having unauthorized possession of any portion of a future, current, or previously administered licensing examination; (2) conduct which violates the standard of test administration, such as communicating with another examinee during administration of the examination, copying another examinee's answers, permitting another examinee to copy one's answers, or possessing unauthorized materials; or (3) impersonating an examinee or permitting an impersonator to take the examination on one's own behalf.

(c) Conviction, during the previous five years, of a felony reasonably related to the practice of medicine or osteopathy. Conviction as used in this subdivision shall include a conviction of an offense which if committed in this state would be deemed a felony without regard to its designation elsewhere, or a criminal proceeding where a finding or verdict of guilt is made or returned but the adjudication of guilt is either withheld or not entered thereon.

(d) Revocation, suspension, restriction, limitation, or other disciplinary action against the person's medical license in another state or jurisdiction, failure to report to the board that charges regarding the person's license have been brought in another state or jurisdiction, or having been refused a license by any other state or jurisdiction.

(e) Advertising which is false or misleading, which violates any rule of the board, or which claims without substantiation the positive cure of any disease, or professional superiority to or greater skill than that possessed by another physician.

(f) Violating a rule promulgated by the board or an order of the board, a state, or federal law which relates to the practice of medicine, or in part regulates the practice of medicine including without limitation sections 148A.02, 609.344, and 609.345, or a state or federal narcotics or controlled substance law.

(g) Engaging in any unethical conduct; conduct likely to deceive, defraud, or harm the public, or demonstrating a willful or careless disregard for the health, welfare or safety of a patient; or medical practice which is professionally incompetent, in that it may create unnecessary danger to any patient's life, health, or safety, in any of which cases, proof of actual injury need not be established.

(h) Failure to supervise a physician's assistant or failure to supervise a physician under any agreement with the board.

continues

Exhibit 1040-2 *continued*

(i) Aiding or abetting an unlicensed person in the practice of medicine, except that it is not a violation of this paragraph for a physician to employ, supervise, or delegate functions to a qualified person who may or may not be required to obtain a license or registration to provide health services if that person is practicing within the scope of that person's license or registration or delegated authority.

(j) Adjudication as mentally incompetent, mentally ill or mentally retarded, or as a chemically dependent person, a person dangerous to the public, or a person who has a psychopathic personality by a court of competent jurisdiction, within or without this state. Such adjudication shall automatically suspend a license for the duration thereof unless the board orders otherwise.

(k) Engaging in unprofessional conduct. Unprofessional conduct shall include any departure from or the failure to conform to the minimal standards of acceptable and prevailing medical practice in which proceeding actual injury to a patient need not be established.

(l) Inability to practice medicine with reasonable skill and safety to patients by reason of illness, drunkenness, use of drugs, narcotics, chemicals or any other type of material or as a result of any mental or physical condition, including deterioration through the aging process or loss of motor skills.

(m) Revealing a privileged communication from or relating to a patient except when otherwise required or permitted by law.

(n) Failure by a doctor of osteopathy to identify the school of healing in the professional use of the doctor's name by one of the following terms: osteopathic physician and surgeon, doctor of osteopathy, or D.O.

(o) Improper management of medical records, including failure to maintain adequate medical records, to comply with a patient's request made pursuant to section 144.335 or to furnish a medical record or report required by law.

(p) Fee splitting, including without limitation:

(1) paying, offering to pay, receiving, or agreeing to receive, a commission, rebate, or remuneration, directly or indirectly, primarily for the referral of patients or the prescription of drugs or devices;

(2) dividing fees with another physician or a professional corporation, unless the division is in proportion to the services provided and the responsibility assumed by each professional and the physician has disclosed the terms of the division;

(3) referring a patient to any health care provider as defined in section 144.335 in which the referring physician has a significant financial interest unless the physician has disclosed the physician's own financial interest; and

(4) dispensing for profit any drug or device, unless the physician has disclosed the physician's own profit interest.

The physician must make the disclosures required in this clause in advance and in writing to the patient and must include in the disclosure a statement that the patient is free to choose a different health care provider. This clause does not apply to the distribution of revenues from a partnership, group practice, nonprofit corporation, or professional corporation to its partners, shareholders, members, or employees if the revenues consist only of fees for services performed by the physician or under a physician's direct supervision, or to the division or distribution of prepaid or capitated health care premiums, or fee-for-service withhold amounts paid under contracts established under other state law.

(q) Engaging in abusive or fraudulent billing practices, including violations of the federal Medicare and Medicaid laws or state medical assistance laws.

(r) Becoming addicted or habituated to a drug or intoxicant.

(s) Prescribing a drug or device for other than medically accepted therapeutic or experimental or investigative purposes authorized by a state or federal agency or referring a patient to any health care provider as defined in section 144.335 for services or tests not medically indicated at the time of referral.

(t) Engaging in conduct with a patient which is sexual or may reasonably be interpreted by the patient as sexual, or in any verbal behavior which is seductive or sexually demeaning to a patient.

(u) Failure to make reports as required by section 147.111 or to cooperate with an investigation of the board as required by section 147.131.

Subd. 2. **Effective dates.** A suspension, revocation, condition, limitation, qualification or restriction of a license shall be in effect pending determination of an appeal unless the court, upon petition and for good cause shown, shall otherwise order.

A license to practice medicine is automatically suspended if (1) a guardian of the person of a licensee is appointed by order of a probate court pursuant to sections 525.54 to 525.61, for reasons other than the minority of the licensee; or (2) the licensee is committed by order of a probate court pursuant to chapter 253B or sections 526.09 to 526.11. The license remains suspended until the licensee is restored to capacity by a court and, upon petition by the licensee, the suspension is terminated by the board after a hearing.

Subd. 3. **Conditions on reissued license.** In its discretion, the board may restore and reissue a license to practice medicine, but as a condition thereof may impose any disciplinary or corrective measure which it might originally have imposed.

Subd. 4. **Temporary suspension of license.** In addition to any other remedy provided by law, the board may, without a hearing, temporarily suspend the license of a physician if the board finds that the physician has violated a statute or rule which the board is empowered to enforce and continued practice by the physician would create a serious risk of harm to the public. The suspension shall take effect upon written notice to the physician, specifying the statute or rule violated. The suspension shall remain in effect until the board issues a final order in the matter after a hearing. At the time it issues the suspension notice, the board shall schedule a disciplinary hearing to be held pursuant to the administrative procedure act. The physician shall be provided with at least 20 days notice of any hearing held pursuant to this subdivision. The hearing shall be scheduled to begin no later than 30 days after the issuance of the suspension order.

Subd. 5. **Evidence.** In disciplinary actions alleging a violation of subdivision 1, paragraph (c) or (d), a copy of the judgment or proceeding under the seal of the court administrator or of the administrative agency which entered the same shall be admissible into evidence without further authentication and shall constitute prima facie evidence of the contents thereof.

Subd. 6. **Mental examination; access to medical data.** (a) If the board has probable cause to believe that a physician comes under subdivision 1, paragraph (1), it may direct the physician to submit to a mental or physical examination. For the purpose of this subdivision every physician licensed under this chapter is deemed to have consented to submit to a mental or physical examination when directed in writing by the board and further to have waived all objections to the admissibility of the examining physicians' testimony or examination reports on the ground that the same constitute a privileged communication. Failure of a physician to submit to an examination when directed constitutes an admission of the allegations against the physician, unless the failure was due to circumstance beyond the physician's control, in which case a default and final order may be entered without the taking of testimony or presentation of evidence. A physician affected under this paragraph shall at reasonable intervals be given an opportunity to demonstrate that the physician can resume the competent practice of medicine with reasonable skill and safety to patients.

In any proceeding under this paragraph, neither the record of proceedings nor the orders entered by the board shall be used against a physician in any other proceeding.

(b) In addition to ordering a physical or mental examination, the board may, notwithstanding section 13.42, 144.651, or any other

continues

Exhibit 1040-2 *continued*

law limiting access to medical or other health data, obtain medical data and health records relating to a licensee or applicant without the licensee's or applicant's consent if the board has probable cause to believe that a physician comes under subdivision 1, paragraph (1). The medical data may be requested from a provider, as defined in section 144.335, subdivision 1, paragraph (b), an insurance company, or a government agency, including the department of human services. A provider, insurance company, or government agency shall comply with any written request of the board under this subdivision and is not liable in any action for damages for releasing the data requested by the board if the data are released pursuant to a written request under this subdivision, unless the information is false and the provider giving the information knew, or had reason to believe, the information was false. Information obtained under this subdivision is classified as private under sections 13.01 to 13.87.

Subd. 7. **Tax clearance certificate.** (a) In addition to the provisions of subdivision 1, the board may not issue or renew a license if the commissioner of revenue notifies the board and the licensee or applicant for a license that the licensee or applicant owes the state delinquent taxes in the amount of $500 or more. The board may issue or renew the license only if (1) the commissioner of revenue issues a tax clearance certificate and (2) the commissioner of revenue or the licensee or applicant forwards a copy of the clearance to the board. The commissioner of revenue may issue a clearance certificate only if the licensee or applicant does not owe the state any uncontested delinquent taxes.

(b) For purposes of this subdivision, the following terms have the meanings given.

(1) "Taxes" are all taxes payable to the commissioner of revenue, including penalties and interest due on those taxes.

(2) "Delinquent taxes" do not include a tax liability if (i) an administrative or court action that contests the amount or validity of the liability has been filed or served, (ii) the appeal period to contest the tax liability has not expired, or (iii) the licensee or applicant has entered into a payment agreement to pay the liability and is current with the payments.

(c) In lieu of the notice and hearing requirements of subdivision 1, when a licensee or applicant is required to obtain a clearance certificate under this subdivision, a contested case hearing must be held if the licensee or applicant requests a hearing in writing to the commissioner of revenue within 30 days of the date of the notice provided in paragraph (a). The hearing must be held within 45 days of the date the commissioner of revenue refers the case to the office of administrative hearings. Notwithstanding any law to the contrary, the licensee or applicant must be served with 20 days' notice in writing specifying the time and place of the hearing and the allegations against the licensee or applicant. The notice may be served personally or by mail.

(d) The board shall require all licensees or applicants to provide their social security number and Minnesota business identification number on all license applications. Upon request of the commissioner of revenue, the board must provide to the commissioner of revenue a list of all licensees and applicants, including the name and address, social security number, and business identification number. The commissioner of revenue may request a list of the licensees and applicants no more than once each calendar year. Notwithstanding sections 290.61 and 297A.43, the commissioner of revenue may release information necessary to accomplish the purpose of this subdivision.

History: *1971 c 485 s 3; 1974 c 31 s 1; 1975 c 213 s 1; 1976 c 222 s 34; 1981 c 83 s 1; 1982 c 581 s 24; 1985 c 21 s 1; 1985 c 247 s 7,24; 1986 c 444; 1Sp1986 c 1 art 7 s 7; 1Sp1986 c 3 art 1 s 82; 1987 c 384 art 2 s 1; 1988 c 557 s 2*

147.10 [Renumbered 147.081]
147.101 [Repealed, 1985 c 247 s 26]
147.11 [Repealed, 1985 c 247 s 26]

147.111 REPORTING OBLIGATIONS.

Subdivision 1. **Permission to report.** A person who has knowledge of any conduct constituting grounds for discipline under sections 147.01 to 147.33 may report the violation to the board.

Subd. 2. **Institutions.** Any hospital, clinic, prepaid medical plan, or other health care institution or organization located in this state shall report to the board any action taken by the institution or organization or any of its administrators or medical or other committees to revoke, suspend, restrict, or condition a physician's privilege to practice or treat patients in the institution, or as part of the organization, any denial of privileges, or any other disciplinary action. The institution or organization shall also report the resignation of any physicians prior to the conclusion of any disciplinary proceeding, or prior to the commencement of formal charges but after the physician had knowledge that formal charges were contemplated or in preparation. Each report made under this subdivision must state the nature of the action taken, state in detail the reasons for the action, and identify the specific patient medical records upon which the action was based. No report shall be required of a physician voluntarily limiting the practice of the physician at a hospital provided that the physician notifies all hospitals at which the physician has privileges of the voluntary limitation and the reasons for it.

Subd. 3. **Medical societies.** A state or local medical society shall report to the board any termination, revocation, or suspension of membership or any other disciplinary action taken against a physician. If the society has received a complaint which might be grounds for discipline under sections 147.01 to 147.33 against a member physician on which it has not taken any disciplinary action, the society shall report the complaint and the reason why it has not taken action on it or shall direct the complainant to the board of medical examiners.

Subd. 4. **Licensed professionals.** A licensed health professional shall report to the board personal knowledge of any conduct which the professional reasonably believes constitutes grounds for disciplinary action under sections 147.01 to 147.33 by any physician, including any conduct indicating that the physician may be medically incompetent, or may have engaged in unprofessional conduct or may be medically or physically unable to engage safely in the practice of medicine. No report shall be required if the information was obtained in the course of a physician-patient relationship if the patient is another physician and the treating physician successfully counsels the other physician to limit or withdraw from practice to the extent required by the impairment.

Subd. 5. **Insurers.** Four times each year as prescribed by the board, each insurer authorized to sell insurance described in section 60A.06, subdivision 1, clause (13), and providing professional liability insurance to physicians shall submit to the board a report concerning the physicians against whom medical malpractice settlements or awards have been made to the plaintiff. The report must contain at least the following information:

(1) the total number of medical malpractice settlements or awards made to the plaintiff;

(2) the date the medical malpractice settlements or awards to the plaintiff were made;

(3) the allegations contained in the claim or complaint leading to the settlements or awards made to the plaintiff;

(4) the dollar amount of each medical malpractice settlement or award;

(5) the regular address of the practice of the physician against whom an award was made or with whom a settlement was made; and

(6) the name of the physician against whom an award was made or with whom a settlement was made.

The insurance company shall, in addition to the above information, report to the board any information it possesses which tends to

continues

Exhibit 1040-2 *continued*

substantiate a charge that a physician may have engaged in conduct violating sections 147.01 to 147.33.

Subd 6. **Courts.** The court administrator of district court or any other court of competent jurisdiction shall report to the board any judgment or other determination of the court which adjudges or includes a finding that a physician is mentally ill, mentally incompetent, guilty of a felony, or guilty of a violation of federal or state narcotics laws or controlled substances act, guilty of an abuse or fraud under Medicare or Medicaid, appoints a guardian of the physician pursuant to sections 525.54 to 525.61 or commits a physician pursuant to chapter 253B or sections 526.09 to 526.11.

Subd. 7. **Self-reporting.** A physician shall report to the board any personal action which would require that a report be filed with the board by any person, health care facility, business, or organization pursuant to subdivisions 2 to 6.

Subd. 8. **Deadlines; forms.** Reports required by subdivisions 2 to 7 must be submitted not later than 30 days after the occurrence of the reportable event or transaction. The board may provide forms for the submission of reports required by this section, may require that reports be submitted on the forms provided, and may adopt rules necessary to assure prompt and accurate reporting.

Subd. 9. **Subpoenas.** The board may issue subpoenas for the production of any reports required by subdivisions 2 to 7 or any related documents.

History: *1985 c 247 s 14; 1986 c 444; 1Sp1986 c 3 art 1 s 82; 1988 c 557 s 3*

147.12 [Repealed, 1985 c 247 s 26]

147.121 IMMUNITY.

Subdivision 1. **Reporting.** Any person, health care facility, business, or organization is immune from civil liability or criminal prosecution for submitting a report to the board pursuant to section 147.111 or for otherwise reporting to the board violations or alleged violations of section 147.091. All such reports are confidential and absolutely privileged communications.

Subd. 2. **Investigation.** Members of the board and persons employed by the board or engaged in the investigation of violations and in the preparation and management of charges of violations of sections 147.01 to 147.33 on behalf of the board are immune from civil liability and criminal prosecution for any actions, transactions, or publications in the execution of, or relating to, their duties under sections 147.01 to 147.33.

History: *1985 c 247 s 15,24*

147.13 [Repealed, 1985 c 247 s 26]

147.131 PHYSICIAN COOPERATION.

A physician who is the subject of an investigation by or on behalf of the board shall cooperate fully with the investigation. Cooperation includes responding fully and promptly to any question raised by or on behalf of the board relating to the subject of the investigation and providing copies of patient medical records, as reasonably requested by the board, to assist the board in its investigation. The board shall pay for copies requested. If the board does not have a written consent from a patient permitting access to the patient's records, the physician shall delete any data in the record which identifies the patient before providing it to the board. The board shall maintain any records obtained pursuant to this section as investigative data pursuant to chapter 13.

History: *1985 c 247 s 16; 1986 c 444*

147.141 FORMS OF DISCIPLINARY ACTION.

When the board finds that a licensed physician has violated a provision or provisions of sections 147.01 to 147.33, it may do one or more of the following:

(1) revoke the license;

(2) suspend the license;

(3) impose limitations or conditions on the physician's practice of medicine, including the limitation of scope of practice to designated field specialties; the imposition of retraining or rehabilitation requirements; the requirement of practice under supervision; or the conditioning of continued practice on demonstration of knowledge or skills by appropriate examination or other review of skill and competence;

(4) impose a civil penalty not exceeding $10,000 for each separate violation, the amount of the civil penalty to be fixed so as to deprive the physician of any economic advantage gained by reason of the violation charged or to reimburse the board for the cost of the investigation and proceeding;

(5) order the physician to provide unremunerated professional service under supervision at a designated public hospital, clinic, or other health care institution; or

(6) censure or reprimand the licensed physician.

History: *1985 c 247 s 17*

147.151 DISCIPLINARY RECORD ON JUDICIAL REVIEW.

Upon judicial review of any board disciplinary action taken under sections 147.01 to 147.33, the reviewing court shall seal the administrative record, except for the board's final decision, and shall not make the administrative record available to the public.

History: *1985 c 247 s 18*

147.16 [Repealed, 1985 c 247 s 26]

147.161 PHYSICIAN ACCOUNTABILITY.

Subdivision 1. **Investigation.** The board shall maintain and keep current a file containing the reports and complaints filed against physicians in the state. Each complaint filed with the board pursuant to section 214.10, subdivision 1, shall be investigated according to section 214.10, subdivision 2.

Whenever the files maintained by the board show that a medical malpractice settlement or award to the plaintiff has been made against a physician as reported by insurers pursuant to section 147.111, the executive director of the board shall notify the board and the board may authorize a review of the physician's practice.

Subd. 2. **Attorney general investigates.** When the board initiates a review of a physician's practice it shall notify the attorney general who shall investigate the matter in the same manner as provided in section 214.10. If an investigation is to be made, the attorney general shall notify the physician, and, if the incident being investigated occurred there, the administrator and chief of staff at the medical care facilities in which the physician serves.

Subd. 3. **Access to hospital records.** The board shall have access to hospital and medical records of a patient treated by the physician under review if the patient signs a written consent permitting such access. If no consent form has been signed, the hospital or physician shall first delete data in the record which identifies the patient before providing it to the board.

History: *1976 c 222 s 39; 1980 c 509 s 47; 1981 c 311 s 39; 1982 c 545 s 24; 1985 c 247 s 10,24; 1Sp1986 c 3 art 1 s 23*

147.162 MEDICAL CARE FACILITIES; EXCLUSION.

Each physician shall file with the board a list of the inpatient and outpatient medical care facilities at which the physician has medical privileges. The list shall be updated when the physician applies for license renewal. Nothing in this chapter grants to any person the right to be admitted to the medical staff of a health care facility.

History: *1976 c 222 s 40; 1985 c 247 s 11,24; 1986 c 444*

Source: Minnesota State Register and Public Documents Division.

Exhibit 1040-3 American Nurses' Association Standards for Nursing Practice

Standard I.

The collection of data about the health status of the client/patient is systematic and continuous. The data are accessible, communicated, and recorded.

Standard II.

Nursing diagnoses are derived from health status data.

Standard III.

The plan of nursing care includes goals derived from the nursing diagnoses.

Standard IV.

The plan of nursing care includes priorities and the prescribed nursing approaches or measures to achieve the goals derived from the nursing diagnoses.

Standard V.

Nursing actions provide for client/patient participation in health capabilities.

Standard VI.

Nursing actions assist the client/patient to maximize his health capabilities.

Standard VII.

Health planning agencies must identify needs of populations and address the development and orderly growth of health care services provided in the home.

Standard VIII.

A national health policy should support research to develop innovative and forward directions for health care at home.

Standard IX.

A national health policy should recognize and reaffirm the individual's responsibility for his own health and should acknowledge the home as the primary site for health care.

Source: Reprinted with permission from *Standards of Nursing Practice*, pp. 1–4, American Nurses' Association, Kansas City, MO, 1973.

Exhibit 1040-4 American Nurses' Association Code for Nurses

1. The nurse provides services with respect for human dignity and the uniqueness of the client, unrestricted by considerations of social or economic status, personal attributes, or the nature of health problems.
2. The nurse safeguards the client's right to privacy by judiciously protecting information of a confidential nature.
3. The nurse acts to safeguard the client and the public when health care and safety are affected by the incompetent, unethical, or illegal practice of any person.
4. The nurse assumes responsibility and accountability for individual nursing judgments and actions.
5. The nurse maintains competence in nursing.
6. The nurse exercises informed judgment and uses individual competence and qualifications as criteria in seeking consultation, accepting responsibilities, and delegating nursing activities to others.
7. The nurse participates in activities that contribute to the ongoing development of the profession's body of knowledge.
8. The nurse participates in the profession's efforts to implement and improve standards of nursing.
9. The nurse participates in the profession's efforts to establish and maintain conditions of employment conducive to high quality nursing care.
10. The nurse participates in the profession's effort to protect the public from misinformation and misrepresentation and to maintain the integrity of nursing.
11. The nurse collaborates with members of the health professions and other citizens in promoting community and national efforts to meet the health needs of the public.

Source: Reprinted with permission from *Code for Nurses with Interpretive Statements*, p. 1, American Nurses' Association, Kansas City, MO, 1985.

Exhibit 1040-5 Legal Standards for Nursing Practice Laws As Indicated by the Minnesota Board of Nursing's Nurse Practice Act

CHAPTER 148
REGISTERED NURSES

148.171 DEFINITIONS.

As used in sections 148.171 to 148.285:

(1) The term "Board" shall mean Minnesota board of nursing.

(2) The term "Registered Nurse" abbreviated R.N., shall mean a natural person licensed by the Minnesota board of nursing to practice professional nursing.

(3) The practice of professional nursing means the performance for compensation or personal profit of the professional interpersonal service of: (a) providing a nursing assessment of the actual or potential health needs of individuals, families, or communities; (b) providing nursing care supportive to or restorative of life by functions such as skilled ministration of nursing care, supervising and teaching nursing personnel, health teaching and counseling, case finding and referral to other health resources; and (c) evaluating these actions.

The practice of professional nursing includes both independent nursing functions and delegated medical functions which may be performed in collaboration with other health team members, or may be delegated by the professional nurse to other nursing personnel. Independent nursing function may also be performed autonomously. The practice of professional nursing requires that level of special education, knowledge, and skill ordinarily expected of an individual who has completed an approved professional nursing education program as described in section 148.211, subdivision 1.

HISTORY: 1945 c 242 s 1; 1955 c 34 s 1; 1959 c 140 s 1; 1974 c 554 s 1

148.18 Repealed, 1945 c 242 s 14

148.181 BOARD OF NURSING; MEMBERSHIP, APPOINTMENTS, VACANCIES, REMOVALS.

Subdivision 1. The board of nursing shall consist of 11 members appointed by the governor, each of whom shall be a resident of this state. Five members shall be registered nurses, each of whom shall have graduated from an approved school of nursing, shall be licensed as a registered nurse in this state, and shall have had at least five years experience in nursing practice, nursing administration, or nursing education immediately preceding appointment. Two of the five shall have had at least two years executive or teaching experience in professional nursing education during the five years immediately preceding appointment, and one of the five shall have had at least two years executive or teaching experience in practical nursing education during the five years immediately preceding appointment. Three members shall be licensed practical nurses each of whom shall have graduated from an approved school of nursing, shall be licensed as a licensed practical nurse in this state, and shall have had at least five years experience in nursing practice immediately preceding appointment. The remaining three members shall be public members as defined by section 214.02. Membership terms, compensation of members, removal of members, the filling of membership vacancies, and fiscal year and reporting requirements shall be as provided in sections 214.07 to 214.09. The provision of staff, 240 s 1; 1975 c 360 s 3; 1976 c 222 s 51; 1983 c 260 s 36

148.20 Repealed, 1945 c 242 s 14

148.201 Repealed, 1975 c 136 s 77

148.21 Repealed, 1945 c 242 s 14

148.211 LICENSING.

Subdivision 1. An applicant for a license to practice as a registered nurse shall apply to the board for license by examination on forms prescribed by the board and pay a fee in an amount determined by rule. An applicant applying for re-examination shall pay a fee in an amount determined by rule. In no case shall fees be refunded.

Before being scheduled for examination the applicant shall provide written evidence verified by oath that he (a) is of good moral character, (b) is in good mental health, (c) meets secondary education requirements as determined by the board and other preliminary qualification requirements the board may prescribe by rule, and (d) either has completed a course of study in a professional nursing program approved by the board or is enrolled in the final term of study in such program. The board shall annually publish and distribute to secondary school counselors the requirements for licensure for practice in Minnesota.

The applicant shall be required to pass a written examination in the subjects the board may determine. Each written examination may be supplemented by an oral or practical examination. An applicant failing to pass any portion of the examination shall be deemed to have failed the examination and may apply for re-examination in the subjects or sections failed.

Refusal to supply information necessary to determine the qualifications of an applicant may result in denial of the application.

Upon submission by the applicant of an affidavit of graduation from an approved nursing program as well as proof that the applicant has passed the examination, paid the required fees and met all other requirements stated in this subdivision, the board shall issue a license to the applicant.

Subd. 2. The board may issue a license to practice professional nursing as a registered nurse without examination to an applicant who has been duly licensed or registered as a registered professional nurse under the laws of another state, territory or foreign country, if in the opinion of the board the applicant has the qualifications equivalent to the qualifications required in this state as stated in subdivision 1, all other laws not inconsistent with this section and rules promulgated by the board.

Subd. 3. Repealed, 1976, c 222 s 209

HISTORY: 1945 c 242 s 5; 1955 c 34 s 4; 1961 c 56 s 1; 1967 c 68 s 1; 1969 c 53 s 1; 1975 c 360 s 4,5; 1976 c 222 s 52, 53; 1981 c 94 s 2

148.22 Repealed, 1945 c 242 s 14

148.221 PERSONS NOW HOLDING CERTIFICATE.

Any person holding a license or certificate of registration to practice nursing as a registered nurse issued by the board which is valid on the effective date of Laws 1945, Chapter 242, shall be deemed to be licensed as a registered nurse under the provisions of sections 148.171 to 148.285.

HISTORY: 1945 c 242 s 6

148.23 Repealed, 1945 c 242 s 14

148.231 TASK FORCE; REGISTRATION; NON-PRACTICING LIST.

Subdivision 1. REGISTRATION. Every person licensed to practice professional nursing must also maintain with the board, a current registration for practice as a registered nurse which must be renewed at regular intervals stipulated by the board by rule. Upon adoption by the board of rules establishing procedures and minimum requirements for successful completion of specified continuing education as hereinafter provided, no certificate of registration shall be issued by the board to a nurse until he or she has submitted satisfactory evidence of compliance with the procedures and minimum requirements established by the board.

The fee for periodic registration for practice as a registered nurse shall be determined by the board by rule. A penalty fee shall be

continues

Exhibit 1040-5 *continued*

added for any application received after the required date as specified by the board by rule. Upon receipt of the application and the required fees, the board shall verify the application and the evidence of completion of continuing education requirements in effect, and thereupon issue to the applicant a certificate of registration for the next renewal period.

Subd. 2. Repealed, 1981 c 94 s 12

Subd. 3. Repealed, 1976 c 222 s 209

Subd. 4. FAILURE TO REGISTER. Any person licensed under the provisions of sections 148.171 to 148.285 who fails to re-register within the period hereinbefore provided shall not be entitled to practice nursing in this state as a registered nurse.

Subd. 5. RE-REGISTRATION. When a person desires to resume practice he or she shall make application for re-registration, and submit satisfactory evidence of compliance with the procedures and minimum requirements established by the board for continuing education, and pay the registration fee for the current period to the board. Thereupon, the registration certificate shall be issued to such applicant, and such person shall immediately be placed on the practicing list as a registered nurse.

Subd. 6. FEE FOR LICENSE VERIFICATION. A person licensed under the provisions of sections 148.171 to 148.285 who requests the board to verify a Minnesota license to another jurisdiction or to an agency, facility, school or institution shall pay a fee to the board for each verification.

HISTORY: 1945 c 242 s 7; 1947 c 286 s 1; 1955 c 34 s 5; 1961 c 8 s 2; 1967 c 68 s 2; 1969 c 53 s 2, 3; 1971 c 131 s 1; 1975 c 240 s 2; 1975 c 360 s 6, 7; 1976 c 149 s 30; 1981 c 94 s 3-6

148.24 Repealed, 1945 c 242 s 14

148.241 EXPENSES.

Subdivision 1. The expenses of administering sections 148.171 to 148.299 shall be paid from the appropriation made to the Minnesota board of nursing.

Subd. 2. All amounts appropriated to the board shall be held subject to the order of the board to be used only for the purpose of meeting necessary expenses incurred in the performance of the purposes of sections 148.171 to 148.285, and the duties imposed thereby as well as the promotion of nursing education and standards of nursing care in this state.

HISTORY: 1945 c 242 s 8; 1955 c 34 s 3; 1973 c 638 s 16; 1976 c 222 s 54

148.25 Repealed, 1945 c 242 s 14

148.251 SCHOOL OF NURSING.

Subdivision 1. An institution desiring to conduct a school of nursing shall apply to the board and submit evidence that:

(1) It is prepared to provide a program of theory and practice in nursing as prescribed in the curriculum adopted by the board. Such instruction and experience may be secured in one or more institutions or agencies approved by the board.

(2) It is prepared to meet other standards established by law and by the board.

Subd. 2. A survey of the institution or institutions with which the school is to be affiliated shall be made by a qualified representative of the board. Such representative shall submit a written report of the survey to the board. If the board determines that the requirements for an approved school of nursing are met, it shall designate the school as an approved school of nursing.

Subd. 3. From time to time as deemed necessary by the board, it shall be the duty of the board, through its representatives, to survey all schools of nursing in the state. Written reports of such surveys shall be submitted to the board by the representative. If the board determines that any approved school of nursing is not maintaining the standards required by the statutes and by the board, notice thereof in writing specifying the defect or defects shall be given to the school. A school which fails to correct these conditions to the satisfaction of the board within a reasonable time shall be removed from the list of approved schools of nursing.

Subd. 4. Associate degree nursing programs approved or seeking to be approved by the board shall provide for advanced standing for licensed practical nurses in recognition of their nursing education and experience. The board shall adopt rules by July 1, 1982 to implement this section.

HISTORY: 1945 c 242 s 9; 1961 c 56 s 2; 1975 c 360 s 8; 1981 c 94 s 7

148.26 Repealed, 1945 c 242 s 14

148.261 REVOCATION OF LICENSE.

Subdivision 1. The board shall have power to deny, suspend, revoke, or restrict the license and registration of any person to practice professional nursing pursuant to sections 148.171 to 148.285, or to otherwise discipline a licensee or applicant upon proof that the person:

(1) Has employed fraud or deceit in procuring or attempting to procure a license to practice nursing as a registered nurse or annual registration for the practice of professional nursing;

(2) Has been convicted of a felony or gross misdemeanor;

(3) Is unfit or incompetent by reason of negligence, habits or other causes;

(4) Is habitually intemperate or is addicted to the use of habit-forming drugs;

(5) Has, in his or her professional capacity, exhibited behavior which creates an undue risk of harm to others;

(6) Is guilty of unethical practice of nursing;

(7) Has wilfully or repeatedly violated any of the provisions of sections 148.171 to 148.285.

Subd. 2. Repealed, 1976 c 222 s 209

Subd. 3. Any registered nurse whose license or registration has been suspended, restricted or revoked, may have his license reinstated and a new registration issued when in the discretion of the board the action is warranted, provided that such nurse may be required by the board to pay 50 percent of the costs of the proceedings resulting in the suspension or revocation of the license or registration certificate and reinstatement of the license or renewal certificate, and in addition thereto, pay the fee for the current year's registration.

HISTORY: 1945 c 242 s 10; 1975 c 360 s 9; 1976 c 222 s 55

148.27 Repealed, 1945 c 242 s 14

148.271 ALLOWABLE UNLICENSED PRACTICES.

The provisions of sections 148.171 to 148.285 shall not prohibit:

(1) The furnishing of nursing assistance in an emergency.

(2) The practice of nursing by any legally qualified nurse of another state who is employed by the United States government or any bureau, division or agency thereof while in the discharge of his or her official duties.

(3) Under the direct supervision of a registered nurse, the practice of nursing by a graduate of a school of professional nursing approved by the board between the date of graduation and the date of notification to the graduate of the board action upon his or her application for licensure hereunder, provided that the graduate will take the first examination for licensure hereunder following graduation given by the board and will be issued a permit by the board to engage in supervised practice of professional nursing while awaiting notification of the results of such examination. The board is authorized to issue permits to such graduates which shall permit the practice of professional nursing under direct supervision from the

continues

Exhibit 1040-5 *continued*

date of graduation until the date that the board shall notify the graduates of the results of their applications for registration conditioned upon the graduates making prompt application for registration and taking the first examination given by the board which they are eligible to take following graduation. These permits shall not be renewable.

(4) The practice of any profession or occupation licensed by the state, other than professional nursing, by any person duly licensed to practice the profession or occupation, or the performance by a person of any acts properly coming within the scope of the profession, occupation or license.

(5) The performance of any act in the nursing care of the sick by a nurse's aide under the direction of a registered nurse.

(6) The practice of nursing by a person licensed as a professional nurse in another jurisdiction and qualified for licensure in the state of Minnesota pursuant to a temporary permit issued by the board of nursing which permit shall be issued by the board pursuant to rules as it may promulgate, for the period between the submission of a proper application for licensure by the person and the date of action upon the application by the board.

(7) The care of the sick, injured or infirm in a private home by any person who does not assume or represent to be a registered or professional nurse.

(8) Care of the sick with or without compensation when done in a nursing home covered by the provisions of section 144A.09, subdivision 1.

(9) The practice of nursing by a graduate of an approved professional nursing program in another jurisdiction provided the graduate has applied for licensure in the state of Minnesota by interstate endorsement and has written the first examination for licensure following graduation. Practice under this clause is allowable only under a temporary permit issued by the board which shall be issued pursuant to rules as the board may promulgate, and which shall be valid only for the period between submission of a proper application and completion of the examination by the person and the date of action upon the application by the board. The examination must be the same examination required of applicants for licensure by examination in Minnesota. The permit shall authorize the practice of nursing only under the direct supervision of a licensed professional nurse. The permit shall not be renewable.

HISTORY: 1945 c 242 s 11; 1959 c 140 s 2; 1975 c 360 s 10; 1977 c 256 s 1; 1981 c 94 s 8

148.272 NURSING PERSONNEL; REGULATIONS

Nothing in sections 148.171 and 148.271 to 148.283, shall affect the requirements of nursing personnel in nursing homes or hospitals as set forth by regulations of the state commissioner of health.

HISTORY: 1959 c 140 s 3; 1977 c 305 s 45

148.28 Repealed, 1945 c 242 s 14

148.281 VIOLATIONS.

Subdivision 1. It shall be unlawful for any person, corporation, or association, to:

(1) Sell or fraudulently obtain or furnish any nursing diploma, license or record, or aid or abet therein;

(2) Practice professional nursing under cover of any diploma, license, or record illegally or fraudulently obtained or signed or issued unlawfully or under fraudulent representation;

(3) Practice professional nursing unless duly licensed and currently registered to do so under the provisions of sections 148.171 to 148.285;

(4) Use any abbreviation or other designation tending to imply licensure as a registered nurse unless duly registered and licensed so to practice professional nursing under the provisions of sections 148.171 to 148.285;

(5) Practice professional nursing in a manner prohibited by the board in any restriction of a license or registration issued under the provisions of sections 148.171 to 148.285;

(6) Practice professional nursing during the time his or her license or current registration issued under the provisions of sections 148.171 to 148.285 shall be suspended or revoked;

(7) Conduct a school of nursing for the training of persons to become registered nurses or professional nurses unless the school or course has been approved by the board.

Subd. 1a. It shall be unlawful to operate any non-governmental partnership, corporation or unincorporated association which is organized primarily to render professional nursing through its agents, unless the partnership, corporation or unincorporated association is registered pursuant to rules adopted by the board.

Subd. 2. Any person, corporation, or association violating any provisions of subdivision 1 shall be guilty of a misdemeanor, and shall be punished according to law.

HISTORY: 1945 c 242 s 12, 13; 1959 c 140 s 4; 1975 c 360 s 11; 1977 c 256 s 2

148.282 Repealed, 1975 c 360 s 25

148.283 UNAUTHORIZED PRACTICE OF PROFESSIONAL NURSING.

The practice of professional nursing by any person who has not been licensed to practice professional nursing under the provisions of sections 148.171 to 148.285, or whose license has been suspended or revoked, or has expired, is hereby declared to be inimical to the public health and welfare and to constitute a public nuisance. Upon complaint being made thereof by the board of nursing, or any prosecuting officer, and upon a proper showing of the facts, the district court of the county where such practice occurred may enjoin such acts and practice. Such injunction proceeding shall be in addition to, and not in lieu of, all other penalties and remedies provided by law.

HISTORY: 1959 c 140 s 6

148.285 TRANSFER OF ASSETS.

All moneys, property, and property rights belonging to and under the control of the board of examiners, are hereby transferred and appropriated to the control and use of the board hereunder and the purpose provided herein.

HISTORY: 1945 c 242 s 14

GRANTS-IN-AID

148.286 NURSING GRANTS-IN-AID.

Subdivision 1. ENTITLEMENT, USE, AMOUNT. The Minnesota board of nursing may award grants-in-aid to students attending a school of nursing in this state approved in accordance with the laws pertaining to registered nurses and licensed practical nurses. Such grants shall be awarded to those students who are residents of this state and who are in need of economic assistance.

Source: State of Minnesota, Office of the Revisor of Statutes.

AMBULATORY HEALTH CARE PROVIDER
QUALITY ASSURANCE
POLICY AND PROCEDURE
1041

Subject: Study Topic	
Drafted by: ______	Date drafted: ______
Revised by: ______	Date revised: ______
Approved by: ______	Date approved: ______
Supersedes date: ______	Page #: ______
Date effective: ______	Page: ______ of ______

POLICY

Selected study topics are studied relative to their impact on patient care and clinical practice.

PURPOSE

1. To study selected health care topics' impact on patient care and/or clinical practice.
2. To ensure that selected health care topics are studied adequately in order to obtain meaningful information.

PROCEDURE

1. Health care topics are studied after they have been selected for study according to Policy and Procedure 1042: Study Topic Selection.
2. Selected health care topics are studied using appropriate and valid study methods to obtain adequate study results by:
   a. developing study topic plan:
      (1) identification of purpose of study topic
      (2) review of literature pertinent to selected health care topic in order to establish theoretical framework for study topic
      (3) delineation of population(s) to be studied
      (4) formulation of selected health care topic into a specific study topic question, problem, or hypothesis, including:
         (a) identification of specific independent and dependent variables to be under study
         (b) formulation of statement that identifies the expected relationship between these variables
      (5) definition of key words so that they have a specific meaning relative to study topic
      (6) selection of study topic approach, including development of a planned approach, as follows:
         (a) historical approach, where current study topic problem is studied in light of understanding what has already been done
         (b) survey approach, where current study topic question, problem, or hypothesis is studied by further description and understanding of current conditions
         (c) experimental approach, where current study topic question, problem, or hypothesis is studied to establish a new situation under controlled situations for more generalized predictions to be made as to what would happen if experimental conditions were instituted on a wider basis
      (7) selection of data collection method, as follows:
         (a) questioning method, where there is verbal interaction between interviewer and participant (i.e., interviews, questionnaires)
         (b) observation method, where observer watches participant function in study situation
         (c) measuring method, where there is an intervening device that individual doing measuring applies to participant to obtain participant's measurements
      (8) selection of data gathering instruments
      (9) selection of data analysis and interpretation methods
      (10) development of data collection method
      (11) development of data gathering instruments
      (12) development of data analysis and interpretation methods
      (13) selection of sample to be asked to participate in study topic
      (14) pilot study of data collection and analysis methods

(15) identification of assumptions and limitations of study topic
(16) the making of requests to selected sample for participation in study topic

b. implementing study topic method:
(1) implementation of data collection method through use of data gathering instruments
(2) implementation of data analysis and interpretation methods

c. reporting study topic results:
(1) documentation of study topic information using a Special Quality Assurance Study Form (see Exhibit 1037-1)
(2) incorporation of conclusions, based on study topic results, in the Special Quality Assurance Study Form
(3) incorporation of recommendations, based on study topic conclusions, in the Special Quality Assurance Study Form
(4) Communication of study topic information to individuals/committees, as appropriate, according to Policy and Procedure 1010: Confidentiality of Quality Assurance Information, and Policy and Procedure 1001: Administrative Control.

AMBULATORY HEALTH CARE PROVIDER
QUALITY ASSURANCE
POLICY AND PROCEDURE
1042

Subject: Study Topic Selection

Drafted by: ______	Date drafted: ______
Revised by: ______	Date revised: ______
Approved by: ______	Date approved: ______
Supersedes date: ______	Page #: ______
Date effective: ______	Page: ____ of ______

POLICY

Health care topics are selected for special quality assurance studies relative to their impact on patient care and clinical practice.

PURPOSE

1. To select appropriate health care topics for special quality assurance studies.
2. To coordinate selection of special quality assurance studies.

PROCEDURE

1. Health care topics are selected for special quality assurance studies in consideration of, but not limited to, the following:
   a. health care trends that warrant study, particularly in relationship to quality of care
   b. actual/potential adverse health care outcomes that warrant study
   c. improvement in delivery of health care that would have a positive impact on patient care and/or clinical practice
   d. benefits for patient care and/or clinical practice that are worthy of cost expenditures for study
   e. probability that adequate resources exist to complete the study
2. The Quality Assurance Manager:
   a. considers impact of health care topic on patient care and clinical practice
   b. makes recommendations for selecting health care topic as a special quality assurance study
   c. documents recommendations for selecting health care topic as a special quality assurance study on a Special Quality Assurance Study Form (see Exhibit 1037-1)
   d. presents completed Special Quality Assurance Study Form to the Ambulatory Health Care Quality Assurance (AHCQA) Committee for review and recommendations
3. The AHCQA Committee:
   a. reviews completed Special Quality Assurance Study Form
   b. considers impact of health care topic on patient care and clinical practice
   c. makes recommendations for selecting health care topic as a special quality assurance study topic
   d. documents its review and recommendations for selecting health care topic as a special quality assurance study on a Special Quality Assurance Study Form
4. Topic selection information is documented on a Special Quality Assurance Study Form.
5. Topic selection information is communicated to appropriate individuals according to Policy and Procedure 1010: Confidentiality of Quality Assurance Information, and Policy and Procedure 1001: Administrative Control.

Section 2000

Patient Care

The following policies and procedures are adaptable to quality assurance functions in the area of patient care.

AMBULATORY HEALTH CARE PROVIDER
QUALITY ASSURANCE
POLICY AND PROCEDURE
2001

Subject: Charting

Drafted by: ______	Date drafted: ______
Revised by: ______	Date revised: ______
Approved by: ______	Date approved: ______
Supersedes date: ______	Page #: ______
Date effective: ______	Page: ______ of ______

POLICY

Ambulatory health care staff and interdisciplinary team members document the patient ambulatory health care given during each ambulatory health care visit. Documentation is made on the day the service is rendered.

PURPOSE

1. To document the ambulatory health care services given to patients.
2. To provide permanent and continuous records of ambulatory health care observations, interventions, and outcomes.

PROCEDURE

1. Ambulatory health care staff and interdisciplinary team members document all patient ambulatory health care on the day the service is rendered.
2. Such documentation includes, but is not limited to, the following:
   a. month, day, and year of ambulatory health care visit
   b. time of ambulatory health care visit
   c. first and last name of individual who made ambulatory health care visit
   d. professional title of individual who made ambulatory health care visit
   e. patient admission data
   f. patient assessment
   g. additional patient assessments
   h. patient interventions
   i. patient outcomes
   j. patient health care education
   k. contacts and visits with physician
   l. patient referral
   m. patient transfer:
      (1) date, time, and mode of transportation
      (2) person accompanying patient
      (3) destination
      (4) reason for transfer
      (5) general patient condition at time of transfer
      (6) notification of physician
      (7) notification of patient family
   n. patient consent
   o. pertinent current and past findings
   p. patient plan of care
   q. appropriate identifying information, such as patient's full name and drug, dietary, treatment, and activity orders
   r. patient summary reports
   s. patient death:
      (1) time and date patient respiration ceased
      (2) patient neurological and vital sign absence
      (3) notification of physician, patient family, and clergy
      (4) notification of coroner
      (5) time and date patient body removed
3. Ambulatory health care staff and interdisciplinary team members:
   a. document patient ambulatory health care information on patient flowsheets, as appropriate
   b. dictate patient ambulatory health care information whenever possible
   c. dictate clearly
   d. document:
      (1) using a black ballpoint pen
      (2) writing legibly
      (3) using objective statements
      (4) writing patient name on every form
      (5) writing complete date for every notation (i.e., month/date/year)

(6) using correct spelling and grammar
(7) charting entries following last charting entry without leaving blank lines or spaces in progress notes
(8) closing each flowsheet entry by signature, professional title, and complete date
(9) closing each narrative entry by signature, professional title, and complete date
(10) never allowing others to chart under or sign name they legally do not have
(11) without copying another staff member's notations
(12) using only common abbreviations
(13) charting only for actual days of delivered ambulatory health care services
(14) including only significant information about the patient
(15) labeling late entries as an addendum, signing them, and including them in the clinical record
(16) correcting one- or two-word errors by making a single line of black ink through the words in error, noting "error" over the words in error, and noting the initials of the individual who made the error
(17) correcting paragraph errors by making a single line of black ink through the paragraph in error, enclosing the paragraph in brackets, writing "error" beside the brackets, and noting initials of individual who made the error

4. Ambulatory health care registered nurses:
   a. document nursing progress notes using a focus charting format:

Data:	Patient behaviors/status
Action:	Nursing actions
Response:	Patient behavior in response to nursing and/or medical care

   b. review completed ambulatory health care aide documentation for appropriate content, delivery of services, and patient information
5. The clinical records clerical staff:
   a. transcribes dictated patient ambulatory health care information
   b. gives transcription to individual who dictated patient ambulatory health care information
   c. places signed, transcribed patient ambulatory health care information in patient's clinical record
   d. monitors patient ambulatory health care documentation, as follows:
      (1) determines if documentation submitted by ambulatory health care staff reflects charting for actual services provided and completes the column, "Services Charted," on a Receipt of Charting Form (see Exhibit 2001-1)
      (2) reviews ambulatory health care staff member documentation for compliance with ambulatory health care provider charting policy and procedure
      (3) informs the ambulatory health care staff member of documentation that does not reflect charting for actual services provided using a Charting Deficiency Memorandum Form (see Exhibit 2001-2)
      (4) informs the ambulatory health care staff member of documentation problems that do not comply with ambulatory health care provider charting policy and procedure using a Charting Deficiency Memorandum Form
      (5) implements corrective action with ambulatory health care staff member for charting deficiencies by requesting ambulatory health care staff member correction of charting deficiencies whenever possible
      (6) informs Administrator of Ambulatory Health Care of problems and concerns with or need of assistance in developing corrective action plan for ambulatory health care staff member charting deficiencies
      (7) monitors distribution of and response to a Charting Deficiencies Memorandum Form using a Distributed/Received Completed Forms Form (see Exhibit 2001-3)
      (8) summarizes charting deficiencies on a Summary of Charting Deficiencies Form (see Exhibit 2001-4)
      (9) submits completed Summary of Charting Deficiencies Form to the Administrator of Ambulatory Health Care
      (10) places adequate and appropriate patient ambulatory health care documentation in patient's clinical record
      (11) files completed Receipt of Charting Form, Charting Deficiencies Memorandum Form, and Distributed/Received Completed Forms Form in the ambulatory health care provider's Receipt of Charting Form, Charting Deficiencies Memorandum Form, and Distributed/Received Completed Forms from administrative files
6. The individual who dictated the patient ambulatory health care information:
   a. reviews transcription of information
   b. signs transcription
   c. returns transcription to clinical records clerical staff
7. The Administrator of Ambulatory Health Care:
   a. reviews submitted Summary of Charting Deficiencies Form
   b. implements corrective action, as necessary, based on identified charting deficiencies
8. Problems identified through the charting process are referred to the Quality Assurance Manager for consideration as a continuous or special quality assurance activity/study.

9. Charting information is communicated to individuals, as appropriate, according to Policy and Procedure 1010: Confidentiality of Quality Assurance Information, and Policy and Procedure 1001: Administrative Control.

10. The completed Summary of Charting Deficiencies Form is filed in the ambulatory health care provider's Summary of Charting Deficiencies administrative file.

Exhibit 2001-1 Receipt of Charting Form

AMBULATORY HEALTH CARE PROVIDER
RECEIPT OF CHARTING

Date This Form Completed	Dates of Reporting Period

PATIENT NAME	Staff Member Name	Services Provided							Services Charted							COMMENTS
		Sat	Sun	M	T	W	Th	F	Sat	Sun	M	T	W	Th	F	

Signature of Individual Completing This Form	Date of Signature

Exhibit 2001-2 Charting Deficiency Memorandum Form

TO: Name of Ambulatory Health Care Staff Member

FROM: Clinical Records Clerical Staff

SUBJECT:

DATE:

We have received a charting form(s) that reflects your documentation for the ambulatory health care services you provided. Your documentation does not comply with the ambulatory health care provider charting policies and procedures as indicated by the following charting deficiency(ies) in the documentation:

____is not done in black ballpoint ink
____is not legible
____is not phrased using objective statements
____is not labeled with patient name on every form
____does not have a complete date for every notation (i.e., month/date/year)
____does not reflect correct spelling and grammar
____does not have charting entries immediately following previous charting entry, thus leaving blank lines or spaces in the progress notes
____does not have a signature, professional title, and complete date for each narrative entry
____does not have a signature, professional title, and complete date for each flowsheet entry
____reflects charting under or signing a name that the staff member legally does not have
____reflects copying of another ambulatory health care staff member's charting
____does not use only common abbreviations
____does not reflect charting for actual days of delivered ambulatory health care services
____does not include only significant information about the patient
____does not have late entries labeled as an addendum that is signed and included in the patient clinical record
____one- or two-word errors are not corrected by making a single line of black ink through the words in error, noting "error" over the words in error, and noting the initials of the individual who made the error
____paragraph errors are not corrected by making a single line of black ink through the paragraph in error, enclosing the paragraph in brackets, writing "error" beside the brackets, and noting the initials of the individual who made the error

Please contact the clinical records clerical staff at (telephone #) as soon as possible for instructions regarding corrective action for your charting deficiency(ies).

Please review the documentation requirements in the Ambulatory Health Care Staff Member Orientation Manual you received upon employment with the ambulatory health care provider. Pease review the documentation requirements carefully, as you are responsible for complying with the same. Strict adherence to the documentation requirements reflects the quality of care we strive to provide to our patients.

Please contact me at (telephone #) if you have any questions.
Thank you for your cooperation.

Exhibit 2001-3 Distributed/Received Completed Forms Form

DISTRIBUTED/RECEIVED COMPLETED FORMS

PATIENT	PATIENT CLINICAL RECORD NO.	NAME OF FORM DISTRIBUTED	NAME OF INDIVIDUAL FORM DISTRIBUTED TO	DATE FORM		FOLLOW-UP LETTER DISTRIBUTED (IF YES, INCLUDE DATE)		COMMENTS
				DISTR'D	REC'D	YES	NO	

Source: Reprinted with permission of Briggs Corporation, Des Moines, Iowa, © 1989.

Exhibit 2001-4 Summary of Charting Deficiencies Form

AMBULATORY HEALTH CARE PROVIDER
SUMMARY OF CHARTING DEFICIENCIES

Date This Form Completed	Dates of Reporting Period	Total Number of Charting Deficiencies

ITEM	TOTAL NUMBER OF DEFICIENCIES				
	YES	NO	DON'T KNOW	N/A	COMMENTS
1. Is not done in black ballpoint ink					
2. Is not legible					
3. Is not phrased using objective statements					
4. Is not labeled with patient name on every form					
5. Does not have a complete date for every notation (i.e., month/date/year)					
6. Does not reflect correct spelling and grammar					
7. Does not have charting entries immediately following previous charting entry, thus leaving blank lines or spaces in the progress notes					
8. Does not have a signature, professional title, and complete date for each flowsheet entry					
9. Does not have a signature, professional title, and complete date for each narrative entry					
10. Reflects that ambulatory health care staff member has charted under or signed a name that the staff member legally does not have					
11. Reflects copying of another ambulatory health care staff member's charting					
12. Does not use only common abbreviations					
13. Does not reflect charting for actual days of delivered ambulatory health care services					
14. Does not include only significant information about the patient					
15. Does not have late entries labeled as an addendum, signed, and included in the patient clinical record					
16. One- or two-word errors are not corrected by making a single line of black ink through the words in error, noting "error" over the words in error, and noting the initials of the individual who made the error					
17. Paragraph errors are not corrected by making a single line of black ink through the paragraph in error, enclosing the paragraph in brackets, writing "error" beside the brackets, and noting the initials of the individual who made the error					
18. Other					

Signature of Individual Completing This Form	Date of Signature

AMBULATORY HEALTH CARE PROVIDER
QUALITY ASSURANCE
POLICY AND PROCEDURE
2002

Subject: Infection Control/Maintenance of Environment/Equipment

Drafted by: ______	Date drafted: ______
Revised by: ______	Date revised: ______
Approved by: ______	Date approved: ______
Supersedes date: ______	Page #: ______
Date effective: ______	Page: ______ of ______

POLICY

Ambulatory health care staff members implement infection control and maintenance procedures for environment and equipment, as appropriate.

PURPOSE

1. To control spread of infection.
2. To protect individuals from transmission of communicable/infectious diseases.
3. To protect individuals from malfunctioning or nonfunctioning equipment.

PROCEDURE

1. Ambulatory health care staff members implement infection control and maintenance procedures with regard to patients, staff, and their environment and equipment.
2. Patient infection control procedures include, but are not limited to, the following:
   a. frequent handwashing by ambulatory health care staff members before and after provision of direct patient care according to ambulatory health care provider policy and procedure
   b. appropriate patient wound and skin dressing techniques according to ambulatory health care provider policy and procedure
   c. appropriate patient skin care according to ambulatory health care provider policy and procedure
   d. appropriate handling and disposal of waste products
   e. maintenance of Foley catheter according to ambulatory health care provider policy and procedure
3. Ambulatory health care staff member infection control procedures include, but are not limited to, the following:
   a. frequent handwashing by ambulatory health care staff members:
      (1) before and after provision of direct patient care
      (2) after handling soiled or contaminated materials
      (3) after going to toilet
   b. covering nose and mouth when coughing or sneezing
   c. covering open sores or cuts on fingers or hands with clean bandages
   d. using personal leave days when ill
4. Environmental and equipment infection control procedures include, but are not limited to, the following:
   a. maintaining a clean work environment, for example, by maintaining clean counters, tables, and shelves
   b. rinsing cans and bottles before disposal in garbage
   c. washing garbage cans, dirty pails, and trash cans with hot soapy water
   d. disposing of garbage properly by draining off liquid before putting garbage in paper or plastic-lined pails
   e. cleaning all areas of bathroom, especially around toilet base
   f. keeping clean and dirty items separate
   g. using sterile items that are not outdated
   h. keeping the patient environment clean, neat, and orderly
   i. regularly cleaning patient supplies, such as commodes, bedpans, urinals, suction machines, and measuring containers
5. Equipment maintenance procedures include, but are not limited to, the following:
   a. inspecting equipment every two weeks to ensure it is appropriately maintained
   b. keeping equipment repaired and in optimal functioning capacity

c. instructing patient, patient family, and ambulatory health care staff members regarding appropriate use of equipment
d. using equipment only for its intended purpose without subjecting it to abuse

6. Ambulatory health care staff members provide information to patients regarding infection control and maintenance of environment and equipment policies and procedures, as appropriate.
7. Ambulatory health care registered nurses:
   a. monitor infection control and maintenance of environment and equipment
   b. document monitored infection control and maintenance of environment and equipment on an Observation of Infection Control/Maintenance of Environment/Equipment Form (see Exhibit 2002-1)
   c. implement corrective action for noncompliance with infection control and maintenance of environment and equipment policies and procedures, as necessary
   d. inform the Nursing Manager when assistance is needed with corrective action for noncompliance with infection control and maintenance of environment and equipment
   e. submit completed Observation of Infection Control/ Maintenance of Environment/Equipment Form to the Administrative Assistant
8. The Administrative Assistant:
   a. summarizes submitted Observation of Infection Control/Maintenance of Environment/Equipment Form on a Summary of Observation of Infection Control/ Maintenance of Environment/Equipment Form (see Exhibit 2002-2)
   b. submits completed Summary of Observation of Infection Control/Maintenance of Environment/Equipment Form to the Nursing Manager
9. The Nursing Manager:
   a. reviews submitted Summary of Observation of Infection Control/Maintenance of Environment/Equipment Form
   b. implements corrective action, as necessary, based on problems with infection control and maintenance of environment and equipment
10. Problems identified through observation of infection control/maintenance of environment/equipment are referred to the Quality Assurance Manager for consideration as a continuous or special quality assurance activity/study.
11. Observation of infection control/maintenance of environment/equipment information is communicated to individuals, as appropriate, according to Policy and Procedure 1010: Confidentiality of Quality Assurance Information, and Policy and Procedure 1001: Administrative Control.
12. The completed Observation of Infection Control/Maintenance of Environment/Equipment Form and Summary of Observation of Infection Control/Maintenance of Environment/Equipment Form are filed in the ambulatory health care provider's Observation of Infection Control/ Maintenance of Environment/Equipment and Summary of Observation of Infection Control/Maintenance of Environment/Equipment administrative files.

Exhibit 2002-1 Observation of Infection Control/Maintenance of Environment/Equipment Form

AMBULATORY HEALTH CARE PROVIDER
OBSERVATION OF INFECTION CONTROL/MAINTENANCE OF ENVIRONMENT/EQUIPMENT

Date This Form Completed	Date of Observation	Location of Observation

ITEM	RESPONSE (PLEASE CHECK [✔] APPROPRIATE RESPONSE)			
	YES	NO	N/A	COMMENTS
I. Patient and Staff Member Infection Control Procedures A. Patient infection control 1. frequent handwashing by staff members *before* provision of direct patient care according to provider policy and procedure				
2. frequent handwashing by staff members *after* provision of direct patient care according to provider policy and procedure				
3. appropriate patient wound and skin dressing techniques according to provider policy and procedure				
4. appropriate patient skin care according to provider policy and procedure				
5. appropriate handling and disposal of waste products				
6. maintenance of Foley catheter according to provider policy and procedure				
B. Staff member infection control 1. frequent handwashing by staff members:				
a. after handling soiled or contaminated materials				
b. after going to toilet				
2. covering nose and mouth when coughing or sneezing				
3. covering open sores or cuts on fingers or hands with clean bandages				
4. using personal leave days when ill				
II. Environmental and Equipment Infection Control Procedures A. Maintaining clean work environment				
B. Rinsing cans and bottles before disposal in the garbage				
C. Washing garbage cans, dirty pails, and trash cans with hot soapy water				
D. Disposing of garbage properly by draining off liquid before putting garbage in paper or plastic-lined pails				
E. Cleaning all areas of bathroom, especially around toilet base				
F. Keeping clean and dirty items separate				
G. Using sterile items that are not outdated				
H. Keeping patient environment clean, neat, and orderly				
I. Regularly cleaning patient supplies				
III. Equipment Maintenance Procedures A. Inspecting equipment every two weeks to ensure it is being appropriately maintained				
B. Keeping equipment repaired and in optimal functioning capacity				
C. Instructing patient, patient family, staff members regarding appropriate use of equipment				
IV. Staff Members Provide Information to Patients Regarding Infection Control and Maintenance of Environment and Equipment Policies and Procedures, As Appropriate				
V. Other				

Signature of Individual Completing This Form	Date of Signature

Exhibit 2002-2 Summary of Observation of Infection Control/Maintenance of Environment/Equipment Form

AMBULATORY HEALTH CARE PROVIDER
SUMMARY OF OBSERVATION OF INFECTION CONTROL/MAINTENANCE OF ENVIRONMENT/EQUIPMENT

Date This Form Completed	Dates of Reporting Period	Total Number of Observations of Infection Control/Maintenance of Environment/Equipment Forms Completed

ITEM	TOTAL NUMBER OF RESPONSES			
	YES	NO	N/A	COMMENTS
I. Patient and Staff Member Infection Control Procedures A. Patient infection control 1. frequent handwashing by staff members *before* provision of direct patient care according to provider policy and procedure				
2. frequent handwashing by staff members *after* provision of direct patient care according to provider policy and procedure				
3. appropriate patient wound and skin dressing techniques according to provider policy and procedure				
4. appropriate patient skin care according to provider policy and procedure				
5. appropriate handling and disposal of waste products				
6. maintenance of Foley catheter according to provider policy and procedure				
B. Staff member infection control 1. frequent handwashing by staff members:				
a. after handling soiled or contaminated materials				
b. after going to toilet				
2. covering nose and mouth when coughing or sneezing				
3. covering open sores or cuts on fingers or hands with clean bandages				
4. using personal leave days when ill				
II. Environmental and Equipment Infection Control Procedures A. Maintaining clean work environment				
B. Rinsing cans and bottles before disposal in the garbage				
C. Washing garbage cans, dirty pails, and trash cans with hot soapy water				
D. Disposing of garbage properly by draining off liquid before putting garbage in paper or plastic-lined pails				
E. Cleaning all areas of bathroom, especially around toilet base				
F. Keeping clean and dirty items separate				
G. Using sterile items that are not outdated				
H. Keeping patient environment clean, neat, and orderly				
I. Regularly cleaning patient supplies				
III. Equipment Maintenance Procedures A. Inspecting equipment every two weeks to ensure it is being appropriately maintained				
B. Keeping equipment repaired and in optimal functioning capacity				
C. Instructing patient, patient family, and staff members regarding appropriate use of equipment				
IV. Staff Members Provide Information to Patients Regarding Infection Control and Maintenance of Environment and Equipment Policies and Procedures, as Appropriate				
V. Other				

Signature of Individual Completing This Form	Date of Signature

AMBULATORY HEALTH CARE PROVIDER
QUALITY ASSURANCE
POLICY AND PROCEDURE
2003

Subject: Medication Errors

Drafted by: ______	Date drafted: ______
Revised by: ______	Date revised: ______
Approved by: ______	Date approved: ______
Supersedes date: ______	Page #: ______
Date effective: ______	Page: ____ of ______

POLICY

All medication errors are reported and documented.

PURPOSE

1. To facilitate timely, accurate, and complete documentation of all medication errors.
2. To implement a quality assurance monitoring system for medication errors.
3. To provide timely interventions for patients involved in medication errors.

PROCEDURE

1. All medication errors are reported as soon as possible to the attending physician and Nursing Manager.
2. All medication errors are documented on a Medication Error Report Form (see Exhibit 2003-1), using one form for each medication error.
3. All medication errors are documented in patient's clinical record and include the following information:
   a. date and time medication error occurred
   b. name, dose, and route of medication given or not given
   c. specific objective description of medication error
   d. nursing assessment of patient following medication error
   e. description of nursing intervention for patient in response to medication error
   f. nursing assessment of patient following nursing intervention in response to medication error
   g. date and time attending physician notified of medication error
   h. physician order relative to medication error
   i. ongoing nursing assessment and intervention, as necessary
4. The completed Medication Error Report Form is submitted to the ambulatory health care staff member's immediate supervisor for review, investigation, corrective action, documentation, and signature.
5. The completed and reviewed Medication Error Report Form is submitted to the Nursing Manager for review, additional investigation, corrective action, documentation, and signature.
6. The completed and reviewed Medication Error Report Form is submitted to the Administrator of Ambulatory Health Care for review and signature.
7. The completed and reviewed Medication Error Report Form is summarized by the Administrative Assistant using a Summary of Medication Error Report Form (see Exhibit 2003-2).
8. Problems identified through medication errors are referred to the Quality Assurance Manager for consideration as a continuous or special quality assurance activity/study.
9. Medication error information is communicated to individuals, as appropriate, according to Policy and Procedure 1010: Confidentiality of Quality Assurance Information, and Policy and Procedure 1001: Administrative Control.
10. The completed and reviewed Medication Error Report Form and Summary of Medication Error Report Form are placed in the ambulatory health care provider Medication Error Report and Summary of Medication Error Report administrative files.

Exhibit 2003-1 Medication Error Report Form

AMBULATORY HEALTH CARE PROVIDER
MEDICATION ERROR REPORT

I. General information (please complete below)

______________________ 1. Name of patient.

______________________ 2. Age of patient.

______________________ 3. Diagnosis of patient.

______________________ 4. Patient clinical record no.

______________________ 5. Date of medication error.

______________________ A.M./P.M. 6. Time of medication error.

______________________ 7. Name(s) of individual(s) involved with medication error.
____

______________________ 8. Address(es) of individual(s) involved with medication error.
____

______________________ 9. Telephone number(s) of individual(s) involved with medication error.
____

______________________ 10. Date of discovery of medication error.

______________________ A.M./P.M. 11. Time of discovery of medication error.

______________________ 12. Name of individual who discovered medication error.

______________________ 13. Name of individual assigned to patient.

II. Information regarding medication involved (please complete below)

MEDICATION INVOLVED IN MEDICATION ERROR

MED NAME: ____________

MED DOSE (Please write dosage below)		MED ROUTE Please check [√] below)										
		ORDERED					GIVEN					
ORDERED	GIVEN	P.O.	I.M.	I.V.	S.Q.	S.L.	P.O.	I.M.	I.V.	S.Q.	S.L.	MED ORDER/ADMIN.
												( ) a. Med ordered and given. ( ) b. Med ordered and not given. ( ) c. Med not ordered and given.

continues

Exhibit 2003-1 *continued*

III. Narrative description of medication error (Please write below and include how medication error was discovered, effect of medication error on patient, sequence of events, and individuals involved.)

____

____

____

____

____

____

____

____

____

____

____

____

IV. Cause(s) of medication error (please check [√] below)

A. Failure to follow procedure.

______ 1. Patient not identified correctly.
______ 2. Comparison of medication container label with physician medication order not done correctly.
______ 3. Administration route of medication not checked correctly.
______ 4. Patient not observed taking medication.
______ 5. Timely charting of medication administration not done.

B. Failure to communicate.

______ 1. Physician medication order not written correctly.
______ 2. Physician medication order not transcribed correctly.
______ 3. Physician medication order not transcribed legibly.
______ 4. Transcribed physician medication order not read correctly.

C. Other.

______ 1. Medication not available.
______ 2. Other (please describe) ______________________________

____

____

____

continues

Exhibit 2003-1 *continued*

V. Type(s) of medication error (please check [√] below)

_________ 1. Wrong patient
_________ 2. Wrong medication
_________ 3. Wrong dose
_________ 4. Wrong date
_________ 5. Wrong time
_________ 6. Wrong route
_________ 7. Transcription error
_________ 8. Medication not given when ordered
_________ 9. Medication given when not ordered
_________ 10. Other (please describe)____
____

VI. Patient outcome (please complete below)

_______ Yes _______ No — 1. Patient seen by physician (please check [√] one; if *no* checked, please explain)
____

______________________________ 2. Date patient seen by physician

______________________________ A.M. / P.M. 3. Time patient seen by physician

______________________________ 4. Intervention(s) implemented for patient
____
____

______________________________ 5. Physician statement of assessment/intervention and signature
____
____

_______ Yes _______ No — 6. Documentation completed in patient clinical record (please check [√] one; if *no* checked, please explain)
____
____
____

continues

Exhibit 2003-1 *continued*

INDIVIDUAL	COMMENTS	SIGNATURE	DATE OF SIGNATURE
1. Individual(s) who made medication error			
2. Individual(s) who discovered medication error			
3. Individual who completed this medication error report			
4. Nursing Manager			
5. Administrator of Ambulatory Health Care			
6. Pharmacist			

Exhibit 2003-2 Summary of Medication Error Report Form

AMBULATORY HEALTH CARE PROVIDER
SUMMARY OF MEDICATION ERROR REPORT

Date This Form Completed	Dates of Reporting Period	Total Number of Medication Error Report Forms Completed

ITEM	TOTAL NUMBER OF RESPONSES				
	YES	NO	DON'T KNOW	N/A	COMMENTS
I. Medication A. Wrong medication					
B. Wrong patient					
C. Wrong time					
D. Wrong dosage					
E. Improper label					
F. Omitted					
G. Not ordered					
H. Not transcribed					
I. Failure to document					
J. Duplicated administration					
K. Wrong route					
L. Allergy/reaction to medication					
M. Administered after medication discontinued/on hold					
N. Other					
II. Intravenous A. Too fast					
B. Too slow					
C. Wrong solution/medication					
D. Wrong patient					
E. Wrong dosage					
F. Wrong time					
G. Wrong administration					
H. Wrong route					
I. Not transcribed					
J. Not infused					
K. Allergy/reaction to medication					
L. Infiltrated					
M. Administered after medication discontinued/on hold					
N. Wrong medication					
O. Other					

Shift When Medication Error Occurred	Patient Experienced Adverse Outcome	Patient Seen by Physician
___ Day ___ Evening ___ Night	___ Yes ___ No	___ Yes ___ No

Signature of Individual Completing This Form	Date of Signature

AMBULATORY HEALTH CARE PROVIDER
QUALITY ASSURANCE
POLICY AND PROCEDURE
2004

Subject: Minor Patient Abuse and/or Neglect: Reporting System

Drafted by: ______	Date drafted: ______
Revised by: ______	Date revised: ______
Approved by: ______	Date approved: ______
Supersedes date: ______	Page #: ______
Date effective: ______	Page: ____ of ______

POLICY

The ambulatory health care provider reports all suspected cases of abuse and/or neglect of minor patients in compliance with relevant state statutes.

PURPOSE

1. To protect minor patients whose health or welfare may be jeopardized through physical, emotional, or sexual abuse or neglect.
2. To ensure that all suspected cases of minor patient abuse and/or neglect are reported under appropriate statutes.
3. To facilitate prompt internal investigation of suspected abuse and/or neglect of minor patients.
4. To implement a quality assurance monitoring system for minor patient abuse and/or neglect.

PROCEDURE

1. Definitions of applicable terms are as follows:*
   a. *minor:* an infant or person who is under the age of legal competence
   b. *physical abuse:* any physical injury inflicted by a person responsible for the minor's care other than by accidental means, or any physical injury that cannot be reasonably explained by the minor's history of injuries
   c. *sexual abuse:* subjection by a person responsible for the minor's care, or by a person in a position of authority where the following acts are committed without the person's consent, except in those cases where consent is not a defense, and committed with sexual or aggressive intent:
      (1) the intentional touching by the actor of the person's intimate parts
      (2) the touching by the complainant of the actor's, the person's, or another's intimate parts effected by coercion or the use of a position of authority, or by inducement if the person is under 13 years of age or mentally impaired
      (3) the touching of the person's intimate parts effected by coercion or the use of a position of authority
      (4) in any of the cases above, the touching of the clothing covering the immediate area of the intimate parts†
   d. *neglect:* failure of a caretaker to supply minor with necessary food, clothing, shelter, or health care when reasonably able to do so or failure to protect a minor from conditions or actions that imminently and seriously endanger the minor's physical and mental health when reasonably able to do so.
   e. *caretaker:* an individual functioning within the family unit and having responsibilities for the care of the minor such as a parent, guardian, or other person having similar care responsibilities, or an individual functioning outside the family and having responsibilities for the care of the minor such as a teacher, school administrator, or other lawful custodian of a minor having either full-time or short-term care responsibilities including, but not limited to, day care, babysitting whether paid or unpaid, counseling, teaching, and coaching
   f. *facility:* a hospital or other entity required to be licensed; an agency, day care facility, or residential facility required to be licensed to serve minors; a

*Derived from Minnesota State Statute 626.556 (1988), Reporting of Maltreatment of Minors.

†Derived from Minnesota State Statute 609.326 (1989), Criminal Code of 1963.

mental health program receiving funds; or an ambulatory health care provider required to be licensed

g. *licensing agency:* the Commissioner of Health, for facilities that are required to be licensed or certified by the state health department; the Commissioner of Public Welfare, for facilities required to be licensed; any licensing board that regulates persons; and any agency responsible for credentialing human services occupations
h. *report:* any report received by the local welfare agency, police department, county sheriff, or licensing agency or a verbal and/or written statement of abuse and/or neglect that states:
   (1) what has happened
   (2) to whom it happened
   (3) when it happened
   (4) where it happened
   (5) who did the abusing or was responsible for the neglect
i. *individual mandated to report:* a professional or the professional's delegate who is engaged in the care of minors or in the practice of the health arts, social services, hospital administration, psychological or psychiatric treatment, child care, education, or law enforcement who knows and has reason to believe a minor is being neglected or physically or sexually abused

2. The action to be taken is as follows:
   a. The individual mandated to report suspected minor patient abuse and/or neglect must report:
      (1) any knowledge of patient abuse and/or neglect
      (2) reasonable cause to suspect patient abuse and/or neglect
      (3) any knowledge that a patient sustained an injury that is not reasonably explained by patient's history of injuries
   b. Individuals not mandated to report suspected minor patient abuse and/or neglect may make such reports if they have:
      (1) any knowledge of patient abuse and/or neglect
      (2) reasonable cause to suspect patient abuse and/or neglect
      (3) any knowledge that a patient has sustained an injury that is not reasonably explained by patient's history of injuries
   c. The individual reporting suspected minor patient abuse and/or neglect:
      (1) immediately informs the Nursing Manager of the suspected minor patient abuse and/or neglect
      (2) immediately completes a Suspected Patient Abuse and/or Neglect Report Form (see Exhibit 2004-1), except for items I.D. and III.F.5.
      (3) submits completed Suspected Patient Abuse and/or Neglect Report Form to the Nursing Manager
   d. Ambulatory health care provider personnel may report suspected cases of minor patient abuse and/or neglect directly to outside licensing agencies.
   e. The Nursing Manager:
      (1) immediately reviews completed Suspected Patient Abuse and/or Neglect Report Form
      (2) informs the Administrator of Ambulatory Health Care of the suspected minor patient abuse and/or neglect
      (3) conducts an immediate initial investigation into the suspected minor patient abuse and/or neglect
      (4) informs the Administrator of Ambulatory Health Care of initial investigation results
      (5) documents review and investigation of the suspected minor patient abuse and/or neglect on the Suspected Patient Abuse and/or Neglect Report Form
      (6) summarizes completed Suspected Patient Abuse and/or Neglect Report Form on a Summary of Suspected Patient Abuse and/or Neglect Report Form (see Exhibit 2004-2)
      (7) sends completed Suspected Patient Abuse and/or Neglect Report Form to the Administrator of Ambulatory Health Care
   f. The Administrator of Ambulatory Health Care:
      (1) immediately submits verbal report of the suspected minor patient abuse and/or neglect to appropriate authority in accordance with relevant statutes
      (2) reviews all suspected minor patient abuse and/or neglect reports
      (3) conducts further investigation of the suspected minor patient abuse and/or neglect, as necessary
      (4) reports all cases of suspected minor patient abuse and/or neglect to appropriate authority in accordance with relevant statutes
      (5) documents review and investigation of the suspected minor patient abuse and/or neglect on a Suspected Patient Abuse and/or Neglect Investigation Report Form (see Exhibit 2004-3)
      (6) sends copy of completed Suspected Patient Abuse and/or Neglect Investigation Report Form to appropriate licensing agency
      (7) places completed Suspected Patient Abuse and/or Neglect Report Form and Suspected Patient Abuse and/or Neglect Investigation Report Form in a locked, confidential ambulatory health care provider administrative file
      (8) places completed Summary of Suspected Patient Abuse and/or Neglect Report Forms in the ambulatory health care provider Summary of Suspected Patient Abuse and/or Neglect Report administrative file
   g. Reports, reviews, and investigations of suspected minor patient abuse and/or neglect are held in strictest confidence.

h. If the Nursing Manager is suspected of committing minor patient abuse and/or neglect, the individual reporting such abuse and/or neglect:
   (1) immediately informs the Administrator of Ambulatory Health Care of the suspected minor patient abuse and/or neglect
   (2) immediately completes a Suspected Patient Abuse and/or Neglect Report Form, except for items I.D. and III.F.5.
   (3) submits completed Suspected Patient Abuse and/or Neglect Report Form to the Administrator of Ambulatory Health Care
i. If the Administrator of Ambulatory Health Care is suspected of committing minor patient abuse and/or neglect, the individual reporting such abuse and/or neglect:
   (1) immediately informs the President of the ambulatory health care provider of the suspected minor patient abuse and/or neglect
   (2) immediately completes a Suspected Patient Abuse and/or Neglect Report Form, except for items I.D. and III.F.5.
   (3) submits completed Suspected Patient Abuse and/or Neglect Report Form to the President of the ambulatory health care provider
j. Problems identified with suspected minor abuse and/or neglect are referred to the Quality Assurance Manager for consideration as a continuous or special quality assurance activity/study.
k. Ambulatory health care staff members shall cooperate fully with those assigned to investigate suspected minor patient abuse and/or neglect.
l. Ambulatory health care staff members shall maintain patient confidentiality and rights during the reporting and investigation of suspected minor patient abuse and/or neglect, as appropriate, according to Policy and Procedure 1009: Confidentiality for Patients.
m. Ambulatory health care administrative staff members may not implement retaliatory action against any individuals who report suspected minor patient abuse and/or neglect.
n. An individual who is mandated to report suspected minor patient abuse and/or neglect and who intentionally fails to report such suspected abuse and/or neglect is guilty of a misdemeanor and liable for damages caused by the failure.
o. An individual who knowingly or recklessly makes a false minor patient abuse and/or neglect report is liable for civil action for any actual damages suffered by the individuals who were reported as suspects in such abuse and/or neglect and for punitive damages set by the court or jury.
p. Information gathered by the ambulatory health care provider relating to minor patient abuse and/or neglect is handled in the following manner:
   (1) If the provider determines the information is false, it destroys the information two years after such determination
   (2) If the provider determines the information is unsubstantiated, it destroys the information four years after such determination
   (3) If the provider determines the information is substantiated, it destroys the information seven years after such determination

Exhibit 2004-1 Suspected Patient Abuse and/or Neglect Report Form

AMBULATORY HEALTH CARE PROVIDER
SUSPECTED PATIENT ABUSE AND/OR NEGLECT REPORT

I. Information regarding patient:

A. Name of patient ______________________
B. Age of patient ______________________
C. Sex of patient (please check [√] one)
_____ Male _____ Female
D. Patient vulnerability risk score (please check [√] one)
_____ High _____ Moderate _____ Low

II. Information regarding alleged perpetrators:

A. Name of alleged perpetrator ______________________
B. Age of alleged perpetrator ______________________
C. Sex of alleged perpetrator (please check [√] one)
_____ Male _____ Female
D. Relationship of alleged perpetrator to patient (please check [√] one)

_____ 1) spouse
_____ 2) son
_____ 3) daughter
_____ 4) brother
_____ 5) sister
_____ 6) relative
_____ 7) neighbor
_____ 8) acquaintance
_____ 9) legal guardian
_____ 10) power of attorney
_____ 11) ambulatory health care staff member
_____ 12) ambulatory health care interdisciplinary team member
_____ 13) ambulatory health care ancillary support staff member
_____ 14) volunteer
_____ 15) unknown
_____ 16) other (please specify)
____

III. Information regarding suspected abuse and/or neglect:

A. Name of individual who reported suspected abuse and/or neglect:
____

B. Relationship of patient to individual who reported suspected abuse and/or neglect (please check [√] one)

_____ 1) spouse
_____ 2) son
_____ 3) daughter
_____ 4) brother
_____ 5) sister
_____ 6) relative
_____ 7) neighbor
_____ 8) acquaintance
_____ 9) legal guardian
_____ 10) power of attorney
_____ 11) ambulatory health care staff member
_____ 12) ambulatory health care interdisciplinary team member
_____ 13) ambulatory health care ancillary support staff member
_____ 14) volunteer
_____ 15) unknown
_____ 16) other (please specify)
____

C. Date of suspected abuse and/or neglect occurrence:
____

D. Name of witness(es) to suspected patient abuse and/or neglect:
____
____

E. Relationship of witness(es) to patient (please check [√] one or more as appropriate)

_____ 1) spouse
_____ 2) son
_____ 3) daughter
_____ 4) brother
_____ 5) sister
_____ 6) relative
_____ 7) neighbor
_____ 8) acquaintance
_____ 9) legal guardian
_____ 10) power of attorney
_____ 11) ambulatory health care staff member
_____ 12) ambulatory health care interdisciplinary team member
_____ 13) ambulatory health care ancillary support staff member
_____ 14) volunteer
_____ 15) unknown
_____ 16) other (please specify)
____

continues

Exhibit 2004-1 *continued*

F. Nature of suspected patient abuse and/or neglect (please check [√] one or more as appropriate)

1. Physical abuse:

_____ a. neglect
_____ b. malnutrition
_____ c. bruise
_____ d. welt
_____ e. abrasion
_____ f. puncture wound
_____ g. laceration
_____ h. burn
_____ i. dislocation
_____ j. fracture
_____ k. internal injury
_____ l. hitting
_____ m. slapping
_____ n. exposure to adverse weather conditions
_____ o. other (please specify) ____________________

2. Verbal abuse:

_____ a. verbal assault
_____ b. verbal humiliation
_____ c. verbal threat
_____ d. other (please specify) ____________________

3. Neglect/failure to provide:

_____ a. physical care
_____ b. emotional care
_____ c. medical care
_____ d. acceptable environment according to community standards
_____ e. adequate supervision
_____ f. appropriate stimulation
_____ g. Other (please specify) ____________________

4. Sexual abuse:

_____ a. sexual abuse
_____ b. sexual assault
_____ c. sexual exploitation
_____ d. other (please specify) ____________________

5. Financial abuse:

_____ a. money misuse
_____ b. property misuse
_____ c. money theft
_____ d. property theft
_____ e. other (please specify) ____________________

6. Description of physical, verbal, sexual, and/or financial abuse, or neglect/failure to provide as checked in Item III-F, 1, 2, 3, 4, and/or 5 (please describe below):

____
____
____
____
____
____
____
____
____
____
____
____
____
____

continues

Exhibit 2004-1 *continued*

7. Violation of patient rights (please describe below):

G. Narrative description of suspected patient abuse and/or neglect (please describe below):

H. Comments:

Signature of Individual Who Completed This Form — Date of Signature

Signature of Individual Who Reviewed This Completed Form — Date of Signature

Exhibit 2004-2 Summary of Suspected Abuse and/or Neglect Report Form

AMBULATORY HEALTH CARE PROVIDER
SUMMARY OF SUSPECTED PATIENT ABUSE AND/OR NEGLECT REPORT

Date This Form Completed	Dates of Reporting Period	Total Number of Adult Abuse and/or Neglect Report Forms Completed Total Number of Child Abuse and/or Neglect Report Forms Completed

Age of Patient
___ Under 1 Yr ___ 12–19 ___ 35–49 ___ 65–79
___ 1–11 ___ 20–34 ___ 50–64 ___ 80 and over

Sex of Patient
___ Male ___ Female

Patient Vulnerability Risk Score
___ High ___ Moderate ___ Low

Age of Alleged Perpetrator
___ 5–11 ___ 20–34 ___ 50–64 ___ 80 and over
___ 12–19 ___ 35–49 ___ 65–79

Sex of Alleged Perpetrator
___ Male ___ Female

Relationship of Alleged Perpetrator to Patient
___Spouse
___Son
___Daughter
___Brother
___Sister
___Relative
___Neighbor
___Acquaintance
___Legal Guardian
___Power of Attorney
___Ambulatory Health Care Staff Member
___Ambulatory Health Care Interdisciplinary Team Member
___Ambulatory Health Care Support Staff Member
___Volunteer
___Unknown
___Other ________________

Relationship of Patient to Individual Who Reported Suspected Abuse and/or Neglect
___Spouse
___Son
___Daughter
___Brother
___Sister
___Relative
___Neighbor
___Acquaintance
___Legal Guardian
___Power of Attorney
___Ambulatory Health Care Staff Member
___Ambulatory Health Care Interdisciplinary Team Member
___Ambulatory Health Care Support Staff Member
___Volunteer
___Unknown
___Other ________________

Relationship of Witness(es) to Patient
___Spouse
___Son
___Daughter
___Brother
___Sister
___Relative
___Neighbor
___Acquaintance
___Legal Guardian
___Power of Attorney
___Ambulatory Health Care Staff Member
___Ambulatory Health Care Interdisciplinary Team Member
___Ambulatory Health Care Support Staff Member
___Volunteer
___Unknown
___Other ________________

Physical Abuse
___Neglect
___Malnutrition
___Bruise
___Welt
___Abrasion
___Puncture Wound
___Laceration
___Burn
___Dislocation
___Fracture
___Internal Injury
___Hitting
___Slapping
___Exposure to Adverse Weather Conditions
___Other ________________

Verbal Abuse
___Verbal Assault
___Verbal Humiliation
___Verbal Threat
___Other ________________

Sexual Abuse
___Sexual Abuse
___Sexual Assault
___Sexual Exploitation
___Other ________________

Financial Abuse
___Money Misuse
___Property Misuse
___Money Theft
___Property Theft
___Other ________________

Neglect/Failure to Provide
___Physical Care
___Emotional Care
___Medical Care
___Acceptable Environment According to Community Standard
___Adequate Supervision
___Appropriate Stimulation
___Other ________________

Signature of Individual Completing This Form	Date of Signature

Exhibit 2004-3 Suspected Patient Abuse and/or Neglect Investigation Report Form

AMBULATORY HEALTH CARE PROVIDER
SUSPECTED PATIENT ABUSE AND/OR NEGLECT INVESTIGATION REPORT

1. Patient name
____

2. Name of individual who reported abuse and/or neglect
____

3. Name of individual who reviewed completed Suspected Patient Abuse and/or Neglect Report Form
____

4. Date completed Suspected Patient Abuse and/or Neglect Report Form reviewed
____

5. Name of individual/agency given report regarding suspected patient abuse and/or neglect
____

6. Date individual/agency given report regarding suspected patient abuse and/or neglect
____

7. Corrective action implemented (please describe)
____
____
____

8. Date corrective action implemented ______________________________

9. Summary of investigation (please describe)
____
____
____
____
____

______________________________________ ______________________
Signature of Individual Completing This Form Date of Signature

______________________________________ ______________________
Signature of Individual Who Investigated Suspected Abuse and/or Neglect Date of Signature

AMBULATORY HEALTH CARE PROVIDER
QUALITY ASSURANCE
POLICY AND PROCEDURE
2005

Subject: Outcome-Oriented Review of Patient Medical Care

Drafted by: ______	Date drafted: ______
Revised by: ______	Date revised: ______
Approved by: ______	Date approved: ______
Supersedes date: ______	Page #: ______
Date effective: ______	Page: ____ of ______

POLICY

Ambulatory health care physicians conduct retrospective outcome-oriented reviews of patient medical care.

PURPOSE

1. To assess patient outcomes against established patient outcome standards.
2. To determine appropriateness of ambulatory health care services.
3. To determine adequacy of patient medical care.
4. To determine effectiveness of patient medical care.
5. To identify problems with patient medical care and outcomes.
6. To identify problems with continuity of patient medical care.
7. To implement quality assurance activities for resolution of identified patient medical care problems.
8. To ensure peer review of patient medical care.
9. To ensure that established policies and procedures are followed in the provision of ambulatory health care services.

PROCEDURE

1. Retrospective outcome-oriented patient medical care reviews:
   a. are completed on a quarterly basis
   b. are completed by ambulatory health care physicians
   c. include assessment of samples of patient medical care records for adherence to established policies and procedures concerning provision of ambulatory health care services
   d. are completed on a quarterly basis to determine:
      (1) patient outcomes based on patient outcome standards
      (2) adequacy of the patient medical care
      (3) appropriateness of ambulatory health care services
   e. are conducted utilizing an outcome auditing and criteria system (see Exhibit 2005-1)
   f. are summarized quarterly utilizing an outcome auditing and criteria system (see Exhibit 2005-1)
2. Results of the outcome-oriented patient medical care reviews are reviewed by the Ambulatory Health Care Utilization Review Committee, Ambulatory Health Care Quality Assurance Committee, and Ambulatory Health Care Advisory Committee.
3. The Ambulatory Health Care Utilization Review Committee, Ambulatory Health Care Quality Assurance Committee, and Ambulatory Health Care Advisory Committee submit the following written report to the Administrator of Ambulatory Health Care: quarterly outcome-oriented patient medical care review results and recommendations for corrective action.
4. Problems identified through medical care reviews are referred to the Quality Assurance Manager for consideration as a continuous and special quality assurance activity/study.
5. Medical care review information is communicated to individuals, as appropriate, according to Policy and Procedure 1010: Confidentiality of Quality Assurance Information, and Policy and Procedure 1001: Administrative Control
6. Patient medical care reviews are filed in the ambulatory health care provider's Outcome-Oriented Review of Patient Medical Care administrative file.

Exhibit 2005-1 Example of Outcome Auditing and Criteria System

SCREENING QUESTIONS
DIABETIC ACIDOSIS

PT. NAME ________________ CLINIC ________________

PT. ID NO. ________________ BIRTHDATE ________ SEX ______ AGE ______

EFF. DATE OF HMO ENROLLMENT ____________ PRIM. M.D. ________________

HOSP. ________________ ADM. DATE ________ DISCH. DATE ________

CONSULTANT ________________

PRIM. DX. ________________

SEC. DX. ________________

SURG. PROCEDURES ________________

CODES: 250.1, 250.2, 250.3, 251

DEFINITION: All hospitalizations for diabetic acidosis with lab reports indicating blood sugar >250 mg./dl, arterial ph $\leq$ 7.30 or venous CO_2<12 and ketonuria or ketonemia.

DATA TO BE COLLECTED REGARDING OUTPATIENT CARE:	**YES**	**NO**
1. Was there a physician visit related to this diagnosis outside the hospital within 10 days prior to admission? (s = same day) Date ________	____	____
2. Was patient seen in ER within 10 days prior to admission? (s = same day) Date ________	____	____
3. Was there telephone contact related to this diagnosis within 10 days prior to admission? (s = same day) Date ________	____	____
4. Was diagnosis of ketoacidosis made more than 24 hours prior to admission?	____	____
5. Was patient a known diabetic?	____	____
6. Was there a history of any of the following within 10 days prior to admission? If yes, circle: a) infection; b) change in diet; c) trauma	____	____
7. Was there a history of any of the following within 10 days prior to admission? If yes, circle: a) weight loss; b) abdominal pain; c) polyuria; d) dehydration	____	____
8. Was patient on insulin prior to admission?	____	____
9. Was patient seen in outpatient setting for diabetes in last 6 months? Date last seen ________	____	____
10. Were blood sugars monitored by patient or clinic within 30 days prior to admission? (s = same day) Date ________	____	____
11. Was patient on home glucose monitoring or had they been instructed in glucose monitoring?	____	____
12. Was there follow-up care within 10 days after discharge? If yes, circle where it occurred: a) clinic; b) nursing home; c) home health care; d) other ________	____	____
13. Was there evidence of patient noncompliance with treatment plan (e.g., drugs, diet, follow-up visits)? If so, comment ________	____	____
14. Was there a readmission or mortality within 30 days after admission? Date ________ Diagnosis ________	____	____
15. Were there other admissions related to this diagnosis within 6 months before or after this admission? Date(s) ________ Diagnosis ________	____	____

☐ Check if comments on back.

continues

Exhibit 2005-1 *continued*

INSTRUCTIONS

"Primary M.D." is the physician who had seen the patient most frequently during the preceding year.

"Consultant(s)" are the one or more physicians, other than the primary care physician, seen either before hospitalization or during preceding year.

Record "yes" or "no" answers from information in either inpatient or outpatient record.

When Emergency Room (ER) is used, the term includes both hospital ER and urgent care clinics outside of hospitals.

When a question asks whether there was a documented history or symptom, record "yes" if there is documentation in chart to answer question in the affirmative; or "no" if there is documentation in chart to answer question in the negative or absence of data requested by the question.

Comments:

continues

Exhibit 2005-1 *continued*

REVIEW CRITERIA
DIABETIC ACIDOSIS

Computer review of answers to screening questions will identify cases with a high likelihood for problems in ambulatory care in the following categories:

1. **DELAYED DIAGNOSIS**		
*a.	1 = Yes (not s)	physician visit
	5 = Yes	patient known diabetic
	4 = No	diagnosis not made more than 24 hours prior to admission
	and one of the following	
	6 = Yes	infection, change in diet, trauma
	7 = Yes	weight loss, abdominal pain, polyuria, dehydration
*b.	2 = Yes (not s)	ER visit
	5 = Yes	patient known diabetic
	4 = No	diagnosis not made more than 24 hours prior to admission
	and one of the following	
	6 = Yes	infection, change in diet, trauma
	7 = Yes	weight loss, abdominal pain, polyuria, dehydration
2. **DELAYED ACCESS**		
*a.	3 = Yes (not s)	telephone contact related to diagnosis
	and one of the following	
	7 = Yes	diagnosis of weight loss, abdominal pain, polyuria, dehydration
	6 = Yes	infection, change in diet, trauma
	and	
	1 = No	no physician visit
3. **INADEQUATE SCREENING/MONITORING**		
a.	5 = Yes	known diabetic
	9 = No	patient not seen in 6 months
b.	8 = Yes	patient on insulin
	10 = No	blood sugar not monitored in 30 days
4. **DELAYED/INADEQUATE TREATMENT**		
*a.	4 = Yes	diagnosis made greater than 24 hours prior to admission
5. **INADEQUATE WORKUP/EVALUATION**		
*a.	1 = Yes (not s) or	physician visit or
	2 = Yes (not s)	ER visit
	5 = Yes	patient known diabetic
	and one of the following	
	7 = Yes	weight loss, abdominal pain, polyuria, dehydration
	6 = Yes	infection, change in diet, trauma
	and one of the following	
	11 = No (not s)	no home monitoring or instruction in monitoring
	13 = No	compliant patient
6. **INADEQUATE MANAGEMENT**		
*a.	15 = Yes	patient hospitalized for DKA within 6 months before or after admission
	11 = No	no home monitoring or instruction in monitoring
7. **INADEQUATE FOLLOW-UP**		
a.	12 = No	no follow-up in 10 days
8. **PATIENT COMPLIANCE**		
a.	13 = Yes	evidence of member noncompliance
9. **UNFAVORABLE OUTCOME**		
*a.	14 = Yes	patient readmitted or died within 30 days

continues

Exhibit 2005-1 *continued*

10. **DOCUMENTATION**

a. 6 = No	no documentation of infection, change in diet, trauma
b. 7 = No	no documentation of weight loss, abdominal pain, etc.

11. **STATISTICAL ANALYSIS**
# of cases with ER visits within 10 days prior to admission

*Charts needing physician review.

Source: Reprinted from *The Minnesota Project* with permission of Group Health Plan Inc., HMO Minnesota, and Share Health Plan, © 1987.

AMBULATORY HEALTH CARE PROVIDER
QUALITY ASSURANCE
POLICY AND PROCEDURE
2006

Subject: Patient Accident/Incident	
Drafted by: ______	Date drafted: ______
Revised by: ______	Date revised: ______
Approved by: ______	Date approved: ______
Supersedes date: ______	Page #: ______
Date effective: ______	Page: ______ of ______

POLICY

Patient accidents/incidents are reported and documented as soon as possible after the patient accident/incident occurs.

PURPOSE

1. To provide necessary timely intervention for patients involved in accidents/incidents.
2. To facilitate timely, accurate, and complete documentation of all patient accidents/incidents.
3. To implement a quality assurance monitoring system for patient accidents/incidents.

PROCEDURE

1. All patient accidents/incidents are reported as soon as possible to the attending physician and Nursing Manager.
2. Patients who have sustained an injury that requires immediate medical care are transferred to an acute care facility.
3. All patient accidents/incidents are documented on a Patient Accident/Incident Report Form (see Exhibit 2006-1).
4. The completed Patient Accident/Incident Report Form is submitted to the ambulatory health care staff member's immediate supervisor for review, investigation, corrective action, documentation, and signature.
5. The completed and reviewed Patient Accident/Incident Report Form is submitted to the Nursing Manager for review, investigation, corrective action, documentation, and signature.
6. The completed and reviewed Patient Accident/Incident Report Form is submitted to the Administrator of Ambulatory Health Care for review and signature.
7. Completed and reviewed Patient Accident/Incident Report Forms are summarized by the Administrative Assistant, using a Summary of Patient Accident/Incident Report Form (see Exhibit 2006-2).
8. The completed Summary of Patient Accident/Incident Report Form is submitted to the Risk Manager, Quality Assurance Manager, Ambulatory Health Care Risk Management Committee, Ambulatory Health Care Quality Assurance Committee, and Ambulatory Health Care Advisory Committee for their review and recommendations for selection of identified patient accident/incident problems as a quality assurance activity.
9. Patient accident/incident information is communicated to individuals, as appropriate, according to Policy and Procedure 1010: Confidentiality of Quality Assurance Information, and Policy and Procedure 1001: Administrative Control.
10. The completed and reviewed Patient Accident/Incident Report Form and Summary of Patient Accident/Incident Report Form are placed in the ambulatory health care provider's Patient Accident/Incident Report and Summary of Patient Accident/Incident Report administrative files.

Exhibit 2006-1 Patient Accident/Incident Report Form

AMBULATORY HEALTH CARE PROVIDER
PATIENT ACCIDENT/INCIDENT REPORT

I. General information (please complete below)

________________________ 1. Name of patient

________________________ 2. Age of patient

________________________ 3. Patient clinical record no.

________________________ 4. Date of actual patient accident/incident

________________________ A.M./P.M. 5. Time of actual patient accident/incident

________________________ 6. Location of patient accident/incident

________________________ 7. Name of individual(s) involved with patient accident/incident

____

________________________ 8. Address(es) of individual(s) involved with patient accident/incident

____

________________________ 9. Telephone number(s) of individual(s) involved with patient accident/incident

____

________________________ 10. Date of discovery of patient accident/incident

________________________ A.M./P.M. 11. Time of discovery of patient accident/incident

________________________ 12. Name of individual who discovered patient accident/incident

________________________ 13. Name of individual assigned to patient

________________________ 14a. Name of witness

________________________ 14b. Address of witness

________________________ 14c. Telephone number of witness

________________________ 15a. Name of witness

________________________ 15b. Address of witness

________________________ 15c. Telephone number of witness

________________________ 16. Description of patient injury

________________________ 17. Description of equipment involved

________________________ 18. Description of property involved

continues

Exhibit 2006-1 *continued*

II. Condition of patient environment (please check [√] below)

Patient/Environmental Conditions	Presence of Conditions		
	Yes	No	Please Explain As Appropriate
1. Call system available to patient?			
2. Call system used by patient?			
3. Bed rails ordered by physician?			
4. Bed rails on bed?			
5. Bed rails in "UP" position?			
6. Bed height adjustable?			
7. Bed height in low position?			
8. Environmental lighting adequate?			
9. Patient oriented to time?			
10. Patient oriented to place?			
11. Patient oriented to person?			
12. Patient under medication?			

III. Narrative description of patient accident/incident (please describe patient accident/incident below and include why and how accident/incident occurred, effect of accident/incident on patient, sequence of events, and any other pertinent information)

____

____

____

____

____

____

IV. Notification of individuals (please complete below)

Individuals Notified	Name of Individual Notified	Date Individual Notified	Time Individual Notified	Name of Individual Who Notified Others
1. Physician			A.M./P.M.	
2. Family			A.M./P.M.	
3. Nursing Manager			A.M./P.M.	
4. Administrator of Ambulatory Health Care			A.M./P.M.	

continues

Exhibit 2006-1 *continued*

V. Patient outcome (please complete below)

_____ a. Yes _____ b. No — 1. Patient seen by physician (please check [√] one; if No checked, please explain)

____

______________________________ 2. Date patient seen by physician

______________________________ A.M./P.M. 3. Time patient seen by physician

______________________________ 4. Intervention(s) implemented for patient

____

____

______________________________ 5. Physician statement of assessment/intervention and signature

____

____

____

_____ a. Yes _____ b. No — 6. Documentation completed in patient clinical record (please check [√] one; if *No* checked, please explain)

____

____

VI. Signatures (please sign below, as applicable)

Individuals	Comments	Signature	Date of Signature
1. Individual involved with patient accident/incident			
2. Individual(s) who discovered patient accident/incident			
3. Individual who completed this Patient Accident/Incident Report Form			
4. Physician			
5. Nursing Manager			
6. Administrator of Ambulatory Health Care			

Exhibit 2006-2 Summary of Patient Accident/Incident Report Form

AMBULATORY HEALTH CARE PROVIDER
SUMMARY OF PATIENT ACCIDENT/INCIDENT

Date This Form Completed	Dates of Reporting Period	Total Number of Patient Accident/Incident Forms Completed

	TOTAL NUMBER OF RESPONSES				
ITEM	**YES**	**NO**	**DON'T KNOW**	**N/A**	**COMMENTS**
I. Type of Patient Accident/Incident A. Patient falls 1. from bed					
2. from commode/toilet					
3. from wheelchair					
4. from chair					
5. on stairs					
6. on wet or slippery surface					
7. fainted					
8. tripped over object					
9. failed to seek assistance					
10. loss of balance					
11. seizure					
12. found on floor; details unknown					
13. other					
B. Patient injury 1. cut or injured by glass					
2. struck against equipment/object					
3. struck by equipment/object					
4. ill from food					
5. burn from fire or explosion					
6. burn from chemical					
7. burn from heated object					
8. burn from spilled food					
9. electrical shock					
10. cut by object/equipment/tool					
11. unexplained sore/cut/blister/burn					
12. other					
C. Patient/family action 1. altercation with family					
2. altercation with staff					
3. attempted suicide					
4. self-inflicted injury					
5. refused treatment					
6. violent/agitated					
7. violation of smoking regulation					
8. possession of illegal drugs					
9. chemical dependency					
10. failure to comply with treatment plan/physician orders					
11. failure to comply with provider policies and procedures					
12. verbal abuse toward staff					

continues

Exhibit 2006-2 *continued*

ITEM	TOTAL NUMBER OF RESPONSES: YES	NO	DON'T KNOW	N/A	COMMENTS
13. physical abuse toward staff					
14. sexual harassment/abuse toward staff					
15. misuse of equipment/supplies					
16. other					
D. Staff action/other					
1. failure to treat					
2. improper treatment method					
3. improper treatment					
4. failure to document					
5. illegible documentation					
6. incomplete documentation					
7. inadequate documentation content					
8. incorrect administration of oxygen					
9. misuse of equipment/supplies					
10. malfunction of equipment					
11. delay in treatment					
12. noncompliance with policy and procedure					
13. failure to obtain adequate consent					
14. wrong patient					
15. mislabeled specimen					
16. unlabeled specimen					
17. property damage/broken					
18. missing money					
19. missing articles					
20. other					
II. Location of Patient Accident/Incident					
1. bathroom					
2. hallway					
3. inside stairs/steps					
4. outside stairs/steps					
5. sidewalk/pathway					
6. parking lot					
7. other					

Shift When Patient Accident/Incident Occurred
___ Day ___ Evening ___ Night ___ Unknown

Individual Involved in Patient Accident/Incident
___ Patient ___ Family Member ___ Staff Member

Restraint:
___ Ordered; In Use ___ Not Ordered; In Use ___ Ordered; Not In Use ___ Not Ordered; Not in Use ___ Warranted; Not in Use ___ N/A

Wheelchair Brakes:
___ On ___ Off ___ N/A

X-ray Taken:
___ Yes; Positive Finding ___ Yes; Negative Finding ___ Not Ordered ___ N/A

Individual Involved Seen by Physician
___ Yes ___ No ___ Not Reported

Signature of Individual Completing This Form ______________________

Date of Signature ______________________

AMBULATORY HEALTH CARE PROVIDER
QUALITY ASSURANCE
POLICY AND PROCEDURE
2007

Subject: Patient Bill of Rights/Responsibilities	
Drafted by:	Date drafted:
Revised by:	Date revised:
Approved by:	Date approved:
Supersedes date:	Page #:
Date effective:	Page: ______ of

POLICY

Ambulatory health care provider staff members implement the patient bill of rights/responsibilities.

PURPOSE

1. To promote patient interests and well-being.
2. To ensure that patient civil and religious liberties are not infringed upon.

PROCEDURE

1. Each patient receiving ambulatory health care services from the provider is given information regarding the patient bill of rights/responsibilities in language the patient can reasonably be expected to understand.
2. The ambulatory health care registered nurse:
   a. reviews Patient Bill of Rights/Responsibilities Form (see Exhibit 2007-1)
   b. requests patient signature on Patient Bill of Rights/Responsibilities Form
   c. gives copy of signed Patient Bill of Rights/Responsibilities Form to patient
   d. places original signed Patient Bill of Rights/Responsibilities Form in patient's clinical record
   e. documents any patient refusal to sign the Patient Bill of Rights/Responsibilities Form
3. Patients are given prompt written information regarding changes in the ambulatory health care patient bill of rights/responsibilities.
4. The Patient Bill of Rights/Responsibilities Form is available upon request.
5. Patients are encouraged to complete a Patient Concerns Form if they believe that their rights have been infringed upon (see Policy and Procedure 2010: Patient Concerns).
6. The completed Patient Concerns Form is processed according to the ambulatory health care provider's policy and procedure.
7. Patients are encouraged to complete a Patient Evaluation of Ambulatory Health Care Services Form (see Policy and Procedure 2011: Patient Evaluation of Ambulatory Health Care Services).
8. The completed Patient Evaluation of Ambulatory Health Care Services Form is processed according to Policy and Procedure 2011: Patient Evaluation of Ambulatory Health Care Services.

Exhibit 2007-1 Patient's Bill of Rights/Responsibilities Form

AMBULATORY HEALTH CARE PATIENT'S BILL OF RIGHTS/RESPONSIBILITIES

As an ambulatory health care patient you have the right to:

1. Be given information about your rights and responsibilities for receiving ambulatory health care services.
2. Receive a timely appointment from the ambulatory health care provider regarding your request for ambulatory health care services.
3. Be given information of the ambulatory health care provider policies and procedures and charges for services, including your eligibility for third party reimbursement.
4. Be given information concerning available ambulatory care services, including after-hours and emergency services.
5. Choose your ambulatory health care providers.
6. Be given appropriate and professional quality ambulatory health care services without discrimination against your race, creed, color, religion, sex, national origin, sexual preference, handicap, or age.
7. Be treated with courtesy, respect, consideration, and dignity by all who provide ambulatory health care services to you.
8. Be free from physical and mental abuse and/or neglect.
9. Be given proper identification by name and title of everyone who provides ambulatory health care services to you.
10. Be given the necessary information so you will be able to give informed consent for your treatment prior to the start of any treatment.
11. Be given complete and current information concerning your diagnosis, treatment, alternatives, risks, and prognosis as required by your physician's legal duty to disclose, in terms and language you can reasonably be expected to understand.
12. A plan of ambulatory health care that will be developed to meet your unique health care needs.
13. Participate in the development of your ambulatory health care plan.
14. Be given an assessment and update of your developed ambulatory health care plan as necessary.
15. Be given data privacy and confidentiality.
16. Review your clinical record at your request.
17. Be given information regarding anticipated transfer of your ambulatory health care to another health care facility and/or termination of ambulatory health care services to you.
18. Voice grievance with and/or suggest change in ambulatory health care services and/or staff without being threatened, restrained, and discriminated against.
19. Refuse treatment within the confines of the law.
20. Refuse to participate in experimental research.
21. Be given information concerning the consequences of refusing treatment or not complying with therapy.

As an ambulatory health care patient you have the responsibility to:

1. Give accurate and complete health information concerning your past illnesses, hospitalization, medications, allergies, and other pertinent items.
2. Assist in maintaining a safe environment.
3. Inform the ambulatory health care provider when you will not be able to keep an ambulatory health care visit.
4. Participate in the development and update of your ambulatory health care plan.
5. Adhere to your developed/updated ambulatory health care plan.
6. Request further information concerning anything you do not understand.
7. Give information regarding concerns and problems you have to an ambulatory health care provider staff member.

I have reviewed and understand my bill of rights/responsibilities as described above.

SIGNATURE OF PATIENT	DATE OF SIGNATURE
SIGNATURE OF AMBULATORY HEALTH CARE PROVIDER REPRESENTATIVE	DATE OF SIGNATURE

AMBULATORY HEALTH CARE PROVIDER
QUALITY ASSURANCE
POLICY AND PROCEDURE
2008

Subject: Patient Case Conferences

Drafted by: ________	Date drafted: ________
Revised by: ________	Date revised: ________
Approved by: ________	Date approved: ________
Supersedes date: ________	Page #: ________
Date effective: ________	Page: ____ of ________

POLICY

Ambulatory health care staff members provide coordination of patient services to establish effective interchange, reporting, and coordinated patient evaluation through patient case conferences.

PURPOSE

To provide complementary services that support patient plan of care objectives.

PROCEDURE

1. Patient case conferences are conducted as necessary.
2. Participation in patient case conferences includes, but is not limited to, all personnel providing services to patients, including:
   a. Nursing Manager
   b. primary care physician
   c. ambulatory health care registered nurse
   d. physical therapist
   e. occupational therapist
   f. speech therapist
   g. social worker
3. The coordinator of patient case conferences is the Nursing Manager.
4. Subjects discussed in patient case conferences include, but are not limited to, the following:
   a. patient assessment
   b. patient intervention
   c. patient reassessment based on patient intervention
   d. development/implementation of patient care plans, covering:
      (1) pertinent patient diagnosis
      (2) patient mental status
      (3) types of ambulatory health care services and equipment required
      (4) frequency of patient visits
      (5) patient prognosis
      (6) patient rehabilitation potential
      (7) patient functional limitations
      (8) patient activities permitted
      (9) patient nutritional requirements
      (10) patient medications and treatments
      (11) safety measures to protect against patient injury
      (12) instructions for timely patient referral
      (13) patient vulnerability to abuse and/or neglect
      (14) other appropriate items
   e. evaluation of patient treatment plan
5. Content and results of patient case conferences are documented on a Patient Case Conference Minutes Form (see Exhibit 2008-1).
6. The completed Patient Case Conference Minutes Form is placed in the ambulatory health care provider's Patient Case Conference Minutes administrative file.
7. Appropriate documentation of patient case conferences, establishing that effective interchange, reporting, and coordinated patient evaluation have occurred, is made in the patient clinical record.

Exhibit 2008-1 Patient Case Conference Minutes Form

AMBULATORY HEALTH CARE PROVIDER
PATIENT CASE CONFERENCE MINUTES

Meeting Date:__________ Meeting Time:__________ Meeting Place:__________

Individuals Present:__________

ISSUE	DISCUSSION	ACTION

AMBULATORY HEALTH CARE PROVIDER
QUALITY ASSURANCE
POLICY AND PROCEDURE
2009

Subject: Patient Case Management

Drafted by: ______	Date drafted: ______
Revised by: ______	Date revised: ______
Approved by: ______	Date approved: ______
Supersedes date: ______	Page #: ______
Date effective: ______	Page: ______ of ______

POLICY

Case management is provided for ambulatory health care patients who require management of their care according to ambulatory health care provider policies and procedures.

PURPOSE

To ensure efficient and effective case management, as necessary.

PROCEDURE

1. Ambulatory health care registered nurses provide patient case management according to ambulatory care provider policies and procedures.
2. The Ambulatory Health Care Registered Nurse:
   a. answers patient and patient family questions and concerns relative to ambulatory health care
   b. requests the patient's signature on appropriate forms
   c. implements a comprehensive nursing assessment of the patient
   d. develops and implements a patient nursing plan of care based on the initial nursing assessment and the attending physician's plan of care
   e. gives information regarding the patient plan of care to the patient and patient family
   f. obtains and implements the physician's orders
   g. orients the patient ambulatory health care staff member to the health care assignment and tasks
   h. informs the Nursing Manager of pertinent information regarding the patient
   i. discusses the patient case's management in the first patient case conference as necessary following Policy and Procedure 2008: Patient Case Conferences
   j. documents the following in patient clinical records:
      (1) a comprehensive patient nursing assessment on an Ambulatory Health Care Patient Nursing Assessment Form (see Exhibit 2009-1).
      (2) the nursing plan of care and patient outcomes in patient clinical record
      (3) implemented physician orders and patient outcomes
      (4) appropriate information relative to the patient

Exhibit 2009-1 Ambulatory Health Care Patient Nursing Assessment Form

AMBULATORY HEALTH CARE PROVIDER
AMBULATORY HEALTH CARE PATIENT NURSING ASSESSMENT

I. General information (please complete below)

______________________ 1. Name of patient

______________________ 2. Address of patient:

______________________ city, state, zip code

______________________ 3. Telephone number of patient

______________________ 4. Patient clinical record number

______________________ 5. Birthdate of patient

______________________ 6. Age of patient

______________________ 7. Sex of patient

______________________ 8. Date of patient admission

______________________ 9. Name of individual referring patient to the ambulatory health care provider

______________________ 10. Name of agency referring patient to the ambulatory health care provider

______________________ 11. Discharge date of patient's most recent hospitalization

______________________ 12. Name of hospital from which patient most recently discharged

______________________ 13. Address of hospital from which patient most recently discharged: city, state, zip code

____

______________________ 14. Other

II. Social information (please complete below)

______________________ 1. Name of patient's informal caregiver

______________________ 2. Address of patient's informal caregiver:

______________________ city, state, zip code

______________________ 3. Telephone number of patient's informal caregiver

Home Work

______________________ 4. Name of patient's closest relative

______________________ 5. Address of patient's closest relative:

______________________ city, state, zip code

______________________ 6. Telephone number of patient's closest relative

Home Work

continues

Exhibit 2009-1 *continued*

III. Medical information (please complete below)

______________________	1. Principal diagnosis of patient
______________________	2. Secondary diagnosis(es) of patient
______________________	
______________________	3. Significant identified problem(s) of patient
______________________	
______________________	4. Significant current medical history of patient
______________________	
______________________	5. Significant past medical history of patient
______________________	
______________________	6. Name, dose, and administration times of medications patient currently taking
______________________	
______________________	
______________________	
______________________	7. Medication allergies of patient
______________________	8. Food allergies of patient
______________________	9. Other allergies of patient
______________________	10. Name of patient's attending physician
______________________	11. Address of patient's attending physician:
______________________	city, state, zip code
______________________ Home Work	12. Telephone number of patient's attending physician
________ Yes (please describe)	13. Equipment required for patient (please check [√] one)
______________________	
________ No	
______________________	14. Other

continues

Exhibit 2009-1 *continued*

Patient Outcome Code Letters

1	=	Nursing action planned for patient.
2	=	Nursing action implemented for patient.
3	=	Medical order implemented for patient.
4	=	Implemented medical order evaluated.
5	=	Verbal information given to patient.
6	=	Written information given to patient.
7	=	Verbal information given to patient's informal caregiver.
8	=	Written information given to patient's informal caregiver.
9	=	Verbal information reviewed with patient.
10	=	Written information reviewed with patient.
11	=	Verbal information reviewed with patient's informal caregiver.
12	=	Written information reviewed with patient's informal caregiver.
13	=	Verbal information repeated by patient.
14	=	Written information repeated by patient.
15	=	Verbal information repeated by patient's informal caregiver.
16	=	Written information repeated by patient's informal caregiver.
17	=	Demonstration given to patient.
18	=	Demonstration given to patient's informal caregiver.
19	=	Demonstration repeated by patient.
20	=	Demonstration repeated by patient's informal caregiver.
21	=	Patient demonstrates independent functioning.
22	=	Patient's informal caregiver demonstrates independent functioning.
23	=	Patient pursuing established care plan.
24	=	Patient not pursuing established care plan.
25	=	Patient's informal caregiver pursuing established care plan.
26	=	Patient significant other not pursuing established care plan.
27	=	Other.

continues

Exhibit 2009-1 *continued*

	First Assessment				Second Assessment				Third Assessment				Fourth Assessment			
	Date:				Date:				Date:				Date:			
	Yes	No	NA	Comments	Yes	No	NA	Comments	Yes	No	NA	Comments	Yes	No	NA	Comments
I. Social history A. Environment 1. Living space adequate																
2. Clean																
3. Safe																
4. Other																
B. Emotional 1. Accepts diagnosis																
2. Altered body image																
3. Using appropriate coping mechanisms																
4. Seeks support from significant others																
5. Other																
C. Spiritual 1. Seeks spiritual support				Religion: ________												
2. Altered ability to participate in religious activities																
3. Resistive to nursing medical interventions based on religious beliefs																
4. Seeks meaning in illness and life experience																
5. Other																
D. Education 1. Speaks English																
2. Illness interfering with educational commitments																
3. Other																
E. Vulnerable to abuse and/or neglect 1. Expresses vulnerability to abuse and/or neglect				Refer to completed Assessment for Patient Vulnerability to Abuse and/or Neglect form				Refer to completed Assessment for Patient Vulnerability to Abuse and/or Neglect form				Refer to completed Assessment for Patient Vulnerability to Abuse and/or Neglect form				Refer to completed Assessment for Patient Vulnerability to Abuse and/or Neglect form
2. Other																

continues

Exhibit 2009-1 *continued*

	First Assessment				Second Assessment				Third Assessment				Fourth Assessment			
	Date:				Date:				Date:				Date:			
	Yes	No	NA	Comments	Yes	No	NA	Comments	Yes	No	NA	Comments	Yes	No	NA	Comments
F. Financial 1. Employed																
2. Significant other employed																
3. Illness interfering with employment commitments																
4. Illness interfering with financial commitments																
5. Other																
II. Activities of daily living A. Needs assistance in: 1. Mobility																
2. Hygiene																
3. Dressing																
4. Feeding																
5. Shopping																
6. Meal preparation																
7. Housework																
8. Laundry																
9. Other																
B. Sleep 1. Sleeps adequately; awakes rested				Hours of sleep/night: ______				Hours of sleep/night: ______				Hours of sleep/night: ______				Hours of sleep/night: ______
2. Naps at intervals				Number of naps: ___ Length of naps: ___ Pattern of naps:				Number of naps: ___ Length of naps: ___ Pattern of naps:				Number of naps: ___ Length of naps: ___ Pattern of naps:				Number of naps: ___ Length of naps: ___ Pattern of naps:
3. Has difficulty falling asleep																
4. Has difficulty waking up																
5. Frequently awakes at night																
6. Other																

C. Leisure activities 1. Reads																
2. Watches TV																
3. Plays games																
4. Does handiwork																
5. Illness interfering with leisure activities																
6. Plays cards																
7. Has visitors																
8. Other																
D. Habits 1. Uses alcohol				Amount of alcohol intake/day: ____ Frequency of alcohol intake/day: ____ Usual timeframe of alcohol intake: ____				Amount of alcohol intake/day: ____ Frequency of alcohol intake/day: ____ Usual timeframe of alcohol intake: ____				Amount of alcohol intake/day: ____ Frequency of alcohol intake/day: ____ Usual timeframe of alcohol intake: ____				Amount of alcohol intake/day: ____ Frequency of alcohol intake/day: ____ Usual timeframe of alcohol intake: ____
2. Alcohol use interfering with normal functioning																
3. Uses tobacco				Amount of tobacco used/day: ____				Amount of tobacco used/day: ____				Amount of tobacco used/day: ____				Amount of tobacco used/day: ____
4. Tobacco use interfering with normal functioning																
5. Uses drugs				Amount of drug intake/day: ____ Frequency of drug intake/day: ____ Usual timeframe of drug intake: ____				Amount of drug intake/day: ____ Frequency of drug intake/day: ____ Usual timeframe of drug intake: ____				Amount of drug intake/day: ____ Frequency of drug intake/day: ____ Usual timeframe of drug intake: ____				Amount of drug intake/day: ____ Frequency of drug intake/day: ____ Usual timeframe of drug intake: ____
6. Drug use interfering with normal functioning																
7. Other																
III. Body systems review A. Skin 1. Color adequate																
2. Texture adequate																
3. Turgor adequate																
4. Temperature normal																
5. Has rash																
6. Has lesions																
7. Has petechiae																
8. Has bruises																
9. Has abrasions																
10. Has deep open wound																
11. Has pressure area																
12. Other																

continues

Exhibit 2009-1 *continued*

	First Assessment				Second Assessment				Third Assessment				Fourth Assessment			
	Date:				Date:				Date:				Date:			
	Yes	No	NA	Comments	Yes	No	NA	Comments	Yes	No	NA	Comments	Yes	No	NA	Comments
B. Vision 1. Vision adequate				Date of previous eye exam: ____ Previous eye exam done by: ____												
2. Wears glasses																
3. Wears contacts																
4. Has blurred vision																
5. Has diplopia																
6. Has eye pain																
7. Has eye inflammation																
8. Has eye discharge																
9. Has cataracts																
10. Has glaucoma																
11. Other																
C. Hearing 1. Hearing adequate																
2. Has limitations imposed by hearing deficit																
3. Wears hearing aid																
4. Has ear pain																
5. Has tinnitus																
6. Has ear discharge																
7. Has cerumen buildup																
8. Other																
D. Speech 1. Tone quality adequate																
2. Pace adequate																
3. Clarity adequate																
4. Sentence structure adequate																
5. Voice strength adequate																
6. Illness interfering with speech																
7. Other																

E. Respiratory 1. Pattern normal				Respiratory rate: ____ Respiratory rhythm: ____ Lung Sound: Left: ____ Right: ____				Respiratory rate: ____ Respiratory rhythm: ____ Lung Sound: Left: ____ Right: ____				Respiratory rate: ____ Respiratory rhythm: ____ Lung Sound: Left: ____ Right: ____				Respiratory rate: ____ Respiratory rhythm: ____ Lung Sound: Left: ____ Right: ____
2. Has pain																
3. Has dyspnea																
4. Has cough																
5. Has sputum drainage																
6. Has frequent epistaxis																
7. Has frequent URI																
8. Current chest x-ray done				Date chest x-ray done: ____ Where chest x-ray done: ____ Chest x-ray results: ____												
9. Other																
F. Cardiovascular 1. Circulation adequate				B.P.: ____ (L) ____ (R) ____ Apical pulse: ____ Pulse rhythm: ____				B.P.: ____ (L) ____ (R) ____ Apical pulse: ____ Pulse rhythm: ____				B.P.: ____ (L) ____ (R) ____ Apical pulse: ____ Pulse rhythm: ____				B.P.: ____ (L) ____ (R) ____ Apical pulse: ____ Pulse rhythm: ____
2. Has edema																
3. Has dizziness																
4. Has syncope																
5. Has chest pain																
6. Has palpitations																
7. Has neck vein distension																
8. Has pacemaker																
9. Other																
G. Mouth 1. Has normal appearance																
2. Has mouth odor																
3. Has swollen and/or bleeding gums																
4. Has coated tongue																
5. Has mouth lesions																
6. Has natural teeth																
7. Has missing teeth																
8. Wears dentures																
9. Has difficulty chewing																
10. Other																

continues

Exhibit 2009-1 *continued*

	First Assessment				Second Assessment				Third Assessment				Fourth Assessment			
	Date:				Date:				Date:				Date:			
	Yes	No	NA	Comments	Yes	No	NA	Comments	Yes	No	NA	Comments	Yes	No	NA	Comments
H. Throat/neck 1. Has sore throat																
2. Has difficulty swallowing																
3. Has hoarseness																
4. Has enlarged nodes																
5. Other																
I. Gastrointestinal 1. Nutrition adequate																
2. Solid intake adequate																
3. Liquid intake adequate																
4. Appetite adequate																
5. Has meal/snack pattern																
6. Weight adequate				Current weight: ___ Current height: ___ Past weight: ___ Past height: ___				Current weight: ___				Current weight: ___				Current weight: ___
7. Has recent weight change																
8. Has diet restriction				Diet type: ___				Diet type: ___				Diet type: ___				Diet type: ___
9. Has food allergies																
10. Has altered method of solid/liquid intake																
11. Has excessive thirst																
12. Has nausea																
13. Has vomiting																
14. Has indigestion																
15. Has abdominal pain																
16. Has abdominal distension																
17. Requires adaptive equipment for eating																
18. Elimination adequate				Stool color: ___ Stool consistency: ___ Stool frequency: ___				Stool color: ___ Stool consistency: ___ Stool frequency: ___				Stool color: ___ Stool consistency: ___ Stool frequency: ___				Stool color: ___ Stool consistency: ___ Stool frequency: ___
19. Bowel sounds present																
20. Bowel pattern adequate																
21. Has constipation																

22. Has diarrhea																
23. Has flatulence																
24. Has stool incontinence																
25. Has ostomy																
26. Uses laxatives																
27. Uses enemas																
28. Has hemorrhoids																
29. Currently on bowel program																
30. Other																
J. Urinary 1. Voids adequately				Urine color: ____ Voiding frequency: ____ Urine amount: ____				Urine color: ____ Voiding frequency: ____ Urine amount: ____				Urine color: ____ Voiding frequency: ____ Urine amount: ____				Urine color: ____ Voiding frequency: ____ Urine amount: ____
2. Urine odor normal																
3. Voids with pain/burning																
4. Has urgency to void																
5. Has difficulty in starting stream of urine																
6. Voids frequently at night																
7. Incontinent of urine																
8. Uses catheter				Catheter size: ____ Catheter type: ____ Reason for catheter: ____ Date catheter inserted: ____ Date catheter removed: ____				Catheter size: ____ Catheter type: ____ Reason for catheter: ____ Date catheter inserted: ____ Date catheter removed: ____				Catheter size: ____ Catheter type: ____ Reason for catheter: ____ Date catheter inserted: ____ Date catheter removed: ____				Catheter size: ____ Catheter type: ____ Reason for catheter: ____ Date catheter inserted: ____ Date catheter removed: ____
9. Has ostomy																
10. Other																
K. Neurological 1. Current mental status a. Oriented to time																
b. Oriented to place																
c. Oriented to person																
d. Forgetful																
e. Hallucinations																
f. Other																

continues

Exhibit 2009-1 *continued*

	First Assessment				Second Assessment				Third Assessment				Fourth Assessment			
	Date:				Date:				Date:				Date:			
	Yes	No	NA	Comments	Yes	No	NA	Comments	Yes	No	NA	Comments	Yes	No	NA	Comments
2. Past mental status a. Oriented to time																
b. Oriented to place																
c. Oriented to person																
d. Forgetful																
e. Hallucinations																
f. Other																
3. Current behavior a. Cooperative																
b. Anxious																
c. Depressed																
d. Demanding																
e. Distrustful																
f. Talkative																
g. Withdrawn																
h. Nervous																
i. Other																
4. Past behavior a. Cooperative																
b. Anxious																
c. Depressed																
d. Demanding																
e. Distrustful																
f. Talkative																
g. Withdrawn																
h. Nervous																
i. Other																
5. Has mood changes																
6. Has behavior changes																
7. Has seizures																
8. Unconscious																
9. Other																

10. Motor a. Has steady gait																
b. Has weakness																
c. Has balance problems																
d. Has paralysis																
e. Has paresis																
f. Has tic																
g. Has tremor																
h. Has spasm																
i. Hand grasps adequate																
j. PERL																
11. Sensory a. Has pain																
b. Has paresthesia																
c. Has tingling/numbness																
d. Other																
L. Musculoskeletal 1. Muscle a. Muscle function adequate																
b. Has muscle cramping/ spasm																
c. Has muscle pain																
d. Has muscle weakness																
e. Has back pain																
f. Other																
2. Bones/joints a. Has joint stiffness																
b. Has joint swelling																
c. Has joint redness																
d. Has joint pain																
e. Has recent injury																
f. Has limitation in range of motion																
g. Other																
3. Has amputated extremities																
4. Uses prosthesis																
5. Other																

continues

Exhibit 2009-1 *continued*

	First Assessment				Second Assessment				Third Assessment				Fourth Assessment			
	Date:				Date:				Date:				Date:			
	Yes	No	NA	Comments	Yes	No	NA	Comments	Yes	No	NA	Comments	Yes	No	NA	Comments
M. Reproductive 1. Reproductive function adequate																
2. Performs self-breast exam																
3. Has breast discharge																
4. Has breast mass																
5. Has breast pain																
6. Has breast dimpling																
7. Has genital lesions																
8. Has labia/testical mass																
9. Has genital pain																
10. Has genital swelling																
11. Has prostrate problems																
12. Has vaginal/penile discharge																
13. Has alteration in sexual activity																
14. Has menses problems																
15. Has menopause problem																
16. Other																

Signature of Nurse	Signature of Nurse	Signature of Nurse	Signature of Nurse
Date of Signature	Date of Signature	Date of Signature	Date of Signature

AMBULATORY HEALTH CARE PROVIDER
QUALITY ASSURANCE
POLICY AND PROCEDURE
2010

Subject: Patient Concerns

Drafted by: ______	Date drafted: ______
Revised by: ______	Date revised: ______
Approved by: ______	Date approved: ______
Supersedes date: ______	Page #: ______
Date effective: ______	Page: ____ of ______

POLICY

Ambulatory health care staff members encourage patients to express their concerns freely.

PURPOSE

To ensure quality ambulatory health care consistent with the ambulatory health care provider's philosophy.

PROCEDURE

1. Ambulatory health care staff members:
   a. listen to concerns expressed by patients
   b. encourage patients to contact the Administrator of Ambulatory Health Care to discuss patient concerns
   c. give Patient Concerns Form (see Exhibit 2010-1) to patients, and request the patients to complete the form
   d. assist patients in returning the completed Patient Concerns Form to the Administrator of Ambulatory Health Care
   e. give information regarding expressed patient concerns to the Administrator of Ambulatory Health Care
2. The Administrator of Ambulatory Health Care:
   a. reviews the completed Patient Concerns Form
   b. delegates the Patient Concerns Form to the appropriate manager for investigation and corrective action
   c. refers the patient concern for a quality assurance activity/study based on the manager's recommendation, as appropriate
   d. summarizes completed Patient Concern Forms using a Summary of Patient Concerns Form (see Exhibit 2010-2)
3. The manager:
   a. reviews the completed Patient Concerns Form
   b. initiates problem-solving process to deal with patient concerns:
      (1) informs patient that the patient's concern has been received and reviewed using a Receipt of Patient Concern Letter Form (see Exhibit 2010-3)
      (2) determines exact nature of concern with patient
      (3) assesses probable cause of patient's concern
      (4) plans appropriate corrective action
      (5) implements corrective action plan
      (6) evaluates implemented corrective action plan to determine if patient's concern has been alleviated
      (7) informs patient that the patient's concern has been investigated and corrective action has been implemented, as necessary, using an Outcome of Patient Concern Letter Form (see Exhibit 2010-4)
      (8) gives information regarding expressed patient concern
      (9) recommends patient concern for a quality assurance activity/study, as appropriate
4. Problems identified from patient concerns are referred to the Quality Assurance Manager for consideration as a continuous or special quality assurance activity/study.
5. Patient concerns are communicated to individuals, as appropriate, according to Policy and Procedure 1010: Confidentiality of Quality Assurance Information, and Policy and Procedure 1001: Administrative Control.
6. Completed quality assurance activities relative to patient concerns are filed in the ambulatory health care provider's Patient Concern Quality Assurance Activity administrative file.

Exhibit 2010-1 Patient Concerns Form

AMBULATORY HEALTH CARE PROVIDER
PATIENT CONCERNS

The ambulatory health care provider staff strive to ensure quality ambulatory health care for patients that is consistent with the ambulatory health care provider philosophy. In order to assist the ambulatory health care staff in addressing your concerns, you are being asked to complete this form. Please promptly complete and return this form to the Administrator of Ambulatory Health Care. Upon receipt of your completed form, you will receive a verbal/written response. Thank you for your assistance in our continuing efforts to provide quality ambulatory health care services to you.

Following Section To Be Completed by Individual Reporting the Concern

Name of Individual(s) Involved in Incident	Date of Incident	Time of Incident A.M. P.M.
Place of Incident	Date This Form Completed	Time This Form Completed A.M. P.M.
Name of Individual Completing This Patient Concern Form	Telephone No. Where Individual Completing This Patient Concern Form Can Be Reached During the Day	

Address of Individual Who Is Completing This Form (Street, City, State, Zip Code)

Objective Narrative Description of Incident (please describe below)

Signature of Individual Completing This Form	Date of Signature

continues

Exhibit 2010-1 *continued*

Following Section To Be Completed by Manager Reviewing Identified Concern

Date This Form Received Completed	Date This Form Reviewed Completed	Time This Completed Form Reviewed A.M. P.M.

Description of Incident Investigation (please describe below)

Description of Identified Problem(s) Resulting from Incident (please describe below)

Corrective Action Implemented? ____ yes ____ no (please explain)	Date Corrective Action Implemented

Description of Implemented Corrective Action (please describe below)

Description of Outcome(s) Resulting from Corrective Action (please describe below)

Identified Problem(s) Recommended for Quality Assurance Activity?
____ yes ____ no (please explain) ____

Signature of Manager	Date of Signature

Following Section To Be Completed by Administrator of Ambulatory Health Care

Identified Problem(s) Referred for Quality Assurance Activity?
____ yes ____ no (please explain) ____

Signature of Administrator of Ambulatory Health Care	Date of Signature

Exhibit 2010-2 Summary of Patient Concerns Form

AMBULATORY HEALTH CARE PROVIDER
SUMMARY OF PATIENT CONCERNS

Date This Form Completed	Dates of Reporting Period	Total Number of Patient Concerns Forms Completed

Item	Total Number of Responses	Comments
I. Identified patient concern A. Inadequate Provision of Quality/Safe Health Care 1. Failure to diagnose		
2. Failure to diagnose appropriately		
3. Failure to treat		
4. Failure to treat appropriately		
5. Failure to monitor results of diagnostic tests/x-rays		
6. Failure to adequately monitor results of diagnostic tests/x-rays		
7. Failure to inform patient of diagnostic test/x-ray results		
8. Failure to provide intervention for patient based on diagnostic test/x-ray results		
9. Failure to provide appropriate intervention for patient based on diagnostic test/x-ray results		
10. Other		
B. Inadequate Provision of Available/Accessible Health Care 1. Failure to provide patient with timely appointment		
2. Failure to provide health care services in a timely manner		
3. Failure to provide after office hours health care services		
4. Failure to provide emergency health care services		
5. Failure to provide emergency health care services in an expedient manner		
6. Failure to provide appropriate referrals		
7. Failure to provide adequate telephone services for health care questions, concerns, & follow-up		
8. Other		
C. Inadequate Administration of Health Care 1. Failure of staff to communicate adequately		
2. Failure of staff to answer questions adequately		
3. Failure of staff to listen adequately		
4. Failure of staff to demonstrate respectful attitude		
5. Failure of staff to provide safe environment		
6. Failure of staff to provide adequate clinical record documentation		
7. Failure of staff to respect patient rights		
8. Other		
D. Other		

continues

Exhibit 2010-2 *continued*

Item	Total Number of Responses	Comments
II. Identified Individuals Involved with Patient Concern A. Physician staff member		
B. Nursing staff member		
C. Laboratory staff member		
D. Radiology staff member		
E. Pharmacy staff member		
F. Physical Therapist		
G. Occupational Therapist		
H. Speech Therapist		
I. Social Worker		
J. Clerical/Reception Staff Member		
K. Administrative/Management Staff Member		
L. Other		
III. Identified Department Involved with Patient Concern A. Administrative Services		
B. Allergy		
C. Cardiology		
D. Chemical Dependency		
E. Dermatology		
F. Gastroenterology		
G. Endocrinology		
H. Family Practice		
I. Internal Medicine		
J. Laboratory Services		
K. Mental Health		
L. Nephrology		
M. Neurology		
N. Nursing Services		
O. Obstetrics/Gynecology		
P. Occupational Therapy Services		
Q. Oncology		
R. Ophthalmology		
S. Optometry		
T. Orthopedics		
U. Pediatrics		
V. Pharmacy Services		
W. Physical Therapy Services		
X. Podiatry		
Y. Pulmonary		
Z. Radiology Services		

continues

Exhibit 2010-2 *continued*

Item	Total Number of Responses	Comments
A1. Rheumatology		
B1. Social Services		
C1. Speech Therapy Services		
D1. Surgery		
E1. Urology		
F1. Other		
IV. Other		

Signature of Individual Completing This Form	Date of Signature

Exhibit 2010-3 Receipt of Patient Concern Letter Form

(Date)

(Patient Name and Address)

Dear (Patient Name):

We have received information that the services provided to you were apparently unsatisfactory.

We encourage patient comments about the services provided by the ambulatory health care provider's employees and appreciate the time you have taken to share your concern(s).

We will be investigating the concern(s) you identified. When we have completed our investigation, we will send you a written response to your concern(s).

Please contact me if you have any questions.

Sincerely,

Administrator of Ambulatory Health Care

Exhibit 2010-4 Outcome of Patient Concern Letter Form

(Date)

(Patient Name and Address)

Dear (Patient Name):

We have concluded our investigation of the concern(s) you identified.

As a result of our investigation, corrective action (was/was not) implemented to address your concern(s).

Thank you for bringing your concern(s) to our attention. It is very important for us to ensure that we continue to provide quality and safe ambulatory health care services.

Please contact me if you have additional questions or concerns.

Sincerely,

Administrator of Ambulatory Health Care

AMBULATORY HEALTH CARE PROVIDER
QUALITY ASSURANCE
POLICY AND PROCEDURE
2011

Subject: Patient Evaluation of Ambulatory Health Care Services

Drafted by: ____________	Date drafted: ____________
Revised by: ____________	Date revised: ____________
Approved by: ____________	Date approved: ____________
Supersedes date: ____________	Page #: ____________
Date effective: ____________	Page: ______ of ____________

POLICY

The ambulatory health care provider provides opportunities for patients to evaluate ambulatory health care services that have been provided to patients.

PURPOSE

1. To collect and assess information regarding patient satisfaction with the ambulatory health care provider's services.
2. To implement a quality assurance monitoring system to address patient concerns.
3. To enhance ambulatory health care provider and patient relationships.

PROCEDURE

1. Ambulatory Health Care Staff members distribute and encourage Ambulatory Health Care patients who have received Ambulatory Health Care Services to complete a Patient Evaluation of Ambulatory Health Care Services Form (see Exhibit 2011-1)
2. Completed Patient Evaluation of Ambulatory Health Care Services Forms are submitted to the Administrative Assistant.
3. The Administrative Assistant:
   a. summarizes the returned, completed Patient Evaluation of Ambulatory Health Care Services Form using a Summary of Patient Evaluation of Ambulatory Health Care Services Form (see Exhibit 2011-2)
   b. gives returned Patient Evaluation of Ambulatory Health Care Services Form and Summary of Patient Evaluation of Ambulatory Health Care Services Form to the Nursing Manager
4. The Nursing Manager:
   a. reviews submitted Patient Evaluation of Ambulatory Health Care Services Form and Summary of Patient Evaluation of Ambulatory Health Care Services Form
   b. implements immediate corrective action, as necessary, based on identified patient concerns
5. Problems identified from patient evaluation of ambulatory health care services are referred to the Quality Assurance Manager for consideration as a continuous or special quality assurance activity/study.
6. Patient evaluation of ambulatory health care services is communicated to individuals, as appropriate, according to Policy and Procedure 1010: Confidentiality of Quality Assurance Information, and Policy and Procedure 1001: Administrative Control.
7. The completed Patient Evaluation of Ambulatory Health Care Services Form and Summary of Patient Evaluation of Ambulatory Health Care Services Form are filed in the ambulatory health care provider's Patient Evaluation of Ambulatory Health Care Services and Summary of Patient Evaluation of Ambulatory Health Care Services administrative files.

Exhibit 2011-1 Patient Evaluation of Ambulatory Health Care Services Form

PATIENT EVALUATION OF AMBULATORY HEALTH CARE SERVICES

Dear Patient: We strive to provide quality care for our patients and would sincerely appreciate your completing this questionnaire. We want to know if you feel that **you** received quality ambulatory health care services. Your reply will be held in strict confidence. Please complete and return this form to the ambulatory health care provider administrative staff. Thank you for assistance in our efforts to provide quality care services.

ITEM	RESPONSE (Please √ appropriate response.)			
	YES	NO	DON'T KNOW	COMMENTS
1. There was a timely response to my initial request for ambulatory health care services.				
2. The staff was prompt in providing services to me.				
3. Staff members identified themselves as ambulatory health care providers by stating their names and titles.				
4. A bill of patient rights was given and explained to me.				
5. The staff members competently demonstrated their professional skills and expertise.				
6. The staff was courteous to me.				
7. The staff gave me privacy whenever necessary.				
8. The staff portrayed a positive and helpful attitude toward me.				
9. The staff was adequately groomed and dressed.				
10. The staff promptly and adequately responded to my needs, concerns, and problems.				
11. My transfer from the ambulatory health care facility was efficient.				
12. The staff gave me adequate information about the charges for ambulatory health care services.				
13. The staff kept me informed about the financial status of my bill.				
14. I would use your services in the future, if necessary.				
15. I would recommend your ambulatory health care services to other individuals.				

Types of services that were provided to me:

☐ Physician ☐ Radiology ☐ Physical Therapy ☐ Other (Please describe)

☐ Nursing ☐ Pharmacy ☐ Occupational Therapy

☐ Laboratory ☐ Social Services ☐ Speech Therapy

Length of time I received ambulatory health care services from your provider.

☐ 0-4 Months ☐ 8-12 Months ☐ 16-20 Months ☐ 24-28 Months ☐ 32-36 Months

☐ 4-8 Months ☐ 12-16 Months ☐ 20-24 Months ☐ 28-32 Months ☐ Over 36 Months

Your Name (Optional)

Source: Reprinted with permission of Briggs Corporation, Des Moines, Iowa, © 1989.

Exhibit 2011-2 Summary of Patient Evaluation of Ambulatory Health Care Services Form

AMBULATORY HEALTH CARE PROVIDER
SUMMARY OF PATIENT EVALUATION OF AMBULATORY HEALTH CARE SERVICES

Date This Form Completed	Dates of Reporting Period	Total Number of Patient Evaluation Forms Completed

	TOTAL NUMBER OF RESPONSES			
ITEM	**YES**	**NO**	**DON'T KNOW**	**COMMENTS**
1. There was a timely response to my initial request for ambulatory health care services.				
2. The staff was prompt in providing services to me.				
3. Staff members identified themselves as ambulatory health care provider employees by stating their names and titles.				
4. A bill of patient rights was given and explained to me.				
5. The staff members competently demonstrated their professional skills and expertise.				
6. The staff was courteous to me.				
7. The staff gave me privacy whenever necessary.				
8. The staff portrayed a positive and helpful attitude toward me.				
9. The staff was adequately groomed and dressed.				
10. The staff promptly and adequately responded to my needs, concerns, and problems.				
11. My transfer from the ambulatory health care provider was efficient.				
12. The staff gave me adequate information about your charges for ambulatory health care services.				
13. The staff kept me informed about the financial status of my bill for your ambulatory health care services.				
14. I would use your ambulatory health care services in the future, if necessary.				
15. I would recommend your ambulatory health care services to other individuals.				

Average number of types of services that were provided to patients:

___ Physician	___ Radiology	___ Physical Therapy	___ Other: Please describe
___ Nursing	___ Pharmacy	___ Occupational Therapy	________________
___ Laboratory	___ Social Services	___ Speech Therapy	________________

Average length of time patient received ambulatory health care services from Ambulatory Health Care Provider:

___ 0–4 Months	___ 8–12 Months	___ 16–20 Months	___ 24–28 Months	___ 32–36 Months
___ 4–8 Months	___ 12–16 Months	___ 20–24 Months	___ 28–32 Months	___ over 36 Months

Signature of Individual Completing This Form	Date of Signature

AMBULATORY HEALTH CARE PROVIDER
QUALITY ASSURANCE
POLICY AND PROCEDURE
2012

Subject: Patient Medical and Nursing Resources	
Drafted by:	Date drafted:
Revised by:	Date revised:
Approved by:	Date approved:
Supersedes date:	Page #:
Date effective:	Page: ______ of

POLICY

Ambulatory health care staff members provide medical and nursing resources to patients on a 24-hour basis.

PURPOSE

1. To provide medical and nursing information to patients.
2. To provide support to patients and patient families.
3. To provide emergency ambulatory health care services.
4. To implement nursing interventions as patient conditions dictate.

PROCEDURE

1. Ambulatory Health Care Registered Nurses provide nursing resources to patients, as required.
2. Physicians provide medical resources to patients, as required.
3. Provision of medical and nursing resources to patients is implemented as follows:
   a. Telephone calls to the ambulatory health care provider during office hours are answered by ambulatory health care provider office staff.
   b. The individual answering the telephone accepts requests for a physician or nurse and records the following information on a Telephone Calls to Ambulatory Health Care Provider Regarding Patient Form (see Exhibit 2012-1):
      (1) name of individual receiving telephone call
      (2) date telephone call received
      (3) time of telephone call
      (4) name of telephone caller
      (5) patient name
      (6) reason for telephone call
      (7) outcome of telephone call
   c. The individual who accepts and records a telephone request for a physician or nurse:
      (1) informs caller that the Ambulatory Health Care Registered Nurse will be contacted
      (2) contacts the Ambulatory Health Care Registered Nurse
      (3) contacts the physician as necessary
      (4) contacts the Nursing Manager if the physician or Ambulatory Health Care Registered Nurse cannot be reached
   d. Normally, the Ambulatory Health Care Registered Nurse responds to telephone requests for a physician or nurse
   e. The Ambulatory Health Care Registered Nurse:
      (1) screens a telephone request for a physician concerning appropriateness of referring telephone requests to the physician
      (2) refers a telephone request for a physician to a physician as appropriate and necessary
      (3) informs the physician of concerns or problems with telephone calls as necessary
      (4) documents telephone calls in the patients' clinical records
   f. The physician:
      (1) responds to a telephone request for a physician as requested and necessary
      (2) documents telephone calls in the patients' clinical records
   g. The Nursing Manager responds to telephone requests for a physician or nurse if the physician or Ambulatory Health Care Registered Nurse cannot be reached.
   h. If the Nursing Manager responds to a telephone request for a physician or nurse, the Nursing Manager provides information to the physician or Ambulatory Health Care Registered Nurse regarding the request and its outcome.
4. Provision of medical and nursing resources to patients during closed provider office hours is implemented through an answering service and beeper system:

a. Individuals rotate on-call responsibilities as documented on the On-Call Schedule (see Exhibit 2012-2)
b. The individual assigned to ambulatory health care on-call coverage:
   (1) responds to answering service when individual's beeper is contacted by same
   (2) records the following information on a Telephone Calls to Ambulatory Health Care Provider Regarding Patient Form:
      (a) name of individual receiving telephone call
      (b) date telephone call received
      (c) time of telephone call
      (d) name of telephone caller
      (e) patient name
      (f) reason for telephone call
      (g) outcome of telephone call
   (3) determines if:
      (a) caller's concern can be handled by telephone communication
      (b) ambulatory health care visit is required
      (c) physician needs to be notified
c. The ambulatory health care on-call nurse provides information to appropriate ambulatory health care staff regarding the telephone request for a nurse and its outcome, as necessary.

5. The Administrative Assistant:
   a. summarizes telephone calls regarding patients on a Summary of Telephone Calls to Ambulatory Health Care Provider Regarding Patient Form (see Exhibit 2012-3)
   b. submits completed Summary of Telephone Calls to Ambulatory Health Care Provider Regarding Patient Form to the Nursing Manager
6. The Nursing Manager:
   a. reviews submitted Summary of Telephone Calls to Ambulatory Health Care Provider Regarding Patient Form
   b. implements corrective action, as necessary, based on problems with on-call system and negative outcomes of telephone calls regarding patients
7. Problems identified with on-call system are referred to the Quality Assurance Manager for consideration as a continuous or special quality assurance activity/study.
8. On-call system information is communicated to individuals, as appropriate, according to Policy and Procedure 1010: Confidentiality of Quality Assurance Information, and Policy and Procedure 1001: Administrative Control.
9. The completed Telephone Calls to Ambulatory Health Care Provider Regarding Patient Form, On-Call Schedule, and Summary of Telephone Calls to Ambulatory Health Care Provider Regarding Patient Form are filed in the ambulatory health care provider's Telephone Calls to Ambulatory Health Care Provider Regarding Patient, On-Call Schedule, and Summary of Telephone Calls to Ambulatory Health Care Provider administrative files.

Exhibit 2012-1 Telephone Calls to Ambulatory Health Care Provider Regarding Patient Form

TELEPHONE CALLS TO AMBULATORY HEALTH CARE PROVIDER REGARDING PATIENT

▶ NAME OF INDIVIDUAL RECEIVING TELEPHONE CALLS: ____________ ▶ DATE TELEPHONE CALLS RECEIVED: ____________

TIME OF TELEPHONE CALL	NAME OF CALLER	PATIENT NAME	REASON FOR CALL	OUTCOME OF TELEPHONE CALL					COMMENTS
				RESOLVED		REFERRED TO	DATE REFERRED	TIME REFERRED	
				YES	NO				

Source: Reprinted with permission of Briggs Corporation, Des Moines, Iowa, © 1986.

Exhibit 2012-2 On-Call Schedule

AMBULATORY HEALTH CARE PROVIDER
ON-CALL SCHEDULE

DAY OF WEEK	DATE	NAME OF INDIVIDUAL ON-CALL		
		PHYSICIAN	NURSE	ADMINISTRATOR
Monday				
Tuesday				
Wednesday				
Thursday				
Friday				
Saturday				
Sunday				
Monday				
Tuesday				
Wednesday				
Thursday				
Friday				
Saturday				
Sunday				

NAME OF INDIVIDUAL	POSITION WITH PROVIDER			TELEPHONE NUMBER	
	PHYSICIAN	NURSE	ADMINISTRATOR	HOME	BEEPER

Exhibit 2012-3 Summary of Telephone Calls to Ambulatory Health Care Provider Regarding Patient Form

AMBULATORY HEALTH CARE PROVIDER
SUMMARY OF TELEPHONE CALLS TO AMBULATORY HEALTH CARE PROVIDER REGARDING PATIENT

DATE THIS FORM COMPLETED	DATES OF REPORTING PERIOD	TOTAL NUMBER OF TELEPHONE CALLS TO PROVIDER REGARDING PATIENT SUMMARIZED

Total Number of Telephone Calls Received/Hour of Day

____ 5–6p. ____ 6–7p. ____ 7–8p. ____ 8–9p. ____ 9–10p. ____10–11p. ____11p.-12mn.
____ 12mn.–1a. ____ 1–2a. ____ 2–3a. ____ 3–4a. ____ 4–5a. ____ 5–6a.

Total Number of Telephone Calls Received/Day of Week

____Mon. ____ Tues. ____ Wed. ____ Thurs. ____ Fri. ____ Sat. ____ Sun.

Total Number Regarding Type of Telephone Caller

____Staff member ____ Patient ____ Family member ____ Physician ____ Therapist ____ Other

Total Number Regarding Reason for Telephone Call

____ Patient Concern
____ Family Member Concern
____ Staff Member Concern
____ Physician Concern
____ Therapist Concern
____ Patient Care Concern
____ Medication Concern
____ I.V. Concern
____ Change In Patient Condition
____ Patient Injury
____ Patient Death
____ Staffing Concern
____ Other ____________

OUTCOME OF TELEPHONE CALL	TOTAL NUMBER OF RESPONSES				COMMENTS
	YES	NO	WHY NOT?	NA	
1. Concern Resolved?					
2. Concern Referred?					
3. Concern Referred in Timely Manner?					

Signature of Individual Completing This Form	Date of Signature

AMBULATORY HEALTH CARE PROVIDER
QUALITY ASSURANCE
POLICY AND PROCEDURE
2013

Subject: Patient Posttransfer Status

Drafted by: ____	Date drafted: ____
Revised by: ____	Date revised: ____
Approved by: ____	Date approved: ____
Supersedes date: ____	Page #: ____
Date effective: ____	Page: ____ of ____

POLICY

Verbal and written contact is made with each patient and patient family one week after the patient is transferred from the ambulatory health care provider.

PURPOSE

1. To monitor the outcomes of the patient transfer plan.
2. To serve as a resource for the patient.
3. To facilitate ongoing ambulatory health care provider/ patient relationships.

PROCEDURE

1. The Ambulatory Health Care Registered Nurse responsible for the patient's case management:
   a. makes telephone contact with the patient and patient family to discuss the patient's transfer status, based on information provided in a Patient Posttransfer Status Form (see Exhibit 2013-1)
   b. informs the Administrative Assistant to mail Patient Posttransfer Status Forms to the patient and patient family for their completion if the patient and patient family cannot be reached by telephone
   c. documents the discussion with the patient and patient family on the Patient Posttransfer Status Form
   d. informs the Nursing Manager if problems with patient transfer plan become evident
2. The Administrative Assistant:
   a. if necessary, mails a blank Patient Posttransfer Status Form to the patient and patient family, accompanied by a Patient Posttransfer Status Letter (see Exhibit 2013-2)
   b. gives the returned Patient Posttransfer Status Form to the registered nurse case manager
3. The registered nurse case manager:
   a. reviews the returned, completed Patient Posttransfer Status Form
   b. gives the reviewed Patient Posttransfer Status Form to the Nursing Manager
4. The Nursing Manager:
   a. reviews the completed Patient Posttransfer Status Form
   b. implements corrective action, as appropriate
5. Reviewed Patient Posttransfer Status Forms are filed in the ambulatory health care provider Patient Posttransfer Status administrative file.

Exhibit 2013-1 Patient Post-Transfer Status Form

AMBULATORY HEALTH CARE PROVIDER
PATIENT POSTTRANSFER STATUS

1. Your name (please complete below)

____

2. Have you had problems with your transfer plan? (please check [√] below)

_______ (a) No

_______ (b) Yes (please describe specific problems)

____

____

____

3. If you have checked 2b above, what do you need to resolve your transfer problems? (please describe below)

____

____

____

____

4. Comments (please complete below)

____

____

____

____

____

____

______________________________ Signature of Individual Completing This Form

______________ Date of Signature

Exhibit 2013-2 Sample Patient Post-Transfer Status Letter

AMBULATORY HEALTH CARE PROVIDER
PATIENT POST TRANSFER STATUS LETTER

Dear Patient

The ambulatory health care staff strive to ensure quality ambulatory health care for patients that is consistent with the ambulatory health care provider philosophy. As a recently transferred patient who has received our ambulatory health care services, you are being asked to complete the enclosed form, due to our unsuccessful attempts to contact you by telephone.

The information you give us on your completed survey form will be used to determine if you are having problems with your transfer plan and, if so, to assist you in resolving those transfer problems.

Please promptly complete and return this form to the Administrator of Ambulatory Health Care or Nursing Manager. Please return a completed form even if you are not having problems with your transfer plan.

Thank you for your assistance in our continuing efforts to provide quality ambulatory health care services to you.

Sincerely,

Administrator of Ambulatory Health Care

AMBULATORY HEALTH CARE PROVIDER
QUALITY ASSURANCE
POLICY AND PROCEDURE
2014

Subject: Patient Transfer	
Drafted by: ______	Date drafted: ______
Revised by: ______	Date revised: ______
Approved by: ______	Date approved: ______
Supersedes date: ______	Page #: ______
Date effective: ______	Page: ______ of ______

POLICY

Planning for patient transfer is initiated for ambulatory health care patients, as necessary.

PURPOSE

To ensure continuity of care when the patient is transferred from the ambulatory health care provider to another health care provider.

PROCEDURE

1. Ambulatory health care staff and interdisciplinary team members assist patients regarding their transfer by:
   a. consulting with patient and patient family regarding need for patient's transfer from the ambulatory health care provider to another health care provider
   b. serving as a referral source for patient and patient family in obtaining follow-up support services
   c. making and documenting contact with patient and patient family one week after patient's transfer from the ambulatory health care provider, following Policy and Procedure 2013: Patient Posttransfer Status
   d. documenting transfer information on the Transfer Summary Form (see Exhibit 2014-1)
   e. consulting with patient and patient family regarding provision of transfer information
   f. sending copy of completed Transfer Summary Form with patient
   g. ensuring that original completed Transfer Summary Form is placed in patient's clinical record
2. Ambulatory health care staff and interdisciplinary team members inform the Nursing Manager in the event problems arise in planning for patient transfer or actual patient transfer that staff or team members are unable to handle.
3. Patient transfers are summarized on a Summary of Patient Transfers Form (see Exhibit 2014-2).
4. Problems identified concerning the process of planning for patient transfers are referred to the Quality Assurance Manager for consideration as a continuous or special quality assurance activity/study
5. Planning for patient transfer information is communicated to individuals as appropriate, according to Policy and Procedure 1010: Confidentiality of Quality Assurance Information, and Policy and Procedure 1001: Administrative Control.
6. The completed Summary of Patient Transfers Form is filed in the ambulatory health care provider's Summary of Patient Transfers administrative file.

Exhibit 2014-1 Transfer Summary Form

TRANSFER SUMMARY

Patient Name (Last, First, Middle) | Attending Physician

Principal Diagnosis | ICD-9-CM

Secondary Diagnosis | ICD-9-CM

Date of Initial Service | Date of Transfer | Clinical Record No.

Type of Services Provided

☐ MD ☐ RN ☐ Lab ☐ X-ray ☐ Pharmacy ☐ PT ☐ OT ☐ ST ☐ SS Other (Please describe) ______

Total No. of Visits Provided

MD ___ RN ___ Lab ___ X-ray ___ Pharmacy ___ PT ___ OT ___ ST ___ SS ___ Other (Please describe) ______

Total Length of Time Services Provided | Other Individuals/Agencies Providing Services

Patient Prognosis

☐ Excellent ☐ Good ☐ Fair ☐ Guarded ☐ Poor

Patient Rehabilitation Potential

☐ Excellent ☐ Good ☐ Fair ☐ Guarded ☐ Poor

Plan of Care Goals

☐ Completely achieved ☐ Partially achieved ☐ Not achieved Please describe why not achieved ______

Transfer Vital Signs

Temp. ______ ☐ Oral ☐ Rectal ☐ Axillary Pulse ______ ☐ Apical ☐ Radial Respiration ______ Blood Pressure ______ ☐ Lying ☐ Sitting ☐ Standing Height ______ Weight ______

ALLERGIES | Diet

PATIENT REQUIREMENTS FOR ACTIVITIES OF DAILY LIVING			
PATIENT ACTIVITY	PATIENT REQUIRES: PARTIAL ASSISTANCE	TOTAL ASSISTANCE	NO ASSISTANCE
Bathing			
Shampoo			
Shave			
Oral hygiene			
Skin care			
Foot soaks			
Nails			
Feeding			
Ambulation			
Transfers			
Sitting			
Range of motion			
Turning & positioning			
Bladder elimination			
Bowel elimination			
Treatments			
Other			

PATIENT CONDITION		
PATIENT:	YES	NO
Is alert		
Is oriented to time, place and person		
Is cooperative		
Has adequate speech		
Speaks English		
Has adequate hearing		
Has adequate vision		
Has adequate touch		
Is under physician's care		
Is confined to home		
Needs equipment		
Takes meds independently		
Other		
Other		
Other		
Other		

TRANSFER MEDICATIONS

MEDICATION NAME	DOSE	FREQUENCY	MEDICATION NAME	DOSE	FREQUENCY

TRANSFER TREATMENTS

TREATMENTS	FREQUENCY	TREATMENTS	FREQUENCY

continues

Exhibit 2014-1 *continued*

REASON FOR TRANSFER

TRANSFERRED BECAUSE PATIENT:

- ❑ Admitted to Acute Care Facility
- ❑ Admitted to Extended Care Facility
- ❑ Admitted to Outpatient Care Facility
- ❑ Moved out of Ambulatory Health Care Provider's geographic service area
- ❑ Obtaining ambulatory health care services from another source
- ❑ Condition does not require ambulatory health care services
- ❑ Needs cannot be met by the Ambulatory Health Care Provider.
- ❑ Non-compliant with the delivery of ambulatory health care services
- ❑ Reimbursement source for ambulatory health care services inadequate
- ❑ Other. (Please describe) ____________________

REFERRALS

REFERRED TO:

- ❑ Attending physician
- ❑ Home Health Care Agency
- ❑ Acute Care Facility
- ❑ Extended Care Facility
- ❑ Outpatient Care Facility
- ❑ Other. (Please describe)____________________

TRANSFER NURSING ASSESSMENT

(Include patient physiological, psychological, psychosocial, financial, spiritual, educational needs and progress, knowledge about illness, coping ability, support systems, etc.)

INSTRUCTIONS GIVEN TO PATIENT/PATIENT'S PRIMARY CAREGIVER

PATIENT/PATIENT'S PRIMARY CAREGIVER DEMONSTRATES UNDERSTANDING OF GIVEN INSTRUCTIONS

❑ Yes ❑ No If No, why not? ____________________

SIGNATURE OF NURSE	DATE OF SIGNATURE

Source: Reprinted with permission of Briggs Corporation, Des Moines, Iowa, © 1986.

Exhibit 2014-2 Summary of Patient Transfers Form

AMBULATORY HEALTH CARE PROVIDER
SUMMARY OF PATIENT TRANSFERS

Date This Form Completed	Dates of Reporting Period	Total Number of Patient Transfers Completed

ITEM	TOTAL NUMBER OF REASONS FOR PATIENT TRANSFERS				
	YES	NO	DON'T KNOW	N/A	COMMENTS
1. Patient condition does not require ambulatory health care services					
2. Patient needs cannot be met by ambulatory health care provider					
3. Patient noncompliant with delivery of ambulatory health care services					
4. Patient physically abusive to ambulatory health care staff					
5. Patient verbally abusive to ambulatory health care staff					
6. Patient sexually harassing ambulatory health care staff					
7. Reimbursement source for ambulatory health care services inadequate					
8. Patient moved out of ambulatory health care provider's geographic area					
9. Patient obtained ambulatory health care services from another source					
10. Patient obtained health care services from: a. acute care facility					
b. extended care facility					
c. outpatient care facility					
11. Other					

Signature of Individual Completing This Form	Date of Signature

AMBULATORY HEALTH CARE PROVIDER
QUALITY ASSURANCE
POLICY AND PROCEDURE
2015

Subject: Physician Evaluation of Ambulatory Health Care Services	
Drafted by:	Date drafted:
Revised by:	Date revised:
Approved by:	Date approved:
Supersedes date:	Page #:
Date effective:	Page: ______ of

POLICY

The ambulatory health care provider provides opportunities for physicians to evaluate ambulatory health care services.

PURPOSE

1. To collect and assess information regarding physician satisfaction with the ambulatory health care provider's services.
2. To implement a quality assurance monitoring system to address physician concerns.
3. To enhance ambulatory health care staff and physician relationships.

PROCEDURE

1. Physicians are encouraged to complete a Physician Evaluation of Ambulatory Health Care Services Form (see Exhibit 2015-1).
2. The Administrative Assistant:
   a. mails Physician Evaluation of Ambulatory Health Care Services Form to physicians every three months
   b. summarizes returned, completed Physician Evaluation of Ambulatory Health Care Services Form using a Summary of Physician Evaluation of Ambulatory Health Care Services Form (see Exhibit 2015-2)
   c. gives returned Physician Evaluation of Ambulatory Health Care Services Form and completed Summary of Physician Evaluation of Ambulatory Health Care Services Form to the Administrator of Ambulatory Health Care
3. The Administrator of Ambulatory Health Care:
   a. reviews submitted Physician Evaluation of Ambulatory Health Care Services Form and Summary of Physician Evaluation of Ambulatory Health Care Services Form
   b. implements immediate corrective action, as necessary, based on identified physician concerns
4. Problems identified through physician evaluation of ambulatory health care services are referred to the Quality Assurance Manager for consideration as a continuous or special quality assurance activity/study.
5. Physician evaluation of ambulatory health care services information is communicated to individuals, as appropriate, according to Policy and Procedure 1010: Confidentiality of Quality Assurance Information, and Policy and Procedure 1001: Administrative Control.
6. The completed Physician Evaluation of Ambulatory Health Care Services Form and Summary of Physician Evaluation of Ambulatory Health Care Services Form are filed in the ambulatory health care provider's Physician Evaluation of Ambulatory Health Care Services and Summary of Physician Evaluation of Ambulatory Health Care Services administrative files.

Exhibit 2015-1 Physician Evaluation of Ambulatory Health Care Services Form

AMBULATORY HEALTH CARE PROVIDER
PHYSICIAN EVALUATION OF AMBULATORY HEALTH CARE SERVICES

Dear Physician: The ambulatory health care staff is dedicated to providing quality ambulatory health care for patients that is consistent with the ambulatory health care provider philosophy. As a physician who provides ambulatory health care services, you are being asked to complete this survey form. The information you give us on your completed survey form will be assessed to measure how well we have provided quality ambulatory health care services to your patients and ways in which we can improve the same services to your patients. Please promptly complete and return this form to the Administrator of Ambulatory Health Care.

Thank you for your assistance in our continuing efforts to provide quality ambulatory health care services to your patients.

ITEM	RESPONSE (PLEASE CHECK [✓] APPROPRIATE RESPONSE)				
	YES	NO	DON'T KNOW	N/A	COMMENTS
I. Ambulatory Health Care Provider					
A. I was given adequate information regarding the ambulatory health care provider's ability/inability to treat patients.					
B. I was given adequate information regarding the ambulatory health care provider policies and procedures.					
C. I was given adequate information regarding ambulatory health care provider patient transfers.					
D. I was given adequate information regarding the ambulatory health care provider charges, including patient eligibility for third party reimbursement.					
II. Ambulatory Health Care Services A. I was treated with courtesy by staff members.					
B. I was treated with a positive and helpful attitude by staff members.					
C. I was given proper identification by name and title of staff members who communicated with me.					
D. I was provided with competent staff members who demonstrated their professional expertise and skills.					
E. I was given a prompt and adequate response to my needs, concerns, and problems regarding my patients.					
F. I was assured of patient confidentiality.					
G. I was provided with efficient patient transfers to other health care providers.					
H. I was provided with prompt implementation of physician orders.					
I. I was involved with the development and implementation of care plans for my patients.					
J. I was provided with prompt, adequate, and available documentation regarding the progress of my patients.					
K. I was promptly and appropriately informed of changes in the conditions of my patients.					
L. I was given adequate information about my patients.					
M. I was provided with available durable medical equipment services for my patients.					
N. I was provided with available therapy services for my patients.					
O. I would recommend the ambulatory health care services to other individuals.					

continues

Exhibit 2015-1 *continued*

Types of services that were provided to patients:

___ Physician	___ Radiology	___ Physical Therapy	___ Other: Please describe
___ Nursing	___ Pharmacy	___ Occupational Therapy	________________
___ Laboratory	___ Social Services	___ Speech Therapy	________________

Average length of time patients received ambulatory health care services from ambulatory health care provider:

___ 0–4 Months	___ 8–12 Months	___ 16–20 Months	___ 24–28 Months	___ 32–36 Months
___ 4–8 Months	___ 12–16 Months	___ 20–24 Months	___ 28–32 Months	___ Over 36 Months

Recommendation(s) for Strengthening Ambulatory Health Care Services

Your Name (optional)

Your Address (optional)

Your Telephone Number (optional)

Exhibit 2015-2 Summary of Physician Evaluation of Ambulatory Health Care Services Form

AMBULATORY HEALTH CARE PROVIDER
SUMMARY OF PHYSICIAN EVALUATION OF AMBULATORY HEALTH CARE SERVICES

Date This Form Completed	Dates of Reporting Period	Total Number of Physician Evaluation Forms Completed

ITEM	TOTAL NUMBER OF RESPONSES				
	YES	NO	DON'T KNOW	N/A	COMMENTS
I. Ambulatory Health Care Provider A. I was given adequate information regarding the ambulatory health care provider's ability/inability to treat patients.					
B. I was given adequate information regarding the ambulatory health care provider policies and procedures.					
C. I was given adequate information regarding ambulatory health care provider patient transfers.					
D. I was given adequate information regarding the ambulatory health care provider charges, including patient eligibility for third party reimbursement.					
II. Ambulatory Health Care Services A. I was treated with courtesy by staff members.					
B. I was treated with a positive and helpful attitude by staff members.					
C. I was given proper identification by name and title of staff members who communicated with me.					
D. I was provided with competent staff members who demonstrated their professional expertise and skills.					
E. I was given a prompt and adequate response to my needs, concerns, and problems regarding my patients.					
F. I was assured of patient confidentiality.					
G. I was provided with efficient patient transfers to other health care providers.					
H. I was provided with prompt implementation of physician orders.					
I. I was involved with the development and implementation of care plans for my patients.					
J. I was provided with prompt, adequate, and available documentation regarding the progress of my patients.					
K. I was promptly and appropriately informed of changes in the conditions of my patients.					
L. I was given adequate information about my patients.					
M. I was provided with available durable medical equipment services for my patients.					
N. I was provided with available therapy services for my patients.					
O. I would recommend the ambulatory health care services to other individuals.					

continues

Exhibit 2015-2 *continued*

Types of services that were provided to patients:

___ Physician	___ Radiology	___ Physical Therapy	___ Other: Please describe
___ Nursing	___ Pharmacy	___ Occupational Therapy	________________
___ Laboratory	___ Social Services	___ Speech Therapy	________________

Average length of time patients received ambulatory health care services from your provider:

___ 0–4 Months	___ 8–12 Months	___ 16–20 Months	___ 24–28 Months	___ 32–36 Months
___ 4–8 Months	___ 12–16 Months	___ 20–24 Months	___ 28–32 Months	___ Over 36 Months

Recommendation(s) for Strengthening Ambulatory Health Care Services

Signature of Individual Completing This Form	Date of Signature

AMBULATORY HEALTH CARE PROVIDER
QUALITY ASSURANCE
POLICY AND PROCEDURE
2016

Subject: Physician Orders and Care Plans	
Drafted by: ______	Date drafted: ______
Revised by: ______	Date revised: ______
Approved by: ______	Date approved: ______
Supersedes date: ______	Page #: ______
Date effective: ______	Page: ______ of ______

POLICY

Physician orders and care plans are signed by the patient's attending physician who gave the order and/or arranged the patient's plan of care.

PURPOSE

1. To comply with legal medical and nursing practice.
2. To facilitate quality assurance for review, approval, and signature of physician orders and care plans.
3. To provide maximum safety standards for review, approval, and signature of physician orders and care plans.

PROCEDURE

1. Physician orders and care plans are signed by the patient's attending physician who gave the order and/or arranged the patient's plan of care.
2. Ambulatory Health Care Registered Nurses:
   a. monitor physician orders and care plans for each attending physician's signature on respective physician order and care plan
   b. inform the Nursing Manager whenever physician orders and care plans do not document attending physician's signature on physician order and care plan
   c. request the Administrative Assistant to give a Rejection of Physician Orders and/or Care Plans Physician Letter (see Exhibit 2016-1) to patient's attending physician
   d. monitor return of physician orders and care plans according to item 2a
3. The Administrative Assistant gives a signed Rejection of Physician Orders and/or Care Plans Physician Letter and rejected physician orders/care plans to the patient's attending physician.
4. The Nursing Manager:
   a. monitors frequency of physician noncompliance with policy regarding signatures for physician orders and care plans
   b. informs the Administrator of Ambulatory Health Care of problems with obtaining physician orders and care plans that do not document attending physician's signature on physician order and care plan
   c. monitors corrective action implemented for correcting identified problems with physician noncompliance with policy regarding signatures for physician orders and care plans
5. The Administrator of Ambulatory Health Care implements additional corrective action, as necessary, to correct physician noncompliance with policy regarding signatures for physician orders and care plans.
6. Problems identified with signatures for physician orders and care plans are referred to the Quality Assurance Manager for consideration as a continuous or special quality assurance activity/study.
7. Information regarding physician noncompliance with signatures for physician orders and care plans are communicated to individuals, as appropriate, according to Policy and Procedure 1010: Confidentiality of Quality Assurance Information, and Policy and Procedure 1001: Administrative Control.
8. Information concerning physician noncompliance with the policy regarding signatures for physician orders and care plans are filed in the ambulatory health care provider's Physician Noncompliance with Policy Regarding Medical Orders and Care Plans administrative file.

Exhibit 2016-1 Rejection of Physician Orders and/or Care Plans Physician Letter

(Date)

(Physician's Name and Address)

Dear (Physician's Name):

The ambulatory health care provider has recently received physician orders and care plans that you apparently did not sign. Please see attached. Because of this problem, we would like to take this opportunity to state our policy regarding signatures for physician orders and care plans. Our policy for obtaining physician signatures on orders and care plans is to accept only those orders and care plans that have been signed by the patient's physician. We believe that physician signatures on orders and care plans demonstrate safe and legal medical and nursing practice due to physician review and approval of the orders and care plans.

Therefore, because of our desire to deliver safe and quality ambulatory health care services to your patients, we cannot accept any of your orders and care plans that you have not signed. Consequently, we are returning the same to you for your signature.

Please contact me if you have any questions.

Sincerely,

Nursing Manager

AMBULATORY HEALTH CARE PROVIDER
QUALITY ASSURANCE
POLICY AND PROCEDURE
2017

Subject: Process- and/or Outcome-Oriented Review of Patient Nursing Care Plans	
Drafted by: ______	Date drafted: ______
Revised by: ______	Date revised: ______
Approved by: ______	Date approved: ______
Supersedes date: ______	Page #: ______
Date effective: ______	Page: ______ of ______

POLICY

Ambulatory health care nursing staff conduct process- and/or outcome-oriented reviews of patient nursing care plans.

PURPOSE

1. To assess patient process/outcomes against established patient process/outcome standards.
2. To determine appropriateness of ambulatory health care services.
3. To determine adequacy of patient nursing care.
4. To determine effectiveness of patient nursing care.
5. To identify problems with patient nursing care, process, and outcomes.
6. To identify problems with continuity of patient nursing care.
7. To implement quality assurance activities for resolution of identified patient nursing care problems.
8. To ensure peer review of patient nursing care.
9. To ensure that established policies and procedures are followed in the provision of ambulatory health care services.

PROCEDURE

1. Process- and/or outcome-oriented patient care plan reviews:
   a. are completed on a quarterly basis
   b. are completed by ambulatory health care provider nursing staff
   c. include assessment of samples of patient care plan records for adherence to established policies and procedures concerning provision of ambulatory health care services
   d. are completed on a quarterly basis to determine:
      (1) patient process/outcomes based on patient process/outcome standards
      (2) adequacy of the nursing care plan
      (3) appropriateness of ambulatory health care services
   e. are conducted utilizing a process and/or outcome auditing and criteria system (see Exhibits 2017-1, 2017-2, and 2017-3)
   f. are summarized quarterly utilizing a process and/or outcome auditing and criteria system (see Exhibits 2017-1, 2017-2, and 2017-3)
2. Results of the process- and/or outcome-oriented patient nursing care plan reviews are reviewed by the Ambulatory Health Care Utilization Review Committee, Ambulatory Health Care Quality Assurance Committee, and Ambulatory Health Care Advisory Committee.
3. The Ambulatory Health Care Utilization Review Committee, Ambulatory Health Care Quality Assurance Committee, and Ambulatory Health Care Advisory Committee submit the following written report to the Administrator of Ambulatory Health Care: quarterly process- and/or outcome-oriented patient nursing care plan review results and recommendations for appropriate action.
4. Problems identified through nursing care plan reviews are referred to the Quality Assurance Manager for consideration as a continuous and special quality assurance activity/study.
5. Nursing care plan review information is communicated to individuals, as appropriate, according to Policy and Procedure 1010: Confidentiality of Quality Assurance Information, and Policy and Procedure 1001: Administrative Control.
6. Patient care plan reviews are filed in the ambulatory health care provider's Process- and/or Outcome-Oriented Reviews of Patient Nursing Care Plans administrative files.

Exhibit 2017-1 Nursing Care Plan Sample

Nursing Care Plan for ______________________ Adm. # ______________ Date ______________
Nursing Diagnosis: Alteration in **nutrition** due to ______________________
Goal: Patient will achieve therapeutic food intake.

NURSING ORDERS

1. Assess patient's current and past food intake (amount, preferences, frequency).
2. Instruct patient/significant other in recommended diet (specify): ______________________
3. Give patient positive reinforcement in following diet plan.
4. Initiate discussion with patient/significant other to clarify perception of food needs.
5. Discuss methods to prepare food for easier ingestion.
6. Provide patient education materials: ______________________

Nurse's Signature ______________________

TEACHING PLAN

Contributing Objectives	Dates Instructed														Goal Date / Date Accom.
Patient/S.O. Will															
List patient's food preferences which are included in prescribed diet.															
Describe how to read packaged food nutrition labels to determine if conforms to diet.															
Identify foods to be avoided and why.															
Discuss how to prepare food to enable patient to eat it.															
List alternatives to manage symptoms.															
Accept and listen to instruction concerning patient education materials.															

Source: Reprinted from *Home Health Nursing Care Plans* by E.J. Gould and J. Wargo, p. 97, with permission of United Medical Services, © 1987.

Exhibit 2017-2 Process-Oriented Review of Patient Nursing Care Plans Form

AMBULATORY HEALTH CARE PROVIDER
PROCESS-ORIENTED REVIEW OF PATIENT NURSING CARE PLANS

Nursing Diagnosis To Be Reviewed	Clinical Record Number	Dates of Reporting Period	Date of Review

PLANNED NURSING ORDER	DATE NURSING ORDER PLANNED	NURSING ORDER IMPLEMENTED APPROPRIATELY			DATE NURSING ORDER IMPLEMENTED	COMMENTS
		YES	NO	WHY NOT?		

Signature of Individual Completing This Form	Date of Signature

Exhibit 2017-3 Outcome-Oriented Review of Patient Nursing Care Plans Form

AMBULATORY HEALTH CARE PROVIDER
OUTCOME-ORIENTED REVIEW OF PATIENT NURSING CARE PLANS

Nursing Diagnosis To Be Reviewed	Clinical Record Number	Dates of Reporting Period	Date of Review

PATIENT OUTCOMES EXPECTED	DATE PATIENT OUTCOME TO BE ACHIEVED	DATE INSTRUCTION GIVEN FOR ACTUALLY ACHIEVING PATIENT OUTCOME	PATIENT OUTCOME ACHIEVED			DATE PATIENT OUTCOME ACTUALLY ACHIEVED	COMMENTS
			YES	NO	WHY NOT?		

Signature of Individual Completing This Form	Date of Signature

AMBULATORY HEALTH CARE PROVIDER
QUALITY ASSURANCE
POLICY AND PROCEDURE
2018

Subject: Process- and/or Outcome-Oriented Review of Specific Patient Diagnosis or Category

Drafted by: ______	Date drafted: ______
Revised by: ______	Date revised: ______
Approved by: ______	Date approved: ______
Supersedes date: ______	Page #: ______
Date effective: ______	Page: ____ of ______

POLICY

Ambulatory health care staff and interdisciplinary team members conduct process- and/or outcome-oriented reviews of specific patient diagnoses or categories.

PURPOSE

1. To assess patient care delivery process.
2. To assess patient outcomes against established patient outcome standards.
3. To assess patient diagnoses and categories having high potential for quality of care problems.
4. To identify both individual and collective care problems and patterns.
5. To determine adequacy of patient care.
6. To determine effectiveness of patient care.
7. To identify problems with continuity of care.

PROCEDURE

1. Reviews of specific patient diagnoses or categories:
   a. are completed on a quarterly basis
   b. are completed by health care professionals representing appropriate components of the ambulatory health care program
   c. include assessment of samples of patient clinical records for review of specific diagnoses or categories
   d. are conducted utilizing a process and/or outcome auditing and criteria system (see Exhibits 2005-1 and 2018-1)
   e. are summarized quarterly utilizing the process and/or outcome auditing and criteria system (see Exhibits 2005-1 and 2018-1)
2. Results of the specific patient diagnosis or category reviews are reviewed by the Ambulatory Health Care Utilization Review Committee, Ambulatory Health Care Quality Assurance Committee, and Ambulatory Health Care Advisory Committee.
3. The Ambulatory Health Care Utilization Review Committee, Ambulatory Health Care Quality Assurance Committee, and Ambulatory Health Care Advisory Committee submit the following written report to the Administrator of Ambulatory Health Care: quarterly specific patient diagnosis or category review results and recommendations for appropriate action.
4. Problems identified through review of specific patient diagnosis or category are referred to the Quality Assurance Manager for consideration as a continuous or special quality assurance activity/study.
5. Patient diagnosis or category reviews are communicated to individuals, as appropriate, according to Policy and Procedure 1010: Confidentiality of Quality Assurance Information, and Policy and Procedure 1001: Administrative Control.
6. Specific patient diagnosis or category reviews are filed in the ambulatory health care provider's Process- and/or Outcome-Oriented Reviews of Specific Patient Diagnoses or Categories administrative file.

Exhibit 2018-1 Sample Audit Tool

Criterion	Exception(s)	Standard	Met	Met by Exception	Not Met	Comments	Instructions to Auditor
1.							Where data is to be found in the record
2.							
3.							
4.							

Source: Reprinted with permission from St. Michael Hospital, Milwaukee, Wisconsin, © 1980.

AMBULATORY HEALTH CARE PROVIDER
QUALITY ASSURANCE
POLICY AND PROCEDURE
2019

Subject: Process-Oriented Review of Individualized Patient Care	
Drafted by: ______	Date drafted: ______
Revised by: ______	Date revised: ______
Approved by: ______	Date approved: ______
Supersedes date: ______	Page #: ______
Date effective: ______	Page: ____ of ______

POLICY

Ambulatory health care staff and interdisciplinary team members conduct process-oriented review of individualized patient care.

PURPOSE

1. To determine adequacy of patient care.
2. To determine appropriateness of continuing ambulatory health care for patients.
3. To identify problems with patient care.
4. To ensure peer review of patient care.
5. To ensure that established policies and procedures are followed in the provision of ambulatory health care services.
6. To meet clinical record review requirements.

PROCEDURE

1. Process-oriented patient care reviews:
   a. are completed on a quarterly basis
   b. are completed by health care professionals representing appropriate components of the ambulatory health care program
   c. include assessment of samples of patient clinical records for adherence to established policies and procedures concerning provision of ambulatory health care services
   d. are completed on a quarterly basis to determine:
      (1) adequacy of treatment plan
      (2) appropriateness of ambulatory health care services
   e. are conducted utilizing a process-oriented auditing and criteria system (see Exhibit 2018-1)
   f. are summarized quarterly utilizing a process-oriented and criteria system Summary Sheet (see Exhibit 2018-1)
2. Results of patient care reviews are reviewed by the ambulatory health care provider's Ambulatory Health Care Advisory Committee, Ambulatory Health Care Quality Assurance Committee, and Ambulatory Health Care Utilization Review Committee.
3. The Ambulatory Health Care Advisory Committee, Ambulatory Health Care Quality Assurance Committee, and Ambulatory Health Care Utilization Review Committee submit the following written report to the Administrator of Ambulatory Health Care: quarterly patient care review results and recommendations for appropriate action based thereon, keyed to items in 1d.
4. Problems identified through process-oriented review of individualized patient care are referred to the Quality Assurance Manager for consideration as a continuous or special quality assurance activity/study.
5. Individualized patient care review information is communicated to individuals, as appropriate, according to Policy and Procedure 1010: Confidentiality of Quality Assurance Information, and Policy and Procedure 1001: Administrative Control.
6. Patient care reviews are filed in the ambulatory health care provider's Process-Oriented Reviews of Individualized Patient Care administrative file.

AMBULATORY HEALTH CARE PROVIDER
QUALITY ASSURANCE
POLICY AND PROCEDURE
2020

Subject: Vulnerable Adult Patient Abuse and/or Neglect: Reporting System	
Drafted by: ______	Date drafted: ______
Revised by: ______	Date revised: ______
Approved by: ______	Date approved: ______
Supersedes date: ______	Page #: ______
Date effective: ______	Page: ______ of ______

POLICY

The ambulatory health care provider reports all suspected cases of abuse and/or neglect of vulnerable adult patients in compliance with relevant state statutes.

PURPOSE

1. To ensure that all suspected cases of adult patient abuse and/or neglect are reported under appropriate statutes.
2. To facilitate prompt internal investigation of suspected abuse and/or neglect of vulnerable adult patients.
3. To implement a quality assurance monitoring system for adult patient abuse and/or neglect.

PROCEDURE

1. Definitions of applicable terms are as follows:*
   a. *vulnerable adult*: anyone 18 years or older who falls into any of the following categories:
      (1) is a resident, inpatient, or outpatient of a facility
      (2) receives services at or from a facility required to be licensed to serve adults, except a person receiving outpatient services for treatment of chemical dependency or mental illness
      (3) receives services from a licensed home health care provider
      (4) regardless of residence or type of service received, is unable or unlikely to report abuse or neglect without assistance because of impairment of mental or physical function or emotional status

   b. *abuse*: any act that constitutes a violation of the prostitution or criminal sexual conduct statutes, the nontherapeutic conduct that produces or could reasonably be expected to produce pain or injury and is not accidental, or any repeated conduct that produces or could reasonably be expected to produce emotional distress; any sexual contact between a facility staff person and a resident or patient of that facility; the illegal use of a vulnerable adult's person or property for another person's profit or advantage, or the breach of a fiduciary relationship through the use of a person or a person's property for any purpose not in the proper and lawful execution of a trust, including but not limited to situations where a person obtains money, property, or services from a vulnerable adult through the use of undue influence, harassment, duress, deception, or fraud; or any aversive and deprivation procedures that have not been authorized, such as those procedures restricting patients' normal access to nutritious diet, drinking water, adequate ventilation, necessary medical care, ordinary hygiene facilities, normal sleeping conditions, necessary clothing, and access to legal counsel and next of kin
   c. *neglect*: failure of a caretaker to supply vulnerable adult with necessary food, clothing, shelter, health care, or supervision or absence or likelihood of absence of necessary food, clothing, shelter, health care, or supervision for vulnerable adult, the absence or likelihood of absence of necessary financial management to protect a vulnerable adult against abuse
   d. *caretaker*: an individual or facility responsible for care of vulnerable adult as a result of a family relationship, such as relative or spouse, or responsible for all or some of the care given voluntarily or by contract or agreement, such as ambulatory health care provider personnel
   e. *facility*: a hospital or other entity required to be licensed; a nursing home required to be licensed to serve adults; an agency, day care facility, or residen-

---

*Derived from Minnesota State Statute 626.557 (1988), Reporting of Maltreatment of Vulnerable Adults.

tial facility required to be licensed to serve adults; a mental health program receiving funds; or a licensed home health care provider

f. *licensing agency*: the Commissioner of Health, for facilities that are required to be licensed or certified by the state health department; the Commissioner of Human Services, for facilities required to be licensed; any licensing board that regulates persons; and any agency responsible for credentialing human services occupations

g. *report*: any report received by the local welfare agency, police department, county sheriff, or licensing agency or a verbal and/or written statement of abuse and/or neglect that states:
   (1) what has happened
   (2) to whom it happened
   (3) when it happened
   (4) where it happened
   (5) who did the abusing or was responsible for the neglect

h. *individual mandated to report*: a professional or the professional's delegate who is engaged in the care of vulnerable adults or in education, social services, law enforcement, or any related occupation; an employee of a rehabilitation facility certified by the Commissioner of Economic Security for vocational rehabilitation; or a person or employee of a person who provides services in a facility who has knowledge of abuse or neglect of a vulnerable adult, has reasonable cause to believe that a vulnerable adult is being or has been abused or neglected, or has knowledge that a vulnerable adult has sustained a physical injury that is not reasonably explained by the history of injuries provided by the caretaker of the vulnerable adult

2. The action to be taken is as follows:

a. The individual mandated to report suspected adult patient abuse and/or neglect must report:
   (1) any knowledge of patient abuse and/or neglect
   (2) any knowledge of patient self-abuse and/or self-neglect
   (3) reasonable cause to suspect patient abuse and/or neglect
   (4) reasonable cause to suspect patient self-abuse and/or self-neglect
   (5) any knowledge that a patient sustained an injury that is not reasonably explained by patient's history of injuries

b. Individuals not mandated to report suspected adult patient abuse and/or neglect may make such reports if they have:
   (1) any knowledge of patient abuse and/or neglect
   (2) any knowledge of patient self-abuse and/or self-neglect
   (3) reasonable cause to suspect patient abuse and/or neglect
   (4) reasonable cause to suspect patient self-abuse and/or self-neglect
   (5) any knowledge that a patient has sustained an injury that is not reasonably explained by patient's history of injuries

c. The individual reporting suspected adult patient abuse and/or neglect:
   (1) immediately informs the Nursing Manager of the suspected adult patient abuse and/or neglect
   (2) immediately completes a Suspected Patient Abuse and/or Neglect Report Form (see Exhibit 2004-1)
   (3) submits completed Suspected Patient Abuse and/or Neglect Report Form to the Nursing Manager

d. Ambulatory health care provider personnel may report suspected cases of adult patient abuse and/or neglect directly to outside agencies.

e. The Nursing Manager:
   (1) immediately reviews completed Suspected Patient Abuse and/or Neglect Report Form
   (2) informs the Administrator of Ambulatory Health Care of the suspected adult patient abuse and/or neglect
   (3) conducts an immediate initial investigation into the suspected adult patient abuse and/or neglect
   (4) informs the Administrator of Ambulatory Health Care of initial investigation results
   (5) documents review and investigation of the suspected adult patient abuse and/or neglect on the Suspected Patient Abuse and/or Neglect Report Form
   (6) sends completed Suspected Patient Abuse and/or Neglect Report Form to the Administrator of Ambulatory Health Care
   (7) summarizes completed Suspected Patient Abuse and/or Neglect Report Form on a Summary of Suspected Patient Abuse and/or Neglect Report Form (see Exhibit 2004-2)

f. The Administrator of Ambulatory Health Care:
   (1) immediately submits verbal report of the suspected adult patient abuse and/or neglect to appropriate authority in accordance with relevant statutes
   (2) reviews all suspected adult patient abuse and/or neglect reports
   (3) conducts further investigation of the suspected adult patient abuse and/or neglect, as necessary
   (4) reports all cases of suspected adult patient abuse and/or neglect to appropriate authority in accordance with relevant statutes
   (5) documents review and investigation of the suspected adult patient abuse and/or neglect on a Suspected Patient Abuse and/or Neglect Investigation Report Form (see Exhibit 2004-3)

(6) sends copy of completed Suspected Patient Abuse and/or Neglect Investigation Report Form to appropriate office of state department of health
(7) places completed Suspected Patient Abuse and/or Neglect Report Form and Suspected Patient Abuse and/or Neglect Investigation Report Form in a locked, confidential ambulatory health care provider administrative file

g. Reports, reviews, and investigations of suspected adult patient abuse and/or neglect are held in strictest confidence.
h. If the Nursing Manager is suspected of committing adult patient abuse and/or neglect, the individual reporting such abuse and/or neglect:
   (1) immediately informs the Administrator of Ambulatory Health Care of the suspected adult patient abuse and/or neglect
   (2) immediately completes a Suspected Patient Abuse and/or Neglect Report Form
   (3) submits completed Suspected Patient Abuse and/or Neglect Report Form to the Administrator of Ambulatory Health Care
i. If the Administrator of Ambulatory Health Care is suspected of committing adult patient abuse and/or neglect, the individual reporting such abuse and/or neglect:
   (1) immediately informs the President of the ambulatory health care provider of the suspected adult patient abuse and/or neglect
   (2) immediately completes a Suspected Patient Abuse and/or Neglect Report Form
   (3) submits completed Suspected Patient Abuse and/or Neglect Report Form to the President of the ambulatory health care provider
j. Problems identified with suspected vulnerable adult abuse and/or neglect are referred to the Quality Assurance Manager for consideration as a continuous or special quality assurance activity/study.
k. Ambulatory health care staff members shall cooperate fully with those assigned to investigate suspected adult patient abuse and/or neglect.
l. Ambulatory health care staff members shall maintain patient confidentiality and rights during the reporting and investigation of suspected adult patient abuse and/or neglect, as appropriate, according to Policy and Procedure 1009: Confidentiality for Patients.
m. Ambulatory health care administrative staff members may not implement retaliatory action against any individuals who report suspected adult patient abuse and/or neglect.
n. An individual who is mandated to report suspected adult patient abuse and/or neglect and who intentionally fails to report such suspected abuse and/or neglect is guilty of a misdemeanor and liable for damages caused by the failure.
o. An individual who willingly makes a false adult patient abuse and/or neglect report is liable for civil action for any damages suffered by the individuals who were reported as suspects in such abuse and/or neglect.
p. Information gathered by the ambulatory health care provider relating to adult patient abuse and/or neglect is handled in the following manner:
   (1) If the provider determines the information is false, it destroys the information two years after such determination.
   (2) If the provider determines the information is unsubstantiated, it destroys the information four years after such determination.
   (3) If the provider determines the information is substantiated, it destroys the information seven years after such determination.

Section 3000

Clinical Records

The following policies and procedures are adaptable to quality assurance functions in the area of clinical record maintenance.

AMBULATORY HEALTH CARE PROVIDER
QUALITY ASSURANCE
POLICY AND PROCEDURE
3001

Subject: Patient Clinical Record Filing System

Drafted by: ______	Date drafted: ______
Revised by: ______	Date revised: ______
Approved by: ______	Date approved: ______
Supersedes date: ______	Page #: ______
Date effective: ______	Page: ______ of ______

POLICY

Patient clinical records are filed according to assigned patient clinical record numbers.

PURPOSE

To facilitate convenient and expedited access to patient clinical records.

PROCEDURE

1. The clinical records clerical staff file patient clinical records according to assigned patient clinical record numbers.
2. Patient clinical records are retrieved following Policy and Procedure 1009: Confidentiality for Patients. The clinical records clerical staff:
   a. locate the patient's last name on the completed Patient Clinical Record Index Card in appropriate patient clinical record index file (see Exhibit 3001-1)
   b. obtain the patient's clinical record number from the Patient Clinical Record Index Card
   c. locate the patient's clinical record in the ambulatory health care provider's patient clinical record files
   d. sign out the appropriate patient clinical record, including the following information on the sign-out card:
      (1) date the patient clinical record was retrieved
      (2) name of the individual who requested that the patient clinical record be retrieved
      (3) name of the individual who retrieved the patient clinical record

Exhibit 3001-1 Patient Clinical Record Index Card

PATIENT CLINICAL RECORD INDEX					
PATIENT NAME:					
PATIENT ADDRESS:					
PATIENT BIRTH DATE:					
PATIENT CLINICAL RECORD NUMBER:					
PATIENT ATTENDING PHYSICIAN:					
PATIENT PRINCIPAL DIAGNOSIS:					
PATIENT SECONDARY DIAGNOSIS(ES):					
PATIENT PAYMENT SOURCE:					
PATIENT VISIT DATE: ______	______	______	______	______	
PATIENT TRANSFER DATE: ______	______	______	______	______	
PATIENT SPOUSE/RELATIVE NAME:					

AMBULATORY HEALTH CARE PROVIDER
QUALITY ASSURANCE
POLICY AND PROCEDURE
3002

Subject: Patient Clinical Record Review	
Drafted by: ______	Date drafted: ______
Revised by: ______	Date revised: ______
Approved by: ______	Date approved: ______
Supersedes date: ______	Page #: ______
Date effective: ______	Page: ____ of ______

POLICY

All patient clinical records are reviewed for compliance with accepted professional and legal standards.

PURPOSE

To ensure patient clinical records are consistently and continually maintained with adequate, complete, current, and legal patient/delivery of health care information.

PROCEDURE

1. Patient clinical records are submitted to clinical records staff for review whenever documentation is added to the records.
2. The clinical records clerical staff member:
   a. documents patient's transfer as applicable on an Ambulatory Health Care Patient Register Log Form by filling in the following information (see Policy and Procedure 1006 and Exhibit 1006-6):
      (1) transfer date
      (2) place to which patient transferred
      (3) reason for transfer
      (4) services patient received
      (5) total number of patient visits
   b. documents patient's transfer on a Patient Clinical Record Index Card (see Exhibit 3001-1)
   c. arranges patient's clinical record forms in appropriate chart order, filing them in reverse order with the most recently dated form on top chronologically if there is more than one form of the same type
   d. analyzes patient's clinical record for record deficiencies, as indicated on the Patient Clinical Record Analysis Form (see Exhibit 3002-1)
   e. documents any record deficiencies on the Patient Clinical Record Analysis Form
   f. notifies appropriate individual of any record deficiencies using a Notification of Patient Clinical Record Deficiencies Form (see Exhibit 3002-2)
   g. places completed Patient Clinical Record Analysis Form in the front of patient's clinical record
   h. files patient's clinical record in the Patient Clinical Record Deficiency file until all record deficiencies are corrected
   i. when record deficiencies are corrected, files patient's clinical record in the patient clinical record file, following Policy and Procedure 3001: Patient Clinical Record Filing System
   j. submits completed Summary of Patient Clinical Record Analysis Form (see Exhibit 3002-3) to the Administrator of Ambulatory Health Care
3. The Administrator of Ambulatory Health Care reviews completed Summary of Patient Clinical Record Analysis Form for commonalities and trends of problems with clinical record analysis.
4. Problems identified with clinical record analysis are referred to the Quality Assurance Manager for consideration as a continuous or special quality assurance activity/study.
5. Clinical record analysis information is communicated to individuals, as appropriate, according to Policy and Procedure 1010: Confidentiality of Quality Assurance Information, and Policy and Procedure 1001: Administrative Control.
6. The completed Patient Clinical Record Analysis Form and Summary of Patient Clinical Record Analysis Form are filed in the ambulatory health care provider's Patient Clinical Record Analysis and Summary of Patient Clinical Record Analysis administrative files.

Exhibit 3002-1 Patient Clinical Record Analysis Form

AMBULATORY HEALTH CARE PROVIDER
PATIENT CLINICAL RECORD ANALYSIS

PATIENT NAME: ______________________ PATIENT CLINICAL RECORD NO.: ______________________
PATIENT PRINCIPAL DIAGNOSIS: ______________________ PATIENT VISIT DATE: ______________________
PATIENT ATTENDING PHYSICIAN NAME: ______________________ PATIENT TRANSFER DATE: ______________________

ITEM	DEFICIENCY				CORRECTIVE ACTION	NAME OF INDIVIDUAL NOTIFIED
	YES	NO	N/A	COMMENTS		
1. Medical record content is legible						
2. Medical record information is documented on standardized forms, whenever possible						
3. Medical record information is documented in a timely manner						
4. Medical record information is documented in a complete manner						
5. Medical record information is documented in a clear and concise manner						
6. Medical record reports, such as medical/nursing progress notes, history and physical examinations, laboratory and radiology reports, consultations, etc., are incorporated into each patient's medical record in a timely manner						
7. Medical record forms are filed according to a defined chart order						
8. Each provider/patient telephone/in-person contact is adequately documented in the medical record, including at least the following information as applicable a. patient name						
b. date of provider/patient contact						
c. time of provider/patient contact						
d. name of department from which patient received care (e.g., Internal Medicine, Surgery, Pediatrics, Obstetrics, and Gynecology, etc.)						
e. provider's signature and proper credentials (e.g., MD, RN, PT, OT, etc.)						
f. chief complaint/purpose of visit/ identified problem of patient						
g. complete and appropriate patient assessment/medical findings						
h. complete and appropriate primary and secondary diagnoses						
i. current problem list						
j. current signed physician orders						
k. appropriate diagnostic tests ordered						

continues

Exhibit 3002-1 *continued*

ITEM	DEFICIENCY				CORRECTIVE ACTION	NAME OF INDIVIDUAL NOTIFIED
	YES	NO	N/A	COMMENTS		
l. diagnostic test results						
m. investigation of diagnostic test/exam results						
n. intervention for abnormal diagnostic test/exam results						
o. treatment plans based on patient assessments						
p. appropriate treatments ordered						
q. treatment outcomes						
r. current progress notes for each service providing health care						
s. prognosis						
t. patient's condition and anticipated clinical course						
u. rehabilitation potential						
v. therapeutic short-term goals						
w. therapeutic long-term goals						
x. current/most recently used medications 1) name 2) dose 3) time of medication administration						
y. nutritional status						
z. activity level						
a1. signs & symptoms/reactions to be observed						
b1. significant current medical history						
c1. significant past medical history						
d1. significant past surgical procedures						
e1. allergies 1) medication 2) food 3) other						
f1. clinical summaries that describe the health care the patient received from another health care provider/facility						
g1. transfer information						
h1. referral information						
i1. patient disposition, with health care recommendations, education, and instructions given to patient						
j1. patient consent for treatment						
k1. patient bill of rights/responsibilities						
l1. patient vulnerability to abuse and/or neglect						
m1. patient death						

continues

Exhibit 3002-1 *continued*

ITEM	DEFICIENCY				CORRECTIVE ACTION	NAME OF INDIVIDUAL NOTIFIED
	YES	NO	N/A	COMMENTS		
9. Medical record content demonstrates: a. that reasonable coordination of health care services exists						
b. that the patient's total health care needs were addressed: 1) physiological 2) psychological 3) psychosocial 4) spiritual						
c. that the patient's total health care needs were addressed in a timely manner						
d. that the patient's total health care needs were addressed in an appropriate manner						
e. an adequate assessment of patient's needs for community resources						
f. adequate action taken to meet assessed patient's needs for community resources						
10. Other (please list)						

Conclusions:

Relationship of care plan and amount and type of service to patient's condition and clinical course indicate:

____Appropriate care provided

____Inappropriate care provided

____Timely care provided

____Untimely care provided

____Underutilized services

____Overutilized services

____Inability to determine relationship due to inadequate medical record information

____Inability to determine relationship due to incomplete medical record information

____Other ____________________

Comments: ____________________

____

____

____

Recommendations: ____________________

____

____

____

Disposition: ____________________

____

____

____

____________________ Signature of Reviewer

____________________ Date of Signature

Exhibit 3002-2 Notification of Patient Clinical Record Deficiencies Form

AMBULATORY HEALTH CARE PROVIDER
NOTIFICATION OF PATIENT CLINICAL RECORD DEFICIENCIES

Patient name: ______________________________

Patient clinical record no.: ______________________________

Patient case manager: ______________________________

Patient attending physician: ______________________________

Patient principal diagnosis: ______________________________

Patient visit date: ______________________________

Patient transfer date: ______________________________

Patient clinical record deficiency(ies): ______________________________

____

____

____

____

____

____

Name of individual notified of patient clinical record deficiency(ies): ______________________________

____

Patient clinical record deficiency(ies): ______________________________

____

____

____

____

____

____

____

____

____

____

______________________________ ______________________________
Signature of Individual Who Performed Patient Clinical Record Analysis Date of Signature

Exhibit 3002-3 Summary of Patient Clinical Record Analysis Form

AMBULATORY HEALTH CARE PROVIDER
SUMMARY OF PATIENT CLINICAL RECORD ANALYSIS

Date This Form Completed	Dates of Reporting Period	Total Number of Patient Clinical Record Analysis Forms

ITEM	TOTAL NUMBER OF DEFICIENCIES			
	YES	NO	N/A	COMMENTS
1. Medical record content is legible				
2. Medical record information is documented on standardized forms, whenever possible				
3. Medical record information is documented in a timely manner				
4. Medical record information is documented in a complete manner				
5. Medical record information is documented in a clear and concise manner				
6. Medical record reports, such as medical/nursing progress notes, history and physical examinations, laboratory and radiology reports, consultations, etc., are incorporated into each patient's medical record in a timely manner				
7. Medical record forms are filed according to a defined chart order				
8. Each provider/patient telephone/in-person contact is adequately documented in the medical record, including at least the following information as applicable				
a. patient name				
b. date of provider/patient contact				
c. time of provider/patient contact				
d. name of department from which patient received care (e.g., Internal Medicine, Surgery, Pediatrics, Obstetrics, and Gynecology, etc.)				
e. provider's signature and proper credentials (e.g., MD, RN, PT, OT, etc.)				
f. chief complaint/purpose of visit/identified problem of patient				
g. complete and appropriate patient assessment/medical findings				
h. complete and appropriate primary and secondary diagnoses				
i. current problem list				
j. current signed physician orders				
k. appropriate diagnostic tests ordered				
l. diagnostic test results				
m. investigation of diagnostic test/exam results				
n. intervention for abnormal diagnostic test/exam results				
o. treatment plans based on patient assessments				
p. appropriate treatments ordered				
q. treatment outcomes				
r. current progress notes for each service providing health care				
s. prognosis				
t. patient's condition and anticipated clinical course				
u. rehabilitation potential				
v. therapeutic short-term goals				
w. therapeutic long-term goals				

continues

Exhibit 3002-3 *continued*

ITEM	TOTAL NUMBER OF DEFICIENCIES YES	NO	N/A	COMMENTS
x. current/most recently used medications 1) name 2) dose 3) time of medication administration				
y. nutritional status				
z. activity level				
a1. signs & symptoms/reactions to be observed				
b1. significant current medical history				
c1. significant past medical history				
d1. significant past surgical procedures				
e1. allergies 1) medication 2) food 3) other				
f1. clinical summaries that describe the health care the patient received from another health care provider/facility				
g1. transfer information				
h1. referral information				
i1. patient disposition, with health care recommendations, education, and instructions given to patient				
j1. patient consent for treatment				
k1. patient bill of rights/responsibilities				
l1. patient vulnerability to abuse and/or neglect				
m1. patient death				
9. Medical record content demonstrates: a. that reasonable coordination of health care services exists				
b. that the patient's total health care needs were addressed: 1) physiological 2) psychological 3) psychosocial 4) spiritual				
c. that the patient's total health care needs were addressed in a timely manner				
d. that the patient's total health care needs were addressed in an appropriate manner				
e. an adequate assessment of patient's needs for community resources				
f. adequate action taken to meet assessed patient's needs for community resources				
10. Other (please list)				

Total # of conclusions:

Relationship of care plan and amount and type of service to patient's condition and clinical course indicate:

____Appropriate care provided

____Inappropriate care provided

____Timely care provided

____Untimely care provided

____Underutilized services

____Overutilized services

____Inability to determine relationship due to inadequate medical record information

____Inability to determine relationship due to incomplete medical record information

____Other ____________________

continues

Exhibit 3002-3 *continued*

Total narrative comments: ____

Total narrative recommendations: ____

Total narrative dispositions: ____

______________________________ Signature of Individual Completing This Form

______________________________ Date of Signature

Section 4000

Education

The following policies and procedures are adaptable to quality assurance functions in the area of education.

AMBULATORY HEALTH CARE PROVIDER
QUALITY ASSURANCE
POLICY AND PROCEDURE
4001

Subject: Education	
Drafted by:	Date drafted:
Revised by:	Date revised:
Approved by:	Date approved:
Supersedes date:	Page #:
Date effective:	Page : ______ of

POLICY

The ambulatory health care provider maintains an effective comprehensive education program for ambulatory health care staff, interdisciplinary team members, patients, and patient families.

PURPOSE

1. To provide necessary orientation, training, and education for ambulatory health care staff members to enable them to fulfill the responsibilities of their ambulatory health care positions.
2. To provide ambulatory health care staff members with current health care information.
3. To provide patients and patient families with current health care information.
4. To increase ambulatory health care staff awareness of the physiological, safety, psychological, self-esteem, and self-actualization needs of patients and patient families.
5. To increase knowledge and technical skills of ambulatory health care staff members.
6. To provide opportunities for ambulatory health care staff members to develop a healthy self-awareness of personal attitudes and feelings about illness, aging, death, and dying.
7. To increase ambulatory health care staff members' understanding and appreciation of the value of each member's role in promoting wellness and positive aging concepts among patients, patient families, and the community.
8. To promote an environment conducive to the acknowledgement and acceptance of innovative ideas and programs by ambulatory health care staff members.

PROCEDURE

1. The ambulatory health care provider's education program is based on the following philosophical principles:
   a. Learning is a lifelong experience.
   b. Adult learning promotes ambulatory health care staff member professional growth and development.
   c. Advancement of ambulatory health care staff member knowledge and skills is likely to improve their job performance and satisfaction.
2. The ambulatory health care provider's educational components include the following:
   a. *Orientation:* the means by which new ambulatory health care staff members are introduced to the philosophy, goals, policies and procedures, role expectations, and special services in a specific work setting
   b. *Continuing education:* any organized, planned program under the direction of the Nursing Manager in which learning experiences are designed to build upon previously acquired knowledge and skills
   c. *Inservice education:* any instructional or training program provided by the ambulatory health care provider in the work setting that is designed to increase its staff members' competence in a specific area of practice
   d. *Incidental learning:* opportunities in the work environment that may or may not be preplanned but provide learning experiences that build upon previously acquired knowledge and skills
3. Patient education includes educational programs and services developed for patients and patient families.
4. Community education includes all educational programs, seminars, conferences, and forums that are developed by the ambulatory health care provider, or by the provider in collaboration with other agencies, and are open for public participation.

AMBULATORY HEALTH CARE PROVIDER
QUALITY ASSURANCE
POLICY AND PROCEDURE
4002

Subject: Inservice Education Programs	
Drafted by:	Date drafted:
Revised by:	Date revised:
Approved by:	Date approved:
Supersedes date:	Page #:
Date effective:	Page : ______ of ______

POLICY

The ambulatory health care provider provides inservice education programs for ambulatory health care staff members.

PURPOSE

1. To increase ambulatory health care staff member competency in a specific area of practice.
2. To provide ambulatory health care staff members with current health care information.

PROCEDURE

1. The Nursing Manager:
   a. plans an annual inservice education program calendar based on:
      (1) needs assessment
      (2) organizational/program objectives
      (3) regulatory requirements
   b. posts a monthly inservice education program calendar in designated areas one month in advance of the program offerings
2. Ambulatory health care staff members are required to attend a minimum of 12 inservice education programs per year.
3. The Nursing Manager completes and files an Inservice Education Program Summary Form (see Exhibit 4002-1).
4. Ambulatory health care staff members document their participation in inservice education programs on an Inservice Education Program Attendance Form (see Exhibit 4002-2) and an Individual Inservice/Continuing Education Record Form (see Exhibit 4002-3).

Exhibit 4002-1 Inservice Education Program Summary Form

AMBULATORY HEALTH CARE PROVIDER
INSERVICE EDUCATION PROGRAM SUMMARY

Inservice education program title: ______________________

Date of inservice education program: ______________________

Time of inservice education program: ______________________

Name of individual who presented inservice education program: ______________________

Summary of inservice education program content: ______________________

____

____

____

____

____

____

Assessment of inservice education program content:

____

____

____

______________________ Signature of Individual Completing This Form

______________________ Date of Signature

Exhibit 4002-2 Inservice Education Program Attendance Form

AMBULATORY HEALTH CARE PROVIDER INSERVICE EDUCATION PROGRAM ATTENDANCE		
DATE	**NAME**	**POSITION TITLE**

Exhibit 4002-3 Individual Inservice/Continuing Education Record Form

AMBULATORY HEALTH CARE PROVIDER
INDIVIDUAL INSERVICE/CONTINUING EDUCATION RECORD

INDIVIDUAL NAME:

DATE	INSERVICE EDUCATION TITLE	AMBULATORY HEALTH CARE STAFF MEMBER SIGNATURE

DATE	CONTINUING EDUCATION TITLE	AMBULATORY HEALTH CARE STAFF MEMBER SIGNATURE

Section 5000

Personnel

The following policies and procedures are adaptable to quality assurance functions in the area of personnel management.

AMBULATORY HEALTH CARE PROVIDER
QUALITY ASSURANCE
POLICY AND PROCEDURE
5001

Subject: Accidents/Incidents of Ambulatory Health Care Staff Members

Drafted by: ______	Date drafted: ______
Revised by: ______	Date revised: ______
Approved by: ______	Date approved: ______
Supersedes date: ______	Page #: ______
Date effective: ______	Page: ______ of ______

POLICY

Ambulatory health care staff members involved in accidents/incidents are treated, as necessary, and the accident/incident is documented as soon as possible after it occurs.

PURPOSE

1. To provide necessary and timely intervention for ambulatory health care staff members involved in an accident/incident.
2. To facilitate timely, accurate, and complete documentation of all accidents/incidents.
3. To implement a quality assurance monitoring system for accidents/incidents involving ambulatory health care staff members.
4. To submit timely workers' compensation information, as appropriate.

PROCEDURE

1. All accidents/incidents involving ambulatory health care staff members are reported as soon as possible to the Nursing Manager.
2. Ambulatory health care staff members who have sustained an injury that requires immediate medical care are taken to the nearest acute care facility.
3. Ambulatory health care staff members who have sustained an injury that does not require immediate medical care must see their personal physician as soon as possible after the injury has occurred.
4. Accidents/incidents involving ambulatory health care staff members are documented on an Employee Accident/Incident Report Form (see Exhibit 5001-1).
5. The completed Employee Accident/Incident Report Form is submitted to the Nursing Manager for review and signature.
6. The Nursing Manager:
   a. investigates accidents/incidents involving ambulatory health care staff members
   b. implements corrective action, as appropriate
   c. documents investigation and corrective action regarding accident/incident on the Employee Accident/Incident Report Form
   d. requests the relevant ambulatory health care staff member's signature on an Authorization To Release Information Form (see Exhibit 5001-2)
   e. sends signed Authorization To Release Information Form to the physician who treated the staff member for the injury, requesting information regarding the staff member's medical care
   f. completes and sends a First Report of Injury Form to the ambulatory health care provider insurance company (see Exhibit 5001-3)
   g. if the staff member was ordered not to work while recovering from the injury, obtains a medical release for the staff member to return to work, citing:
      (1) specific work restrictions
      (2) length of time restrictions to be enforced
      (3) next physician examination, as appropriate
   h. informs the Administrator of Ambulatory Health Care of the staff member's accident/incident, as appropriate
7. The completed and reviewed Employee Accident/Incident Report Form is submitted to the Administrator of Ambulatory Health Care for review and signature.
8. The completed and reviewed Employee Accident/Incident Report Forms are summarized by the Administrative Assistant using a Summary of Employee Accidents/Incidents Form (see Exhibit 5001-4).

9. Problems identified with employee accidents/incidents are referred to the Quality Assurance Manager for consideration as a continuous or special quality assurance activity/study.
10. Employee accident/incident information is communicated to individuals, as appropriate, according to Policy and Procedure 1010: Confidentiality of Quality Assurance Information, and Policy and Procedure 1001: Administrative Control.
11. The completed, reviewed Employee Accident/Incident Report Form and Summary of Employee Accidents/Incidents Form are filed in the ambulatory health care provider's Employee Accident/Incident Report and Summary of Employee Accidents/Incidents administrative files.

Exhibit 5001-1 Employee Accident/Incident Report Form

AMBULATORY HEALTH CARE PROVIDER
EMPLOYEE ACCIDENT/INCIDENT REPORT

I. General information (please complete below)

______________________ 1. Name of employee

______________________ 2. Age of employee

______________________ 3. Date of employee accident/incident

______________________ 4. Time of employee accident/incident

______________________ 5. Location of employee accident/incident

______________________ 6. Name of individual(s) involved in employee accident/incident

______________________ 7. Address(es) of individual(s) involved in accident/ incident

____

____

____

______________________ 8. Telephone number(s) of individual(s) involved in employee accident/incident

____

____

______________________ 9. Name of witness

______________________ 10. Address of witness

____

____

______________________ 11. Telephone number of witness

______________________ 12. Name of witness

______________________ 13. Address of witness

______________________ 14. Telephone number of witness

______________________ 15. Description of employee injury

______________________ 16. Description of equipment involved

____

continues

Exhibit 5001-1 *continued*

II. Narrative description of employee accident/incident (please describe employee accident/incident below and include why and how accident/incident occurred, effect of accident/incident on employee, sequence of events, and any other pertinent information)

____

____

____

____

____

____

____

____

III. Notification of individuals (please complete below)

Individuals Notified	Name of Individual Notified	Date Individual Notified	Time Individual Notified	Name of Individual Notifying
Physician				
Family				
Nursing Manager				
Administrator of Ambulatory Health Care				
Other				

FOLLOWING SECTION TO BE COMPLETED BY PHYSICIAN

IV. Employee outcome (please complete below)

_______ Yes _______ No 1. Employee seen by physician (please check (√)one; if *no* checked, please explain)

____

____ 2. Date employee seen by physician

____ 3. Time employee seen by physician

continues

Exhibit 5001-1 *continued*

____________________	4. Intervention(s) implemented for employee
____________________	
____________________	
____________________	5. Physician statement of assessment/intervention and signature
____________________	
____________________	
________ Yes ________ No	6. Documentation completed in employee clinical record (please check (√) one; if *no* checked, please explain)
____________________	

FOLLOWING SECTION TO BE COMPLETED BY NURSING DIRECTOR

V. Investigation of employee accident/incident (please complete below)

1. Review of employee accident/incident (please complete below)

____________________	Review date of this completed Employee Accident/Incident Report Form
____________________	Review time of this completed Employee Accident/Incident Report Form

2. Description of employee accident/incident investigation (please describe below)

____

____

____

____

____

3. Action that could have been taken to prevent recurrence of employee accident/incident (please describe below)

____

____

____

continues

Exhibit 5001-1 *continued*

4. Additional corrective action implemented? (please check (√) one below

_____ Yes

_____ No (please explain) ____________________

____

5. Date additional corrective action implemented (please complete below)

____

6. Description of implemented additional corrective action (please describe below)

____

____

____

____

7. Description of outcome(s) resulting from implemented corrective action (please describe below)

____

____

____

____

VI. Signatures (please sign below, as applicable)

Individuals	Comments	Date of Signature	Signature
Individual involved with employee accident/incident			
Individual(s) who completed this Employee Accident/Incident Report Form			
Physician			
Nursing Manager			
Administrator of Ambulatory Health Care			

Exhibit 5001-2 Authorization to Release Information Form

AMBULATORY HEALTH CARE PROVIDER
AUTHORIZATION TO RELEASE INFORMATION

To:

From:

Date:

Subject: Authorization to release information

I consent to the release of my insurance, employment, and medical information and other records. Specifically, I authorize and request you to allow______________________________to examine my
(name of individual/agency requesting to review records)
personal and medical records now heldby______________________________ and
(name of individual/agency requesting to review records)
to make photocopies of said records. I authorize ______________________________to
(name of individual/agency requesting to review records)
examine my personal and medical records for the following purpose(s) only:

1. ______________________________

2. ______________________________

3. ______________________________

I hereby release you from all legal responsibility or liability that may arise from compliance with the consent and request contained herein.

______________________________ ____________________

Signature of Individual Requesting Release of Information — Date of Signature

Exhibit 5001-3 First Report of Injury Form

ACORD. **WORKERS COMPENSATION EMPLOYER'S FIRST REPORT OF INJURY OR ILLNESS**
CONTAINS ALL ITEMS REQUIRED BY OSHA FORM 101 (Enter all dates in MM/DD/YY format)

OSHA CASE/FILE #

EMPLOYER (Name & State Mailing Address incl. County & Zip)

CARRIER CLAIM NUMBER

JURISDICTION CLAIM NUMBER

DO NOT WRITE IN SPACE BELOW

EMPLOYER'S LOCATION ADDRESS (If Different)

INDIVIDUAL PARTNERSHIP CORPORATION SIC CODE UNEMPLOY I.D. NO.: PHONE NUMBER (A/C No. Ext.)

OTHER FED TAX

NATURE OF BUSINESS (Mfg. Trade, Construction Etc.) SPECIFIC PRODUCTS # EMPLOYEES

INSURANCE

CARRIER (Name, Address & Phone No.)

POLICY/SELF-INSURED NUMBER

POLICY PERIOD

TO

CHECK IF APPROPRIATE SELF INSURANCE STATE FUND

EMPLOYEE

NAME (Last, First, Middle) SOCIAL SECURITY NUMBER PHONE NO. (A/C, No.)

ADDRESS (Include County & Zip) DATE OF BIRTH MARITAL STATUS EXEMPTION INFO. OVER 65 BLIND

EMPLOYEE

OFFICER/PARTNER? MALE SPOUSE

YES NO FEMALE # DEPENDENT CHILDREN

REGULAR DEPT. OR DIVISION DATE HIRED STATE WHERE HIRED

OTHER DEPENDENTS

OCCUPATION HOW LONG AT CURRENT JOB CERTIFICATE NUMBER (If Under 18)

WAGE INFORMATION

RATE PER HOUR WEEK OTHER

DAY MONTH

DATE RETURNED TO WORK FULL PAY FOR DAY OF INJURY? DID SALARY CONTINUE?

YES NO YES NO

AVERAGE WAGE/WEEK AT TIME OF INJURY

DOES EMPLOYEE RECEIVE PAY IN KIND?

NO YES (Explain)

OCCURRENCE

PLACE OF ACCIDENT OR OCCURRENCE (Incl. State) COUNTY OF INJURY DATE OF INJURY/ILL. TIME OF OCCURRENCE TIME WORKDAY BEGAN

AM PM AM PM

LAST WORKDATE DATE EMPL'R NOTIF'D INDIVIDUAL NOTIFIED

EMPLOYER'S PREMISES?

DESCRIBE NATURE OR INJURY OR ILLNESS IN DETAIL (Include part of body affected, eg. amputation of right index finger at 2nd joint, fractured arm, lead poisoning)

DESCRIBE EMPLOYEE'S ACTIVITIES WHEN INJURY OCCURRED WITH DETAILS OF HOW EVENT OCCURRED (Include name of other individuals involved, tools, machinery, objects, vapors, chemicals, radiations, unnatural motions of employee)

IF FATAL, GIVE DATE OF DEATH:

WERE SAFEGUARDS OR SAFETY EQUIPMENT PROVIDED? YES NO

WERE THEY USED? YES NO

PHYSICIAN (Name & Address)

HOSPITALIZED HOSPITAL (Name & Address)

OUT PATIENT

EMERGENCY ROOM

IN-HOUSE TREATMENT

FIRST AID

WITNESS (Name & Phone Number)

DATE MAILED TO INSURER PREPARER'S NAME & TITLE PHONE NUMBER (A/C, No., Ext.)

ACORD 4 (10/88) **SEND REPORT IMMEDIATELY - DO NOT WAIT FOR DOCTOR'S REPORT** **© ACORD CORPORATION 1988**

Note: The Workers Compensation Employers First Report of Injury or Illness (ACORD 4), has been endorsed as a standard form by the IAIABC. To date, a number of states either have or are in the process of adopting the form. Please check with the Industrial Commission or Department of Labor within your state to see if the form has been approved.

Source: ACORD Corporation, White Plains, New York, 1988.

Exhibit 5001-4 Summary of Employee Accidents/Incidents Form

AMBULATORY HEALTH CARE PROVIDER
SUMMARY OF EMPLOYEE ACCIDENTS/INCIDENTS

Date This Form Completed	Dates of Reporting Period	Total Number of Staff Member Accident/ Incident Forms Completed

ITEM	TOTAL NUMBER OF RESPONSES				
	YES	NO	DON'T KNOW	N/A	COMMENTS
I. Type of Employee Accident/Incident A. Employee injury 1. sprain/strain					
2. contusion					
3. laceration					
4. abrasion					
5. burn					
6. fracture					
7. dislocation					
8. foreign body					
9. human bite					
10. animal bite					
11. needle puncture					
12. other					
II. Type of Activity A. Employee					
1. handling equipment or supplies					
2. medication preparation					
3. medication administration					
4. patient assistance at bedside					
5. patient assistance away from bedside					
6. treatment preparation					
7. treatment administration					
8. other					
III. Action Related to Injury A. Employee 1. caught in or between objects					
2. fall					
3. lifting or pulling object					
4. lifting or pulling patient					
5. struck by equipment/object					
6. struck against equipment/object					
7. other					
B. Patient/Family Member 1. abusive; uncooperative					
2. other					
IV. Location of Employee Accident/Incident A. Provider office					
B. Parking lot					
C. Other					

continues

Exhibit 5001-4 *continued*

Shift When Employee Accident/Incident Occurred _____ Day _____ Evening _____ Night _____ Unknown	Job Category of Employee _____ RN _____ LPN _____ AHCA _____ Other _____________
Employee Involved Seen by Physician _____ Yes _____ No _____ Not Reported	X-Ray Taken: _____ Yes; Positive Finding _____ Yes; Negative Finding _____ Not Ordered _____ N/A
Signature of Individual Completing This Form	Date of Signature

AMBULATORY HEALTH CARE PROVIDER
QUALITY ASSURANCE
POLICY AND PROCEDURE
5002

Subject: Ambulatory Health Care Staff Member Orientation Manual

Drafted by: ____________	Date drafted: ____________
Revised by: ____________	Date revised: ____________
Approved by: ____________	Date approved: ____________
Supersedes date: ____________	Page #: ____________
Date effective: ____________	Page: ______ of ______

POLICY

The ambulatory health care provider maintains an orientation manual for use by its staff members.

PURPOSE

1. To provide written documentation of provider policies and procedures for staff members.
2. To define general standards for provider job performances and work expectations.

PROCEDURE

1. An *Ambulatory Health Care Provider Staff Member Orientation Manual* (see Exhibit 5002-1) is distributed to and discussed with each new ambulatory health care staff member.
2. The *Orientation Manual* does not necessarily contain all applicable ambulatory health care provider policies and procedures.
3. The Administrator of Ambulatory Health Care annually reviews and revises the *Orientation Manual* as necessary.
4. New or revised policies and procedures that are to be included in the *Ambulatory Health Care Provider Staff Member Orientation Manual* are first posted on the ambulatory health care provider's office bulletin board.
5. Ambulatory health care staff members may request and receive copies of new additions to the *Orientation Manual*.
6. Ambulatory health care staff members sign the last page of the *Orientation Manual* they received to indicate receipt of the same.
7. A copy of the signed last page of the *Orientation Manual* is placed in the ambulatory health care staff member's personnel file.
8. The ambulatory health care provider consistently enforces all ambulatory health care provider policies and procedures.

Exhibit 5002-1 Staff Member Orientation Manual

AMBULATORY HEALTH CARE PROVIDER
AMBULATORY HEALTH CARE STAFF MEMBER
ORIENTATION MANUAL

CONTENTS

* * * *

GENERAL INFORMATION FOR AMBULATORY HEALTH CARE STAFF

1. The ambulatory health care provider (AHCP) provides 24-hour ambulatory health care services, seven days a week.
2. The AHCP office hours are from 8:00 A.M. to 5:00 P.M., Monday through Friday.
3. The AHCP on-call hours are:
   a. 5:00 P.M. to 8:00 A.M., Monday through Friday
   b. 5:00 P.M. to 8:00 A.M., Friday through Monday (weekend hours)
4. An AHCP staff member who has accepted employment with the AHCP must submit the following:
   a. negative results from a Mantoux test or chest x-ray completed within two weeks of applying for the position, and annually thereafter
   b. completed staff member health examination form no later than two weeks after the first worked assignment if the staff member has not had a physical within a two-year period
5. The AHCP considers an AHCP staff member to have voluntarily quit employment with the AHCP if the staff member has not complied with the AHCP policies and procedures.
6. A minimum two-week written notice must be given if the AHCP staff member wishes voluntarily to quit employment with the AHCP. If a two-week notice is not given, the staff member will not be eligible for rehire by the AHCP.
7. AHCP staff members must represent the AHCP in a positive manner.

AMBULATORY HEALTH CARE PROVIDER
RESPONSIBILITIES OF AMBULATORY HEALTH CARE STAFF MEMBERS

PATIENT CARE

1. Communicate patient condition/changes, questions, and concerns to the AHCP nursing services department in a timely manner.
2. Do not violate patient confidentiality. Strict laws exist for protection of patient rights to confidentiality. This means that anything about the patients for whom services are provided is not to be discussed with anyone not affiliated with the AHCP. The patient's medical condition/diagnosis etc. may not be discussed with anyone not affiliated with the AHCP. Information may not be given to any attorney or individual that would violate patient confidentiality. When asked to give information about the patient, inform the requesting individual to contact the Nursing Manager.
3. Do not violate the patient/employee relationship:
   a. Do not share your personal life with patients, especially personal problems and concerns.
   b. Do not assume responsibility for patients' lifestyles but instead remember that patients choose to live certain lifestyles and that you must respect the same.
   c. Do not request or accept money from any patient or patient family members.
   d. Do not accept personal gifts from patients or patient family members. If a patient or family absolutely insists that the gift be taken, inform your supervisor of the same so that documentation can be placed in your personnel file to explain that the item was given to you. This action will protect you in the event there is a question as to why you are in possession of the item.
   e. Do not give personal gifts to any patient or patient family members.
   f. Do not take patients home.
   g. Do not discuss salary with patients, patient family members, and other staff members.
   h. Unlicensed staff members:
      (1) *do not contact the patient's physician without approval from the AHCRN or Nursing Manager.* If the patient or patient's family member requests that you contact the physician, inform him/her that you are not permitted to do so, but that you can contact the AHCRN so that the AHCRN can give assistance as necessary. Under no circumstances are unlicensed staff members allowed to receive physician orders.
      (2) *do not administer medications to patients.* Contact the appropriate AHCRN or the Nursing Manager if the

continues

Exhibit 5002-1 *continued*

patient is unable to take the medications, or if there is any other problem with the patient taking medications.
- (3) *do not apply medicated ointments for patients*
- (4) *do not administer eye or ear drops for patients*
- (5) *do not administer oxygen to patients*
- (6) *do not irrigate any tubes inserted in patients*
- (7) *do not suction any patient*

i. Do not personally transport patients in automotive vehicles.

j. Report suspected child abuse and/or neglect according to Child Abuse Act and the AHCP Policies and Procedures.

k. Report suspected vulnerable adult patient abuse and/or neglect according to the Vulnerable Adult Act and the AHCP policies and procedures:
- (1) Examples of adult abuse and neglect:
  - (a) *physical abuse*: physical act by caregiver that causes pain, suffering, injury, or hurt to a patient; physical acts by caregiver that chastise, belittle, embarrass, humiliate, or degrade a patient; use of unapproved or excessive physical or chemical restraint techniques toward a patient by caregiver
  - (b) *verbal abuse*: any derogatory, threatening, derisive, or demeaning language, whether oral or with gestures, directed toward a patient by caregiver; any profane language directed toward a patient by caregiver
  - (c) *neglect*: failure or refusal to attend to the necessary care and necessary treatment of a patient by caregiver; action or inaction by caregiver that denies patients the prescribed care and treatment to which they are entitled; actions by caregiver contrary to the prescribed treatment or program; unauthorized removal or unauthorized denial of a patient's personal possessions (e.g., cigarettes, radio, phonograph, toiletries, etc.); unauthorized removal or unauthorized denial of a patient's scheduled meals or snacks; failure to implement individual treatment programs as designed by the interdisciplinary treatment team; unauthorized use of seclusion and/or restraint; failure to secure proper or sufficient clothing and to see that patient is properly clothed; preventing a patient during normal waking hours from communicating by letter, telephone, or personal visit with the patient's lawyer, physician, patient advocate, or guardian; preventing a patient from having visits from relatives unless such visits are unauthorized; failure to intervene or protect patient from abuse/mistreatment by another patient or staff member; removal or denial of a patient's normal comfort needs (e.g., bed, hot water, lights, heat, clothing)
  - (d) *sexual abuse*: any sexual activity between a caregiver and a patient, even if such actions are consented to by the patient, or that a person in the caregiver's position should have reasonably known that the patient would perceive as sexual activity; caregiver using his/her position for sexual gratification or exploitation of patients

l. Report patient sexual harassment to the AHCP nursing services department.

m. Give a verbal and written report of patient incidents/accidents (e.g., patient falls, patient missing personal item, medication error) to the AHCP nursing services department immediately when the same is known.

n. Do the following for patient accidents/incidents:
- (1) Dial 911 for assistance in an emergency situation.
- (2) Report the incident to the nursing services department for further direction and instructions as necessary.
- (3) Contact patient's physician as necessary (licensed staff members).
- (4) Document the patient accident/incident without stating in the patient's clinical record that any error has been made. Record only an objective, factual account of the actual patient accident/incident, as illustrated by the following example:

  Situation: Demerol 50 mg ordered and Demerol 75 mg given.
  Charting: 5-10-88, 4:00 P.M. Demerol 100 mg IM given. Dr. Pain notified at 4:15 P.M. J. Nurse, R.N.

- (5) Send the completed AHCP patient accident/incident report to the Nursing Manager.

o. Follow infection control guidelines:
- (1) Wash hands frequently:
  - (a) before and after provision of direct patient care
  - (b) after handling soiled or contaminated materials
  - (c) after going to the toilet
- (2) Cover nose when coughing or sneezing.
- (3) Cover open sores or cuts on fingers or hands with clean bandages.
- (4) Maintain a clean work environment by maintaining clean counters, tables, and shelves.
- (5) Rinse cans and bottles before disposal in the garbage.
- (6) Wash garbage cans, dirty pails, and trash cans with hot soapy water.
- (7) Dispose of garbage properly.
- (8) Keep clean and dirty items separate.
- (9) Use sterile items that are not outdated.
- (10) Regularly clean patient supplies, such as commodes, bedpans, urinals, suction machines, and measuring containers.

STAFFING

1. AHCP staff members must be dependable and responsible for their work schedule and assignments, as follows:
   a. Have all schedule changes and work assignments arranged, coordinated, and approved by your supervisor.
   b. Report for accepted work assignments.
   c. Arrange schedules to avoid conflict with accepted AHCP work assignments, especially if you are working for another employer in addition to working for the AHCP.
   d. Give an advance four-hour minimum notice to your supervisor if a work assignment is canceled due to unforeseen events such as illness, injury, or emergency situations. If the answering service is contacted after AHCP office hours, inform the answering service of the need to speak to an on-call nurse. The answering service will contact the on-call nurse, who will contact the staff member.
   e. Be on time for scheduled work assignments. If you are not able to be on time due to a legitimate emergency, you must contact your supervisor.
   f. The hours you work, as reflected on your time card, must coincide with the hours approved by your supervisor in order for you to be paid for the hours worked.

continues

Exhibit 5002-1 *continued*

JOB PERFORMANCE

1. Report to your supervisor who supervises, evaluates, and monitors your job performance.
2. Participate in annual job performance reviews done by your supervisor.
3. Function according to your job description.
4. Contact your supervisor if you are requested to perform tasks that are not in your job description.
5. Contact your supervisor if the work assignment changes drastically from your job description.
6. Adhere to the following AHCP standards in dress, appearance, and conduct:
   a. Wear casual clothes, such as skirts, slacks, and shirts.
   b. Maintain a neat appearance.
   c. Wear a clean uniform.
   d. *For women*: wear hemlines at knee length; comfortable, enclosed toe and heel shoes; and nylons or socks.
   e. Wear an AHCP identifying name tag.
   f. Keep fingernails clean.
   g. Wear jewelry sparingly, for example, a ring and small earrings.
   h. Function within limits set by the AHCP's policies and procedures.
   i. Do not use slang or foul language.
   j. Be considerate and courteous in contacts with patients and other persons.
   k. Treat patients with respect and recognize their need for privacy.
   l. Ensure confidentiality with respect to patients' conditions, histories, and behaviors.
   m. Do not accept gratuities from patients.
   n. Maintain a calm and reassuring attitude in crisis situations.
   o. Be tactful in manners and attitudes when dealing with patients and other persons.
   p. Complete all assignments satisfactorily.
   q. Seek clarification of assignments as necessary.
   r. Seek assistance when unable to complete assignments.
7. Contact your supervisor within 24 hours if injured while on duty. Failure to notify your supervisor within the 24-hour period may disqualify you from receiving workers compensation benefits.
8. Do not abuse chemical substances, e.g., alcohol or drugs.
9. Do not sleep on duty. Any medication that might make you drowsy is not to be taken while on duty.
10. Do not witness signatures on any papers, e.g., sale of a house, last will and testament.
11. Do not violate staff member confidentiality. This means that staff members' addresses and telephone numbers are not to be released to patients or any person not affiliated with the AHCP. If a request is received to release the same information, tell the individual to contact the personnel manager.
12. Do not falsify time slips. The time that is written on the time slip is to reflect the time that is actually scheduled and worked.
13. Do not discuss salary with patients or patient family members.

DOCUMENTATION

1. Document all patient ambulatory health care on the day the service is rendered.
2. Document patient ambulatory health care information on patient flowsheets, as appropriate.
3. Document:
   a. using black ballpoint ink
   b. writing legibly
   c. using objective statements
   d. putting patient name on every form
   e. putting complete date for every notation, i.e., month, date, year
   f. using correct spelling and grammar
   g. charting entries following last charting entry without leaving blank lines or spaces in progress notes
   h. ending each narrative entry by signature, professional title, and complete date
   i. ending each flowsheet entry by signature, professional title, and complete date
   j. never charting under or signing name that you legally do not have
   k. without copying another staff member's notations
   l. using only common abbreviations
   m. charting only for actual days of delivered ambulatory health care services
   n. including only significant information about the patient
   o. labeling late entries as an addendum, signing them, and including them in the clinical record
   p. correcting one-word or two-word errors by making a single line of black ink through the words in error, noting "error" over the words in error, and noting the initials of the individual who made the error
   q. correcting paragraph errors by making a single line of black ink through the paragraph in error, enclosing the paragraph in brackets, writing "error" beside the brackets, and noting the initials of the individual who made the error

COMMUNICATION

1. Conduct yourself in a friendly, cooperative, and professional manner with everyone.
2. Ask if something is not understood.
3. Use a normal speaking tone when talking with others. Raising your voice or sounding angry is unacceptable behavior.
4. Use respectful language when talking with others. Use of foul language is unacceptable behavior.
5. Listen when other individuals are talking. Hanging up in the middle of a telephone conversation is unacceptable behavior.
6. Communicate appropriate information to the appropriate individuals, e.g., communicate patient condition/changes to the nursing services department and not to the finance department.

PERSONNEL

1. Keep professional licenses updated.
2. Give copy of updated professional license to the Personnel Manager.
3. Attend continuing education classes to keep professional knowledge and skills current.
4. Advise the Personnel Manager of any change in home address, telephone number, or availability to work.
5. Contact the Personnel Manager if new skills are learned or enough experience is gained that may increase salary level.
6. Contact Personnel Manager regarding any physical limitations you have regardless of where the physical limitation occurred.

continues

Exhibit 5002-1 *continued*

7. Give the Personnel Manager a signed physician release statement for continued employment when treated for any communicable disease, back injury, mental illness, chemical dependency, or pregnancy.
8. Contact the Personnel Manager within 24 hours if injured while on duty. Failure to notify the Personnel Manager within 24 hours may disqualify you from receiving workers compensation benefits.
9. Contact the Personnel Manager regarding incidents/accidents immediately upon awareness of the same, e.g., staff member injury.
10. Document incidents/accidents immediately.
11. Report sexual harassment to the Personnel Manager.

I am in receipt and have reviewed of the entire orientation manual

______________________	______________________
Ambulatory Health Care Staff Member Signature	Date of Signature

---

BIBLIOGRAPHY

Bulau, Judith M. *Clinical Policies and Procedures for Home Health Care*. Rockville, Md.: Aspen Publishers, Inc., 1986.

Connaway, Nancy. *Documenting Patient Care in the Home: Legal Issues for Home Health Nurses*, Home Health Care Nurse Hospital Publications Incorporated, New Jersey, Sept./Oct. 1985, Vol. 3, No. 5, pp. 6–8.

AMBULATORY HEALTH CARE PROVIDER
QUALITY ASSURANCE
POLICY AND PROCEDURE
5003

Subject: Discipline of Ambulatory Health Care Staff Members	
Drafted by: ______	Date drafted: ______
Revised by: ______	Date revised: ______
Approved by: ______	Date approved: ______
Supersedes date: ______	Page #: ______
Date effective: ______	Page: ______ of ______

POLICY

Discipline of ambulatory health care staff members for inappropriate behavior is imposed in a fair and consistent manner.

PURPOSE

1. To assist individual ambulatory health care staff members in addressing inappropriate behavior.
2. To provide a fair and consistent approach in addressing inappropriate behavior demonstrated by ambulatory health care staff members.

PROCEDURE

1. Definition of *inappropriate behavior*: ambulatory health care staff member actions that adversely affect the quality of care, personal safety, or comfort of patients or the proper functioning of the ambulatory health care provider's operations, services, programs, activities, and staff.
2. Action:
   a. Inappropriate behavior demonstrated by an ambulatory health care staff member is documented on a Staff Concern Form (see Exhibit 5003-1) by the individual who observed the behavior.
   b. The completed Staff Concern Form is submitted to the staff member's immediate supervisor.
   c. The staff member's immediate supervisor:
      (1) investigates staff concern, as appropriate
      (2) reviews and discusses staff concern with the ambulatory health care staff member who allegedly demonstrated the inappropriate behavior to determine extent of problem behavior and corrective action that may be necessary
      (3) considers the following courses of action with regard to the ambulatory health care staff member's reported inappropriate behavior:
         (a) formal counseling
         (b) verbal warning
         (c) written warning
         (d) suspension notice
         (e) voluntary quit notice
      (4) discusses the inappropriate behavior with the ambulatory health care staff member
      (5) clarifies relevant issues or problems from a management perspective
      (6) notes desired corrective action to be taken within defined time period
      (7) notes possibility of further disciplinary action if such corrective action is not taken in stipulated time period
      (8) notes that all documentation regarding the inappropriate behavior will be placed in the ambulatory health care staff member's personnel file
      (9) encourages the ambulatory health care staff member to prepare a written explanation for the inappropriate behavior
   d. The staff member's immediate supervisor subsequently:
      (1) documents the meeting with the ambulatory health care staff member on an Inappropriate Behavior Documentation Form (see Exhibit 5003-2)
      (2) documents and signs a written warning on a Written Warning Letter Form (see Exhibit 5003-3)
      (3) documents any implemented disciplinary action on the Disciplinary Action Report Form (see Exhibit 5003-4)
      (4) gives copy of completed Inappropriate Behavior Documentation Form to the ambulatory health care staff member

(5) gives copy of completed Written Warning Letter Form to the ambulatory health care staff member if a written warning is issued
(6) gives copy of completed Disciplinary Action Report Form to Personnel Manager who places documentation in ambulatory health care staff member's personnel file
(7) arranges subsequent meetings as appropriate with the ambulatory health care staff member to assess progress with plan of corrective action
(8) documents subsequent meetings with the staff member on the Inappropriate Behavior Documentation Form
(9) gives copy of completed Inappropriate Behavior Documentation Form on such meetings to the ambulatory health care staff member

e. If the corrective action is not taken by the ambulatory health care staff member within the defined time period, or if the staff member demonstrates further inappropriate behavior, the staff member's immediate supervisor in consultation with the supervisor's immediate supervisor:
(1) implements next step of disciplinary process:
(a) first step: formal counseling
(b) second step: verbal warning
(c) third step: written warning
(d) fourth step: suspension
(e) fifth step: voluntary quit
(2) documents next step of disciplinary process as described in item d(1), (2), and (3)
(3) gives copy of documentation describing next step of disciplinary process as detailed in item d(4), (5), and (6) to the ambulatory health care staff member

f. Ambulatory health care staff members may be considered to have voluntarily quit their employment with the ambulatory health care provider for demonstrating critical inappropriate behavior following Policy and Procedure 5005: Involuntary Termination of Employment.

Exhibit 5003-1 Staff Concern Form

AMBULATORY HEALTH CARE PROVIDER
STAFF CONCERN

Following Section To Be Completed by Individual Reporting the Concern

Name of Individual(s) Involved in Incident	Date of Incident	Time of Incident a.m. p.m.
Place of Incident	Date This Form Completed	Time This Form Completed a.m. p.m.

Objective Narrative Description of Incident (Please Describe Below)

Description of Identified Problems Resulting from Incident (Please Describe Below)

Corrective Action Implemented? ____ yes ____ no (Please Explain) ________	Date Corrective Action Implemented

Description of Implemented Corrective Action (Please Describe Below)

Signature of Individual Completing This Form	Date of Signature

Following Section To Be Completed by Supervisor Reviewing Identified Concern

Date This Completed Form Received	Date This Completed Form Reviewed	Time This Completed Form Reviewed a.m. p.m.

Description of Incident Investigation (Please Describe Below)

continues

Exhibit 5003-1 *continued*

Description of Identified Problem(s) Resulting from Incident (Please Describe Below)

Additional Corrective Action Implemented?
_____ yes _____ no (Please Explain) ____________________

Description of Implemented Additional Corrective Action (Please Describe Below)

Description of Outcome(s) Resulting from Corrective Action (Please Describe Below)

Signature of Supervisor	Date of Signature

Exhibit 5003-2 Inappropriate Behavior Documentation Form

AMBULATORY HEALTH CARE PROVIDER
INAPPROPRIATE BEHAVIOR DOCUMENTATION

To: (Employee with inappropriate behavior)

From: (Employee's immediate supervisor)

Date:

Subject: Inappropriate behavior

This is to provide documentation of our ____________________ (date) discussion regarding your inappropriate behavior, apparently demonstrated, as follows:

- Individuals present during our discussion:
- Reason for our discussion was to give you information about how other individuals perceive your behavior and to give you a:
  ______ formal counseling session
  ______ verbal warning notice
  ______ written warning notice
  ______ suspension notice
  ______ termination notice
- Description of documented inappropriate behavior you apparently demonstrated:
- Summary of discussion issues from:
  - your perspective
  - management perspective
- Plan of corrective action will be as follows:
  - you will be expected to:
- The consequences for you if you do not meet the defined expectations and if you demonstrate any further inappropriate behaviors will be:

Please be informed that all documentation related to your inappropriate behavior will be placed in your personnel file.

Please contact me if I can be of any assistance to you or if you have any questions and/or concerns.

____ ______________________

Signature of Employee's Immediate Supervisor Date of Signature

Exhibit 5003-3 Written Warning Letter Form

(Date)

(Name and Address of Ambulatory Health Care Staff Member)

Dear (Name of Ambulatory Health Care Staff Member):

This is to inform you that because you have demonstrated inappropriate behavior, disciplinary action is being implemented for the same.

The inappropriate behavior demonstrated by you and the disciplinary action being implemented for your inappropriate behavior is as follows:

_____ Incompetence
_____ Misconduct
_____ Malicious, verbal abuse to patient, patient family, peers, supervisors, or others
_____ Physical abuse of patient, patient family, peers, supervisors, or others
_____ Not reporting for accepted work assignments without supervisory approval
_____ Leaving accepted work assignment without supervisory approval
_____ Chemical abuse while on duty at accepted work assignments
_____ Sleeping while on duty at accepted work assignments
_____ Refusal to comply with requests and assignments of supervisors
_____ Current professional license has not been submitted
_____ Professional license outdated
_____ Current Mantoux or chest x-ray results have not been submitted within timeframe defined by ambulatory health care policy and procedure
_____ Current physical has not been submitted within timeframe defined by ambulatory health care provider policy and procedure
_____ Violation of acknowledged and known ambulatory health care provider policies and procedures
_____ Other: ______________________________

Comments: ______________________________
____
____
____
____
____

In the event you demonstrate additional inappropriate behavior and noncompliance with ambulatory health care provider policies and procedures, we will have no alternative but to consider that you have voluntarily decided to quit your employment with the provider.
Please contact me if you have any questions.

Sincerely,

(Employee's Immediate Supervisor)

cc: Ambulatory health care staff member's personnel file

Exhibit 5003-4 Disciplinary Action Report Form

DISCIPLINARY ACTION

DATE: ______________________

EMPLOYEE NAME	DISCIPLINE:		DEPARTMENT WHERE PROBLEM BEHAVIOR DEMONSTRATED:	WORK RESTRICTIONS
	DATE	TYPE		

AMBULATORY HEALTH CARE PROVIDER
QUALITY ASSURANCE
POLICY AND PROCEDURE
5004

Subject: Discipline of Ambulatory Health Care Staff Members Involved in Patient Abuse and/or Neglect

Drafted by: ______	Date drafted: ______
Revised by: ______	Date revised: ______
Approved by: ______	Date approved: ______
Supersedes date: ______	Page #: ______
Date effective: ______	Page: ____ of ______

POLICY

The ambulatory health care provider implements disciplinary action when there is reasonable cause to believe that an ambulatory health care staff member has engaged in patient abuse and/or neglect.

PURPOSE

1. To implement corrective action in the case of patient abuse and/or neglect by an ambulatory health care staff member.
2. To prevent further patient abuse and neglect.

PROCEDURE

1. Appropriate disciplinary action is taken when there is reasonable cause to believe that an ambulatory health care staff member has engaged in patient abuse and/or neglect.
2. In such cases, the employment of the ambulatory health care staff member with the ambulatory health care provider is immediately terminated.
3. The disciplinary action is documented on a Termination of Employment Form, following Policy and Procedure 5005: Involuntary Termination of Employment (see Exhibit 5005-2).
4. The completed Termination of Employment Form is filed in the relevant staff member's personnel file.

AMBULATORY HEALTH CARE PROVIDER
QUALITY ASSURANCE
POLICY AND PROCEDURE
5005

Subject: Involuntary Termination of Employment	
Drafted by: ______	Date drafted: ______
Revised by: ______	Date revised: ______
Approved by: ______	Date approved: ______
Supersedes date: ______	Page #: ______
Date effective: ______	Page: ____ of ______

POLICY

The ambulatory health care provider consistently processes ambulatory health care staff members' involuntary termination of employment, following appropriate provider policies and procedures.

PURPOSE

1. To address ambulatory health care staff members' inappropriate behavior.
2. To facilitate the processing of the termination of ambulatory health care staff members' employment with the ambulatory health care provider.

PROCEDURE

1. Definition
   Involuntary termination: the termination of an ambulatory health care staff member who has not volunteered to terminate employment with the ambulatory health care provider and who has demonstrated critical inappropriate behavior, regardless of whether the staff member has previously demonstrated inappropriate behavior or been disciplined.
2. Action
   a. The ambulatory health care staff member's immediate supervisor:
      (1) consults with the Administrator of Ambulatory Health Care regarding need for involuntary termination of employment of an ambulatory health care staff member
      (2) informs the ambulatory health care staff member that the staff member will be terminated from employment with the ambulatory health care provider
      (3) informs the staff member of the opportunity to participate in an exit interview
      (4) gives an Ambulatory Health Care Staff Member Evaluation of Employment with the Ambulatory Health Care Provider Form to the terminating ambulatory health care staff member (see Policy and Procedure 5011 and Exhibit 5011-1)
      (5) requests the terminating ambulatory health care staff member to complete and sign a Health Insurance Coverage for Terminating Employees Form (see Exhibit 5005-1)
      (6) places the original signed copy of the Health Insurance Coverage for Terminating Employees Form in the terminating staff member's personnel file
      (7) gives a copy of the signed Health Insurance Coverage for Terminating Employees Form to the terminating staff member
      (8) documents the involuntary termination of employment on Termination of Employment Form (see Exhibit 5005-2)
      (9) documents additional information concerning the termination, following Policy and Procedure 5003: Discipline of Ambulatory Health Care Staff Members
      (10) submits completed documentation regarding the involuntary termination of employment to the Administrator of Ambulatory Health Care
      (11) collects keys, equipment, and other provider property from the staff member prior to issuing the final paycheck to the staff member
      (12) ascertains the status of any outstanding financial obligations to the ambulatory health care provider, such as payments in educational programs, before issuing the final paycheck to the terminating staff member
      (13) ensures that the final paycheck is released to the terminating ambulatory health care staff mem-

ber within 48 hours of the involuntary termination of employment

(14) places completed documentation regarding the involuntary termination of employment in the staff member's personnel file

b. The Personnel Manager:

(1) sends the appropriate forms concerning the involuntary termination to the Department of Economic Security

(2) gives a copy of a completed Separation Notice Form to the terminating ambulatory health care staff member (see Exhibit 5005-3)

(3) completes an Employee Change Form (see Exhibit 5005-4)

(4) sends the completed Employee Change Form to the Bookkeeping Department

c. The last employment day worked is the staff member's official date of involuntary termination of employment.

Exhibit 5005-1 Form for Health Insurance Coverage for Terminating Employees

AMBULATORY HEALTH CARE PROVIDER
HEALTH INSURANCE COVERAGE FOR TERMINATING EMPLOYEES

To: (Ambulatory health care staff member)

From:

Date:

Subject: Health insurance coverage for terminating employees

Due to your termination with the ambulatory health care provider, your health insurance coverage will be affected. However, state law provides you with the option to continue health insurance coverage at your own expense, until you are employed again or for a period of six (6) months after your termination of employment with the ambulatory health care provider, whichever is shorter.

If you choose to continue this health insurance coverage, it will be your responsibility to pay the entire cost of the health insurance premium to the ambulatory health care provider. The ambulatory health care provider will then make payment to the health insurance carrier. Please make your payment checks payable to the ambulatory health care provider by ______________________ (date payment due). If you fail to make timely health insurance coverage payments, your health insurance coverage for the month in which payment is not received will be terminated.

Please check (√) one of the options below. Please sign and date your signature at the bottom of this form.

___I have read the above information and want to cancel my current health insurance coverage after I terminate my employment with the ambulatory health care provider.

___I have read the above information and want to continue my current health insurance coverage after I terminate employment with the ambulatory health care provider. I understand and agree to all of the terms stated above.

______________________________ ______________________________
Signature of Ambulatory Health Care Staff Member — Date of Signature

______________________________ ______________________________
Signature of Individual Sending This Form — Date of Signature

Exhibit 5005-2 Termination of Employment Form

AMBULATORY HEALTH CARE PROVIDER
TERMINATION OF EMPLOYMENT

To:

From:

Subject: Termination of employment

Date:

Last date of employment: ____________________

Reason(s) for termination: ____________________

____

____________________ ____________________

Signature of Ambulatory Health Care Staff Member Date of Signature

____________________ ____________________

Signature of Ambulatory Health Care Staff Members Immediate Supervisor Date of Signature

Exhibit 5005-3 Separation Notice Form

INSTRUCTIONS TO EMPLOYER

- DO NOT USE THIS FORM TO SHOW A SEPARATION DUE TO LACK OF WORK.
- WHEN A SEPARATION IS FOR ANY OTHER REASON OR IF A WORKER REFUSES REEMPLOYMENT, MAIL CARD COPY TO THE DEPARTMENT AT THE ADDRESS BELOW WITHIN 7 DAYS OF THE SEPARATION.
- DELIVER DUPLICATE TO WORKER. RETAIN TRIPLICATE FOR YOUR FILES.
- ADDITIONAL SUPPLIES OF THESE FORMS MAY BE SECURED WITHOUT COST FROM THE DEPARTMENT.

MINNESOTA UNEMPLOYMENT TAX ACCOUNT NUMBER

☐☐☐☐☐☐☐ • ☐ • ☐☐

EMPLOYER'S NAME AND ADDRESS

MINNESOTA DEPARTMENT OF ECONOMIC SECURITY
390 N. Robert Street
St. Paul, Minnesota 55101

SEPARATION NOTICE

WORKER'S NAME

SSA# ☐☐☐ ☐☐ ☐☐☐☐

LAST DAY OF ACTUAL WORK ____________________

DATE WORK BEGAN ____________________

REASON FOR NOTICE

☐ VOLUNTARY QUIT ☐ DISCHARGE FOR MISCONDUCT
☐ OTHER REASON ☐ REFUSAL OF RE-EMPLOYMENT

EXPLANATION ____________________

____

EMPLOYER'S SIGNATURE DATE

INSTRUCTIONS TO WORKER

- SAVE THIS NOTICE AND PRESENT IT IF YOU CLAIM UNEMPLOYMENT COMPENSATION.
- LOSS COULD DELAY PAYMENT OF BENEFITS.

Exhibit 5005-4 Employee Change Form

GRAMCO

Great American Computer Systems, Inc.
2419 Nicollet Avenue
Minneapolis, MN 55404
871-1459

EMPLOYEE CHANGE FORM

Client Name ______________________ Number ________ of ________

1. Department/Class/Level	15. Pay Type	46. Standard 7	37. Benefit Eligible	52. Irregular Frequency
2. Reset	16. Rate of Pay	47. Standard 8	38. Vacation Plan No.	53 Deduct Calculation
5. Name	17. Different Rt. 1	27. Standard 9	39. Activate	54. Calculation Rate
6. Address	18. Differential Rt. 2	28. Standard 10	40. Terminate and Date 2	59. Code & Date 3 xx xx/xx/xx
7. City/State	19. Additional F. W. H.	29. Standard 11	41. Weeks Worked	60. Code & Date 4 xx xx/xx/xx
8. Hire Date 1	20. Additional S. W. H.	30. Zip Code	42. Over Maximum	61. Code & Date 5 xx xx/xx/xx
9. Social Security No.	21. Standard 1	31. Vacation Hours Worked	43. Passive Rate Increase	75. Uniform Cycle
10. Federal Dependents	22. Standard 2	32. Vacation Hours Taken	45. Irregular State	76. Uniform Hours
11. State Dependents	23. Standard 3	33. Vacation Hours Available	48. Vacation Earned	80. Month/Date of Birth
12. Marital Status	24. Standard 4	34. Sick Worked	49. Sick Earned	81. Date of Last Increase
13. Officer	25. Standard 5	35. Sick Taken	50. Federal Withholding %	82. Prior Pay Rate
14. FICA	26. Standard 6	36. Sick Available	51. State Withholding %	83. Hours Wkd. Since Last Increase
				84. Hours Wkd. Since Date of Hire

D	C	L	BASE	EMPLOYEE NAME	CODE NAME	CODE	ENTRY TO BE	ENTRY WAS

1. Information given will replace information currently on file. Hour or dollar values will not be added to or subtracted from what is currently on file.
2. All changes are made prior to processing. Thus if an employee is to get a final check do not terminate until following period.
3. When a department, class, or level of care is changed it must also be changed on the input form.

____
Authorization

____
Date

Source: Reprinted with permission of Great American Computer Systems, Inc., 1982.

AMBULATORY HEALTH CARE PROVIDER
QUALITY ASSURANCE
POLICY AND PROCEDURE
5006

Subject: Job Descriptions	
Drafted by: ______	Date drafted: ______
Revised by: ______	Date revised: ______
Approved by: ______	Date approved: ______
Supersedes date: ______	Page #: ______
Date effective: ______	Page: ______ of ______

POLICY

Ambulatory health care staff positions are defined by written job descriptions.

PURPOSE

1. To define standards for ambulatory health care staff role performance.
2. To document ambulatory health care staff member job responsibilities and expectations.

PROCEDURE

1. The written job description includes:
   a. *job title:* name by which position is identified
   b. *scope of position:* overall statement of responsibilities and duties
   c. *qualifications:* necessary education or competencies, years of experience, and other necessary requirements
   d. *physical requirements:* expectations of what is physically required to fulfill the responsibilities of the position
   e. *performance responsibilities:* job performance expectations
   f. *organizational relationship:* the position's inter- and intradepartmental reporting/cooperative relationships
   g. *acceptance of position:* staff member's signing of the following statement: "I have read and understand the job description for *(position)* and agree to fulfill the position's responsibilities to meet the defined standards."
   h. *signatures:* the signatures of the ambulatory health care staff member and the staff member's supervisor and the date of their signatures.
2. Job descriptions are documented for each ambulatory health care provider position, for example, Administrator of Ambulatory Health Care (see Exhibit 5006-1), Nursing Manager (see Exhibit 5006-2), Quality Assurance Manager (see Exhibit 5006-3), Ambulatory Health Care Registered Nurse (see Exhibit 5006-4), Ambulatory Health Care Licensed Practical Nurse (see Exhibit 5006-5), and Ambulatory Health Care Aide (see Exhibit 5006-6).
3. Provider job descriptions are reviewed and revised on an annual basis.

Exhibit 5006-1 Job Description of Position of Administrator of Ambulatory Health Care

AMBULATORY HEALTH CARE PROVIDER
ADMINISTRATOR OF AMBULATORY HEALTH CARE JOB DESCRIPTION

Date approved: ________________

SUPERSEDES ALL PREVIOUS ADMINISTRATOR OF AMBULATORY HEALTH CARE JOB DESCRIPTIONS

Approved by: ____
Signature of President of the Ambulatory Health Care Provider

continues

Exhibit 5006-1 *continued*

Position title:

Administrator of Ambulatory Health Care

Position scope:

To ensure quality and safe delivery of ambulatory health care services.

To coordinate provision of ambulatory health care services that reflect the ambulatory health care provider philosophy and standards of ambulatory health care.

To plan, develop, implement, and evaluate ambulatory health care provider services, programs, and activities.

Position qualifications:

Graduate of an accredited college with a bachelor's degree required.

Graduate from an accredited college with a master's degree in health care administration or business preferred.

Minimum of five years progressively responsible administrative experience in health care or related field, demonstrating management and leadership expertise, preferred.

Demonstrated ability in application of organizational/communication skills required.

Physical requirements

Visual/hearing ability sufficient to comprehend written/verbal communication.

Ability to perform tasks involving physical activity, which may include heavy lifting and extensive bending and standing.

Ability to deal effectively with stress.

Performance responsibilities and standards:

1. Ensures quality and safe delivery of ambulatory health care services.
   a. Developed and implemented written ambulatory health care provider policies and procedures reflect quality and safe delivery of ambulatory health care services.
   b. Patient clinical records are reviewed per policy and procedure.
   c. Activities of committees, including Ambulatory Health Care Advisory Committee and Ambulatory Health Care Quality Assurance Committee are monitored on a regular basis.
   d. Quality of ambulatory health care services given by contract personnel are monitored on a regular basis.
   e. Adequate and appropriate supplies and equipment are available and maintained at all times.
   f. Ambulatory health care staff members' job performance is monitored and evaluated on a regular basis.
   g. Performance responsibilities are delegated to appropriate individuals as necessary.
2. Performs additional performance responsibilities as assigned and as necessary.
   a. Additional performance responsibilities are accurately completed in a timely manner.
3. Develops and implements written policies and procedures that reflect ambulatory health care provider philosophy and objectives.
   a. Developed and implemented written policies and procedures reflect ambulatory health care provider philosophy and objectives.
   b. Developed and implemented long-range plan reflects ambulatory health care provider philosophy and objectives.
   c. Ambulatory health care administrative and clinical policies and procedures are reviewed and revised annually.
   d. Ambulatory health care administrative and clinical policies and procedures are evaluated for effectiveness in delivery of quality and safe ambulatory health care services.
   e. Corrective action is implemented for ambulatory health care administrative and clinical policies and procedures that are not effective in delivery of quality and safe ambulatory health care services.
4. Ensures compliance of ambulatory health care provider operations with federal, state, and local rules and regulations.
   a. Documentation of ambulatory health care provider and patient clinical records demonstrates compliance with ambulatory health care provider policies and procedures and federal, state, and local rules and regulations.
   b. Ambulatory health care administrative and clinical policies and procedures are reviewed and revised as necessary to reflect compliance with federal, state, and local rules and regulations.
   c. The Administrator of Ambulatory Health Care is available at all times during ambulatory health care provider operating hours.

continues

Exhibit 5006-1 *continued*

- d. The Administrator of Ambulatory Health Care is on-call for emergencies involving ambulatory health care staff members and patients.
- e. Participation in ambulatory health care activities is demonstrated.

5. Promotes effective written/verbal communication.
   - a. Skill in conflict resolution is demonstrated.
   - b. Positive work environment is promoted for ambulatory health care staff members.
   - c. Monthly ambulatory health care staff meetings with management team members are conducted and documented.
   - d. Changes in ambulatory health care provider operations and policies and procedures are communicated to ambulatory health care provider staff members in a timely manner.
   - e. Consistent and concise lines of authority and responsibility are interpreted and maintained among ambulatory health care staff members.
   - f. Participation in appropriate committee meetings is demonstrated per policy and procedure.
   - g. Communication of appropriate information regarding ambulatory health care provider operations is communicated to ambulatory health care provider Board of Directors.
   - h. Submission of written reports to the ambulatory health care provider Board of Directors in a timely manner is demonstrated.
   - i. Cooperation with ambulatory health care provider Board of Directors pursuant to ambulatory health care provider philosophy and objectives is demonstrated.
   - j. Participation in ambulatory health care provider events is demonstrated.
   - k. Positive interpretation of ambulatory health care provider philosophy, objectives, and long-range plan is provided to ambulatory health care staff members on a regular basis.
   - l. Consultation with ambulatory health care provider Board of Directors is initiated as issues and concerns require.
   - m. Cooperation with federal, state, and local agencies is demonstrated.
6. Develops, implements, and evaluates adequate staffing to address staffing needs for delivery of ambulatory health care services.
   - a. Assigned responsibility for ambulatory health care provider operations in absence of Administrator and Nursing Manager is demonstrated.
   - b. Developed, implemented, and evaluated ambulatory health care staff recruitment policies and procedures reflect staffing needs of ambulatory health care provider.
   - c. Ambulatory health care staff recruitment policies and procedures are demonstrated in the interviewing and hiring of qualified ambulatory health care staff members according to written job descriptions.
   - d. Attendance and replacement of ambulatory health care staff members are monitored for compliance with ambulatory health care provider policies and procedures.
   - e. Ambulatory health care staffing patterns are assessed to ensure that staffing needs of the ambulatory health care provider are adequately fulfilled.
7. Monitors supervision and evaluation of ambulatory health care staff job performance.
   - a. Job descriptions are reviewed and revised annually.
   - b. Performance appraisals of ambulatory health care staff members are monitored.
   - c. Performance appraisal of Nursing Manager is documented.
   - d. Performance appraisal of Nursing Manager is communicated to Nursing Manager annually and as necessary.
   - e. Consultation with Nursing Manager regarding professional growth is demonstrated.
   - f. Disciplinary action is instituted, interpreted, and documented per policy and procedure.
   - g. Review of disciplinary action of ambulatory health care staff members is documented.
   - h. Performance appraisals of contract personnel are documented.
8. Develops, implements, evaluates, and monitors ambulatory health care provider financial policies and procedures and records.
   - a. Financial policies and procedures and records comply with federal, state, and local rules and regulations.
   - b. Patient financial records are consistently accurate, current, and accessible.
   - c. Statistical financial records are current and accurate.
   - d. Billing for ambulatory health care provider services provided to patients and third party payers is current and presented in a timely manner.
9. Develops, implements, and evaluates budget plan and cost control policies and procedures.
   - a. Ambulatory health care provider salary/equipment/supply budgets are submitted in a timely manner to the ambulatory health care provider Board of Directors.
   - b. Recommendations for capital expenditures are submitted in a timely manner to the ambulatory health care provider Board of Directors.
   - c. Proposals for salary changes are submitted to the Board of Directors for approval.
   - d. Ambulatory health care provider budget reports and statistics are accurately written and submitted in a timely manner to the ambulatory health care provider Board of Directors.
   - e. Cost control policies and procedures are developed, implemented, and evaluated.
   - f. Cost reports are reviewed and discussed with management team members as necessary.
   - g. Cost reports are monitored.
   - h. Corrective action plans are implemented for cost control problems.
   - i. The ambulatory health care provider budget is monitored to ensure operation within the approved budget.

continues

Exhibit 5006-1 *continued*

10. Develops and implements salary program within approved ambulatory health care provider policies and procedures.
    a. Ambulatory health care provider staff member salaries are determined within approved salary budgets.
    b. Salary increases are recommended according to ambulatory health care provider policies and procedures.
    c. New ambulatory health care staff member salaries and salary adjustments are implemented according to ambulatory health care provider policies and procedures.
    d. Ambulatory health care staff member salaries and salary adjustments are approved by the Administrator of Ambulatory Health Care.
    e. Time card and payroll documentation is done accurately and in a timely manner.
    f. Ambulatory health care staff member paychecks are distributed according to the ambulatory health care provider policy and procedure.
11. Complies with ambulatory health care provider policies and procedures.
    a. Ambulatory health care staff member job performance is demonstrated to be in compliance with ambulatory health care provider policies and procedures.
    b. Administrator of Ambulatory Health Care job performance is demonstrated to be in compliance with ambulatory health care provider policies and procedures.
    c. Participation in developing ambulatory health care administrative and clinical policies and procedures is demonstrated.
    d. Appropriate changes in ambulatory health care administrative and clinical policies and procedures are demonstrated.
    e. Contract personnel services are monitored for compliance with ambulatory health care provider policies and procedures.
    f. Ambulatory health care provider systems for evaluating ambulatory health care provider services are developed and implemented on a regular basis.
    g. Development and implementation of emergency policies and procedures are demonstrated.
12. Promotes and maintains a provider environment that is in compliance with federal, state, and local regulatory agencies.
    a. Federal, state, and local rules and regulations are shared with ambulatory health care provider staff members.
    b. Consultation with ambulatory health care staff members regarding federal, state, and local rules and regulations is demonstrated.
    c. Ambulatory health care staff member compliance with appropriate policies and procedures regarding patient rights is monitored.
    d. A patient complaint system is developed and implemented.
    e. Current professional licensure and qualifications for ambulatory health care staff members are monitored.
    f. Ambulatory health care staff member compliance with infection control and safety policies and procedures is monitored.
    g. Requirements of regulatory agencies for the ambulatory health care provider are met through satisfactory regulatory agency surveys.
13. Promotes education for ambulatory health care staff members.
    a. Needs assessment of ambulatory health care staff members is documented.
    b. Educational programs are developed and implemented to address needs assessment.
    c. Management team members are encouraged to participate in appropriate educational meetings that address job performance responsibilities.
    d. Needs assessment of management team members is documented.
    e. Orientation and education of management team members are closely monitored.
    f. Consultation with management team members regarding professional growth objectives relative to job performance is documented.
    g. Educational programs for ambulatory health care staff members are conducted by Administrator of Ambulatory Health Care as appropriate.
14. Participates in personal professional growth and development.
    a. Professional career objectives are developed and implemented.
    b. Current knowledge regarding professional career development in the delivery of health care services is demonstrated.
    c. Participation in education programs is consistently demonstrated.
    d. Review of current literature regarding health care is demonstrated.
    e. Current knowledge of leadership and management principles is demonstrated.
    f. Participation in development and presentation of education programs is demonstrated.

Performance responsibilities and standards that exceed defined job description:

(Include performance responsibilities and standards that are not included in the above job description, that may exceed the requirements of the above job description, or that should be identified as unique to the individual currently in the Administrator of Ambulatory Health Care position. For example, the current Administrator of Ambulatory Health Care may also act as a consultant for labor relations because of specific expertise in labor relations. In contrast, the past Administrator of Ambulatory Health Care may have had expertise in personnel management. In both cases, the above job description should be expanded to include the additional, appropriately defined performance responsibilities and standards.)

continues

Exhibit 5006-1 *continued*

Job description review:

I have read and understand the job description for the position of Administrator of Ambulatory Health Care.

Signature of Administrator of Ambulatory Health Care	Date of Signature

Exhibit 5006-2 Job Description of Position of Nursing Manager

AMBULATORY HEALTH CARE PROVIDER
NURSING MANAGER JOB DESCRIPTION

Date approved: ________________

SUPERSEDES ALL PREVIOUS NURSING MANAGER
JOB DESCRIPTIONS

Approved by: ____
Signature of Administrator of Ambulatory Health Care

Approved by: ____
Signature of President of Ambulatory Health Care Provider

continues

Exhibit 5006-2 *continued*

Position title:

Nursing Manager

Position scope:

To ensure quality and safe delivery of ambulatory health care services.

To coordinate provision of ambulatory health care services that reflect the ambulatory health care provider philosophy and standards of ambulatory health care.

To plan, develop, implement, and evaluate ambulatory health care provider services, programs, and activities.

To ensure quality and safe delivery of nursing care services.

Position qualifications:

Graduate of an accredited school of nursing required.

Current registered nurse registration with the state board of nursing required.

Minimum of three (3) to five (5) years progressively responsible management experience in health care or related field, demonstrating leadership expertise, preferred.

Demonstrated knowledge regarding ambulatory health care and/or public health nursing preferred.

Physical requirements:

Visual/hearing ability sufficient to comprehend written/verbal communication.

Ability to perform tasks involving physical activity, which may include heavy lifting and extensive bending and standing.

Ability to deal effectively with stress.

Performance responsibilities and standards:

1. Ensures quality and safe delivery of ambulatory health care services.
   a. Developed, documented, and implemented ambulatory health care provider policies and procedures reflect quality and safe delivery of ambulatory health care services.
   b. Developed and implemented nursing standards are evaluated on an annual basis.
   c. Patient plans of care are developed, implemented, and evaluated per ambulatory health care provider policy and procedure.
   d. Ambulatory health care staff member nursing practice is assessed per nursing standards and ambulatory health care provider policy and procedure.
   e. Patient clinical records are reviewed per ambulatory health care provider policy and procedure.
   f. Patient case conferences are conducted per ambulatory health care provider policy and procedure.
   g. Communication regarding patient care and nursing practices is demonstrated on a regular basis.
   h. Quality of ambulatory health care services provided by contract personnel is monitored on a regular basis.
   i. Adequate and appropriate supplies and equipment are available and maintained at all times.
   j. Assessment of patients for appropriateness of the ambulatory health care services they are receiving is demonstrated.
   k. Ambulatory health care staff members' job performance is assessed and documented on a regular basis.
   l. Performance responsibilities are delegated to appropriate individuals as necessary.
   m. Ability to perform nursing functions in emergency staffing situations is demonstrated.
   n. Consultation with ambulatory health care staff members regarding nursing concerns and practices is demonstrated on a regular basis.
2. Performs additional assigned performance responsibilities as necessary.
   a. Additional performance responsibilities are fulfilled accurately and completed in a timely manner.
3. Develops and implements written policies and procedures that reflect ambulatory health care provider philosophy and objectives.
   a. Developed, documented, and implemented written policies and procedures reflect ambulatory health care provider philosophy and objectives.
   b. Ambulatory health care administrative and clinical policies and procedures are reviewed and revised annually.

continues

Exhibit 5006-2 *continued*

   c. Developed and revised ambulatory health care provider philosophy and objectives are submitted to the Administrator of Ambulatory Health Care.
   d. Ambulatory health care administrative and clinical policies and procedures are evaluated and revised for effectiveness in delivery of quality and safe ambulatory health care services.
   e. Corrective action is implemented for ambulatory health care administrative and clinical policies and procedures that are not effective in delivery of quality and safe ambulatory health care services.
   f. Assessments and recommendations for alternative methods of health care delivery are submitted to the Administrator of Ambulatory Health Care as appropriate.

4. Assumes assigned responsibility for ambulatory health care provider operations in absence of Administrator of Ambulatory Health Care.
   a. Compliance of ambulatory health care provider operations with federal, state, and local rules and regulations is demonstrated.
   b. The Nursing Manager is available at all times during ambulatory health care provider operating hours.
   c. The Nursing Manager is on-call for emergencies involving health care staff members and patients.
   d. Participation in ambulatory health care activities is demonstrated.

5. Promotes effective written/verbal communication.
   a. Skill in conflict resolution is demonstrated.
   b. Positive work environment is promoted for ambulatory health care staff members.
   c. Monthly meetings with ambulatory health care staff members are conducted and documented.
   d. Changes in ambulatory health care provider operations and policies and procedures are communicated to ambulatory health care provider staff members in a timely manner.
   e. Consistent and concise lines of authority and responsibility are interpreted and maintained among ambulatory health care staff members.
   f. Participation in appropriate committee meetings is demonstrated per ambulatory health care provider policy and procedure.
   g. Submission of written reports to the Administrator of Ambulatory Health Care in a timely manner is demonstrated.
   h. Cooperation with ambulatory health care provider staff members and the Administrator of Ambulatory Health Care pursuant to ambulatory health care provider philosophy and objectives is demonstrated.
   i. Participation in ambulatory health care provider events is demonstrated.
   j. Positive interpretation of ambulatory health care provider philosophy, objectives, and long-range plans is provided to ambulatory health care staff members on a regular basis.
   k. Consultation with Administrator of Ambulatory Health Care is initiated as issues and concerns require.
   l. Cooperation with federal, state, and local agencies is demonstrated.

6. Develops, implements, and evaluates adequate staffing to address staffing needs for delivery of ambulatory health care services.
   a. Assigned responsibility for job functions assigned in absence of Nursing Manager is demonstrated.
   b. Developed, implemented, and evaluated ambulatory health care staff recruitment policies and procedures reflect staffing needs of ambulatory health care provider.
   c. Ambulatory health care staff recruitment policies and procedures are demonstrated in the interviewing and hiring of qualified ambulatory health care staff members according to written job descriptions.
   d. Developed and implemented ambulatory health care provider staffing patterns that meet ambulatory health care provider needs are demonstrated.
   e. Ambulatory health care staffing patterns are assessed to ensure that staffing needs of the ambulatory health care provider are adequately fulfilled.
   f. Implemented staffing patterns are posted in a timely manner.
   g. Attendance and replacement of ambulatory health care staff members are demonstrated.
   h. Ambulatory health care staff members' work assignments are clearly defined and documented.
   i. Ambulatory health care staff members' work hours are in compliance with federal, state, and local rules and regulations and ambulatory health care provider policies and procedures.

7. Monitors supervision and evaluation of ambulatory health care staff job performance.
   a. Job descriptions are reviewed and revised annually.
   b. Job descriptions reflect ambulatory health care staff members' job performances.
   c. Performance as role model for ambulatory health care staff members is demonstrated.
   d. Orientation programs for ambulatory health care staff members are demonstrated and documented.
   e. Performance appraisals of ambulatory health care staff members are demonstrated and documented.
   f. Performance appraisals of ambulatory health care staff members are communicated to ambulatory health care staff members annually and as necessary.
   g. Consultation with ambulatory health care staff members regarding professional growth is demonstrated.
   h. Disciplinary action is instituted, interpreted, and documented per ambulatory health care provider policy and procedure.
   i. Information regarding job performance of contract personnel is submitted to the Administrator of Ambulatory Health Care as appropriate.
   j. Monitoring of ambulatory health care staff member job performance is demonstrated.
   k. The Nursing Manager is on-call for emergencies involving ambulatory health care staff members and patients.

continues

Exhibit 5006-2 *continued*

8. Develops, implements, evaluates, and monitors ambulatory health care provider financial policies and procedures and records.
   a. Implemented financial policies and procedures and records comply with federal, state, and local rules and regulations.
   b. Patient financial records are consistently accurate, current, and accessible.
   c. Statistical financial records are current and accurate.
   d. Billing for ambulatory health care provider services provided to patients and third party payers is current and presented in a timely manner.
9. Develops, implements, and evaluates budget plan and cost control policies and procedures.
   a. Ambulatory health care provider salary/equipment/supply budgets are submitted in a timely manner to the Administrator of Ambulatory Health Care.
   b. Recommendations for capital expenditures are submitted in a timely manner to the Administrator of Ambulatory Health Care.
   c. Proposals for salary changes are submitted to the Administrator of Ambulatory Health Care for approval.
   d. Ambulatory health care provider budget reports and statistics are accurately written and submitted in a timely manner to the Administrator of Ambulatory Health Care.
   e. Cost control policies and procedures are developed, implemented, and evaluated.
   f. Cost reports are reviewed and discussed with the Administrator of Ambulatory Health Care.
   g. Cost reports are monitored.
   h. Corrective action plans are implemented for cost control problems.
   i. The ambulatory health care provider budget is implemented and monitored to ensure operation within the approved budget.
10. Develops and implements salary program within approved ambulatory health care provider policies and procedures.
   a. Ambulatory health care provider staff member salaries are determined within approved salary budgets.
   b. Salary increases are recommended to the Administrator of Ambulatory Health Care according to ambulatory health care provider policies and procedures.
   c. New ambulatory health care staff member salaries and salary adjustments are implemented according to ambulatory health care provider policies and procedures.
   d. Time card and payroll documentation is done accurately and in a timely manner.
   e. Ambulatory health care staff member paychecks are distributed according to ambulatory health care provider policy and procedure.
11. Complies with ambulatory health care provider policies and procedures.
   a. Ambulatory health care staff member job performance is demonstrated to be in compliance with ambulatory health care provider policies and procedures.
   b. Nursing Manager job performance is demonstrated to be in compliance with ambulatory health care provider policies and procedures.
   c. Participation in developing ambulatory health care administrative and clinical policies and procedures is demonstrated as appropriate.
   d. Appropriate changes in ambulatory health care administrative and clinical policies and procedures are demonstrated as appropriate.
   e. Contract personnel services are monitored for compliance with ambulatory health care provider policies and procedures.
   f. Ambulatory health care provider systems for evaluating ambulatory health care provider delivery of services are developed and implemented on a regular basis.
   g. Development and implementation of emergency policies and procedures are demonstrated.
   h. Maintenance of confidentiality of patient information is demonstrated per ambulatory health care provider policy and procedure.
   i. Infection control and safety policies and procedures are implemented per ambulatory health care provider policy and procedure.
   j. Patient concerns are consistently addressed per ambulatory health care provider policy and procedure.
   k. Current professional licenses of ambulatory health care staff members and the Nursing Manager are documented and maintained.
12. Promotes and maintains a provider environment that is in compliance with federal, state, and local regulatory agencies.
   a. Federal, state, and local rules and regulations are shared with ambulatory health care provider staff members.
   b. Consultation with ambulatory health care staff members regarding federal, state, and local rules and regulations is demonstrated.
   c. Ambulatory health care staff member job performance is monitored for compliance with appropriate policies and procedures regarding patient rights.
   d. A patient complaint system is developed and implemented.
   e. Current professional licensure and qualifications for ambulatory health care staff members are monitored.
   f. Ambulatory health care staff member compliance with infection control and safety policies and procedures is monitored.
   g. Requirements of regulatory agencies for the ambulatory health care provider are met through satisfactory regulatory agency surveys.
   h. Completed regulatory documentation forms are submitted in a timely manner.

continues

Exhibit 5006-2 *continued*

13. Promotes education for ambulatory health care staff members.
    a. Needs assessment of ambulatory health care staff members is demonstrated and documented.
    b. Educational programs are developed and implemented to address ambulatory health care staff members' needs assessment.
    c. Participation in educational programs is documented in ambulatory health care staff members' personnel files.
    d. Assessment of additional educational needs of ambulatory health care staff members is ongoing and documented.
    e. Educational programs for ambulatory health care staff members to maintain professional skill levels and to perform job functions are provided as necessary.
    f. Ambulatory health care staff members are encouraged to participate in educational programs.
    g. Educational programs for ambulatory health care staff members are conducted by the Nursing Manager as appropriate.
14. Promotes education for patients, patient families, and the community.
    a. Participation in community education programs is demonstrated.
    b. Identification of patient, patient family, and community education needs is demonstrated.
    c. Educational programs are developed and implemented to address identified patient, patient family, and community education needs.
15. Promotes research and study of adult learning theory and concepts related to ambulatory health care services.
    a. Participation in professional and nursing practice meetings is demonstrated and documented.
    b. Literature review of current trends in ambulatory health care and nursing practice is demonstrated.
16. Participates in personal professional growth and development.
    a. Professional career objectives are developed and implemented.
    b. Current knowledge regarding professional career development in the delivery of health care services is demonstrated.
    c. Participation in education programs is consistently demonstrated.
    d. Review of current literature regarding health care is demonstrated.
    e. Current knowledge of leadership and management principles is demonstrated.
    f. Participation in development and presentation of education programs is demonstrated.

Performance responsibilities and standards that exceed defined job description:

(Include performance responsibilities and standards that are not included in the above job description, that may exceed the requirements of the above job description, or that should be identified as unique to the individual currently in the Nursing Manager position. For example, the Nursing Manager may also act as a consultant for management information systems because of specific expertise in such systems. In contrast, the past Nursing Manager may have had expertise in education. In both cases, the above job description should be expanded to include the additional, appropriately defined performance responsibilities and standards.)

Job description review:

I have read and understand the job description for the position of Nursing Manager.

____ ____________________

Signature of Nursing Manager Date of Signature

Exhibit 5006-3 Job Description of Position of Quality Assurance Manager

AMBULATORY HEALTH CARE PROVIDER
QUALITY ASSURANCE MANAGER JOB DESCRIPTION

Date approved: ________________

SUPERSEDES ALL PREVIOUS QUALITY ASSURANCE MANAGER JOB DESCRIPTIONS

Approved by: ____
Signature of Administrator of Ambulatory Health Care

Approved by: ____
Signature of President of the Ambulatory Health Care Provider

continues

Exhibit 5006-3 *continued*

Position title:

Quality Assurance Manager

Position scope:

To ensure quality and safe delivery of ambulatory health care services.

To develop, implement, and evaluate quality assurance program and activities that support the ambulatory health care provider's objectives in delivering quality and safe ambulatory health care services.

To coordinate quality assurance program and activities that reflect the ambulatory health care provider's philosophy and standards of ambulatory health and nursing care of patients.

To monitor quality assurance program and activities for ensuring that desired outcomes are achieved and maintained.

To ensure quality and safe delivery of nursing care and therapy services.

Position qualifications:

Graduate of an accredited school of nursing required.

B.S.N. degree or equivalent experience in acute and ambulatory health care settings required.

Current registered nurse registration with the state board of nursing required.

Experience in developing, implementing, and evaluating quality assurance programs and activities in both acute and ambulatory health care settings required.

Excellent verbal and written communication skills required.

Excellent administrative, organizational, and leadership skills required.

Physical requirements:

Visual/hearing ability sufficient to comprehend written/verbal communication.

Ability to deal effectively with stress.

Performance responsibilities and standards:

1. Ensures quality and safe delivery of ambulatory health care services.
   a. Quality assurance program and activities are developed, implemented, and evaluated per ambulatory health care provider policy and procedure.
   b. Quality assurance reports are completed in a timely manner per ambulatory health care provider policy and procedure.
   c. Ambulatory Health Care Quality Assurance Committee meeting agendas are developed prior to committee meetings.
   d. Ambulatory Health Care Quality Assurance Committee meetings are conducted in a timely manner according to ambulatory health care provider policy and procedure.
   e. Quality assurance activities reflect current, identified quality of care problems.
   f. Information regarding quality assurance activities is given to ambulatory health care staff members in a timely manner.
   g. Ambulatory health care provider staff members are involved in developing quality assurance activities whenever possible.
2. Fulfills additional performance responsibilities as assigned and as necessary accurately and in a timely manner.
3. Promotes effective written/verbal communication.
   a. Skill in conflict resolution is demonstrated.
   b. Positive work environment is promoted for ambulatory health care staff members.
   c. Participation in assigned meetings is demonstrated and documented.
   d. Communication of information regarding changes in ambulatory health care provider operations and policies and procedures to ambulatory health care provider staff members, in a timely manner, is demonstrated.
   e. Consistent and concise lines of authority and responsibility are maintained.

continues

Exhibit 5006-3 *continued*

f. Participation in appropriate committee meetings is demonstrated per ambulatory health care provider policy and procedure.
g. Cooperation and collaboration with ambulatory health care provider staff members, the Administrator of Ambulatory Health Care, and physicians pursuant to ambulatory health care provider philosophy, standards, and objectives are demonstrated.
h. Participation in ambulatory health care provider events is demonstrated.
i. Documentation of information regarding quality assurance program and activities is demonstrated.
j. Quality assurance administrative files are maintained according to ambulatory health care provider policy and procedure.
k. Consultation with the Administrator of Ambulatory Health Care is initiated as issues and concerns require.
l. Cooperation with federal, state, and local agencies is demonstrated.

4. Gives accurate information to ambulatory health care staff members regarding costs for quality assurance program and activities.
   a. Knowledge of ambulatory health care provider policies and procedures and regulations regarding costs for quality assurance program and activities is demonstrated.
   b. Consultation with the Administrator of Ambulatory Health Care regarding financial matters is demonstrated.
5. Provides information regarding equipment and supply needs for quality assurance program and activities.
   a. Information regarding equipment and supply needs for quality assurance program and activities is submitted to the Administrator of Ambulatory Health Care in a timely manner.
   b. Recommendations for capital expenditures are submitted to the Administrator of Ambulatory Health Care in a timely manner.
   c. Statistics for quality assurance program and activities are written accurately and submitted to the Administrator of Ambulatory Health Care in a timely manner.
   d. Participation in the development of cost control policies and procedures is demonstrated.
   e. Cost reports are reviewed and discussed with the Administrator of Ambulatory Health Care as appropriate.
   f. Cost reports are monitored as appropriate.
   g. Participation in corrective action plans to deal with cost control problems is demonstrated.
   h. Participation in the implementation and monitoring of the quality assurance program budget to ensure operation within approved limits is demonstrated.
6. Uses equipment and supplies effectively and efficiently.
   a. Utilization of equipment and supplies in a cost-effective manner is demonstrated.
   b. Accurate utilization of equipment and supplies is demonstrated.
   c. Information regarding malfunctioning equipment and inadequate supplies is given to the appropriate individuals.
   d. Charges for equipment and supplies used for quality assurance program and activities are documented.
7. Participates in salary programs following approved ambulatory health care provider policies and procedures. Time card documentation is done accurately and in a timely manner per ambulatory health care provider policy and procedure.
8. Complies with ambulatory health care provider policies and procedures.
   a. Job performance of the Quality Assurance Manager is demonstrated to be in compliance with ambulatory health care provider policies and procedures.
   b. Participation in developing ambulatory health care administrative and clinical policies and procedures is demonstrated as appropriate.
   c. Need for changes in ambulatory health care administrative and clinical policies and procedures is communicated to the Administrator of Ambulatory Health Care.
   d. Participation in developing systems for evaluating ambulatory health care provider delivery of services is demonstrated.
   e. Participation in the development and implementation of emergency policies and procedures is demonstrated.
   f. Maintenance of confidentiality of patient information is demonstrated per ambulatory health care provider policy and procedure.
   g. Patient concerns are consistently addressed per ambulatory health care provider policy and procedure.
   h. Current professional license of Quality Assurance Manager is maintained and documented.
9. Promotes and maintains a provider environment that is in compliance with federal, state, and local regulatory agencies.
   a. Federal, state, and local rules and regulations are shared with ambulatory health care staff members.
   b. Consultation with ambulatory health care staff members regarding federal, state, and local rules and regulations is demonstrated.
   c. Participation in development and implementation of a patient complaint system is demonstrated.
   d. Compliance of ambulatory health care staff members with infection control and safety policies and procedures is monitored.
   e. Participation in meeting requirements for regulatory surveys of ambulatory health care provider is demonstrated.
   f. Regulatory documentation forms are completed and submitted in a timely manner.
10. Promotes quality assurance education for ambulatory health care staff members.
    a. Participation in development and implementation of quality assurance educational programs to address ambulatory health care staff members' needs is demonstrated.
    b. Documentation of quality assurance educational programs in ambulatory health care staff members' personnel files is demonstrated.

continues

Exhibit 5006-3 *continued*

   c. Assessment of additional quality assurance educational needs of ambulatory health care staff members is ongoing and demonstrated.
   d. Participation in quality assurance educational programs to enable ambulatory health care staff members to maintain professional skill levels and perform job functions is demonstrated.
   e. Encouragement of ambulatory health care staff members to participate in quality assurance educational programs is demonstrated.
   f. Conducting of quality assurance educational programs for ambulatory health care staff members as appropriate is demonstrated.

11. Promotes quality assurance education for patients, patient families, and the community.
   a. Participation in community quality assurance education programs is demonstrated.
   b. Identification of patient, patient family, and community quality assurance education needs is demonstrated.
   c. Development and implementation of quality assurance educational programs that address identified patient, patient family, and community educational needs are demonstrated.
12. Participates in research and study of adult learning theory and concepts related to nursing practice, ambulatory health care, and quality assurance.
   a. Participation in professional, nursing practice, and quality assurance meetings is demonstrated and documented.
   b. Literature review of current trends in ambulatory health care, nursing practice, and quality assurance is demonstrated.
13. Participates in personal professional growth and development.
   a. Professional career objectives are developed and implemented.
   b. Current knowledge regarding professional career development in the delivery of health care services is demonstrated.
   c. Participation in education programs is consistently demonstrated.
   d. Review of current literature regarding health care is demonstrated.
   e. Current knowledge of quality assurance, communication, administrative, organizational, and leadership principles is demonstrated.
   f. Participation in development and presentation of quality assurance education programs is demonstrated.

Performance responsibilities and standards that exceed defined job description:

(Include performance responsibilities and standards that are not included in the above job description, that may exceed the requirements of the above job description, or that should be identified as unique to the individual currently in the Quality Assurance Manager position. For example, the current Quality Assurance Manager may also act as a consultant regarding documentation of patient care because of specific expertise in documentation. In this case, the above job description should be expanded to include the additional, appropriately defined performance responsibilities and standards.)

Job description review:

I have read and understand the job description for the position of Quality Assurance Manager.

______________________________ ______________________________

Signature of Quality Assurance Manager   Date of Signature

Exhibit 5006-4 Job Description of Position of Ambulatory Health Care Registered Nurse

AMBULATORY HEALTH CARE PROVIDER
AMBULATORY HEALTH CARE REGISTERED NURSE JOB DESCRIPTION

Date approved: ________________

SUPERSEDES ALL PREVIOUS AMBULATORY HEALTH CARE REGISTERED NURSE JOB DESCRIPTIONS

Approved by: ______________________________
Signature of Administrator of Ambulatory Health Care

Approved by: ______________________________
Signature of Nursing Manager

continues

Exhibit 5006-4 *continued*

Position title:

Ambulatory Health Care Registered Nurse

Position scope:

To ensure quality and safe delivery of ambulatory health care services.

To coordinate provision of ambulatory health care services that reflect the ambulatory health care provider philosophy and standards of ambulatory health and nursing care of assigned patients.

To ensure quality and safe delivery of nursing care services.

Position qualifications:

Graduate of an accredited school of nursing required.

Current registered nurse registration with the state board of nursing required.

Public health nursing certification preferred.

Experience in ambulatory health care or public health nursing preferred.

Evidence of independent nursing practice in delivering nursing care required.

Physical requirements:

Visual/hearing ability sufficient to comprehend written/verbal communication.

Ability to perform tasks involving physical activity, which may include heavy lifting and extensive bending and standing.

Ability to deal effectively with stress.

Performance responsibilities and standards:

1. Ensures quality and safe delivery of ambulatory health care services.
   a. Patient plans of care are developed, implemented, and evaluated per ambulatory health care provider policy and procedure.
   b. Nursing assessment forms are completed in a timely manner per ambulatory health care provider policy and procedure.
   c. Individual nursing plans of care are developed prior to patient case conferences.
   d. Patient case conferences are conducted in a timely manner according to ambulatory health care provider policy and procedure.
   e. Individual nursing plans of care reflect current patient needs.
   f. Information regarding patient plans of care is given to ambulatory health care staff members, patients, and patient families in a timely manner.
   g. Patients and patient families are involved in developing patient plans of care whenever possible.
   h. Patient clinical record documentation reflects delivery of quality and safe ambulatory health care services.
2. Implements current nursing practice.
   a. Patient conditions are assessed in every ambulatory health care visit.
   b. Patient assessments are communicated to appropriate individuals.
   c. Nursing interventions are implemented to meet patient needs and changed conditions.
   d. Patient clinical record documentation is done per ambulatory health care provider policy and procedure.
   e. Physician orders are accurately transcribed, implemented, and evaluated for patient outcome in a timely manner.
   f. Transfers of patients to other health care providers are done per ambulatory health care provider policy and procedure.
   g. Transfer information is documented accurately, completely, and in a timely manner.
   h. Infection control and safety measures are implemented per ambulatory health care provider policy and procedure.
   i. Recommendations and requirements for additional ambulatory health care services for patients are communicated to the appropriate individuals in a timely manner.
   j. Clinical care is implemented per ambulatory health care provider policies and procedures.
   k. Patient care is monitored for compliance with defined patient plans of care.
3. Fulfills additional performance responsibilities as assigned and as necessary.
   a. Additional performance responsibilities are accurately fulfilled in a timely manner.

continues

Exhibit 5006-4 *continued*

4. Assumes assigned responsibility for ambulatory health care provider operations in the absence of the Administrator and Nursing Manager.
   a. Compliance of ambulatory health care provider operations with federal, state, and local rules and regulations is demonstrated.
   b. Ambulatory Health Care Registered Nurse is available at all times during ambulatory health care provider operating hours.
   c. Ambulatory Health Care Registered Nurse is on-call for emergencies involving health care staff members and patients.
   d. Participation in ambulatory health care activities is demonstrated.
5. Promotes effective written/verbal communication.
   a. Skill in conflict resolution is demonstrated.
   b. Positive work environment is promoted for ambulatory health care staff members.
   c. Participation in monthly ambulatory health care staff meetings is demonstrated and documented.
   d. Communication of information regarding changes in ambulatory health care provider operations and policies and procedures to ambulatory health care provider staff members in a timely manner is demonstrated.
   e. Consistent and concise lines of authority and responsibility are maintained.
   f. Participation in appropriate committee meetings is demonstrated per ambulatory health care provider policy and procedure.
   g. Cooperation with ambulatory health care provider staff members and the Nursing Manager pursuant to ambulatory health care provider philosophy and objectives is demonstrated.
   h. Participation in ambulatory health care provider events is demonstrated.
   i. Documentation of information regarding interpretation of ambulatory health care provider philosophy, objectives, and long-range plan is demonstrated as necessary.
   j. Consultation with the Nursing Manager is initiated as issues and concerns require.
   k. Cooperation with federal, state, and local agencies is demonstrated.
6. Develops written staff assignments according to staffing patterns, patient needs, and ambulatory health care staff member competencies.
   a. Information regarding patient needs and patient plans of care are given to ambulatory health care staff members.
   b. Information regarding assignments is reviewed with ambulatory health care staff members as necessary.
   c. Consultation with ambulatory health care staff members regarding assignments is demonstrated.
   d. Ambulatory health care staff member completion of assignments is monitored.
   e. Ambulatory health care staff member assignments are clearly defined and documented.
7. Supervises ambulatory health care licensed practical nurses and ambulatory health care aides.
   a. Performance as role model for ambulatory health care staff members is demonstrated.
   b. Participation in orientation of ambulatory health care staff members is demonstrated.
   c. Job performances of ambulatory health care licensed practical nurses and ambulatory health care aides are monitored.
   d. Reports of the job performances of ambulatory health care licensed practical nurses and ambulatory health care aides are communicated to the Nursing Manager.
   e. Monitoring of ambulatory health care services delivered by ambulatory health care staff members is demonstrated.
8. Gives accurate information to patients, patient families, and ambulatory health care staff members regarding costs for ambulatory health care services.
   a. Knowledge of ambulatory health care provider policies and procedures and regulations regarding reimbursement for ambulatory health care services is demonstrated.
   b. Consultation with the Nursing Manager regarding financial matters is demonstrated.
   c. Referral of patients and patient families to appropriate individuals/agencies for assistance with financial concerns is demonstrated.
9. Provides information regarding equipment and supply needs of the ambulatory health care provider.
   a. Information regarding equipment and supply needs for the ambulatory health care provider is submitted to the Nursing Manager in a timely manner.
   b. Recommendations for capital expenditures are submitted in a timely manner to the Nursing Manager.
   c. Ambulatory health care provider statistics are written accurately and submitted in a timely manner to the Nursing Manager.
   d. Participation in the development of cost control policies and procedures is demonstrated.
   e. Cost reports are reviewed and discussed with the Nursing Manager as appropriate.
   f. Cost reports are monitored as appropriate.
   g. Participation in corrective action plans to deal with cost control problems is demonstrated.
   h. Participation in the implementation and monitoring of the ambulatory health care provider budget to ensure operation within approved limits is demonstrated.
10. Uses equipment and supplies effectively and efficiently.
   a. Utilization of equipment and supplies in a cost-effective manner is demonstrated.
   b. Accurate utilization of equipment and supplies is demonstrated.
   c. Consultation with ambulatory health care staff members regarding utilization of equipment and supplies accurately and in a cost-effective manner is demonstrated.

continues

Exhibit 5006-4 *continued*

d. Information regarding malfunctioning equipment and inadequate supplies is given to the appropriate individuals.
e. Charges for equipment and supplies used for patient care are documented for appropriate reimbursement.
f. Information is given to patients and patient families regarding effective and efficient use of equipment and supplies.
g. Information is given to patients and patient families regarding reimbursement of equipment and supplies needed for ambulatory health care.

11. Participates in salary programs following approved ambulatory health care provider policies and procedures.
    a. Time card documentation is done accurately and in a timely manner per ambulatory health care provider policy and procedure.
12. Complies with ambulatory health care provider policies and procedures.
    a. Job performances of ambulatory health care licensed practical nurses and ambulatory health care aides are demonstrated to be in compliance with ambulatory health care provider policies and procedures.
    b. Job performance of the Ambulatory Health Care Registered Nurse is demonstrated to be in compliance with ambulatory health care provider policies and procedures.
    c. Participation in developing ambulatory health care administrative and clinical policies and procedures is demonstrated as appropriate.
    d. Need for changes in ambulatory health care administrative and clinical policies and procedures is communicated to the Nursing Manager.
    e. Contract personnel services are monitored for compliance with ambulatory health care provider policies and procedures.
    f. Participation in developing systems for evaluating ambulatory health care provider delivery of services is demonstrated.
    g. Participation in the development and implementation of emergency policies and procedures is demonstrated.
    h. Maintenance of confidentiality of patient information is demonstrated per ambulatory health care provider policy and procedure.
    i. Infection control and safety measures are implemented per ambulatory health care provider policy and procedure.
    j. Patient concerns are consistently addressed per ambulatory health care provider policy and procedure.
    k. Current professional licenses of Ambulatory Health Care Registered Nurses are maintained and documented.
13. Promotes and maintains a provider environment that is in compliance with federal, state, and local regulatory agencies.
    a. Federal, state, and local rules and regulations are shared with ambulatory health care provider staff members.
    b. Consultation with ambulatory health care staff members regarding federal, state, and local rules and regulations is demonstrated.
    c. Job performances of ambulatory health care licensed practical nurses and ambulatory health care aides are monitored for compliance with appropriate policies and procedures regarding patient rights.
    d. Participation in development and implementation of a patient complaint system is demonstrated.
    e. Compliance of ambulatory health care licensed practical nurses and ambulatory health care aides with infection control and safety policies and procedures is monitored.
    f. Participation in meeting requirements for regulatory agency surveys of ambulatory health care provider is demonstrated.
    g. Regulatory documentation forms are completed and submitted in a timely manner.
14. Promotes education for ambulatory health care staff members.
    a. Participation in needs assessment of ambulatory health care staff members is demonstrated.
    b. Participation in development and implementation of educational programs to address ambulatory health care staff members' needs is demonstrated.
    c. Educational programs are documented in Ambulatory Health Care Registered Nurse personnel files.
    d. Assessment of additional educational needs of Ambulatory Health Care Registered Nurses is ongoing and demonstrated.
    e. Participation in educational programs to enable ambulatory health care staff members to maintain professional skill levels and perform job functions is demonstrated.
    f. Ambulatory health care staff members are encouraged to participate in educational programs.
    g. Educational programs for ambulatory health care staff members are conducted by the Ambulatory Health Care Registered Nurse as appropriate.
15. Promotes education for patients, patient families, and the community.
    a. Participation in community education programs is demonstrated.
    b. Identification of patient, patient family, and community education needs is demonstrated.
    c. Educational programs are developed and implemented to address identified patient, patient family, and community education needs.
16. Participates in research and study of adult learning theory and concepts related to ambulatory health care services.
    a. Participation in professional and nursing practice meetings is demonstrated and documented.
    b. Literature review of current trends in ambulatory health care and nursing practice is demonstrated.
17. Participates in personal professional growth and development.
    a. Professional career objectives are developed and implemented.
    b. Current knowledge regarding professional career development in the delivery of health care services is demonstrated.

continues

Exhibit 5006-4 *continued*

c. Participation in education programs is consistently demonstrated.
d. Review of current literature regarding health care is demonstrated.
e. Current knowledge of leadership and management principles is demonstrated.
f. Participation in development and presentation of education programs is demonstrated.

Performance responsibilities and standards that exceed defined job description:

(Include performance responsibilities and standards that are not included in the above job description, that may exceed the requirements of the above job description, or that should be identified as unique to the individual currently in the Ambulatory Health Care Registered Nurse position. For example, the current Ambulatory Health Care Registered Nurse may also act as a consultant in the management of a diabetic client because of specific expertise in diabetes. In this case, the above job description should be expanded to include the additional, appropriately defined performance responsibilities and standards.)

Job description review:

I have read and understand the job description for the position of Ambulatory Health Care Registered Nurse.

____ ________________

Signature of Ambulatory Health Care Registered Nurse | Date of Signature

Exhibit 5006-5 Job Description of Position of Ambulatory Health Care Licensed Practical Nurse

AMBULATORY HEALTH CARE PROVIDER
AMBULATORY HEALTH CARE LICENSED PRACTICAL NURSE JOB DESCRIPTION

Date approved: ________________

SUPERSEDES ALL PREVIOUS AMBULATORY HEALTH CARE LICENSED PRACTICAL NURSE JOB DESCRIPTIONS

Approved by: ____
Signature of Administrator of Ambulatory Health Care

Approved by: ____
Signature of Nursing Manager

continues

Exhibit 5006-5 *continued*

Position title:

Ambulatory Health Care Licensed Practical Nurse

Position scope:

To ensure quality and safe delivery of ambulatory health care services.

To assist in the provision of ambulatory health care services that reflect the ambulatory health care provider philosophy and standards of ambulatory health and nursing care of assigned patients.

To ensure quality and safe delivery of nursing care services.

Position qualifications:

Graduate of an accredited school of nursing required.

Current licensed practical nurse registration with the state board of nursing required.

Experience in ambulatory health care or related health care field preferred.

Physical requirements:

Visual/hearing ability sufficient to comprehend written/verbal communication.

Ability to perform tasks involving physical activity, which may include heavy lifting and extensive bending and standing.

Ability to deal effectively with stress.

Performance responsibilities and standards:

1. Ensures quality and safe delivery of ambulatory health care services.
   a. Participates in development and implementation of patient plans of care per ambulatory health care provider policy and procedure.
   b. Participates in patient case conferences according to ambulatory health care provider policy and procedure as appropriate.
   c. The provided nursing care reflects patient plans of care.
   d. Information regarding patient plans of care is submitted to the Ambulatory Health Care Registered Nurse in a timely manner.
   e. Patient clinical record documentation reflects delivery of quality and safe ambulatory health care services.
2. Implements current nursing practice.
   a. Patient plans of care are discussed with the Ambulatory Health Care Registered Nurse on a regular basis.
   b. Nursing interventions are implemented for patient plans of care.
   c. Patient clinical records are documented per ambulatory health care provider policy and procedure.
   d. Patient assignments and reports are received from the Ambulatory Health Care Registered Nurse.
   e. Infection control and safety policies and procedures are implemented per ambulatory health care provider policy and procedure.
   f. Identified patient needs are communicated to the Ambulatory Health Care Registered Nurse in a timely manner.
   g. Clinical care is implemented per ambulatory health care provider policies and procedures.
   h. Patients' overall appearance reflects good personal hygiene.
   i. Patient environment is neat and orderly.
   j. Procedures and treatments are implemented accurately and documented appropriately.
   k. Observations of patient condition are accurately reported to the Ambulatory Health Care Registered Nurse.
   l. Patients are assisted to meet socialization needs.
   m. Assignments are organized and completed on time.
   n. Patient requests are responded to promptly.
   o. Proper body mechanics are utilized consistently.
   p. The Ambulatory Health Care Registered Nurse is notified upon return to the ambulatory health care provider.
   q. Daily patient reports are given to the Ambulatory Health Care Registered Nurse.
3. Fulfills additional performance responsibilities as assigned and as necessary.
   a. Additional performance responsibilities are fulfilled accurately and in a timely manner.
4. Promotes effective written/verbal communication.
   a. Skill in conflict resolution is demonstrated.
   b. A positive work environment is promoted for ambulatory health care staff members.

continues

Exhibit 5006-5 *continued*

   c. Participation in monthly ambulatory health care staff meetings is demonstrated and documented.
   d. Information regarding changes in ambulatory health care provider operations and policies and procedures is communicated to ambulatory health care provider staff members in a timely manner.
   e. Consistent and concise lines of authority and responsibility are maintained.
   f. Participation in appropriate committee meetings is demonstrated per ambulatory health care provider policy and procedure.
   g. Cooperation with ambulatory health care provider staff members and the Nursing Manager pursuant to ambulatory health care provider philosophy and objectives is demonstrated.
   h. Participation in ambulatory health care provider events is demonstrated.
   i. Documentation of information regarding interpretation of ambulatory health care provider philosophy, objectives, and long-range plan is demonstrated as necessary.
   j. Consultation with the Ambulatory Health Care Registered Nurse or Nursing Manager is initiated as issues and concerns require.
5. Gives accurate information to patients and patient families regarding costs for ambulatory health care services.
   a. Consultation with the Ambulatory Health Care Registered Nurse regarding financial matters is demonstrated.
   b. Referral of patients and patient families to appropriate individuals/agencies for assistance with financial concerns is demonstrated.
6. Provides information regarding equipment and supply needs of the ambulatory health care provider.
   a. Information regarding equipment and supply needs of the ambulatory health care provider is submitted to the Nursing Manager in a timely manner.
   b. Recommendations for capital expenditures are submitted in a timely manner to the Nursing Manager.
   c. Participation in the development of cost control policies and procedures is demonstrated.
   d. Participation in corrective action plans to deal with cost control problems is demonstrated.
   e. Participation in the implementation of the ambulatory health care provider budget to ensure operation within approved limits is demonstrated.
7. Uses equipment and supplies effectively and efficiently.
   a. Utilization of equipment and supplies in a cost-effective manner is demonstrated.
   b. Accurate utilization of equipment and supplies is demonstrated.
   c. Information regarding malfunctioning equipment and inadequate supplies is given to the appropriate individuals.
   d. Information is given to patients and patient families regarding effective and efficient use of equipment and supplies.
8. Participates in salary programs following approved ambulatory health care provider policies and procedures.
   a. Time card documentation is done accurately and in a timely manner per ambulatory health care provider policy and procedure.
9. Complies with ambulatory health care provider policies and procedures.
   a. Job performance of Ambulatory Health Care Licensed Practical Nurse is demonstrated to be in compliance with ambulatory health care provider policies and procedures.
   b. Participation in developing ambulatory health care administrative and clinical policies and procedures is demonstrated as appropriate.
   c. Need for changes in ambulatory health care administrative and clinical policies and procedures is communicated to the Ambulatory Health Care Registered Nurse or Nursing Manager.
   d. Participation in implementing systems for evaluating ambulatory health care provider delivery of services is demonstrated.
   e. Participation in the development and implementation of emergency policies and procedures is demonstrated.
   f. Maintenance of confidentiality of patient information is demonstrated per ambulatory health care provider policy and procedure.
   g. Infection control and safety measures are implemented per ambulatory health care provider policy and procedure.
   h. Patient concerns are consistently addressed per ambulatory health care provider policy and procedure.
   i. Current professional licenses of Ambulatory Health Care Licensed Practical Nurses are maintained and documented.
10. Promotes and maintains a provider environment that is in compliance with federal, state, and local regulatory agencies.
   a. Consultation with the Ambulatory Health Care Registered Nurse and Nursing Manager regarding federal, state, and local rules and regulations is demonstrated.
   b. Participation in implementation of a patient complaint system is demonstrated.
   c. Regulatory documentation forms are completed and submitted in a timely manner.
11. Promotes education for ambulatory health care staff members.
   a. Participation in needs assessment of ambulatory health care staff members is demonstrated.
   b. Participation in development and implementation of educational programs to address ambulatory health care staff members' needs is demonstrated.
   c. Educational programs are documented in Ambulatory Health Care Licensed Practical Nurse personnel files.
12. Promotes education for patients, patient families, and the community.
   a. Identification of patient, patient family, and community education needs is demonstrated.
   b. Participation in educational programs to address identified patient, patient family, and community education needs is demonstrated.

continues

Exhibit 5006-5 *continued*

13. Participates in personal professional growth and development.
    a. Professional career objectives are developed and implemented.
    b. Current knowledge regarding professional career development in the delivery of health care services is demonstrated.
    c. Participation in education programs is consistently demonstrated.
    d. Review of current literature regarding health care is demonstrated.

Performance responsibilities and standards that exceed defined job description:

(Include performance responsibilities and standards that are not included in the above job description, that may exceed the requirements of the above job description, or that should be identified as unique to the individual currently in the Ambulatory Health Care Licensed Practical Nurse position. For example, the current Ambulatory Health Care Licensed Practical Nurse may also have expertise in pain management. In this case, the above job description should be expanded to include the additional, appropriately defined performance responsibilities and standards.)

Job description review:

I have read and understand the job description for the position of Ambulatory Health Care Licensed Practical Nurse.

____ ____________________

Signature of Ambulatory Health Care Licensed Practical Nurse Date of Signature

Exhibit 5006-6 Job Description of Position of Ambulatory Health Care Aide

AMBULATORY HEALTH CARE PROVIDER
AMBULATORY HEALTH CARE AIDE JOB DESCRIPTION

Date approved: ____________

SUPERSEDES ALL PREVIOUS AMBULATORY HEALTH CARE AIDE JOB DESCRIPTIONS

Approved by: ______________________________
Signature of Administrator of Ambulatory Health Care

Approved by: ______________________________
Signature of Nursing Manager

continues

Exhibit 5006-6 *continued*

Position title:

Ambulatory Health Care Aide

Position scope:

To ensure quality and safe delivery of ambulatory health care services.

To assist in the provision of ambulatory health care services that reflect the ambulatory health care provider philosophy and standards of ambulatory health and nursing care of assigned patients.

To ensure quality and safe delivery of ambulatory health care aide services.

Position qualifications:

High school graduation required.

Ambulatory health care aide certification required.

Experience in ambulatory health care or related health care field preferred.

Physical requirements:

Visual/hearing ability sufficient to comprehend written/verbal communication.

Ability to perform tasks involving physical activity, which may include heavy lifting and extensive bending and standing.

Ability to deal effectively with stress.

Performance responsibilities and standards:

1. Ensures quality and safe delivery of ambulatory health care services.
   a. Participates in development and implementation of patient plans of care per ambulatory health care provider policy and procedure.
   b. Participates in patient case conferences according to ambulatory health care provider policy and procedure, as appropriate.
   c. The provided ambulatory health care aide services reflect patient plans of care.
   d. Information regarding patient plans of care is submitted to the Ambulatory Health Care Registered Nurse in a timely manner.
   e. Patient clinical record documentation reflects delivery of quality and safe ambulatory health care services.
2. Implements current ambulatory health care aide services.
   a. Patient plans of care are discussed with the Ambulatory Health Care Registered Nurse on a regular basis.
   b. Patient clinical records are documented per ambulatory health care provider policy and procedure.
   c. Patient assignments and reports are received from the Ambulatory Health Care Registered Nurse.
   d. Infection control and safety policies and procedures are implemented per ambulatory health care provider policy and procedure.
   e. Identified patient needs are communicated to the Ambulatory Health Care Registered Nurse in a timely manner.
   f. Clinical care is implemented per ambulatory health care provider policies and procedures.
   g. Patients' overall appearance reflects good personal hygiene.
   h. Patient environment is neat and orderly.
   i. Procedures and treatments are implemented accurately and documented appropriately.
   j. Observations of patient condition are accurately reported to the Ambulatory Health Care Registered Nurse in a timely manner.
   k. Patients are assisted to meet socialization needs.
   l. Assignments are organized and completed on time.
   m. Patient requests are responded to promptly.
   n. Proper body mechanics are utilized consistently.
3. Fulfills additional performance responsibilities as assigned and as necessary.
   a. Additional performance responsibilities are fulfilled accurately and in a timely manner.
4. Promotes effective written/verbal communication.
   a. Skill in conflict resolution is demonstrated.
   b. A positive work environment is promoted for ambulatory health care staff members.
   c. Participation in monthly ambulatory health care staff meetings is demonstrated and documented.

continues

Exhibit 5006-6 *continued*

   d. Documentation of information regarding changes in ambulatory health care provider operations and policies and procedures is communicated to ambulatory health care provider staff members in a timely manner.
   e. Consistent and concise lines of authority and responsibility are maintained.
   f. Participation in appropriate committee meetings is demonstrated per ambulatory health care provider policy and procedure.
   g. Cooperation with ambulatory health care provider staff members and the Nursing Manager pursuant to ambulatory health care provider philosophy and objectives is demonstrated.
   h. Participation in ambulatory health care provider events is demonstrated.
   i. Documentation of information regarding interpretation of ambulatory health care provider philosophy, objectives, and long-range plans is demonstrated as necessary.
   j. Consultation with the Nursing Manager is initiated as issues and concerns require.
5. Uses equipment and supplies effectively and efficiently.
   a. Utilization of equipment and supplies in a cost-effective manner is demonstrated.
   b. Accurate utilization of equipment and supplies is demonstrated.
   c. Information regarding malfunctioning equipment and inadequate supplies is given to the appropriate individuals.
6. Participates in salary programs following approved ambulatory health care provider policies and procedures.
   a. Time card documentation is done accurately and in a timely manner per ambulatory health care provider policy and procedure.
7. Complies with ambulatory health care provider policies and procedures.
   a. Ambulatory Health Care Aide job performance is demonstrated to be in compliance with ambulatory health care provider policies and procedures.
   b. Participation in developing ambulatory health care administrative and clinical policies and procedures is demonstrated as appropriate.
   c. Need for changes in ambulatory health care administrative and clinical policies and procedures is communicated to the Ambulatory Health Care Registered Nurse or Nursing Manager.
   d. Participation in the development and implementation of emergency policies and procedures is demonstrated.
   e. Maintenance of confidentiality of patient information is demonstrated per ambulatory health care provider policy and procedure.
   f. Infection control and safety measures are implemented per ambulatory health care provider policy and procedure.
   g. Patient concerns are consistently addressed per ambulatory health care provider policy and procedure.
8. Promotes and maintains a provider environment that is in compliance with federal, state, and local regulatory agencies.
   a. Consultation with Ambulatory Health Care Registered Nurse and Nursing Manager regarding federal, state, and local rules and regulations is demonstrated.
   b. Participation in implementation of a patient complaint system is demonstrated.
   c. Regulatory documentation forms are completed and submitted in a timely manner.
9. Promotes education for ambulatory health care staff members.
   a. Participation in needs assessment of ambulatory health care staff members is demonstrated.
   b. Participation in development and implementation of educational programs to address ambulatory health care staff members' needs is demonstrated.
   c. Educational programs are documented in Ambulatory Health Care Aide personnel files.
10. Promotes education for patients, patient families, and the community.
   a. Participation in educational programs to address identified patient, patient family, and community education needs is demonstrated.
11. Participates in personal professional growth and development.
   a. Personal job objectives are developed and implemented.
   b. Current knowledge regarding career development and delivery of health care services is demonstrated.
   c. Participation in education programs is consistently demonstrated.
   d. Review of current literature regarding health care is demonstrated.

Performance responsibilities and standards that exceed defined job description:

(Include performance responsibilities and standards that are not included in the above job description, that may exceed the requirements of the above job description, or that should be identified as unique to the individual currently in the Ambulatory Health Care Aide position. For example, the current Ambulatory Health Care Aide may also have expertise in transfer techniques. In this case, the above job description should be expanded to include the additional, appropriately defined performance responsibilities and standards.)

Job description review:

I have read and understand the job description for the position of Ambulatory Health Care Aide.

____________________________________ ________________
Signature of Ambulatory Health Care Aide — Date of Signature

AMBULATORY HEALTH CARE PROVIDER
QUALITY ASSURANCE
POLICY AND PROCEDURE
5007

Subject: Maintenance of Licensure, Certification, and/or Credentialing Records

Drafted by: ______	Date drafted: ______
Revised by: ______	Date revised: ______
Approved by: ______	Date approved: ______
Supersedes date: ______	Page #: ______
Date effective: ______	Page: ______ of ______

POLICY

The ambulatory health care provider maintains current licensure, certification, and/or credentialing records for professional ambulatory health care staff members and contract personnel required to have the same in order to provide health care services.

PURPOSE

1. To ensure that professional ambulatory health care staff members and contract personnel function with current, valid licensure, certification, and/or credentials.
2. To monitor ambulatory health care staff members and contract personnel for inappropriately providing health care services with restrictions placed on their license, certification, and/or credentials.
3. To monitor individuals for inappropriately providing health care services without possessing valid licensure, certification, and/or credentials.

PROCEDURE

1. A copy of current, valid licensure, certification, and/or credentials is submitted by newly hired professional ambulatory health care staff members and contract personnel prior to or on the date of hire to the Personnel Manager.
2. Verification of current, valid licensure, certification, and/or credentials for newly hired professional ambulatory health care staff members and contract personnel is obtained by:
   a. requesting such verification from the respective state licensure, certification, and/or credentialing agency/organization
   b. requesting such verification from the respective out-of-state licensure, certification, and/or credentialing agency/organization when staff member/contract personnel alleges out-of-state licensure, certification, and/or credentialing
3. A copy of current, valid licensure, certification, and/or credentials is submitted by hired professional ambulatory health care staff members and contract personnel annually and as requested.
4. Ambulatory health care staff members and contract personnel licensure, certification, and/or credentials are monitored for:
   a. expiration
   b. lack of submission prior to or on the date of hire/contract approval
   c. lack of submission on an annual basis
   d. having been obtained falsely, fraudulently, deceitfully, illegally, etc.
   e. having been forged or counterfeited
   f. having had restrictions/sanctions imposed on the same
   g. other when circumstances require
5. Monitoring current, valid licensure, certification, and/or credentialing records includes review of public information concerning restrictions/sanctions placed on the same.
6. Hired professional ambulatory health care staff members and contract personnel are subject to a hold being placed on their hire to the ambulatory health care provider or to disciplinary action, including a voluntary quit with the provider, when circumstances require or if the licensure, certification, and/or credentials:
   a. have expired
   b. have not been submitted prior to or on the date of hire/contract approval
   c. have not been submitted annually
   d. have been obtained falsely, fraudulently, deceitfully, illegally, etc.

   e. have been forged or counterfeited
   f. have had restrictions/sanctions imposed on the same
7. Any newly hired or currently employed ambulatory health care staff members or contract personnel possessing an invalid or restricted licensure, certification, and/or credentials are reported to the respective state/out-of-state licensure, certification, and/or credentialing agency/organization.
8. The receipt of current, valid licensure, certification, and credentialing is monitored by use of a Receipt of Licensure, Certification, and/or Credentials Form (see Exhibit 5007-1).
9. Summarized information regarding the maintenance of licensure, certification, and/or credentials records is submitted to the Administrator of Ambulatory Health Care.
10. The Administrator of Ambulatory Health Care:
    a. reviews the summarized licensure, certification, and/or credentials information
    b. is informed about problems with obtaining current, valid licensure, certification, and/or credentials from ambulatory health care staff members and contract personnel
    c. responds to problems with obtaining current, valid licensure, certification, and/or credentials from ambulatory health care staff members and contract personnel
11. Problems identified with licensure, certification, and/or credentials are referred to the Quality Assurance Manager for consideration as a continuous or special quality assurance activity/study.
12. Licensure, certification, and/or credentials information is communicated to individuals, as appropriate, according to Policy and Procedure 1010: Confidentiality of Quality Assurance Information, and Policy and Procedure 1001: Administrative Control.
13. The completed Receipt of Licensure, Certification, and/or Credentials Form is filed in the ambulatory health care provider's Receipt of Licensure, Certification, and/or Credentials administrative file.

Exhibit 5007-1 Receipt of Licensure, Certification, and/or Credentials Form

AMBULATORY HEALTH CARE PROVIDER RECEIPT OF LICENSURE, CERTIFICATION, AND/OR CREDENTIALS						
NAME OF STAFF MEMBER/ CONTRACT PERSONNEL	ITEM REQUESTED			DATE		COMMENTS
	LICENSURE	CERTIFICATION	CREDENTIALS	REQUESTED	RECEIVED	

AMBULATORY HEALTH CARE PROVIDER
QUALITY ASSURANCE
POLICY AND PROCEDURE
5008

Subject: Mandatory Reporting Requirements in Cases of Patient Abuse	
Drafted by: ______	Date drafted: ______
Revised by: ______	Date revised: ______
Approved by: ______	Date approved: ______
Supersedes date: ______	Page #: ______
Date effective: ______	Page: ______ of ______

POLICY

The ambulatory health care provider administrative staff informs all provider staff members of the mandatory reporting requirements imposed by state statute in cases of patient abuse.

PURPOSE

To provide information regarding the ambulatory health care provider's patient abuse reporting system and its disciplinary action in cases of patient abuse and/or neglect by ambulatory health care staff members.

PROCEDURE

1. Each ambulatory health care staff member orientation and education program includes a review of the following:
   a. disciplinary action in cases of patient abuse and/or neglect by ambulatory health care staff members
   b. the internal reporting system relating to patient abuse and/or neglect
   c. the related mandatory reporting requirements imposed on the ambulatory health care staff members by state statute
   d. the fact that anyone may report suspected cases of patient abuse and/or neglect directly to the appropriate outside licensing agencies
2. The ambulatory health care provider orientation and education programs are documented to reflect the above review by ambulatory health care staff members.

AMBULATORY HEALTH CARE PROVIDER
QUALITY ASSURANCE
POLICY AND PROCEDURE
5009

Subject: Performance Appraisal	
Drafted by: ______	Date drafted: ______
Revised by: ______	Date revised: ______
Approved by: ______	Date approved: ______
Supersedes date: ______	Page #: ______
Date effective: ______	Page: ____ of ______

POLICY

Ambulatory health care staff members are given performance appraisals after six months of employment and annually thereafter.

PURPOSE

1. To ensure that ambulatory health care staff members' performances meet job description standards.
2. To provide opportunities for ambulatory health care staff member personal and professional growth.
3. To identify ambulatory health care staff member strengths and problems.
4. To develop ambulatory health care staff member objectives for job performance.
5. To communicate management expectations for appropriate job performance.
6. To reinforce ambulatory health care staff member strengths.

PROCEDURE

1. The Nursing Manager:
   a. schedules meetings with staff members who are to receive a performance appraisal
   b. instructs the staff members to appraise their own job performances using a Performance Appraisal Form (see Exhibits 5009-1 through 5009-6) and relevant job descriptions
   c. appraises the individual staff member's job performance based on the submitted Performance Appraisal Form and relevant job description.
   d. discusses the director's and staff member's performance appraisals with the staff member
   e. assists the staff member in identifying his or her strengths and problems
   f. assists the staff member in assessing progress toward his or her career objectives
   g. assists the staff member in developing future objectives
   h. communicates to the staff member management expectations for appropriate job performance
   i. gives positive reinforcement for staff member strengths
   j. documents discussion with staff member regarding his or her job performance on Performance Appraisal Form
   k. obtains staff member's signature on completed Performance Appraisal Form
   l. submits completed Performance Appraisal Form to the Administrator of Ambulatory Health Care
   m. completes and submits Summary Performance Appraisal Forms (see Exhibits 5009-7, 5009-8, and 5009-9) to the Administrator of Ambulatory Health Care
2. The Administrator of Ambulatory Health Care reviews and signs the completed Performance Appraisal Form.
3. Problems identified through summarized ambulatory health care staff members' performance appraisals without identifying staff members' names are referred to the Quality Assurance Manager for consideration as a continuous or special quality assurance activity/study.
4. The reviewed Performance Appraisal Form is placed in the relevant ambulatory health care staff member's personnel file.
5. The completed Summary Performance Appraisal Forms are filed in the respective ambulatory health care provider's Summary Performance Appraisal administrative files.

Exhibit 5009-1 Administrator of Ambulatory Health Care Performance Appraisal Form

AMBULATORY HEALTH CARE PROVIDER
ADMINISTRATOR OF AMBULATORY HEALTH CARE PERFORMANCE APPRAISAL

PERFORMANCE RESPONSIBILITY	PERFORMANCE RATING*				COMMENTS
	1	2	3	NOT OBSERVED	
1. Ensures quality and safe delivery of ambulatory health care services.					
2. Performs additional performance responsibilities as assigned and as necessary.					
3. Develops and implements written policies and procedures that reflect ambulatory health care provider philosophy and objectives.					
4. Ensures compliance of ambulatory health care provider operations with federal, state, and local rules and regulations.					
5. Promotes effective written/verbal communication.					
6. Develops, implements, and evaluates adequate staffing to address staffing needs for delivery of ambulatory health care services.					
7. Monitors supervision and evaluation of ambulatory health care staff job performance.					
8. Develops, implements, evaluates, and monitors ambulatory health care provider financial policies and procedures and records.					
9. Develops, implements, and evaluates budget plan and cost control policies and procedures.					
10. Develops and implements salary program within approved ambulatory health care provider policies and procedures.					
11. Complies with ambulatory health care provider policies and procedures.					
12. Promotes and maintains a provider environment that is in compliance with federal, state, and local regulatory agencies.					
13. Promotes education for ambulatory health care staff members.					
14. Participates in personal professional growth and development.					
15. Other (please describe).					

*RATING SCALE
1 = Job performance does not meet requirements
2 = Job performance meets requirements
3 = Job performance exceeds requirements

Signature of Administrator of Ambulatory Health Care ____________ Date of Signature ____________

Signature of President ____________ Date of Signature ____________

Exhibit 5009-2 Nursing Manager Performance Appraisal Form

AMBULATORY HEALTH CARE PROVIDER
NURSING MANAGER PERFORMANCE APPRAISAL

PERFORMANCE RESPONSIBILITY	PERFORMANCE RATING*				COMMENTS
	1	2	3	NOT OBSERVED	
1. Ensures quality and safe delivery of ambulatory health care services.					
2. Performs additional assigned performance responsibilities as necessary.					
3. Develops and implements written policies and procedures that reflect ambulatory health care provider philosophy and objectives.					
4. Assumes assigned responsibility for ambulatory health care provider operations in absence of Administrator of Ambulatory Health Care.					
5. Promotes effective written/verbal communication.					
6. Develops, implements, and evaluates adequate staffing to address staffing needs for delivery of quality and safe ambulatory health care services.					
7. Monitors supervision and evaluation of ambulatory health care staff job performance.					
8. Develops, implements, evaluates, and monitors ambulatory health care provider financial policies and procedures and records.					
9. Develops, implements, and evaluates budget plan and cost control policies and procedures.					
10. Develops and implements salary program within approved ambulatory health care provider policies and procedures.					
11. Complies with ambulatory health care provider policies and procedures.					
12. Promotes and maintains a provider environment that is in compliance with federal, state, and local regulatory agencies.					
13. Promotes education for ambulatory health care staff members.					
14. Promotes education for patients, patient families, and the community.					
15. Promotes research and study of adult learning theory and concepts related to ambulatory health care services.					
16. Participates in personal professional growth and development.					
17. Other (please describe).					

*RATING SCALE
1 = Job performance does not meet requirements
2 = Job performance meets requirements
3 = Job performance exceeds requirements

____________________________ Signature of Nursing Manager

____________________________ Date of Signature

____________________________ Signature of Administrator of Ambulatory Health Care

____________________________ Date of Signature

Exhibit 5009-3 Quality Assurance Manager Performance Appraisal Form

AMBULATORY HEALTH CARE PROVIDER
QUALITY ASSURANCE MANAGER PERFORMANCE APPRAISAL

PERFORMANCE RESPONSIBILITY	TOTAL NUMBER RELATIVE TO PERFORMANCE RATING*				COMMENTS
	1	2	3	NOT OBSERVED	
1. Ensures quality and safe delivery of ambulatory health care services.					
2. Performs additional assigned performance responsibilities as necessary.					
3. Develops and implements written policies and procedures that reflect ambulatory health care provider quality assurance philosophy and objectives.					
4. Assumes assigned responsibility for ambulatory health care provider operations in absence of Administrator of Ambulatory Health Care.					
5. Promotes effective written/verbal communication.					
6. Develops, implements, and evaluates quality assurance activities to address the delivery of quality and safe ambulatory health care services.					
7. Monitors supervision of ambulatory health care quality assurance staff job performance.					
8. Develops, implements, evaluates, and monitors ambulatory health care provider quality assurance financial policies and procedures and records.					
9. Develops, implements, and evaluates quality assurance budget plan and cost control policies and procedures.					
10. Develops and implements salary program for quality assurance staff within approved ambulatory health care provider policies and procedures.					

continues

Exhibit 5009-3 *continued*

PERFORMANCE RESPONSIBILITY	TOTAL NUMBER RELATIVE TO PERFORMANCE RATING*				COMMENTS
	1	2	3	NOT OBSERVED	
11. Complies with ambulatory health care provider policies and procedures.					
12. Promotes and maintains a provider environment that is in compliance with federal, state, and local regulatory agencies.					
13. Promotes quality assurance education for ambulatory health care staff members.					
14. Promotes quality assurance education for patients, patient families, and the community.					
15. Promotes research and study of adult learning theory and concepts related to quality assurance.					
16. Participates in personal professional growth and development.					
17. Other (please describe).					

*RATING SCALE
1 = Job performance does not meet requirements
2 = Job performance meets requirements
3 = Job performance exceeds requirements

______________________________ ____________________
Signature of Quality Assurance Manager — Date of Signature

______________________________ ____________________
Signature of Administrator of Ambulatory Health Care — Date of Signature

Exhibit 5009-4 Ambulatory Health Care Registered Nurse Performance Appraisal Form

AMBULATORY HEALTH CARE PROVIDER
AMBULATORY HEALTH CARE REGISTERED NURSE PERFORMANCE APPRAISAL

PERFORMANCE RESPONSIBILITY	PERFORMANCE RATING*				COMMENTS
	1	2	3	NOT OBSERVED	
1. Ensures quality and safe delivery of ambulatory health care services.					
2. Implements current nursing practice.					
3. Fulfills additional performance responsibilities as assigned and as necessary.					
4. Assumes assigned responsibility for ambulatory health care provider operations in the absence of the Administrator and Nursing Manager.					
5. Promotes effective written/verbal communication.					
6. Develops written staff assignments according to staffing patterns, client needs, and ambulatory health care staff member competencies.					
7. Supervises ambulatory health care licensed practical nurses and ambulatory health care aides.					
8. Gives accurate information to patients, patient families, and ambulatory health care staff members regarding costs for ambulatory health care services.					
9. Provides information regarding equipment and supply needs of the ambulatory health care provider.					
10. Uses equipment and supplies effectively and efficiently.					
11. Participates in salary programs following approved ambulatory health care provider policies and procedures.					
12. Complies with ambulatory health care provider policies and procedures.					
13. Promotes and maintains a provider environment that is in compliance with federal, state, and local regulatory agencies.					
14. Promotes education for ambulatory health care staff members.					
15. Promotes education for patients, patient families, and the community.					
16. Participates in research and study of adult learning theory and concepts related to ambulatory health care services.					
17. Participates in personal professional growth and development.					
18. Other (please describe).					

*RATING SCALE
1 = Job performance does not meet requirements
2 = Job performance meets requirements
3 = Job performance exceeds requirements

Signature of Ambulatory Health Care Registered Nurse ____________ Date of Signature ____________

Signature of Nursing Manager ____________ Date of Signature ____________

Exhibit 5009-5 Ambulatory Health Care Licensed Practical Nurse Performance Appraisal Form

AMBULATORY HEALTH CARE PROVIDER
AMBULATORY HEALTH CARE LICENSED PRACTICAL NURSE PERFORMANCE APPRAISAL

PERFORMANCE RESPONSIBILITY	PERFORMANCE RATING*				COMMENTS
	1	2	3	NOT OBSERVED	
1. Ensures quality and safe delivery of ambulatory health care services.					
2. Implements current nursing practice.					
3. Fulfills additional performance responsibilities as assigned and as necessary.					
4. Promotes effective written/verbal communication.					
5. Gives accurate information to patients and patient families regarding ambulatory health care provider costs for ambulatory health care services.					
6. Provides information regarding equipment and supply needs of the ambulatory health care provider.					
7. Uses equipment and supplies effectively and efficiently.					
8. Participates in salary programs following approved ambulatory health care provider policies and procedures.					
9. Complies with ambulatory health care agency policies and procedures.					
10. Promotes and maintains a provider environment that is in compliance with federal, state, and local regulatory agencies.					
11. Promotes education for ambulatory health care staff members.					
12. Promotes education for patients, patient families, and the community.					
13. Participates in personal professional growth and development.					
14. Other (please describe).					

*RATING SCALE
1 = Job performance does not meet requirements
2 = Job performance meets requirements
3 = Job performance exceeds requirements

______________________________ ______________________________
Signature of Ambulatory Health Care Licensed Practical Nurse — Date of Signature

______________________________ ______________________________
Signature of Nursing Manager — Date of Signature

Exhibit 5009-6 Ambulatory Health Care Aide Performance Appraisal Form

AMBULATORY HEALTH CARE PROVIDER
AMBULATORY HEALTH CARE AIDE PERFORMANCE APPRAISAL

PERFORMANCE RESPONSIBILITY	PERFORMANCE RATING*				COMMENTS
	1	2	3	NOT OBSERVED	
1. Ensures quality and safe delivery of ambulatory health care services.					
2. Implements current ambulatory health care aide services.					
3. Fulfills additional performance responsibilities as assigned and as necessary.					
4. Promotes effective written/verbal communication.					
5. Uses equipment and supplies effectively and efficiently.					
6. Participates in salary programs following approved ambulatory health care provider policies and procedures.					
7. Complies with ambulatory health care provider policies and procedures.					
8. Promotes and maintains a provider environment that is in compliance with federal, state, and local regulatory agencies.					
9. Promotes education for ambulatory health care staff members.					
10. Promotes education for patients, patient families, and the community.					
11. Participates in personal career growth and development.					
12. Other (please describe).					

*RATING SCALE
1 = Job performance does not meet requirements
2 = Job performance meets requirements
3 = Job performance exceeds requirements

_______________________________ Signature of Ambulatory Health Care Aide

_______________ Date of Signature

_______________________________ Signature of Nursing Manager

_______________ Date of Signature

Exhibit 5009-7 Summary of Ambulatory Health Care Registered Nurse Performance Appraisal Form

AMBULATORY HEALTH CARE PROVIDER
SUMMARY OF AMBULATORY HEALTH CARE REGISTERED NURSE PERFORMANCE APPRAISAL

Date This Form Completed	Dates of Reporting Period	Total Number of RN Performance Appraisal Forms Completed

PERFORMANCE RESPONSIBILITY	TOTAL NUMBER RELATIVE TO PERFORMANCE RATING*				
	1	2	3	NOT OBSERVED	COMMENTS
1. Ensures quality and safe delivery of ambulatory health care services.					
2. Implements current nursing practice.					
3. Fulfills additional performance responsibilities as assigned and as necessary.					
4. Assumes assigned responsibility for ambulatory health care provider operations in the absence of Administrator and Nursing Manager.					
5. Promotes effective written/verbal communication.					
6. Develops written staff assignments according to staffing patterns, patient needs, and ambulatory health care staff member competencies.					
7. Supervises ambulatory health care licensed practical nurses and ambulatory health care aides.					
8. Gives accurate information to patients, patient families, and ambulatory health care staff members regarding costs for ambulatory health care services.					
9. Provides information regarding equipment and supply needs of the ambulatory health care provider.					
10. Uses equipment and supplies effectively and efficiently.					
11. Participates in salary programs following approved ambulatory health care provider policies and procedures.					
12. Complies with ambulatory health care provider policies and procedures.					
13. Promotes and maintains a provider environment that is in compliance with federal, state, and local regulatory agencies.					
14. Promotes education for ambulatory health care staff members.					
15. Promotes education for patients, patient families, and the community.					
16. Participates in research and study of adult learning theory and concepts related to ambulatory health care services.					
17. Participates in personal professional growth and development.					
18. Other (please describe).					

*RATING SCALE
1 = Job performance does not meet requirements
2 = Job performance meets requirements
3 = Job performance exceeds requirements

Signature of Individual Completing This Form	Date of Signature

Exhibit 5009-8 Summary of Ambulatory Health Care Licensed Practical Nurse Performance Appraisal Form

AMBULATORY HEALTH CARE PROVIDER
SUMMARY OF AMBULATORY HEALTH CARE LICENSED PRACTICAL NURSE PERFORMANCE APPRAISAL

Date This Form Completed	Dates of Reporting Period	Total Number of LPN Performance Appraisal Forms Completed

PERFORMANCE RESPONSIBILITY	TOTAL NUMBER RELATIVE TO PERFORMANCE RATING*				
	1	2	3	NOT OBSERVED	COMMENTS
1. Ensures quality and safe delivery of ambulatory health care services.					
2. Implements current nursing practice.					
3. Fulfills additional performance responsibilities as assigned and as necessary.					
4. Promotes effective written/verbal communication.					
5. Gives accurate information to patients and patient families regarding ambulatory health care provider costs for ambulatory health care services.					
6. Provides information regarding equipment and supply needs of the ambulatory health care provider.					
7. Uses equipment and supplies effectively and efficiently.					
8. Participates in salary programs following approved ambulatory health care provider policies and procedures.					
9. Complies with ambulatory health care provider policies and procedures.					
10. Promotes and maintains a provider environment that is in compliance with federal, state, and local regulatory agencies.					
11. Promotes education for ambulatory health care staff members.					
12. Promotes education for patients, patient families, and the community.					
13. Participates in personal professional growth and development.					
14. Other (please describe).					

*RATING SCALE
1 = Job performance does not meet requirements
2 = Job performance meets requirements
3 = Job performance exceeds requirements

Signature of Individual Completing This Form	Date of Signature

Exhibit 5009-9 Summary of Ambulatory Health Care Aide Performance Appraisal Form

AMBULATORY HEALTH CARE PROVIDER
SUMMARY OF AMBULATORY HEALTH CARE AIDE PERFORMANCE APPRAISAL FORM

Date This Form Completed	Dates of Reporting Period	Total Number of AHCA Performance Appraisal Forms Completed

PERFORMANCE RESPONSIBILITY	TOTAL NUMBER RELATIVE TO PERFORMANCE RATING*				
	1	2	3	NOT OBSERVED	COMMENTS
1. Ensures quality and safe delivery of ambulatory health care services.					
2. Implements current ambulatory health care aide services.					
3. Fulfills additional performance responsibilities as assigned and as necessary.					
4. Promotes effective written/verbal communication.					
5. Uses equipment and supplies effectively and efficiently.					
6. Participates in salary programs following approved ambulatory health care provider policies and procedures.					
7. Complies with ambulatory health care provider policies and procedures.					
8. Promotes and maintains a provider environment that is in compliance with federal, state, and local regulatory agencies.					
9. Promotes education for ambulatory health care staff members.					
10. Promotes education for patients, patient families, and the community.					
11. Participates in personal career growth and development.					
12. Other (please describe).					

*RATING SCALE
1 = Job performance does not meet requirements
2 = Job performance meets requirements
3 = Job performance exceeds requirements

Signature of Individual Completing This Form	Date of Signature

AMBULATORY HEALTH CARE PROVIDER
QUALITY ASSURANCE
POLICY AND PROCEDURE
5010

Subject: Positive Ambulatory Health Care Staff Job Performance	
Drafted by: ______	Date drafted: ______
Revised by: ______	Date revised: ______
Approved by: ______	Date approved: ______
Supersedes date: ______	Page #: ______
Date effective: ______	Page: ____ of ______

POLICY

Positive ambulatory health care staff job performance is recognized and acknowledged by ambulatory health care provider management.

PURPOSE

1. To recognize and acknowledge positive ambulatory health care staff job performance that represents staff efforts in monitoring and enhancing the delivery of quality and safe ambulatory health care services to patients.
2. To encourage continued positive ambulatory health care staff job performance.

PROCEDURE

1. Information regarding positive ambulatory health care staff job performance is given to the Administrator of Ambulatory Health Care.
2. The Administrator of Ambulatory Health Care:
   a. reviews information regarding the positive ambulatory health care staff job performance
   b. asks Administrative Assistant to prepare a Positive Staff Job Performance Letter (see Exhibit 5010-1) to be mailed to the respective staff member
   c. signs prepared Positive Staff Job Performance Letter
   d. gives signed Positive Staff Job Performance Letter to the Administrative Assistant
   e. communicates the distribution of the Positive Staff Job Performance Letter to other staff members
3. The Administrative Assistant:
   a. copies signed Positive Staff Job Performance Letter
   b. mails signed Positive Staff Job Performance Letter to the respective ambulatory health care staff member
   c. files copy of Positive Staff Job Performance Letter in the staff member's personnel file
4. Positive ambulatory health care staff job performance letters are considered in the determination of staff members' merit salary increases.

Exhibit 5010-1 Positive Staff Job Performance Letter

(Date)

(Ambulatory Health Care Staff Member Name and Address)

Dear (Ambulatory Health Care Staff Member Name):

We have received information regarding the positive way in which you performed your job responsibilities.

It gives us great pleasure to congratulate you for your outstanding job performance. We appreciate how well you represent the quality and safe ambulatory health care services that we provide to patients.

We are certain that you will continue to perform in the same positive manner, and we look forward to having more patients tell us how well you perform your job responsibilities.

Again, thank you for a job well done!

Sincerely,

Administrator of Ambulatory Health Care

cc: Ambulatory Health Care Staff Member's personnel file

AMBULATORY HEALTH CARE PROVIDER
QUALITY ASSURANCE
POLICY AND PROCEDURE
5011

Subject: Staff Member Evaluation of Employment with the Ambulatory Health Care Provider

Drafted by: ______	Date drafted: ______
Revised by: ______	Date revised: ______
Approved by: ______	Date approved: ______
Supersedes date: ______	Page #: ______
Date effective: ______	Page: ______ of ______

POLICY

The ambulatory health care provider provides opportunities for staff members to evaluate employment with the ambulatory health care provider.

PURPOSE

1. To collect and assess information regarding staff member satisfaction with employment with the ambulatory health care provider.
2. To implement a quality assurance monitoring system to address staff member concerns.
3. To enhance ambulatory health care provider and staff member relationships.

PROCEDURE

1. Staff members are encouraged to complete an Ambulatory Health Care Staff Member Evaluation of Employment with the Ambulatory Health Care Provider Form (see Exhibit 5011-1).
2. The Administrative Assistant:
   a. distributes an Ambulatory Health Care Staff Member Evaluation of Employment with the Ambulatory Health Care Provider Form to staff members every three months
   b. summarizes returned, completed Ambulatory Health Care Staff Member Evaluation of Employment with the Ambulatory Health Care Provider Forms using a Summary of Staff Member Evaluation of Employment with the Ambulatory Health Care Provider Form (see Exhibit 5011-2)
   c. gives returned Ambulatory Health Care Staff Member Evaluation of Employment with the Ambulatory Health Care Provider Form and Summary of Staff Member Evaluation of Employment with the Ambulatory Health Care Provider Form to the Administrator of Ambulatory Health Care
3. The Administrator of Ambulatory Health Care:
   a. reviews submitted Ambulatory Health Care Staff Member Evaluation of Employment with the Ambulatory Health Care Provider Form and Summary of Staff Member Evaluation of Employment with the Ambulatory Health Care Provider Form
   b. implements immediate corrective action, as necessary, based on identified staff member concerns
4. Problems identified with staff member evaluation of employment with the ambulatory health care provider are referred to the Quality Assurance Manager for consideration as a continuous or special quality assurance activity/study.
5. Staff member evaluation of employment with the ambulatory health care provider information is communicated to individuals, as appropriate, according to Policy and Procedure 1010: Confidentiality of Quality Assurance Information, and Policy and Procedure 1001: Administrative Control.
6. The completed Ambulatory Health Care Staff Member Evaluation of Employment with the Ambulatory Health Care Provider Form and Summary of Staff Member Evaluation of Employment with the Ambulatory Health Care Provider Form are filed in the ambulatory health care provider's Ambulatory Health Care Staff Member Evaluation of Employment with the Ambulatory Health Care Provider and Summary of Staff Member Evaluation of Employment with the Ambulatory Health Care Provider administrative files.

Exhibit 5011-1 Staff Member Evaluation of Employment with the Ambulatory Health Care Provider Form

AMBULATORY HEALTH CARE PROVIDER
AMBULATORY HEALTH CARE STAFF MEMBER EVALUATION OF EMPLOYMENT WITH THE AMBULATORY HEALTH CARE PROVIDER

The ambulatory health care provider is dedicated to providing satisfying employment for ambulatory health care staff members. As an employee who has been employed with our home health care provider, you are being asked to complete this survey form. The information you give us on this form will be assessed to measure how well we have provided satisfying employment for you and the ways in which we can improve our employment opportunities. Please promptly complete and return this form to the Administrator of Ambulatory Health Care. Thank you for your assistance in our continuing efforts to provide satisfying employment opportunities.

ITEM	YOUR AGREEMENT WITH EACH ITEM			
	AGREE	DO NOT AGREE	NO OPINION	NOT APPLICABLE
1. My work was interesting to me.				
2. I was encouraged to take initiatives in my work.				
3. I was encouraged to make suggestions about my work.				
4. My work gave me a chance to use my knowledge and skills.				
5. I had adequate time to keep up with my work.				
6. My work assignments were usually fair.				
7. I was given adequate instruction regarding my work assignments.				
8. I was given adequate information about situations that might affect my work.				
9. The orientation program I participated in was adequate.				
10. The education programs I participated in were adequate.				
11. The ambulatory health care provider "atmosphere" seemed to be one of cooperation.				
12. Adequate equipment was available for performing my work tasks.				
13. Adequate career advancement opportunities were available to me.				
14. Adequate personnel benefits were available to me.				
15. My salary compared favorably with salaries elsewhere for comparable work.				
16. The ambulatory health care provider management staff were fair with me concerning provider policies and procedures.				
17. The ambulatory health care provider management staff adequately dealt with my patient/staff member concerns and problems.				

continues

Exhibit 5011-1 *continued*

ITEM	YOUR AGREEMENT WITH EACH ITEM			
	AGREE	DO NOT AGREE	NO OPINION	NOT APPLICABLE
18. I felt comfortable in asking questions of the ambulatory health care provider management staff.				
19. I felt comfortable voicing concerns and problems to the ambulatory health care provider management staff.				
20. Other comments:				

Please complete the following:

21. Your position title: ______

22. Your work shift: ______

23. Your work hours: ______

24. Number of days you worked per pay period: ______

25. Your length of employment: ______

26. Your reason(s) for leaving: ______

27. Type of position you may seek/have obtained: ______

28. Would you recommend employment with the ambulatory health care provider?

    ____ Yes

    ____ No (please explain) ______

    ______

29. Comments: ______

    ______

    ______

Exhibit 5011-2 Summary of Staff Member Evaluation of Employment with the Ambulatory Health Care Provider Form

AMBULATORY HEALTH CARE PROVIDER
SUMMARY OF STAFF MEMBER EVALUATION OF EMPLOYMENT WITH THE AMBULATORY HEALTH CARE PROVIDER

Date This Form Completed	Dates of Reporting Period	Staff Member Job Category Summarized ☐ RN ☐ LPN ☐ AHCA ☐ Other ___	Total Number of Staff Evaluation Forms Completed

ITEM	TOTAL NUMBER OF RESPONSES			
	AGREE	DO NOT AGREE	NO OPINION	NOT APPLICABLE
1. My work was interesting to me.				
2. I was encouraged to take initiatives in my work.				
3. I was encouraged to make suggestions about my work.				
4. My work gave me a chance to use my knowledge and skills.				
5. I had adequate time to keep up with my work.				
6. My work assignments were usually fair.				
7. I was given adequate instruction regarding my work assignments.				
8. I was given adequate information about situations that might affect my work.				
9. The orientation program I participated in was adequate.				
10. The education programs I participated in were adequate.				
11. The ambulatory health care provider "atmosphere" seemed to be one of cooperation.				
12. Adequate equipment was available for performing my work tasks.				
13. Adequate career advancement opportunities were available to me.				
14. Adequate personnel benefits were available to me.				
15. My salary compared favorably with salaries elsewhere for comparable work.				
16. The ambulatory health care provider management staff were fair with me concerning provider policies and procedures.				
17. The ambulatory health care provider management staff adequately dealt with my patient/staff member concerns and problems.				
18. I felt comfortable asking questions of the ambulatory health care provider management staff.				
19. I felt comfortable voicing concerns and problems to the ambulatory health care provider management staff.				

_____ Average Length of Employment with the Ambulatory Health Care Provider

_____ Total Number Recommending Employment with the Ambulatory Health Care Provider

Signature of Individual Completing This Form _______________________ Date of Signature _______________________

Section 6000

Provider Services

The following policies and procedures are adaptable to quality assurance functions in the area of provider services.

AMBULATORY HEALTH CARE PROVIDER
QUALITY ASSURANCE
POLICY AND PROCEDURE
6001

Subject: Contract Arrangements

Drafted by: ____	Date drafted: ____
Revised by: ____	Date revised: ____
Approved by: ____	Date approved: ____
Supersedes date: ____	Page #: ____
Date effective: ____	Page: ____ of ____

POLICY

The ambulatory health care provider requires written contracts with other entities that provide services for the ambulatory health care provider.

PURPOSE

To maintain quality control of services provided by other agencies and individuals under contract arrangements.

PROCEDURE

1. A current written contract is required before an outside provider or individual is permitted to provide services for the ambulatory health care provider.
2. The written contract must clearly stipulate:
   a. understanding that patients are to be accepted for care only by the primary ambulatory health care provider
   b. ambulatory health care services to be provided
   c. necessity to conform to all applicable ambulatory health care provider policies and procedures, including those concerning personnel qualifications and the development of patient plans of care, and quality assurance
   d. manner in which the services are to be controlled, coordinated, and evaluated by the primary ambulatory health care provider
   e. policies and procedures for submitting patient clinical and progress notes, for scheduling patient visits, and for periodic patient evaluations
   f. policies and procedures for determining charges and reimbursements
3. Written contracts with outside entities are reviewed, revised, and approved on an annual basis.

AMBULATORY HEALTH CARE PROVIDER
QUALITY ASSURANCE
POLICY AND PROCEDURE
6002

Subject: Personnel under Hourly or Per-Visit Contracts	
Drafted by: ______	Date drafted: ______
Revised by: ______	Date revised: ______
Approved by: ______	Date approved: ______
Supersedes date: ______	Page #: ______
Date effective: ______	Page:______ of ______

POLICY

The ambulatory health care provider requires written contracts with outside personnel who are utilized by the provider under hourly or per-visit arrangements.

PURPOSE

To maintain quality control of personnel who provide services for the ambulatory health care provider.

PROCEDURE

1. A current written contract that specifies hourly or per-visit arrangements for the provision of services is required before outside personnel are permitted to provide such ambulatory services for the provider.
2. The written contract must clearly stipulate:
   a. understanding that patients are to be accepted for care only by the primary ambulatory health care provider
   b. ambulatory health care services to be provided
   c. necessity to conform to all applicable ambulatory health care provider policies and procedures, including those concerning personnel qualifications and the development of patient plans of care, and quality assurance
   d. manner in which the services are to be controlled, coordinated, and evaluated by the primary ambulatory health care provider
   e. policies and procedures for submitting patient clinical and progress notes, for scheduling patient visits, and for periodic patient evaluations
   f. policies and procedures for determining charges and reimbursements
3. Written contracts with outside personnel under hourly or per-visit arrangements are reviewed, revised, and approved on an annual basis.

Index

A

About the Author

Judith M. Bulau is Health Care Program Investigator in the Health Systems Development Division, Alternative Delivery Systems Section, at the Minnesota Department of Health, Minneapolis, Minnesota. In this capacity, she is primarily responsible for the development and implementation of regulatory examinations for quality of care programs of health maintenance organizations. She belongs to Sigma Theta Tau, the National Honor Society of Nursing. She has written three books: *Administrative Policies and Procedures for Home Health Care*, *Clinical Policies and Procedures for Home Health Care*, and *Quality Assurance Policies and Procedures for Home Heath Care* published by Aspen Publishers, Inc., Rockville, Maryland. Her work has been published in *The Journal of Nursing Administration*. She has held numerous nurse administrative positions and has lectured on administrative, organizational, health care, and quality of care topics. She holds degrees from the University of Minnesota (M.S.N.; B.S.) and the Arthur B. Ancker Memorial School of Nursing (R.N.) and is certified in public health nursing (P.H.N.) by the Minnesota Department of Health.

9 780834 201385

Printed in Dunstable, United Kingdom

91342608R00208